The Opium War
1840–1842

francine jacobs

The Opium War
1840-1842

Barbarians in the Celestial Empire

in the Early Part of the Nineteenth Century

and the War by Which They Forced Her Gates Ajar

by Peter Ward Fay

The University of North Carolina Press
Chapel Hill

Copyright © 1975, 1997 by
The University of North Carolina Press
All rights reserved
Manufactured in the United States of America
Library of Congress Catalog Card Number 74-30200
03 02 01 00 99   7 6 5 4 3

Library of Congress Cataloging-in-Publication Data
Fay, Peter Ward, 1924–
   The Opium War, 1840–1842: barbarians in the Celestial Empire
   in the early part of the nineteenth century and the war by which they
   forced her gates ajar = [Ya p' ien chan cheng] / by Peter Ward Fay.
     p. cm.
   Parallel title in Chinese characters.
   Originally published: 1975.
   Includes bibliographical references and index.
   ISBN 0-8078-4714-3 (pbk.: alk. paper)
   1. China—History—Opium War, 1840–1842. I. Title.
   DS757.5.F39   1997
   951'.033—dc21   97-35261
                               CIP

Contents

Maps

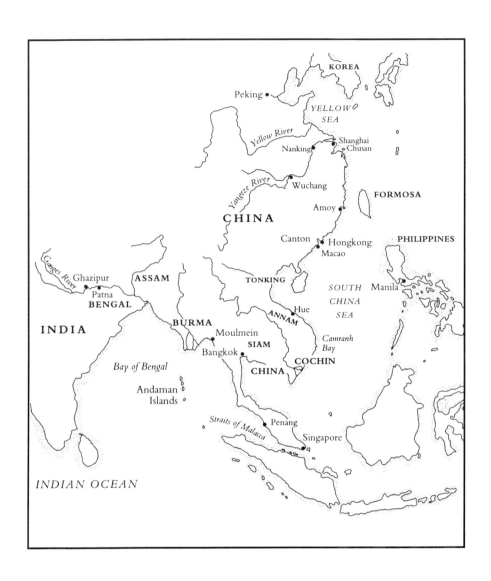

KOREA

Peking •

YELLOW SEA

Yellow River

Nanking • Shanghai
Chusan

Wuchang •

FORMOSA

Amoy •

CHINA

Canton • Hongkong
Macao

PHILIPPINES

Ganges River Ghazipur •

ASSAM

TONKING

SOUTH CHINA SEA Manila

Patna •

BENGAL

Hue •

ANNAM

INDIA

BURMA

Moulmein •

SIAM

Camranh Bay

Bangkok •

Bay of Bengal

CHINA

COCHIN

Andaman
Islands

Straits of Malacca Penang •

Singapore

INDIAN OCEAN

Preface to the Paperback Edition

It's a place all ups and downs, the hills rising to gaunt granite peaks, the gullies falling to narrow beaches and rocky coves. Two large islands and quite a few small ones embrace the Kowloon peninsula, which pushes gently into the South China Sea, and if you could somehow bring the land parts tidily together, you'd have a square only twenty miles on a side. So it's no more than a patch, this, possessing no natural resources; in fact, not even gifted, given the narrowness of the shoreline and the steepness of the approach, as a place nature intended for a port. A patch of ground that in the 1840s, when it first began to get attention, could point to only a handful of inhabitants, most of them farmers and fishermen, and offered no compelling reason why it should ever attract more. In short, a piece of China that on the face of it ought never to have become what today it *has* become: a place packed with over six million people, almost all of whom are Chinese, and almost none of whom farm or fish. A place well known to westerners, many of them Americans, who come and go and even settle down, brought less by the tourist attractions than by the business opportunities it offers—the money to be made—at the highest levels of commerce and finance. A place well known to a particular group among these westerners, a group brought for the same reasons but harboring a feeling—a keen and now somewhat bitter feeling—that they have always been more than visitors: they *belong* there. And a government, distant, acidly determined, that insists they never have and don't. The place, of course, is Hong Kong.

No one looking back to the moment when Hong Kong began to make a name for itself should have expected that because it was barren and empty, barren and empty it would always be. Circumstances have a way of invalidating expectation. The circumstance in this case was a decision on the part of the British, shortly before the Opium War began, to take refuge there. Hong Kong island (eventually it passed its name on to the colony as a whole) is some eight miles long and up to four miles wide. It lies east to west just below the Kowloon peninsula and forms a "U" about Kowloon's tip but always a mile or more away. The water there is deep but the bottom is not beyond the reach of an anchor. The wind is muffled (not always—a typhoon at Hong Kong can be disastrous) on the west by Lantao, the other big island in the group, and on the east by an extension of the mainland. As a place to drop anchor in, nothing more secure is available anywhere else about the Gulf of Canton. Indeed, so effectively does the topography lock Hong Kong in that if you arrive one evening by sea, as tourists often do, when you come on deck in the morning you may wonder how your ship got in at all.

ix

A safe anchorage—that was all the British at the time wanted. There was no thought of landing or taking on goods. The narrowness of the seafront would not have been helpful, and anyway, there were no docks or landing slips. But on a day late in August 1839, they came, several score merchant ships accompanied by the few small men-of-war available to Charles Elliot—he was the chief superintendent of trade, and in that capacity Britain's only official representative on the China coast. Besides officers and crew and men from the agency houses, the ships carried the whole of the British community—men, women, and children—at Macao. They had left at the insistence of the Portuguese governor because Chinese troops were threatening Macao from the north. In the gulf itself there had already been some bloody scraps. Off Lantao one night, boatloads of Chinese had attacked a passage schooner, killed every lascar except the bosun (who jumped into the water and clung to the rudder), and so knocked about the single English passenger—cutting off one ear and stuffing it into his mouth—that it was a mercy he survived. No doubt these had been pirates. There were many about the gulf. But war junks of the Chinese maritime service were making threatening gestures, too. And behind all this was a much more annoying development. In March, at the height of the trading season, a special high commissioner sent direct from Peking (Beijing) had reached Canton (Guangzhou), lectured the local mandarins and the Hong merchants into a state of shock, and made arrangements to bring the barbarians, particularly the British barbarians, to order. His first step had been to cut the barbarians off from all contact with Macao or their ships. His second had been to force, as a condition of their release, the surrender of merchandise worth several million dollars. Next, he had declared all further trade with the British closed until other conditions were met, conditions with which the British had made it plain they would not comply. And at the same time he had signaled, by the suddenly vigorous behavior of his war junks and troops, that if they wouldn't, they would pay.

The merchandise was opium, twenty thousand chests of it, brought into the gulf and up to the mouth of the Canton (or Pearl) river, surrendered there to the special high commissioner Lin Tse-Hs, and destroyed by being dumped into salt water. Twenty thousand chests worth perhaps six million dollars, or two-and-a-half million pounds sterling. Elliot had persuaded the merchants involved (Lin, no fool, had a pretty good idea who they were and how much of the stuff they had) to send for the chests. Naturally, they were not in the river, but in receiving ships (floating warehouses) out in the gulf or up the coast, or in the opium clippers that had brought them from Calcutta. Getting word to these vessels had taken time. There was a good deal of resistance to the giving of the necessary orders, in part because most of the chests belonged to distant persons who had entrusted them to these merchants to be sold. But Elliot had assured them that he asked for the surrender on behalf of his government. Surely it would find the money to cover the loss. Failing that, it would compel the Chinese to do so.

Meanwhile, the British were looking for their safe anchorage, not because they walked in fear and trembling of what Lin Tse-Hs would do now, but because they intended to make his next move impossible. He had taken them for a tidy sum by catching them up a river. He must not be allowed to catch them thus again—not him, not others, ever. Lin knew where they were. British vessels had dropped anchor at Hong Kong before and had not hesitated to meet impertinent behavior—in their confidence that was how they instinctively perceived it—with solid shot. They would not hesitate now. And if things turned violent Lin would be instantly alerted. But the Hong Kong roadstead, a mile wide, with exits at both ends and no forts save a small battery at Kowloon, was a far cry from the Canton River. He could never repeat his maneuver here.

Wisely, he did not try. As for the British, for a while they stayed on, nearly seventy vessels which, if you include their crews, meant several thousand men, some armed, all restless, living aboard ship but going ashore for water and recreation. To Jack Tar, going ashore no doubt meant women and drink. There were clashes. Rumor had it some of the springs were poisoned, and when three war junks suspected of directing it refused to move off, Elliot sent a cutter and two other craft and almost blew them, much larger though they were, out of the water. Was this the beginning of the war, the Opium War? In those days, formality and habit required at the start of a war a declaration to that effect, a declaration accompanied by the withdrawal of ambassadors. But neither Peking nor London had ambassadors positioned and ready to be withdrawn; Peking because it could perceive about the world no equal to whom an ambassador could possibly be sent, London because Peking could not possibly, of course, receive one. Perhaps, then, we should fix the war's opening at the moment when London decided to send an expeditionary force. Or at the moment, chosen in this book, when the force arrived and made serious fighting possible.

The force arrived in June 1840, paused briefly off the gulf, left a few ships and troops behind, and (as the reader will discover) went on up the coast. Chusan was its first serious objective, direct diplomatic contact with Peking the goal. What the reader will also discover is that although the men and ships left behind recovered command of the gulf (men, women, and children went back to Macao), Hong Kong was not abandoned. On the contrary, it gradually became the anchorage of choice for men-of-war and merchant vessels both.

Its very emptiness was inviting. Men-of-war could drop anchor, load provisions, take on water, and replace canvas, rigging, and spars, free from interference or even observation on the part of the Chinese. *They*, after all, had little presence on the Kowloon side of the roadstead. They had no presence at all on the island, and made no attempt to establish any, which was not surprising given their habitual inability to take seriously barbarians who approached by sea. An attempt would have failed anyway. Reaching the roadstead by land would have proved difficult. They could not have laid out and built a proper fort, even on the Kowloon side, quickly enough to withstand what a frigate's broadsides were sure to send their way at the very first sign of the intent. But the same frigate, anchored in this roadstead, was in an excellent position to sally out instantly into the gulf, or set off up the coast. The advantages were obvious. And they corresponded nicely with what London had in mind.

For with the expeditionary force had come certain instructions from Her Majesty's Government, and among them was one that directed the establishing, somewhere along China's coast, of a base and refuge for Her Majesty's forces, perhaps temporary, but eventually to be made permanent by a formal act of cession. The why of all this was not explicit. No doubt London, however, had not forgotten what had happened a few years back to Lord Napier—peer, naval officer, and the first superintendent of trade—when he went up to Canton and (among other things) tried to approach the governor-general directly. The governor-general had not taken kindly to this. He had ordered Napier away, and when he would not leave, forcibly confined him to the factories. Napier had two frigates at the Bogue. He summoned them up. With some difficulty they got as far as Whampoa, within sight of the factories, but there their own deep draft, and the sight of chop boats weighted with rocks (being sunk in a way calculated to trap them), gave their skippers pause. They went no farther. Napier hung on a little longer and then, sick and dispirited, let himself be sent down slowly, almost alone, and by a devious route. Within hours of reaching Macao he was dead.

Napier was surely not forgotten. In London the humiliation had inflamed, among others, the Duke of Wellington. But this was not the first time an effort to meet the Middle Kingdom on equal terms had failed, and the cost—one man's death—cannot have seemed exorbitant. Not so the cost, even if measured simply in pounds, shillings, and pence, of the forcible confinement a little more than a year back of the entire British merchant community at the very same place. The expeditionary force had been sent to China to efface that unjust and humiliating act, and to recover the value of the confiscated chests plus expenses. It could not, of course, remain on the China coast forever. A secure enclave was necessary while the task of coaxing or forcing China into relations of equality and openness went forward. And Hong Kong, it seemed to Elliot and others on the spot, would do nicely.

Without waiting, therefore, for Her Majesty's Government to specify the when and where of the required enclave, Sir Gordon Bremer, the senior naval officer on the station, took formal possession of Hong Kong in Britain's name on January 26, 1841, at a little promontory thereafter known as Possession Point. Her Majesty's Government was not altogether pleased when it heard. The island as described struck Lord Palmerston, the foreign secretary, as rather a barren place, which of course it was. A small group of Protestant missionaries, who came over from Macao to look around, thought as little of its prospects. "A continued chain of uncouth, naked, rocky, poor, uncultivated, and uncultivable mountains,"[1] one is reported to have said. But there was no going back on Bremer's action. The naval officers were happy with the selection.

So were the merchants. If the anchorage was useful for men-of-war, it was even more useful for their opium ships. The traffic in that commodity had never required warehousing on a large scale. A careful selection among samples, a leisurely bargaining over price, and the other ordinary procedures of trade in teas, cotton, and the like had not been required. Opium's bulk was modest, relatively speaking. If packed properly it did not spoil. Best of all, as long as the demand was high, you did not have to go looking for customers: they came to you, paid you on the spot in silver, and went away with what they had ordered. Your only worry was interference by pirate or mandarin boats, and for that you armed your vessels well. But if you lay in an anchorage that men-of-war frequented, so much the better—they would lend you a fighting hand. Hong Kong was such. With its possession now formal, the merchants should be able to expand. "Elliot says that he sees no objection to our storing opium there," James Matheson wrote to one of the Jardines, "and as soon as the New Year holidays are over I shall set about building."[2] Build he did. Others, who like Matheson did business in much more than just the drug, built too. Before the Opium War was over, the north shore of the island boasted a road some four miles in length, with a straggling ribbon of a town along it. The mat sheds of the Chinese were relieved from time to time by houses built of a mixture of clay, lime, and broken stone, the whole pounded between wooden forms. There were even a few bungalows and godowns in granite or brick.

Hong Kong and opium. The place, the British, the drug. A natural, deadly, three-way symbiosis. The one inconceivable without the other two, particularly if you have been listening to what official China tells us and whole masses of Chinese believe. Hong Kong itself had a dose of this as the appointed surrender, scheduled to take place on the last day of June 1997, came near. The theme was homecoming. Taking Hong Kong back from the British was to be a homecoming, not just for the Hong Kong Chinese but for Chinese everywhere. Homecoming "driven home without pause" (reported Ian Buruma of the *New York Review Of Books*, who was there), "in official speeches, a new movie, mass stadium demonstrations, newspaper headlines, buttons and badges, T-shirts and posters, and slogans in wooden Chinese."[3] The homecoming was to be a patriotic victory that wiped out 150 years of humiliation and shame inflicted by the British and the despicable native hucksters through whom they did their smuggling. For it was at Hong Kong, seized impudently and brazenly so many, many years ago, that the British had pushed for so long, and with such dreadful consequences to China's millions, their unconscionable traffic in opium.

You will be inclined to agree that there is something to that indictment, more so because this book begins with opium, never leaves opium for long, and toward the end devotes an entire chapter to Hong Kong. But there is an explanation for this. The book does indeed begin with opium. This is because opium leads directly to the book's subject, which is—I draw upon the original preface—westerners in China in the early decades of the nineteenth century and the war, the Opium War, that they brought on. The war is the centerpiece. And at the time I wrote, in the late sixties and early seventies, I intended (save for a few generalizations) nothing beyond the chronological limit of the story and paid no particular attention to place. Canton city, the Canton River upon which it lies, the Gulf of Canton into which that river flows, and Macao perched upon the gulf's western rim, dominated the early chapters because that was where the westerners mostly were, less by choice than by necessity. Later, with the war on, they spread up China's coast, and the book's narrative followed them there. Hong Kong (in those days often spelled "Hongkong") fell into that category. The war brought westerners to the archipelago. I gave it a chapter. It did not occur to me to think beyond that.

But almost a quarter of a century has passed since the book was written. And in the interval a lot has changed in the world. The Cold War is over, replaced not by the "One World" so many of us looked forward to so fondly, but by one a good deal less attractive. A world fractured by hostilities that might more politely be called differences. Differences over who has what, of course. But differences, too, over cultures. Cultural differences, often local, but sometimes so large (especially if religion is involved), and so keenly felt, that they cross the boundaries of ideology and national identity and qualify as a "clash of cultures"—the expression is currently on many lips. Meanwhile, almost everywhere in Europe, Asia, and elsewhere around the globe, Communism, in its two dimensions—political and economic—has faltered, been quietly dismantled, or in some cases has simply crumbled and collapsed, as in the springtime ice jammed against a river bridge so often will. But in China the process has taken a turn that promises to pit the repudiation of an ideology against the preservation of a cultural position. For in China, though Communism as a political system is as firmly in command as it has ever been, Communism as an economic system is not. Consequently, whereas the first confirms and pursues the traditional duties of a Chinese government, namely, to command from the center, elevate the community above the individual, and allow nothing to undermine or break the harmony of the common course, the second moves in quite the opposite direction. No less an agency than the Party itself has turned its back upon Marxist economic theory. With that lead to follow, a significant proportion of China's population, particularly in the south, has for some years now been devoting itself with great gusto to free market theory and free market enterprise. Every man for himself, runs the prescription. Wealth is power. To get rich is glorious. And as that not only draws from the western mind, but also brings the practitioner into contact with westerners in the flesh, there is in this the makings of a cultural clash. Particularly in Hong Kong, a Hong Kong spectacularly different from the anchorage of that name a century and a half ago.

The difference is partly a matter of scale. Take Shanghai. Lay Hong Kong against it, side by side. When, in January 1841, the British in Bremer's person made Hong Kong into the royal colony that the Chinese did not "bring home" until midnight on a late June day 156 years later—when Hong Kong went British, and thereby slipped into the history books, it really *was* (bar the odd village here and there) barren and empty, whereas Shanghai, 800 miles to the north, was already a considerable city, as Sir Hugh Gough's men discovered when they stormed it without difficulty in the early summer of 1842. Shanghai was not, it is true, an administrative center, which meant it had no Manchu quarter (and that in turn explains why it fell so easily: the Manchu bannermen were formidable, the Green Standard men were not). It had, however, walls. It had stone warehouses along the banks of the Hwangpu, which flows into the Yangtse's mouth. The Hwangpu itself was thick with junks. Shanghai was the terminus not just for the Yangtse, which drains half of China, but for the trade along great stretches of China's coast. By the turn of the century, it had easily surpassed Hong Kong in population, size, and sheer economic power. (Hong Kong had meanwhile added first Kowloon, then the New Territories, at times and in ways that need not be dealt with here, beyond observing that in terms of breathing space, the additions simply produced the twenty-miles-on-a-side first mentioned.) It held that position right up to the Second World War, and when the war was over recovered it for several years more. But Shanghai as a great commercial city has never elicited, not then and not now, language to match what Hong Kong has prompted lately.

Here is a specimen, from a recent study of Hong Kong, Taiwan, and China at large by the freelance journalist and correspondent Willem Van Klemenade. "Hong Kong," he begins in a chapter that introduces the reader to the place, "is number one in the show of extravagance and ostentatious luxury, and number two (after New York) in the possession of an imposing skyline." From whatever hilltop you choose, the view is magnificent: coastline of "mini-fjords," skyscrapers rearing, villas gay against a background of green hills and rocky slopes. If you spend some time there you will discover that the city holds "an endless list" of world records: the largest per capita number of Rolls-Royces, Mercedes-Benzes, and BMWs, "the highest consumption rate of VSOP cognacs, the highest levels of stress, the highest prices for real estate (considerably higher than Tokyo's)." Its per capita income is already higher than that of its "stepmother country," England, and forty times that of its "historical motherland," China. "One of the world's top five cities." "One of the most spectacularly successful city-states in world history." Never, not even in Venice in the late Middle Ages or in Amsterdam in the seventeenth century, has such an immense wealth been accumulated in such a short time.[4]

And as he continues his analysis of this "megalopolis spread out over a craggy, sprawling archipelago," this dynamo of entrepreneurial energy that he knows so well (Van Klemenade has spent the past twenty years in Hong Kong and Peking), you are made aware of two things. That the "homecoming" may spoil everything. And that, on the contrary, the marriage (if you may call it that) may pull China at large into the orbit not simply of free markets, but of free politics and thought.

Buruma says the same thing. So does the *Economist*. "How Hong Kong Can Change China" runs the caption on the leading article in its June 28, 1997 issue. Everywhere the attention given those June days by the serious press hovers between apprehension and hope. But nowhere does the press assure us that half a dozen other Chinese cities are moving Hong Kong's way. In the matter of market economics, all probably are. But that is not what the press has in mind. For what rivets attention, one might say world attention, upon those twenty square miles is not simply its commercial and financial success. It is the independence in thought and action of these "Hong-Kongers," to borrow the *Economist*'s term. That these Hong-Kongers exist is confirmed by a statistic: whereas a dozen years ago more than half the inhabitants of the colony were main-land-born immigrants, today just under two-thirds were born in Hong Kong. They are not fond of the British per se but are anxious over what they may lose with that country's departure. They do not pretend, or even think, that they are not Chinese. They are somewhere in the middle. And that, in the circumstances of enormous energy in a very tight space, is exciting.

It would be beyond my competence to explain adequately just how all this came to be, even had I months and my publisher the patience. One comment only: how curious that a place and its use that so offended a whole people should metamorphose over time into something quite attractive. They say you cannot make a silk purse out of a sow's ear. But perhaps you can.

As for the book, it will have to stand by itself. Readers may discover that though I am quite aware what damage opium did, I do not believe that the Opium War was really *about* opium at all. It was about other particular things, shaped by circumstances as most history is; and it was, if you look for an overarching principle, about somehow getting the Chinese to open up. The desire is still very much with us today.

I am delighted that the University of North Carolina Press has undertaken this reprint, and grateful for the encouragement and editorial attention given the process by Mary Laur, my editor, and Michael Taeckens, my copyeditor, and their colleagues. Nothing has been added to the existing Note on Sources, in part because in the years since it was drawn up, nothing that seriously added to or challenged the narrative has to my knowledge appeared. Of more general works on China, and Hong Kong in particular, I have nothing to suggest beyond what bibliographies more effectively offer. There is one exception: Willem Van Klemenade's *China, Hong Kong, Taiwan, Inc.* (New York: Alfred A. Knopf, 1997).

Place names have been rendered as they were in the original edition, partly to make the reprinting less difficult, partly for the reason given in the first preface. That explains why "Hong Kong," now so current, becomes "Hongkong" when you start reading.

Pasadena, California
August 1997

1. *Canton Press*, 27 February 1841.

2. 22 January 1841, James Matheson Private Letter Books, vol. 6, Jardine Matheson Papers.

3. 12 June 1997, p. 54.

4. Willem Van Klemenade, *China, Hong Kong, Taiwan, Inc.* (New York: Alfred A. Knopf, 1997).

Preface

There does not exist, for the West's first major intrusion into China, what the subject deserves and a reader is entitled to. The popular books on the war leave it a piece in the larger story of the "awakening dragon" or treat it decidedly hurriedly. The scholarly monographs approach it from one angle or another, rarely making much of an effort at narrative. Neither give the missionaries, particularly the Catholic missionaries, their due; neither do as much with opium and the opium traffic as they should. To write a comprehensive account of westerners in China in the fourth decade of the nineteenth century and of the Opium War that they brought on—an account that begins with opium, of course, and never lets opium go, but allows other interests and ambitions to take their rightful parts, and with the firms, missions, ships, regiments, and men, play those parts out—has been my purpose and the book's excuse.

I should like to thank the trustees and staff of the several libraries, archives, and missions on which I have drawn, among them Father Guennou of the Missions Etrangères, Father Combaluzier of the Congrégation de la Mission, and the United Church Board for World Ministries (which allowed me to use the ABCFM papers). I am grateful to Matheson and Company, Ltd., of London, and to Alan Reid thereof, for access to the invaluable Jardine Matheson archive at Cambridge University and for permission to quote from the letters it contains.

A number of people have helped me personally: the same Alan Reid with various notes and observations; H. A. Crosby Forbes and my cousin Commander P. B. Beazley, R.N., with maps; Peter de Jong with tea; Randle Edwards with classical Chinese law. A. B. Malik, then director of industries for Uttar Pradesh, kindly arranged a visit to the Ghazipur opium factory. Charlton M. Lewis got me to improve several sections on things Chinese. Jacques Downs, who probably knows more about Americans in China in the early nineteenth century than any man alive, made available to me xerox copies of a portion of the Carrington papers and read a large part of the manuscript with a critical eye. Many other friends and colleagues read parts too—I should like to thank Heinz Ellersieck and Susan Sidle particularly, and Shirley Marneus most of all.

The book is very much better for the skillful editing of Gwen Duffey of the University of North Carolina Press. I owe the index to Carol B. Pearson, the Chinese characters (which translate "opium war") to Mingshui Hung of Brooklyn College, the typing and retyping to Joy Hansen and her colleagues in the Humanities Division secretarial pool, the maps to Pat Lee and hers. Years ago Hallett D. Smith, then chairman of the division, encouraged me to begin the book and found me the wherewithal to work in London and Paris. The present chairman, Robert A. Huttenback, has been equally encouraging and helpful in a number of ways—not least by making it possible for me and my family to live in India, where I began the writing. My wife Mariette has read and reread the many drafts and final copy, has advised me shrewdly on matters both of substance and of style, and has put up with a great deal beside. My children have wondered sympathetically when I would finish. The book is for her and for them.

Pieces of it in somewhat different shape have appeared in *Bengal Past and Present*, *Modern Asian Studies*, and the *Pacific Historical Review*. I am grateful to their respective editors for permission to repeat some of the material here.

In the matter of Chinese names I have kept particularly in mind the intelligent general reader (I hope I am one), who sees no point in being constantly reminded that Leghorn is really Livorno, and in the case of transliterations from other scripts prefers something easily recognizable the second time around. Often I have spelled places and people as foreigners spelled them a century ago.

California Institute of Technology
Kanpur, U.P., 1966——Beaminster, Dorset, 1974

Introduction

In the summer of 1846 several enterprising Englishmen on the island of Hongkong decided to buy a junk and sail her home.

Though their government had only recently signed a victorious peace with the Chinese, though the union jack flew over the island and merchants from Europe and America traded with relative freedom at Canton and four other ports, they had to go about their business with caution; for Chinese law still forbade the sale of vessels to foreigners. Unobtrusively they located a likely deep-water junk, bought her, named her after Kiying (Ch'i-ying), the Chinese governor-general at Canton, engaged a crew two-thirds Chinese and one-third European, and prepared for sea. By early December the *Kiying* was ready. Sir John Francis Davis, first civil governor of Hongkong, paid her the courtesy of a visit; and on the sixth, to a salute from warships, she sailed. Strong headwinds in the Indian Ocean stretched her passage to the Cape past sixteen weeks. Another two brought her to St. Helena. Then continuous gales drove her so far to the west that she was obliged to put into New York. There she lay for several months, refitting, while thousands of the curious trooped across her deck. Early in 1848 she moved up to Boston, sailed from that port for England, sighted Land's End twenty-one days later (a fast passage even for the packets of the Black Ball Line), and on the last Monday of March entered the Thames and anchored at Gravesend. The *Illustrated London News* sent a man down to have a look.

The papers that spring were full of revolution on the Continent. Louis Philippe of France had lost his throne, patriots and liberals were up in arms in Italy and Germany, Metternich had fled Vienna. The *News* was naturally much occupied with these events and filled its pages with eyewitness accounts of street fighting and pen and ink drawings of barricades. But towards the back of the first issue in April the editor found room for the *Kiying*. To the story he attached a sketch. His readers saw a floating halfmoon of a vessel 160 feet long and a little over 30 feet wide, her stern towering above the waterline, her bow rising almost as high. With masts quite naked of yards or standing rigging, sails of matting ribbed with bamboo, ropes of plaited rattan, anchors of ironwood, and a large eye painted in brilliant colors on either side of her bow, there was not on the Thames, nor had there ever been, a ship remotely like her. And that was not surprising. For the *Kiying* was the first Chinese vessel ever to reach England.

After some time she moved up the river to Blackwall. There she was visited by Queen Victoria, Prince Albert, and the Duke of Wellington. Presumably they were as struck by her curious lines and strange appearance as the man from the *News* had been. What ought to have astonished them, however—though it probably did not—was the fact that she had been brought to London at all, and by Englishmen. How could there be, on the island of Hongkong in the summer of 1846, Englishmen in a position to buy a junk and fit her out? How could there be an English governor to pay her a courtesy call and a union jack to do it under?

For at the beginning of the nineteenth century the English were scarcely to be found east of Calcutta. There were Dutch on the island of Java and Spanish at Manila, but their being at those places constituted only a modest extension of the West past the Bay of Bengal, one that reached into southeast Asia only. China, the heart and the bulk of the true East, remained almost untouched—remained, in fact, closed; if not fully closed like Japan, nevertheless much more nearly closed than were India and the Arab world. A tiny Russian colony at Peking, a few dozen Catholic missionaries scattered furtively about the interior, a few hundred Portuguese roosting idle and neglected on the tiny peninsula of Macao, and a handful of merchants carrying on a limited trade at Canton made up the sum of the western presence in the immense Chinese Empire. And the sum was not significantly inflated during the first third of the century.

By 1846, however, things were different. Different in actuality. Very different in prospect. China was not closed any more. A war had decided she must open. And though she had not opened very far by the time the English bought the *Kiying*, it was already clear that the process, for some time at least, was irreversible. China was going to open further.

This book is about the first step in the opening, not the whole process. It is about the first China War, not western relations with China. Nevertheless it may be worth observing how odd, how unexpected, that process and those relations have been. For suppose the Chinese had been the openers instead of the opened.

Suppose the sighting of Land's End by an expedition sent from China early in the sixteenth century. Suppose mandarins in silk gowns demanding audience of James I, merchant junks discharging teas and loading wool and tin at London Bridge, the breaking out in 1801 of the so-called "Gin War" (it began when Pitt tried to stop the importation into England of grain spirits from the great Chinese dependency on the Mississippi and ended when twenty-five junks of war caught Nelson's numerically superior squadron off the Goodwin Sands and destroyed it), the consequent cession to the Chinese of the Isle of Wight and a strip of the mainland along Southampton Water, the irresistible demand of the Japanese and the Straits Malays for equivalent trading concessions at

Bristol and Hull, and the development of the International Settlement at Liverpool with its smartly drilled mixed Oriental police and its famous Institute for the Propagation of Confucian Ethics. Suppose, finally, a party of Chinese buying one day a Glasgow sidewheeler and steaming her home around the Horn.

You might, in short, have expected China to force herself upon Europe. She had, after all, such a head start. When Confucius taught his sophisticated ethics in the sixth century B.C., Rome was only a village and England a savage waste. Two thousand years later, when a united and highly civilized China prospered under the Ming, Christian Europe was hardly more than the sum of her kings and princes, with moribund Moors at her western extremity and Turks battering at the east. Over all this extent of time the flow of influence, if any, had been from China towards Europe—not the other way around. Paper, porcelain, printing, gunpowder, the compass, the wheelbarrow, and the fore-and-aft rig are among the things China gave Europe. And when, early in the eighteenth century, European admiration for Chinese society and things Chinese was at its height, the admirers still imagined (as they had always and with perfect accuracy imagined) that the object of their admiration was as powerful as it was advanced. Yet for all that it was Europe that shortly forced herself upon China—bringing Christ and opium.

List of Characters

A list alphabetically arranged, by no means complete, yet including many who, though not particularly important of themselves, appear often enough so that the reader may wish a handy means of reminding himself who or what they are.

Abeel	American missionary who, reaching China temporarily in 1830 and settling permanently in 1839, observes at first hand the opium crisis and the war.
Alligator	26-gun frigate.
Ann	Jardine Matheson coastal opium brig (Denham is her skipper).
Atalanta	wooden steamer.
Auckland	Whig governor-general of India when the war begins; replaced early in 1842 by the Tory Ellenborough.
Baldus	French Lazarist missionary.
Belcher	captain of the survey bark *Sulphur* and one of those officers who later write about the war.
Bingham	lieutenant for most of the war aboard the corvette *Modeste*. He too writes a long narrative based on his experiences.
Blonde	42-gun heavy frigate (Bourchier is her captain).
Bremer	naval officer appointed (briefly) joint plenipotentiary with Charles Elliot and recalled when Elliot is.
Bridgman	continuously at Canton and Macao from 1830 onward, this American missionary

	founds the *Chinese Repository,* and through its pages reports the thirties, the opium crisis, and the war fully and to much moral purpose.
Burrell	senior regimental officer and commander of the land forces of the expedition—until, not a moment too soon, Gough arrives to take his place.
Cambridge	armed ex-Indiaman that assists Charles Elliot and eventually becomes a Chinese man-of-war.
Conway	26-gun frigate (Bethune is her captain).
Dent	senior partner in the English agency house that bears his name and, at the time of the opium crisis, the factory community's leading merchant member.
Druid	44-gun heavy frigate (Smith eventually gets her).
Charles Elliot	chief superintendent at the time of the opium crisis; joint plenipotentiary and de facto political director of the expedition in its first year; recalled in 1841 to nobody's surprise (not even his own).
George Elliot	admiral and in 1840 joint plenipotentiary with his younger cousin Charles, lets Charles take the reins and goes home ill.
Faivre	French Lazarist missionary who reaches his interior post with the aid of the *Red Rover.*
Forbes	American merchant with Russell and Company.
Good Success	Bombay country ship regularly bringing raw cotton and opium to Jardine's.

Gough	taking Burrell's place early in 1841, he makes one in the triumvirate (Parker and Pottinger are the others) that conducts the war to its victorious conclusion at Nanking.
Gutzlaff	German Protestant missionary and old China hand who serves the Superintendency and the expedition in various civil capacities.
Hellas	Jardine Matheson coastal opium schooner (Jauncey is her skipper).
Hercules	Jardine Matheson receiving ship.
Hobhouse	in Melbourne's Whig government the cabinet minister responsible for India.
Howqua	first among the hong merchants in wealth and standing.
Hunter	American merchant with Russell and Company. During the opium crisis he keeps a journal; much later he publishes his memoirs.
Hyacinth	18-gun corvette.
Innes	private (very private) English merchant and old China hand.
Jamsetjee Jeejeebhoy	Bombay Parsee merchant doing business with Jardine's.
Jardine	William Jardine is senior partner in Jardine Matheson until his departure for England early in 1839. Two nephews, Andrew and David, remain behind.
Jocelyn	military secretary to the plenipotentiaries through 1840—when he rushes home and into print.

Johnston	deputy chief superintendent and eventually acting governor of Hongkong.
Joset	procurator of the Propaganda, i.e., the Italian Franciscan mission.
King	American merchant with Olyphant and company, he has strong moral views and pushes them.
Kishen	Chinese high commissioner encountered first at the Peiho, later in the negotiations that lead to the abortive Chuenpi Convention of January, 1841.
Kiying	Chinese high commissioner who negotiates the Treaty of Nanking.
Larne	18-gun corvette (Blake is her captain).
Lay	China agent for the English Bible Society and, later, interpreter with the expedition.
Legrégeois	procurator of the Missions Etrangères until early in 1842 he goes home—when Libois succeeds him.
Lin	Chinese high commissioner who precipitates the opium crisis and is eventually sacked for it. A hero to today's Chinese—and irresistibly attractive to almost everybody else (now, not then).
Lintin	Russell and Company receiving ship.
Lockhart	English medical missionary who stays the war out (whereas Parker does not) and reports what he sees.
Mackenzie	military secretary to the plenipotentiaries after Jocelyn; like Jocelyn he hurries home and writes it up.

MacPherson	observant surgeon with the 37th Madras Native Infantry.
Madagascar	wooden steamer.
Matheson	James Matheson follows William Jardine as senior partner in the house that bears their names; when early in 1842 he too goes home, his nephew Alexander takes his place.
Milne	two English missionaries, father (d. 1822) and son.
Mor	Jardine Matheson opium clipper ship.
Morrison	Robert Morrison, the first Protestant missionary to reach China, is at his death in 1834 chief interpreter to the superintendency. His son John succeeds him in that office.
Mountain	staff officer first with Burrell, later with Gough.
Napier	hapless peer and naval officer who assumes the superintendency in 1834 and is crushed by it.
Nemesis	extraordinary armed iron steamer (Hall is captain).
Nye	American merchant.
Palmerston	foreign secretary in Melbourne's Whig governments; the man whom both Napier and Charles Elliot must somehow contrive to satisfy.
Admiral Parker	commands the expedition's fleet from mid-1841 until the end.

Peter Parker	the American missionary who first attempts to put medicine to the service of Christ. His Hog Lane hospital opens in 1835.
Perboyre	French Lazarist missionary who reaches the interior in 1836 and dies there four years later.
Phlegethon	armed iron steamer very like the *Nemesis*.
Pinto	Portuguese governor of Macao.
Pottinger	sent out to take Charles Elliot's place, he is sole plenipotentiary and political director of the expedition from mid-1841 until the end.
Queen	armed wooden steamer.
Rameaux	French Lazarist missionary.
Red Rover	Jardine Matheson opium clipper bark, the first of her kind (Clifton builds her).
Senhouse	captain of the *Blenheim*, a 74-gun ship-of-the-line, and senior naval officer in the Canton operations of 1841.
Slade	publisher of the weekly *Canton Register*.
Squire	China agent for the English Church Missionary Society.
Stanton	English divinity student who comes to Macao as a tutor and is kidnapped there.
Teng	Chinese governor-general at Canton before and during the opium crisis.
Thom	Jardine Matheson clerk who learns Chinese and becomes an interpreter with the expedition.

Torrette	procurator of the French Lazarists until death removes him in 1840. Guillet takes his place.
Volage	26-gun frigate (Smith is her captain until he gets the *Druid*).
Wellesley	74-gun flagship of the East Indian squadron for most of the war.
Williams	American missionary printer who joins Bridgman at the *Repository*; like Bridgman he observes and reports the opium crisis and the war.

PART ONE

The Old China Trade

1

Papaver Somniferum

On the banks of the Ganges some distance east of Benares, in the most wretched and neglected part of the north Indian state of Uttar Pradesh, lies the little town of Ghazipur. It is not much of a place. In April and May, when the thermometer stands at well over a hundred in the shade and terrible dry storms drive the dust so high into the air you may look the sun full in the face without flinching, it is hard to imagine anyone doing anything at Ghazipur save wait for the rains of the summer monsoon to sweep up from the Bay of Bengal. But in fact there is activity here even at this time of the year. For Ghazipur is one of the few places in the world where opium is still openly and legitimately prepared for market. And it is during these particularly trying months that the raw drug comes in from the villages.

It is brought directly to the Government of India Opium and Alkaloid Works, a collection of brick buildings scattered about ten or twenty acres on the north bank of the river. A high brick wall broken by watchtowers surrounds the area. There are guards on the towers; if you are rash enough to approach along the river bank (the channel long ago shifted leaving a quarter of a mile of blinding white sand between the bank and the water), an officer will appear and lead you firmly around to the main gate. There you will be asked your business and perhaps relieved of your camera, for the Government of India does not welcome tourists to its Ghazipur factory. Though Benares is only a few dozen miles away, the literature about that famous city does not mention the place. It may be that New Delhi is not anxious to have its opium activities made much of, entirely respectable and aboveboard though they are. It may be, too, that it does not care to have its factory cased. A dacoity there would fetch a king's ransom in opium.

Opium is obtained by collecting the latex that exudes from the partially ripe seed capsule of *papaver somniferum,* the opium poppy. If you slit

3

a capsule just after the petals have fallen but before it is fully ripe, a thick milky-white juice will ooze from the cut and harden upon the surface into a dark brown gum. This gum is raw opium. It is secreted by the skin of the capsule; it does not come from the seeds themselves, which may be used quite safely for other things. There are fields of the poppy right in Ghazipur District. But most of the opium received at Ghazipur, the only major opium factory left in India, comes from distant parts of Uttar Pradesh and from the neighboring states of Madhya Pradesh and Rajasthan. The year's crop begins to arrive about the middle of April. After inspection and weighing it is poured into large rectangular stone vats standing side by side in a warehouse. The smell is the smell of new-mown hay, but the look is the look of tar. Later, in the dry weather before the rains come and in the dry weather after, the drug is taken out of the vats a little at a time and carried to an open space near the high brick wall. There it is spread in shallow wooden trays set upon concrete platforms. Mechanical stirrers on rails move noiselessly across the trays, stirring the gummy stuff to expose it fully to the air. Monkeys wander here and there; and though they do not touch the opium, they perhaps drink from the ditch just outside the wall, for they seem always a little bit dopey.

At any given moment there will be hundreds of gallons of opium drying thus—opium is soluble in water, absorbs moisture readily, and must be hardened before it can be packed—and it is hard to imagine that all of it oozed a drop at a time from multiple incisions on the surface of seed capsules no bigger than crab apples. These incisions, explains a certain John Scott in a *Manual of Opium Husbandry* published at Calcutta in 1877, are made by a knife called *nashtar* or *nurnee*. "It consists of four concave-faced, sharp-pointed blades tied together with cotton at about the one-thirtieth of an inch apart, the parallel lines of incisions rarely exceeding one-eighth of an inch." (Except that the blades used nowadays span as much as three-eighths of an inch, a century seems to have made little difference in the knife.) "When the plants have been in bloom for some time," explains another manual, this one published at Benares in 1861,[1] "the green capsules become slightly coated over with a fine transparent white colored surface and the pods become less yielding to the touch." It is then time to cut, and on an afternoon in February the work begins. "The lancers," continues Scott, "move backwards through the fields and expertly catch with their left hand the sufficiently mature capsule, draw their lancets perpendicularly over it, slip it, catch another, and so on." To cut properly requires patience and some skill; for if the incision is too shallow no juice exudes, and if it pierces the capsule the juice flows inward and is lost among the seeds. Twenty lancers should be able to cover one acre in an afternoon. Next morning they return to collect the opium that has exuded during the night. Moving this time forwards so as not to brush against the drug-bearing capsules, they grasp a capsule in one hand, scrape its incised surface with an iron scoop held in the other, and from time to time empty the scoop into earthenware pots. Two days later the capsules are incised again at a different place. The process is repeated at intervals—perhaps as little as four times, perhaps as often as eight—until nothing more seeps out.

To produce an appreciable quantity of opium requires, therefore, the repeated incision of a great number of capsules: at half a gram a capsule (the figure suggested by the chief chemist at the Ghazipur factory), about eighteen thousand capsules to yield the twenty pounds that appears to be the minimum return per acre throughout India—today as well as a hundred years ago. Of course an acre of *papaver somniferum* produces other things as well: about two hundred pounds of poppy seeds, which in India are used in curries or pressed for oil; and several dozen pounds of the petals once thought essential to the preparation of the drug for export. But opium itself is obtained only by the application of a great deal of labor. With the consequence that though the opium poppy will grow wherever the corn poppy does, it is not likely to be cultivated in areas of high labor cost—not as long as it can be cultivated in areas where cost is low. In 1830 an Edinburgh man succeeded in getting fifty-six pounds of raw opium from one acre of the plants. The experiment was apparently never repeated. Cheap as agricultural labor was in Great Britain, it was not as cheap there as on the Ganges plain.

From the drying yard hardened opium is taken to an adjoining shed. There it is pressed into blocks, wrapped in polyethylene, and put into mango-wood chests the size of small footlockers. That is the end of the process in this part of the factory; nothing more is done to the drug before it is shipped. Exactly how much is turned out it is not easy to discover. In 1954 the Ghazipur factory produced not quite four hundred and eighty tons of opium, drawing for the purpose on 50,000 acres of the poppy. Of this quantity 290 tons—at 170 pounds of opium to the chest, about 3,400 chests—left Ghazipur for points overseas, enough to satisfy between a quarter and a third of the world's annual legitimate medical requirements. The figures for the years since cannot have been much greater and may have been less.

More or less, however, 3,400 chests is a very small figure next to what used to leave India in the late nineteenth century. Then the Ghazipur works drew on over 400,000 acres of the poppy. Then another factory down the river at Patna, since closed, received the juice from almost half a million. From these two places, and from the Malwa area of west central India, not three or four thousand chests but twenty times that number went overseas each year, not a few hundred tons but approximately six thousand! In the shipping season, which for the Ganges plain meant late autumn when the rains were over and the heat had gone, enough chests were made ready at Ghazipur alone to fill a special train to Calcutta every fourth day. Even in the 1830s half a century earlier, though Ghazipur lagged well behind Patna in production of the drug, it turned out more chests than it does today. It was opium that made it the "very handsome place" a contemporary gazetteer calls it. Opium, not the tomb of Cornwallis or the government stud farm, built it up to a civil station of sufficient size to justify the brick and granite church that stands to all appearances empty and abandoned now. In 1838 over seven thousand chests of Benares were sold at the Calcutta auctions—twice as many as left Ghazipur for that city in 1954.

Then as now a part of each year's production was consumed right in India. Known as *akbari* or excise opium, it was prepared much as it is prepared today. "The opium intended for *akbaree* purposes," an English opium examiner named Eatwell wrote in 1850,[2] "is brought to a consistence of 90 percent by direct exposure to the sun, in which state it is as firm and as easily moulded as wax. It is then formed by means of a mould into square bricks of one seer weight each, and these are wrapped in oiled Nepaul paper and packed in boxes." If you ignore the division into two-pound bricks and read polyethylene for "Nepaul paper," nothing at first sight has changed.

Yet there is a difference. A large part of today's *akbari* is converted right at the Ghazipur factory into the opium alkaloids morphine and codeine. In Eatwell's day none of it was. Morphine had been isolated about the time of Waterloo. Codeine, and the synthetic alkaloid heroin with which we are so painfully familiar, appeared later in the century. But until the development of the hypodermic needle, these alkaloids were not much used. Instead physicians prescribed opium in water—or more usually, opium in alcohol. It was tincture of opium that the druggist handed De Quincey when the latter tried to get relief from the neuralgic pains of the head and face that were torturing him. Coleridge began taking laudanum (camphorated tincture of opium) about the same time and for much the same reason. At that moment in *Middlemarch* when his tormentor Raffles lies dying, it is an "almost empty opium phial" that Bulstrode puts out of sight lest Lydgate discover that his patient has been given an overdose. Opium, not its alkaloids, was the essential ingredient in the innumerable remedies dispensed in Europe and America for the treatment of diarrhea, dysentery, asthma, rheumatism, diabetes, malaria, cholera, fevers, bronchitis, insomnia, and pains of any sort. At a time when the physician's cabinet was almost bare of alternative drugs, it was impossible to practice medicine without it.

The ancient Mediterranean world knew opium and used it widely. From the eastern Mediterranean and the lands immediately beyond, where the opium poppy was then principally cultivated, the Arabs carried the drug to India. In India, however, opium came to be accepted not simply as a medicine but as a general restorative, its qualities in this direction being readily apparent to all who took it, and there being no wine to compete. An English doctor serving with the 3rd Bombay Native Infantry describes how his men, when a halt in a long march sounded, "would break themselves up into small groups of four or five, and sit for a while, and then one of the group would in a quiet way take from his pocket a little lump of opium and proceed to divide it with those sitting with him; and there they would sit awhile meditating, swallowing the opium and meditating; and by the time the halt was at an end and the regiment reformed and marched on, they were fully refreshed and perfectly steady."[3] Rajput camel drivers fortified themselves with opium water before setting off across the deserts of Sind. "I have often thought," observed one retired Indian civil servant before the Royal Commission on Opium of 1893, "that the best practical answer to those who inveigh against the use of opium would be, if such a thing were practicable, to bring one of our crack opium-drinking Sikh regiments to London and exhibit them in Hyde Park."[4] Of course it was not practicable. But in its final report the commission did recommend that opium in India ought not to be confined to occasional medical use. So the drug remained the ordinary Indian's remedy for malaria, his rejuvenator in old age, the agent of his relief from fatigue and pain—no more to be frowned upon than bhang or hashish.

There was, however, another way to take opium, and that was to smoke it. Within India very few people did. Though the "half-caste" woman who looked after Kim smoked, the much more usual reference in literature is that of the heroine in Tagore's *The Home and the World,* whose sight is clouded over "like an opium-eater's eyes." But in parts of Assam and Burma, in Thailand and Cambodia, in Laos and Vietnam, throughout the East Indies, and above all in China, the person who turned to opium for relaxation or stimulation usually used the pipe. Indeed, in the nineteenth century, when opium was everywhere consumed more publicly than it is today, this change in the manner of taking the drug became so marked east of Calcutta that one was tempted to associate opium smoking quite simply with Mongoloid features, with high cheekbones and the epicanthic fold.

Yet no one can really say why the peoples east of the Indian Ocean got into the habit of assimilating the drug in this way. Opium came to them as it had come to the Indians, through the Arabs. For years they ate and drank it as the Indians did. After a while they began to combine it with chopped tobacco or betel leaves in a mixture called *madak.* (Some Assamese still smoke it this way or did so forty years ago.) From the East Indies *madak* passed to the South China coast, as plain tobacco had done before it. And somewhere along the way the leaf was allowed to drop out—or so we must suppose, though it leaves unexplained why Indians (or Europeans for that matter) did not make the same experiment and arrive at the same result.★ Whatever the reason, however, by the second half of the eighteenth century the Chinese were in firm possession of the technique of smoking opium, a technique whose delicate ritual and profound physiological effects may afford the devotee a higher and a keener pleasure than he will ever get by simply eating or drinking the drug. Thereafter wherever the Chinese went, to railroad construction sites in Nevada and canal digging in Panama, they carried the technique with them.

To smoke opium you need, of course, a pipe. But it is a pipe like no other, a pipe you cannot stuff with anything and for which matches are useless. In the memoirs he wrote as he sailed home an invalid in the middle of the Opium War, Lieutenant Bingham of Her Majesty's corvette *Modeste* describes an opium pipe he happened to pick up on an island at the mouth of the Canton River. "The stem of this pipe, in cane, perfectly black from use," he writes, "is seventeen inches long, and one inch in diameter, having a turned mouthpiece of buffalo's horn; six inches of the opposite end are encased in copper beautifully inlaid with silver. Midway on this is a round copper socket three inches in circumference, in which is placed the bowl, formed of fine clay handsomely chased, and resembling in shape a flattened turnip, with a puncture about the size of a pin's head on the upper side; the diameter of this bowl is nearly three inches."[5] Apparently Bingham did not attempt to use his handsome souvenir. But Duncan MacPherson, a surgeon with the 37th Madras Native Infantry in the same campaign, was more daring. "I had the curiosity to try the effects of a few pipes upon myself," he explains.[6] If he mastered the technique, what he did must have gone something as follows.

Settling himself comfortably on his side upon a couch, he took up a drop of gum-like opium on the point of a long needle and held it over a spirit lamp. Under the heat of the flame the drop gradually turned pale, softened, swelled, and began to bubble and sputter. Before it could actually turn to vapor, MacPherson carried it still on the point of the needle to the

---

★The crude opium used in *madak* yields about 0.2% of morphia by volume, the refined opium that is "smoked" yields 9% to 10%; thus "the moderate pleasures of madak—perhaps equivalent to taking a few inhalations of marijuana—were rejected by many smokers when they discovered the smoking of pure opium." Thus Jonathan Spence's reasonable explanation (in "Opium Smoking in Ch'ing China," a paper given at the ACLS University of California Conference on Local Control and Social Protest in the Ch'ing, Honolulu, July 1971). But, of course, someone had to experiment with pure opium first.

surface of the pipe bowl, tipped the bowl over the flame, put the stem of the pipe to his lips, and inhaled. The opium passed into his lungs in the form of a heavy white smoke. Two or three puffs entirely consumed the drop; MacPherson repeated the operation several times; and very soon he began to feel the effects of the drug.

What these effects were MacPherson does not really say. Perhaps he was lucky, like the American traveler Bayard Taylor, who tried opium smoking at Canton a few years later; after his sixth pipe he began to see brilliant colors that floated before his eyes "in a confused and cloudy way, sometimes converging into spots like the eyes in a peacock's tail, but oftenest melting into and through each other, like the hues of changeable silk."[7] Perhaps the opium only made him sick, as it often does beginners. Whatever his first reaction, however, with time the smoker (and the eater too) learns to expect the sensations that the heroin user of today is accustomed to. The cares and distractions of daily life drop quite away. Though in reality dulled, the senses appear to have become keener, and the user feels intensely aware, able to perceive the imperceptible, on the point of passing on weightless feet into——but words desert him, the thing is ineffable. If he is a Coleridge and his opium habit only in its infancy, he may subsequently manage to rework the linked words and images of his opium reverie into a fragment the like of *Kubla Khan*.★ Otherwise he simply lies wrapped in a tranquil and sustaned euphoria. Opium dens are quiet places. Jean Cocteau describes one he visited in the 1920s, the crew's quarters in a steamer on the Marseilles-Saigon run. The purser, a friend of his and an opium smoker, took him there one night, slipping him stealthily past the watch. Sixty Annamite "boys" lay smoking on two tiers of planks. Opium cooked over a row of lamps. Except for one man whom a nightmare convulsed, the smokers were as inert as vegetables. "Opium," observes Cocteau with remarkable single-mindedness, as if the other natural narcotics are to be dismissed, "is the only vegetable substance that communicates the vegetable state to us."[8] A person under the influence

---

★Twenty years ago Elizabeth Schneider, in a book called *Coleridge, Opium, and Kubla Khan*, reached the conclusion that opium does nothing constructive for writers and poets, that Coleridge deceived the public when he represented his famous verse to be the unpremeditated and unedited product of an opium dream. Now along comes Alethea Hayter to argue most persuasively that Schneider was wrong (and M. H. Abrams, in his much older but recently reprinted *The Milk of Paradise*, substantially right), that early as it was in Coleridge's opium habit, and peculiarly gifted as he was, he did in fact produce a first draft of *Kubla Khan* while under the influence of laudanum—produced it, remembered it, wrote it down, and later revised and polished it.

But this does not make Miss Hayter an apologist for opium. Far from it. Opium, she says, became the curse of Coleridge's life, and of De Quincey's and others' too, killing by degrees their powers and their will, consigning them to ever lower and darker levels of that underground temple whose description forms the chilling conclusion to her *Opium and the Romantic Imagination*. No one can read the book and still take narcotics lightly.

does not talk, does not sing, does not quarrel with his neighbor or fall upon him in maudlin good fellowship. There is no such thing as an opium-crazed mob or an opium-induced orgy; nor does opium arouse the sexual appetite, though its withdrawal may. (The scene in Perelaer's late nineteenth-century novel *Baboe Dalima or the Opium Fiend* in which a Javanese villager shamelessly attacks his wife while under the influence of the drug, does not prove the contrary. It simply reflects the widespread feeling that opium addiction ought to be titillating as well as bad.) The taker of opium turns in upon himself and attends an experience entirely passive. He does not try to create a masterpiece. He becomes one, a masterpiece without form and without judges; or rather, he becomes the *scene* of a masterpiece, "the meeting place for the phenomena which art sends to us from outside." Thus it is useless to remonstrate with a man who is taking opium, to tell him he degrades himself. For it is like saying to paper that Shakespeare soils it, to silence that it is broken by Bach.

But when the drug wears off, the euphoria wears off with it, and the opium user is back where he began. And if he makes opium a habit (Cocteau regularly smoked three pipes in the morning, four in the afternoon, three more at night), sooner or later he will experience, should he try to stop, not simply the absence of bliss but positive misery: the withdrawal pains—as if that modest phrase could convey the agony of it!—that the heroin addict expects if deprived. Coleridge suffered from vomiting, stomach cramps, and excruciating pains in the head and limbs. De Quincey felt himself freezing to death while heaped with blankets by a blazing fire in midsummer. And both endured torments of the mind and of the feelings: extreme nervousness, fits of uncontrollable weeping, fear, shame, anger, and dreadful nightmares. "I recommend the patient who has been deprived for eight days," says Cocteau, "to bury his head in his arm, to glue his ear to that arm, and wait. Catastrophe, riots, factories blowing up, armies in flight, flood—the ear can detect a whole apocalypse in the starry night of the human body."

After a while, of course, the tortures of withdrawal diminish. Eventually they disappear. Yet it is a weary road, and at the end of it the penitent may find himself face to face with whatever it was that drove him to the drug in the first place. In which case the cure is not likely to last.

Why resist the craving anyway? To borrow again from Cocteau, moralizing to an opium addict is like saying to Tristan: "Kill Iseult, you will feel much better afterwards."

Cocteau did the cure in 1929. A century earlier neither Coleridge nor De Quincey could manage it.

It was partly that in the early nineteenth century the harmful properties of opium were very far from being adequately recognized. Every year ten to twenty tons entered England, to be eaten and drunk there; yet McCulloch's *Commercial Dictionary*, which reports this interesting statistic, expresses no alarm and even suggests that "the Chinese, by whom it is principally consumed, are a highly industrious, sober, frugal people."[9] Several of the encyclopedias of the first half of the century do better. They inform us that opium is a narcotic; that in large quantities it damages the system and may even cause death; and that ignorant or careless mothers frequently kill their infants by giving them overdoses of Godfrey's Cordial, A Pennyworth of Peace, and other nostrums containing the drug. But working mothers paid no attention to such warnings. They had to leave their infants in the care of old women or very young children when they went off to the mills; there was nothing else they could do; and it was only common prudence to quiet the infants first. One perfectly respectable Manchester druggist regularly supplied seven hundred households for this purpose, mixing his particular brand of "quietness" one hundred drops of laudanum to the ounce, and selling five gallons of it a week! And not just the lower classes used the stuff. Wilkie Collins took it regularly, by the glassful, and saw no shadow of impropriety in introducing it (this as late as 1868) into his immensely popular detective novel *The Moonstone*, where its deliberate administration to Mr. Franklin Blake not only solves the mystery of the missing diamond but restores to that gentleman's affections the lovely Miss Rachel. Even in medical circles its addictive properties were not really understood. Doctors sometimes prescribed it for the very symptoms (diarrhea was one) produced by its withdrawal! So for one reason or another numbers of people went right on taking opium, without embarrassment, without apparent harm, abused by none except those who were more abusive still of drink. In all that follows, and particularly whenever the word "drug" threatens to strike a contemporary note, this is something that has to be remembered.

The opium westerners consumed did not come from India. It came from Turkey, from Egypt, and as the century advanced and commercial cultivation spread, from Holland, France, Italy, and the Balkans. Of India's immense export hardly a chest found its way around the Cape of Good Hope. It moved instead in the opposite direction. Some of it came to rest along the Malacca Straits and in the East Indian archipelago; you encountered the drug at Penang, at Singapore, at Anjer where vessels negotiating the Straits of Sunda usually paused, and elsewhere on Java. But the great majority of Indian chests were landed on the coast of China, from the coast filtered into the interior, and so reached the pipes of the Chinese. Just why the Chinese chose to obtain their supplies from India is no clearer than why, having obtained it, they smoked instead of ate it. Perhaps it was because the practice of smoking developed first on the south China coast, exactly that part of the country that happened to be in contact with India—and India already grew the poppy in abundance. Its cultivation had been an important source of revenue to the Moghul emperors. When the Moghul Empire fell apart, the English simply salvaged and improved a system of state control to which they fell heir. From supplying the domestic Indian market to supplying China was a simple step; once the Chinese had fallen into the habit of buying Indian opium, there was very little to induce them to stop. In the end they came to prefer the Indian product to their own.

It was a preference carefully nourished and attended to by the Government of India—which in the early nineteenth century meant the East India Company. "The great object of the Bengal opium agencies," explained a former opium examiner writing in a Calcutta journal in the 1830s, "is to furnish an article suitable to the peculiar tastes of the population of China."[10] By peculiar he did not mean odd, let alone disgraceful. It was simply that the Chinese would not buy the bricks of unrefined *akbari* opium from which the Rajput camel rider made his stirrup cup and which the Bombay sepoy cut into lumps and chewed. What the Chinese required was something they could turn into *chandu*, the smokable extract. You made *chandu* by boiling opium in water, filtering the solution, then boiling it again until it reached the consistency of treacle. *Akbari* opium did not take well to this treatment because it was of too great a degree of "spissitude," too dried out, to dissolve properly. The problem was how to get opium to China in a partially moist state, and in the case of the Bengal agencies this was solved by shipping the drug in the form of cakes.

There were two Bengal agencies, each comprising ten or a dozen subagencies: one covered part of Bengal proper and all of Bihar; the other stretched from the borders of Bihar northwest as far as Agra and Meerut. The first had the Patna factory producing cakes under that name. The second manufactured at Ghazipur, though what it turned out was called Benares (from the proximity of that more famous place). Each year towards the end of the summer monsoon rains, the officers of the subagencies went out into the villages and contracted with individual peasants for the acreage they were to sow. Advances were paid; the sowing was completed by early November. In December the poppy plants were thinned. By late January they stood two to four feet high and were coming into bloom. The petals, generally white but sometimes rose or purple, fell or were picked shortly before the capsules were due to be lanced and were then collected, pressed into sheets the size of tortillas or the north Indian *chupatti*, and baked in shallow iron pans over an ordinary clay cooking oven. Bundles of these poppy petal sheets came to the Patna and Ghazipur factories in March. The opium itself followed from the rural collection centers in April and early May. At the factories the opium was tipped into big stone vats. Later it was weighed, examined for impurities (peasants sometimes mixed it with sand, brown sugar, or cow dung), and stirred until the intense dry heat of the north Indian plain had lowered the water content to 30 percent. Then it and the poppy petal sheets went together to the caking room.

Down the sides of the caking room sat the cake-makers. Beside each was a brass cup not quite six inches in diameter, several bundles of petal sheets, a container of inferior opium in the semiliquid form known as *lewah*, and a box of crushed, dried poppy stems and leaves called "poppy trash." Taking up the cup, the cake-maker lined it with petal sheets, smearing each with *lewah* and pasting sheet upon sheet until he had formed a shell half an inch thick. Next he received from an assistant a lump of opium a little over three pounds in weight and dropped it into the shell. Steadying the lump with one hand, he applied petal sheets to it with the other, tucking the sheets in to meet the already constructed shell and building steadily upwards until they met at the top and were sealed with a last sheet and a final smear of *lewah*. The finished cake was then rolled in poppy trash and removed to an earthenware cup the size of the brass one. "As thus formed," says Eatwell, "the well-finished cake is a pretty regular sphere not unlike in size and appearance a twenty-four pound shot." (A New England man would say it looked like an oversized duckpin bowling ball.) An average cake-maker turned out a dozen cakes an hour; at the height of the manufacturing season, which ran from May to early September, the 100 or so cake-makers at the Ghazipur factory in mid-century—Patna then employed 150—produced 6,000 to 7,000 cakes a day.

The finished cake in its earthenware cup went for several days to the drying room. As the cake dried, it was turned and examined; "and if, as is frequently the case, it should become distended and puffy, it is at once torn open, the extricated gas allowed to escape, and the cake again tightly closed." But a certain amount of swelling and contracting was to be expected, opium having that property under variations in temperature; indeed, it was for their capacity to yield without splitting or cracking that petal sheets had taken the place of tobacco leaves as the covering for the cake. From the drying room the cake still in its cup was carried to one of the airing sheds, a place with racks from floor to ceiling, and there it remained, turned and examined from time to time and rubbed once more in poppy trash if it showed signs of mildew, until the opium inside ceased transmitting moisture and the surface was completely dry to the touch. Then the cake was well on the way to resembling three specimens Eatwell was shown at Ghazipur. "Some fifteen years old, they are as solid as balls of wood, and may be thrown from a height upon a stone floor without injury."

Meanwhile thousands of mango-wood chests were arriving at the factories. In October and November they were packed. On the floor of each chest was set a wooden frame with twenty compartments. One compartment received one cake, poppy trash filled the cracks and crevices, and down went a mat and a second frame. Forty cakes in two layers completed one chest; at slightly over four pounds a cake, three of them pure opium and the rest petals and *lewah*, a chest contained perhaps 120 pounds of smokable drug. The chests were then sealed with pitch, sewn up in gunny or hides, and loaded at the river gate into boats; and in four or five fleets, the first departing Ghazipur and Patna as early as November and the last as late as March, the boats passed down the Ganges, into the Hooghly, and so at last reached Calcutta. There the chests were taken out and piled up in the opium godowns to await the public auctions.

These took place at the exchange rooms on Tank Square, a few blocks north of Government House. It was an appropriate proximity. For until it was actually knocked down by the auctioneer, opium was the property exclusively of the Government of India's Board of Customs, Salt, and Opium. No one but the board could legally commission the cultivation of the poppy. No one but it could buy the dried exudation and prepare it for market. And the difference between what it paid for the stuff and what it sold it for became, after expenses, the Government of India's profit in the business.

Nevertheless the moment the auctioneer's ivory hammer fell, the Government of India (alias the East India Company) turned its back on the chests. The vessels in which they quit Calcutta, moving with an ebb tide past the magnificent octagon of Fort William, seat and symbol of English rule, past the lawns and white-columned villas along Garden Reach, and down the eighty miles of dreary, jungle-bordered river to the sea, belonged not to the Company but to private merchants. The Company knew perfectly well where these vessels were going. As the years passed it became more and more enthusiastic for their getting there. But it did almost nothing to facilitate their going. And it did nothing to assist them when they arrived.

At Calcutta opium was made much of. It received a very different treatment at Canton.

2

Canton and Macao

The south China city of Canton lies in the latitude of Calcutta, Mecca, and Havana, on the left bank of the Canton River seventy-five miles from the sea. Between city and sea there stretches what appears to be a delta but is actually a partly filled-in bay. The islands in this bay have become hills rising sharply out of low flat ground, the innumerable tidal passages grow narrower and more shallow every year. But at the southeast corner of the bay there is deep water still: an A-shaped gulf forty miles on a side, with the mountains of Hongkong at its right foot, the little peninsula of Macao at its left, and a screen of barren islands across the bottom. Towards the top of this gulf the waters grow shallow and split up among mud flats. Paddy fields and gardens appear, clumps of trees, villages, an occasional piece of high ground. And at the very point of the A lies a cluster of low hills and hilly islands through which runs a wide, deep channel. This is the Bocca Tigris or Bogue, the main entrance to the Canton River—in the old days the entrance to China itself.

China proper began at the Bogue. Once past the Bogue and the forts that commanded it, a vessel was deemed to have entered the inner waters of the Celestial Empire. But the vessel that entered did not immediately drop anchor. Whampoa was almost certainly her destination—and Whampoa was still thirty miles away. Famous later as the site of the Kuomintang's military academy, Whampoa in the early nineteenth century was simply a large dirty village on a flat and unprepossessing island at a point in the Canton River where the channel grows narrower, shallower, and turns from north to west. About Whampoa are a number of reaches suitable for anchoring, and it was here that merchantmen halted, small vessels above First Bar, large vessels below. There they lay for a part or all of the trading season, sometimes as many as fifty or sixty together. At their head were ships that flew the distinctive red and white striped flag of the East India Company and carried cargoes marked with her heart-shaped mark.

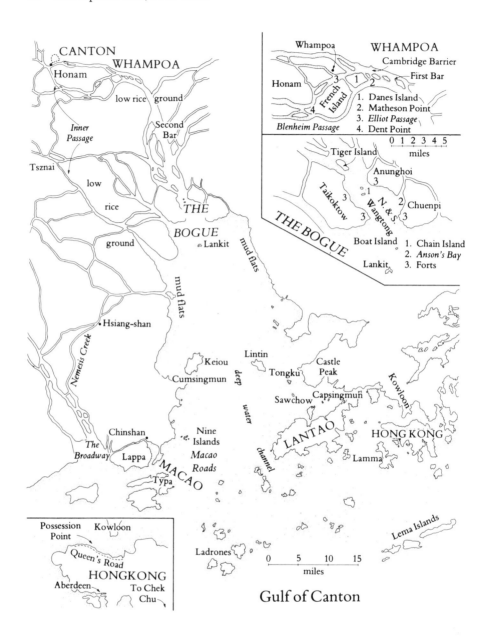

Gulf of Canton

East Indiamen were impressive craft, of a thousand tons burden or more, with the appearance and some of the armament of a 74-gun man-of-war. Each year in the winter or early spring a score of them left the Thames, some sailing for China directly, others calling at Bombay, Madras, or the Straits of Malacca, but all reaching the China Sea in time to roll up it before the southwest winds of summer. Arriving at the Gulf of Canton, they stopped off Macao to obtain entry "chops" or permits and take aboard pilots, at the Bogue to pay a variety of fees, then worked their way up to Whampoa. There "chop boats" (lighters) with barrel hulls and mat sails came alongside to receive cargoes of woolens and lead from England; raw cotton from Bombay; tin, rattans, and fish maws from the Straits of Malacca; the balance in coin or silver with perhaps a few dozen Birmingham clocks and musical snuffboxes thrown in. Up the last dozen miles to Canton went the chop boats, past rows of seagoing junks with huge single masts and painted saucer eyes, past war junks in red and black with barn doors for rudders, upcountry tea boats in plain varnish, mandarin boats delicate as dragonflies, floating brothels known as "flower boats," duck boats with sloping planks for the ducks to waddle to the water by, and hundreds and hundreds of little houseboats with oval roofs; until at last, forcing their way through river traffic as thick as a city street's, they reached the dock front of the appropriate warehouse and discharged. As the trading season advanced and markets opened, back they came with silks and teas, sugar and rhubarb root, porcelain, lacquered cabinets, vermilion to turn English sealing wax the proper shade of red; and one by one the Indiamen weighed, dropped down the river, cleared the Bogue, and were off and running before the winter monsoon for the Straits of Sunda and the direct passage home. A complete round trip, London to Canton to London again, took more than a year.

This was the routine of the old China trade. These were the commodities traditionally brought to China and traditionally carried away. And at the heart of the trade was tea. It came from no other place. India did not then produce any, nor Ceylon, Java, or Formosa; Japan was inaccessible; the world perforce drank China teas. Above all, the English drank them. Russia took a few million pounds annually, most of it overland and in the form of bricks. The Dutch and the Americans took a few million by sea. But as early as the opening of the nineteenth century England was consuming twenty million pounds and by the late 1820s almost thirty. It was enough to give every man, woman, and child two pounds of the leaf a year.

And only the East India Company could legally furnish it. Private merchants would have liked to. The law said they might not. The Company no longer kept its monopoly of England's trade with India. It simply taxed and governed there, and it had for so long allowed private merchants to ship goods between one eastern port and another that everyone assumed that this "country trade" (as it was unaccountably called) was naturally for private hands. But the China trade proper—the long haul around the Cape from London and back again—remained the Company's exclusive property, carefully confirmed at the reissue of its charter. It was a privilege the Company continued to take seriously. Tea it prized above all things.

His Majesty's government prized it too. The duty levied on the leaf brought annually never less than £3 million into the exchequer. That was half the expense of the Royal Navy.

Then as now there were two sorts of tea, black and green. The Americans bought mostly the second. The East India Company might have done so too had its vessels been less long at sea, and its market less protected. To thread the Straits of Sunda, cross the Indian Ocean, round the Cape of Good Hope, and fetch the Channel, required four to six months and meant crossing the equator twice; and though the tea chests were lined with lead, and the ships' hatches carefully fastened down and caulked, moist salt air always got to their contents. Then a further delay occurred. The Company was required by law to keep a year's stock on hand. Naturally it sold at any given moment the oldest; the consequence of this was that a flush picked in August, arriving at Canton too late to catch that season's fleet, stored until the following autumn, loaded at last in time to reach London the next summer and then stored again, would be at least three years old before it reached the teapot. Only black teas could be treated this way and still be drinkable, perhaps because they were roasted more than greens were, perhaps because they really had (as alleged) less delicacy of flavor. So the Company slipped easily into the habit of shipping blacks (which meant that the English slipped willy-nilly into the habit of drinking them). Every year huge quantities of bohea and of the slightly better congou passed through its hands at Canton, together with small quantities of the choicer blacks—and very few greens indeed.

Except for a sort so rubbishy it had to be mixed with congou, no teas of any sort were produced near the city itself. All grew far to the north and east, in districts western tea men never set foot in. Blacks came from Fukien province, especially from the Bohea hills (the name is a European corruption of Wu-i) about four hundred miles northeast of Canton. Greens grew still further north and west, in parts of Kiangsi, Chekiang, and Anhwei five to six hundred miles from Canton. Each year towards the end of March or early in April the tea growers moved along their rows of bushes, plucking the newly formed buds and a few of the fresh young leaves just below. These made up the first flush and yielded (when rolled, roasted, and passed over sieves) the finest teas: pekoe among the blacks, imperial and gunpowder among the greens. A second flush was picked about the middle of May, a third late in June; there might be a fourth picking in August, and in the autumn a fifth even—though this last would yield bohea or twankay so coarse as to be almost undrinkable. As soon as a flush had been picked and processed, the chests in which it was packed began to move towards Canton. From the Bohea hills they went westward into Kiangsi on the backs of porters, thence by river boat south and west to the mountains that separate that province from Kwangtung, by porter again over the low Meiling Pass, and by boat down to the city. Greens, though they came a greater distance, traversed in the later stages of their portage the same ground. Teas picked early in the spring began arriving at Canton in October; the bulk of the crop reached the city during November, December, and January; late pickings might straggle in through March.

At Canton the chests were unloaded into the same warehouses (or hongs) that received cargo from foreign vessels at Whampoa. Long, narrow brick buildings ranged side by side, their ends to the water; they lined the north bank of the Canton River between it and the city wall. In these warehouses damaged teas were unpacked, dried out, and repacked. Delicate greens were sometimes transferred to small leaden canisters, varieties of the middle rank were often put into boxes; for the Americans in particular, with their smaller ships, liked consignments broken up in this way. But most of the teas remained in the wooden chests they had come down in. Only samples were carried to the factories, where the foreigners who bought the leaf lived.

The factories occupied fifteen acres of river bank just to the west of the warehouses. Approaching by boat, you stepped first onto a piece of open ground the size of two football fields laid end to end. To your right was the New English factory garden, with warehouses visible beyond. To your left other warehouses came down to the water's edge. Facing you like a row of dominoes were the factories themselves, their brick and granite walls plastered white, the blinds on their terraces a pleasantly contrasting green, and all presenting an appearance the neater and more substantial for the confusion of crowded river and suburbs out of which they rose.

They were thirteen in number. Some were called after the European states whose chartered companies had once shared the China trade with England; a few had Chinese names; one, the Creek, was known by the stinking little ditch that formed the eastern boundary of the compound. You entered a factory by an arched passage that led into it from the square. Doors opened from the passage into Number 1 house; but unless your business lay there, you continued along the passage to the little court behind, from which a second passage led under Number 2—and so on, through 3, 4, perhaps even 5 and 6, to the very last house of all. On the ground floor of each was a cookhouse, a strongroom, servants' quarters, and a godown or two. The second floor, and the third where it existed,

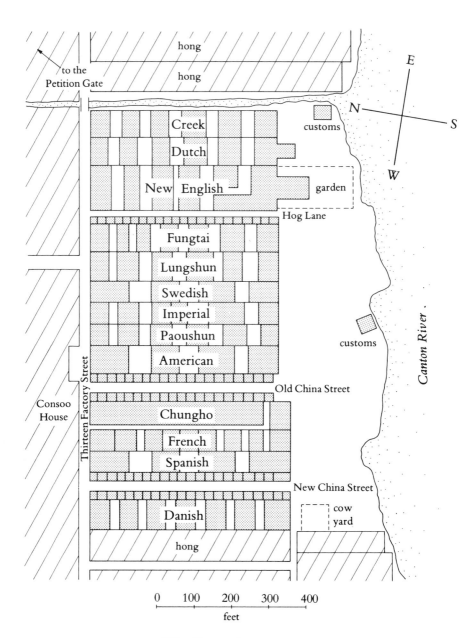

The Factories

were given over to offices, living rooms, and bedrooms. A house could not be any wider than the factory of which it was a part; and the factories, though long, were narrow—all, that is, except the New English where the East India Company men lived. As rebuilt after the great fire of 1822 it was 120 feet wide, almost twice the normal, and graced on its river end with the walled garden already mentioned into which jutted a large veranda. From this veranda you passed into a great hall used principally for dining. On your left was the library, on your right the billiard room; just beyond rose a small chapel with a belfry and clock; the living quarters lay further back still. To sit down to dinner by the light of the best spermaceti candles, a life-size portrait of George IV upon the wall, a servant behind each chair, and the Company's plate upon the table was an experience not to be duplicated at any other English station east of Calcutta.

The Dutch factory had a veranda and a hall too. But they were on a smaller scale; and in the other factories there were no public rooms at all, only living quarters. In the front houses these were reasonably livable. It was a pleasure to sit in the second-floor drawing room of Number 1 the American factory—rented by Olyphant and Company and known from the piety of its occupants as Zion's Corner—and through the windows watch the people passing in the square below. But the houses behind, which were reached through a labyrinth of passages and staircases, afforded no view but of the houses in front or to the rear and were never touched by a breeze off the river. "If you could see the packed-up way in which we have to live here—crammed as close to each other as jars of sweetmeats in a box of bran," wrote Wells Williams, the American missionary, twenty years later when things were if anything a little better, "no yard, no out-houses, no trees, no back door even—you would feel as keenly as I do the pleasure of sometimes seeing growing green things."[1] To Williams and most of the residents these back houses seemed like prisons, dark, cramped, and in summer impossibly stuffy.

For Canton summers could be trying. As early as March it grew decidedly warm, with fog and drizzle that the arrival of the full monsoon in May turned to rain. It rained intermittently all summer, occasionally bringing the river up over the square, and in the intervals the air was hot and humid. Centipedes crawled into clothes and bedding. Lizards dropped from ceilings. Westerners slept under mosquito netting, on rattan mats or mattresses of bamboo shavings, and lounged during the day in cane chairs while the great rectangular mat punkahs pulled by coolies swept lazily above their heads.

Then in October the northeast monsoon returned. It stopped raining, the thermometer dropped, and for three or four months Canton enjoyed clear, invigorating weather. Foreigners got out their woolens. Coal fires burned in factory grates and warehouse braziers. The bite in the air (one February it even snowed) sharpened appetites and made eating a pleasure. The day began with coffee or tea, white bread, perhaps some eggs or fish with rice. The tea was taken sometimes with milk (the foreigners kept a few cows in mat sheds in front of the Danish factory), more often simply with a spoonful of native rock candy pounded into powder. Lunch at noon, with bottled ale from Calcutta, was followed by an early dinner at three or four. After dinner the younger clerks played leapfrog and hop-scotch or lounged at the water's edge trying to talk to the boat girls, while their elders walked up and down smoking Manila cheroots cut square at both ends.

This was the season when shipping crowded the anchorages at Whampoa—the season, too, when malaria abated. In the reach below First Bar lay the East Indiamen, enormous vessels very grand in their black-and-white Nelson chequer. Daily the senior captain hoisted his pennant as commodore, and if he did not invite some of the factory residents down to dinner aboard his ship, a colleague would. Or a visit might be made in the other direction. When a captain had sent off the last of the chop boats, he was obliged to come to Canton to sign his bills of lading and retrieve his canvas letter bag. Very likely he stayed there to dinner before regaining his anchorage, collecting his pilot, and departing with the tide.

Sailors too came up to the factories. Unlike visitors of a more genteel sort they headed not for the little shops in New and Old China streets that sold silks and lacquer ware, ivory chess men, and other traditional curiosities but for Hog Lane. Hog Lane was narrow and dark and filthy. Against the wall of the Fungtai factory, which formed one of its sides, ran a line of hovels offering shawls, fans, canvas shoes, joss sticks, miserable canaries in tiny cages, and other trash as come-ons for food and strong drink. "First Chop Rum" read a sign in clumsy English letters, but what Jack probably got was *samshu,* a rice liquor reputed to contain arsenic and tobacco juice and calculated to make him roaring drunk. Then there would be fights, up and down Hog Lane, spilling over the square and along the adjoining alleys, until at last the sailors fought themselves out and were ready to be coaxed back to the water stairs; and the boats, worked two or three oars on a side by the more nearly sober, crept back to Whampoa.

There was little liquor at Zion's Corner, of course. The Factory, as the East India Company's establishment was called, was another matter. In one particular year it consumed the astonishing total of 330 dozen bottles of madeira, all fortified with brandy against travel and the climate.

As long as the East India Company preserved its monopoly of English trade with China, the Factory remained at the head of the foreign

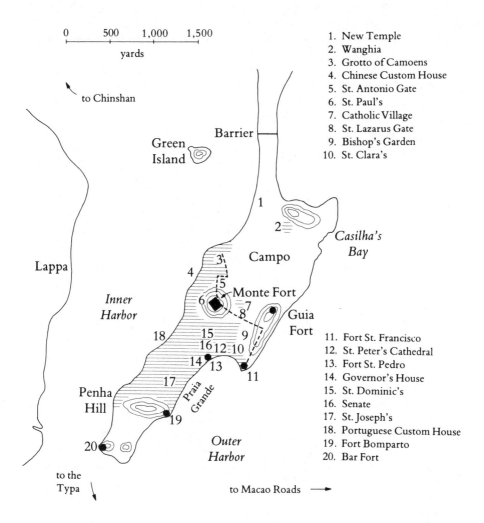

0   500   1,000   1,500

yards

to Chinshan

Green
Island

Barrier

Lappa

1

2

Casilha's
Bay

Campo

3
4
5
Monte Fort
6
7
8
Guia
Fort

Inner
Harbor

18   15   9
16 12 10
14 13
11

17   Praia Grande

Penha
Hill

19

20

Outer
Harbor

to the
Typa

to Macao Roads

1. New Temple
2. Wanghia
3. Grotto of Camoens
4. Chinese Custom House
5. St. Antonio Gate
6. St. Paul's
7. Catholic Village
8. St. Lazarus Gate
9. Bishop's Garden
10. St. Clara's

11. Fort St. Francisco
12. St. Peter's Cathedral
13. Fort St. Pedro
14. Governor's House
15. St. Dominic's
16. Senate
17. St. Joseph's
18. Portuguese Custom House
19. Fort Bomparto
20. Bar Fort

Macao

community at Canton, But neither the Factory nor the community spent the whole year there. Life on the China coast meant a twice-yearly migration. From April to October the foreigners lived in the little Portuguese settlement of Macao, sixty-five miles to the south.

Macao is not what it used to be. Fill dredged from the shallow waters around has swollen it quite out of its original shape. Buildings crowd all the usable ground, and there is a bursting-at-the-seams quality about the place that Hongkong, with its magnificent backdrop of untouched heights, does not have. A century and a half ago, however, Macao was simply a spit of land over two miles long and nowhere more than half a mile wide; indeed, at its sandy neck the width shrank to a few hundred yards. The town proper was confined to the south end, where it climbed the low saddle between the Penha hill at the very tip and the Guia and Monte hills in the middle. There were two harbors, the inner on the west side (with the hilly island of the Lappa beyond), the outer on the east. But the inner harbor could not take vessels larger than schooners and coasting junks, and the outer harbor was so silted up it could hardly take anything at all. So Indiamen and other westerners anchored in the Typa to the southeast or in the roads due east. It was from Macao Roads that the traveler first approached the town, perhaps in a hired sampan—long, narrow, partially roofed and looking a little like a child's old-fashioned covered cradle. A Chinese girl in trousers pulled cheerfully at the bow. Another sculled over the stern. The traveler sank back against the cushions and watched Macao draw near. Half a mile of gently curving shore formed the outer harbor. Along it ran a treeless esplanade, the Praia Grande, backed by a line of two-and three-story houses. There stood the governor's mansion. Next to it rose the sixteen-pillared portico of the Factory's establishment. Other houses in the European style climbed the slope of the saddle. Bits of garden showed, and here and there a church tower. Small forts crowned the summits of the hills. Beyond rose the barren slopes of the Lappa, and off to the north were the still higher hills of the mainland. But Macao itself was elegant, compact, familiar—a piece of Portugal or a miniature Naples, set like a jewel on the threshold of immense and unknown China.

Close up the town was disappointing. A square with the old Senate House at one end and the Church of St. Dominic at the other, the grotto of the poet Camoens, the bishop's garden just below the Guia hill, the Penha hill on whose slopes small boys flew kites cleverly contrived to look like birds and fishes, the Praia Grande itself—these were the extent of its attractions. "The streets are horrid. You cannot conceive of anything more irregular," wrote Harriet Low, an American girl who spent four years at Macao in the early 1830s.[2] In fact they were mere alleys, laid out to no apparent plan and so badly paved that you risked a broken leg if you hurried. Foreigners generally navigated them in sedan chairs. Harriet, who was young and curious, insisted on exploring them on foot. So she met her first Parsee, dressed in a long white robe and a red turban, and saw her first bound feet, a sight that no matter how often repeated always left her sick and angry. In the Chinese quarter her nose was tickled by a hundred smells, her eye caught by the swarthy complexions and black pigtails of cooks crying their steaming dishes; blacksmiths carrying bellows, anvil, coal, and tools in baskets; moneychangers with strings of copper cash and portable scales for weighing silver; dentists displaying pulled teeth as testimonials to their skill; herbsellers and pedlars of knick-knacks; and sweating half-naked coolies with great pails of water at either end of their carrying poles—Macao had no piped water, and only the larger houses had wells. And everywhere she went she encountered beggars, grotesque shapes in stinking rags that rattled clapdishes and shoved ulcerous stumps at her until she distributed a cash or two apiece.

It was better, often, to get outside the town. The town wall ran from the base of the Guia hill over the Monte hill and down to a point on the shore of the inner harbor not far from the grotto of Camoens, and on the other side of it lay more or less open country. If Harriet and her companions went out by the St. Lazarus gate, they came to the Campo, a pleasant place to walk. Beyond the Campo was Casilha's Bay, where in 1622 the Dutch had been stopped and driven off by a handful of Portuguese soldiers and their drunken black slaves in what was probably the only battle between Europeans ever fought on Chinese soil. (People bathed there now.) To the left several paths led over the high ground to the race course and the Barrier. One path went through the Chinese village of Wanghia (Mongha); when Harriet and her friends passed that way, the dogs flew barking at them, children shrieked, hideous-looking hogs almost knocked them down, "and to add to our fright we met two large buffaloes, which looked very wild. All this happened in a little narrow place, but by chin-chinning an old woman she kept the buffaloes from us and we got safely through this little bedlam."[3]

So Harriet, like other westerners, grew accustomed to Macao and to the life there. She learned to expect the thick March fog, "pea soup" the English called it, that pressed upon the town for days and made everything damp and nasty. In the late summer she watched typhoons strip the tiles off roofs, toss ten-foot blocks of granite sea wall about the Praia Grande, and leave trees so burned from the salt spray you would suppose they had been licked by fire. When winter came, and her uncle was gone to Canton with the other men of Russell and Company, she and her aunt huddled before coal fires that hardly began to warm their great barns of rooms, while in the streets the Chinese walked about wearing so many layers of clothing they looked as thick as they were tall—and some Portuguese went to bed and stayed there.

Not all the foreigners observed the seasonal migration, however, and not all who did observed it simultaneously. So Harriet got to know quite a number of people. She met merchants, of course: Company ones, and private ones too, like William Hunter of Russell and Company, who was actually younger than she yet had already lived in China for five or six years. She met Mowqua, the hong merchant, "a great character. He had on his winter dress, which is rather singular. The cap is blue in front, the crown scarlet, with a blue glass button on the top. The whole dress is blue, of different shades." (When she asked him boldly why foreign women were not allowed at the factories, he replied "too muchy man want to look" and "Canton too small, no walky.")[4] She met Thomas Colledge, the senior Company surgeon, very old-fashioned but a darling; George Chinnery, the painter, a remarkably ugly man who had come to Macao from Calcutta many years before to escape, it was said, debts he could not pay and a wife he could not stand; and old Thomas Beale, a curious person who had gone bankrupt long ago and now occupied himself with an enormous open-air aviary in which he kept peacocks, exotic varieties of pheasant, and a real bird of paradise. From time to time there were dances. Such was the shortage of English and American girls that Harriet never lacked for partners. There were glees and amateur theatricals too, the last usually got up by the English—Harriet noticed with surprise that on these occasions they quite dropped their stiff and supercilious manners and became a good deal more willing than her own countrymen to make themselves ridiculous. Once a little company of Italian singers paused on its way from South America to Calcutta and gave a number of operas, Rossini mostly, on a stage sixteen feet wide. And her first winter Harriet was invited to eat Christmas dinner with the Company. "Everything on the table was splendid—a whole service of massive plate." Threescore people sat down to eat, there were toasts and addresses, and afterwards the candles were snuffed out and brandy poured over raisins and set alight. "We were all to put our hands into these blue flames and pull out the raisins beneath. This is called snapdragon, and is a favorite Christmas amusement in England."[5]

But it was unusual for the Factory to remain at Macao until Christmas. The move back to Canton ordinarily took place long before then. Indiamen began arriving in August, bringing to the English colony (whom Harriet rather envied at such moments) the excitement of new books and new faces, as well as the pleasure of friends and acquaintances returning from home leave after an absence of nearly two years. Six or eight weeks later the Factory collected itself and went aboard chop boats in the inner harbor. Some of these chop boats carried books and papers, plate, crockery, linen, drink and provisions, milk cows even. Others, fitted up with cabins, received the supercargoes and writers, the tea tasters, surgeon Colledge, interpreter Robert Morrison, the chaplain, steward, butler, and

Anglo-Indian clerks. What with the Chinese comprador and his assistants, what with cooks, coolies, and boat crews, over 250 persons crowded aboard. Off went the boats, not rounding the southern tip of Macao but heading directly north up the waterways that laced the delta country; sailing the roomier ones, pulling with great sweeps through the narrower, a linguist seeing to it that the Company's "chop" or permit passed scrutiny at the magistrates' stations along the route, the Factory relieving its confinement with ale, roast capon, and fresh milk from the floating dairy; until on the evening of the third day the little flotilla came out into the main channel of the Canton River west of the city, turned right, and swept down to the factories.

There, from its quarters in the New English, the gentlemen of the Company applied themselves to four or five months of serious winter business. They transacted that business exclusively with the hong merchants. From them alone they purchased teas, to them alone sold such articles as their vessels brought to China. For to the hong merchants, to the Cohong (as this loose merchant guild was called), belonged in theory at least the monopoly of all foreign trade at Canton.

This was not because the hong merchants wished it so. There had been a time when the privileges of the Cohong were lucrative, when the hong merchants fought to obtain them, and then fought again to preserve them from the encroachments of the Canton "shopmen." That time was over. Compelled to buy short and sell long, peculiarly susceptible to pressure from the local authorities (who cared nothing for commerce but knew how to garner the fruits thereof), forced to contribute handsomely to the Yellow River conservancy or to the suppression of bandits, the hong merchants found it difficult to make their monopoly pay. They borrowed heavily from the very foreigners they did business with, teetered on the brink of insolvency—sometimes even went over, so that a special "Consoo Fund" (fed by a levy on foreign trade) had to be milked to repay their creditors. Not all were in trouble, to be sure. One or two were still worth millions. But by 1830 it was a real question why a Kwangtung or Fukien merchant (most came from those provinces) would wish to enter the Cohong at all.

Enter they nevertheless continued to do—the authorities made sure of that. For there existed a particular reason for the Cohong, a reason not at all commercial, a reason of state. As long as the foreigners traded only with the hong merchants, the hong merchants were in an excellent position to keep an eye on the foreigners. And keeping an eye on foreigners was something Peking was determined to do.

It was perfectly understandable given the way China had developed, given the way she was.

China in the Early Nineteenth Century

3

Managing the Barbarians

She was huge, ancient, and magnificently insular. Two hundred years before the birth of Christ, the several states of the Yangtze and Yellow River valleys had, by a process of conquest and decay, become one; and ever since that moment there had existed, over the area we regard as China proper, a Chinese state single in conception and more often than not single in fact. Dynasties might come and go, dynasties might even be in origin alien, but China remained, obstinately reverting to oneness even as physical geography tried to pull her apart. Thus the latest of her dynasties, the Ch'ing or Manchu, simply expressed with great splendor a political idea already two thousand years old. For even longer, for at least three thousand years, China had been the cultural center of the Far East—indeed of the whole world, as far as she could see. From that culture all peoples on the periphery had borrowed, the Japanese for example their script. So it was perfectly right that she should call herself the central country, the Middle Kingdom, perfectly right that her emperor assume cosmic dimensions and be everywhere recognized as the Son of Heaven, Lord of Ten Thousand Years.

He ruled according to the precepts of Confucius, who had taught that the good life consists of establishing harmonious relations with nature and with one's fellow men. In the Confucian view the emperor intervened between mankind and Heaven, inspiring in the former the same filial respect he paid the latter, so that he governed by the influence of his own right conduct—as the good father governs the family. But the emperor's goodness was not without the means of practical enforcement. From the yellow-roofed halls of the Forbidden City, he and his ministers directed a quite extraordinary corps of civil servants. The foreigners called these civil servants "mandarins" and identified their several ranks by the color of the button worn upon the cap. They might better have called them, as modern students of China usually call them, "literati." For these mandarins were a great deal more than civil servants in the conventional western sense. They came (in practice though not necessarily in theory) exclusively from the gentry. But what was particularly striking about them was the extent to which they were conversant with their country's literature. Not bureaucrats who had happened to take up letters—which even in the West, after all, was possible—they were instead men of letters who chose to be bureaucrats, or rather who were chosen to be, by virtue of surviving a graduated series of extremely competitive examinations in that portion of China's accumulated literature deemed canonical.

It was a remarkable arrangement, this staffing of the circuit, prefectural, and district yamens of the eighteen provinces with the very finest of China's essayists and poets. It made sure there could be no division in the upper ranks of society between learning and power. It helped unify the empire culturally, for both the successful *chin-shih* (metropolitan degree-holder) and the much greater number who got no further than the prefectural or provincial examinations were by virtue of their training masters of a formal written language that was common to all China where the provincial dialects were not. There was another consequence. A gentleman, a scholar, a government officer—each finds reason to think himself superior. A gentleman-scholar who is at the same time a government officer finds reason to think himself incomparable. So it was with the mandarins. Favored simply through being Chinese, further elevated by membership in the gentry, they were propelled by the winning of the *chin-shih* to heights where the air was of the purest and most rarefied. From those heights they looked down upon soldiers, merchants, everybody—above all upon peoples from outer lands.

It was not that they were contemptuous of outsiders' military prowess. China had been conquered too many times to have any special confidence in her own arms. But a peculiar circumstance guaranteed that repeated conquests would only strengthen China's inclination to think well of herself. Her geographical position, locked in as she was between the ocean to her east, and the desert, mountains, and high plateau country to her west, meant that her invaders were almost always the crude and unlettered barbarians of Inner Asia, of whom the Mongols were the most famous and the Manchus the latest. And these Inner Asian barbarians invariably discovered that while they could conquer China easily enough, to change and reshape her in any significant way was quite beyond their primitive capacities. If they wanted to enjoy her, they had to take her over as she was, mandarins, classics, and all. Otherwise they risked spoiling everything, as small children spoil expensive toys and the Germans spoiled the Roman Empire.

So each wave of Inner Asian barbarians adopted China's own culture and politics. As adoption succeeded adoption, the Chinese came naturally to feel that to their culture and politics there was simply no civilized alternative. Conquest brought, as it were, brief pain followed by sustained self-satisfaction. Between conquests, moreover, the barbarians on China's periphery slipped easily into a subordinate position. They admitted the cultural superiority of the Chinese and proved it by periodically paying tribute. Westerners observed Siamese vessels at Whampoa and knew that they were simply pausing there with emissaries bound for Peking; even Nepal, beyond the highest peaks of the Himalayas, sent tribute once every five years. Elaborate in its ritual, tribute-bearing became in practice hardly more than a cloak for trade. But the Chinese were unwilling to pull the cloak aside. Right relations meant more to them than money, keeping the barbarians in their place more than a flourishing commerce.

Thus when Europeans, with their rough manners and irresistible broadsides, first came sailing up from the southwest, the Chinese received them as just another breed of Inner Asians. One European they easily confused with another: the Portuguese, for example, they mistook for the *fo-lang-chi* or Franks whom Arab traders had told them about, with the consequence that when real Frenchmen turned up it became a question what to call them. Not that it mattered very much. Westerners seemed to the Chinese of no more consequence than the other outsiders they were accustomed to. They came in ships instead of on horseback, but they were barbarians just the same—hairy barbarians, foreign devils, *fan kuei*!

The trouble with this attitude was that Europeans did not admit to being just another barbarian breed. They did not see themselves as bearers of tribute to anyone; and at the end of the eighteenth century the English, for one, deliberately attempted to repudiate that role. An Irish peer named Macartney was sent on an embassy to Peking. The barges that transported him and his party from the coast towards the capital carried inscriptions reading "envoy bearing tribute," as if my lord were leading an embassy from Korea or Siam. Macartney, however, was determined to be treated as the representative of an equal power. The decisive struggle, he supposed, would occur over the kowtow. Bearers of tribute knelt three times before the emperor, and at each kneeling put their faces three times to the floor. It was a thing the emperor himself did before Heaven and his ancestral tablets; it was a thing successfully required of previous envoys from Russia, from Portugal, from Holland; it was, oddly, also a thing that Chinese Catholics voluntarily accorded European missionaries—as Jean-Gabriel Perboyre discovered when he first penetrated into the interior forty years later. "Chinese Christians perform it before the priest when he arrives and when he leaves, when they come to see him for something, when they take communion," he wrote home in some surprise.[1]

But Macartney was not going to oblige, or rather he would perform the three-times-three only if some mandarin also kowtowed before his own sovereign George III, a portrait of whom he had thoughtfully included in his baggage. The condition was refused. The emperor was equally unobliging in the twin matters of receiving a resident English ambassador at Peking and opening ports other than Canton to English trade. "I do not forget," he wrote King George, "the lonely remoteness of your island, cut off from the world by intervening wastes of sea. Nor do I overlook your excusable ignorance of the usages of Our Celestial Empire." But to permit Macartney or an envoy from any other place to live permanently at Peking would be quite contrary to those usages. Indeed, it must have puzzled the emperor that the question should even be asked; he himself maintained no ministry of foreign affairs, placed resident ambassadors in no one else's capitals, and saw about him in the world no equals from whom ambassadors could possibly come! As for expanding trade, it was quite unnecessary. The Chinese needed nothing and traded a little with tribute-bearing barbarians only out of affectionate condescension. Let Macartney go quietly away! Let King George, his master, display the proper respect and devotion by refraining in the future from importunate embassies! Only, suppose he misunderstood, suppose he took courtesy for weakness? England, so distant, so unpredictably bumptious, must be held firmly in the posture of submission. "Tremblingly obey and show no negligence. A special mandate!"[2]

Macartney exchanged presents. Macartney managed to avoid knocking his head upon the ground by dropping on one knee instead. In every other respect he was defeated. Kowtow or no kowtow—and the Chinese let it be generally understood that Macartney had performed it—England continued to be enrolled among the tributary states. A second embassy led by a peer named Amherst a quarter of a century later did nothing to change this. As a special favor to persons so far from home, and also (it had to be admitted) because Peking recognized that trade with the West was worth something and could be carried on in no other way, English and other western merchants were allowed to remain on the coast the year around instead of being obliged to leave after each tribute-bearing visit as the barbarians normally were forced to do. This did not mean, however, that they might go where they wished or do as they pleased. On the contrary they were to be supervised closely and continuously by the hong merchants.

As supervisors, barbarian watchers, animal trainers—two of the Chinese characters used to designate foreigners suggested dogs and sheep—the hong merchants were from the foreigners' point of view not half bad. There were usually six to ten of them. Each represented a family hong or firm—it was really with the firm that foreigners dealt. But foreigners were in the habit of calling the firms by the names of their leading members, or rather by corruptions of those names ending in an honorific *qua* (thus Howqua, Mowqua, Puankequa), and as these corruptions were passed on from father to son (so that there was always a Howqua to do business with and a Mowqua too), it was difficult not to imagine that this particular breed of Chinese had somehow stumbled upon the secret of eternal life. Technically hong merchants were mandarins of the ninth or lowest rank—hence the *qua*. A few had worked their way higher, usually by purchase, which explains why Mowqua wore the blue button when Harriet Low met him. But Mowqua, Howqua (who also wore the blue button and was first in the group in wealth and standing), and the others remained merchants under the skin. So between them and the foreign devils it was their duty to watch, there was not much of a drop.

In the trading season the two groups saw a good deal of each other, for reasons not always commercial. On the second or third day of the Chinese New Year, down Old China Street came a servant wearing a conical rattan hat and carrying a card; after him, bearing a sedan chair, four coolies dressed and padded against the cold in the universal blue of the lower classes. Out of the chair stepped a hong merchant. He wore an elegant fur-lined silk robe and black satin boots with soft, thick soles that made no sound as he walked across the flags and into the Swedish factory to exchange the season's compliments with Hunter and the other Americans living there. Hunter, who describes the scene, also relates how shortly after reaching Canton in 1825, he went by invitation to the city residence of Howqua's eldest son. There he was entertained by the women of the household, striking creatures with "black eyes, splendid eyebrows, and teeth of ivory whiteness. Some smoked the long thin delicate pipe with jade mouthpiece, having attached to it the small embroidered silk tobacco bag." Their silk dresses were of subdued "plum, chocolate, pink, or pea green, the sleeves and edges of the outer garment being embroidered in bright colors on a broad black or blue ground," and they wore their hair in the fashion "such as one sees on old porcelain, secured with long silver or gold ornaments."[3] Actually to be received by Chinese women of station was an extraordinary thing, explicable only by the fact that Hunter was then a boy of thirteen or fourteen, but it was common for foreigners to visit the hong merchants' houses. Years afterwards, when Hunter and his friends rowed regularly on the river, they would sometimes stop at Puankequa's villa a little west of Canton and, once through the great double teak doors, wander along the gravel walks admiring the camelias and the chrysanthemums, the cumquat and peach trees; cross the little ornamental lakes on granite bridges; penetrate the several residences with their broad verandahs and curved roofs to examine the furnishings and objects they found there. Visits such as these gave Hunter an indelible sense of the exquisite cultivation of Chinese life and contributed to the pleasing nostalgia he later infused into his reminiscences. One hong merchant returned the compliment. He learned to play whist and made almost a pest of himself by hanging around the New English factory looking for a game.

But the hong merchants did not content themselves with opening their homes and gardens to the foreigners and playing cards with them. They exercised a much closer and more continuous supervision. They owned the factories and leased them to the *fan kuei*. They gave instructions to the linguists, who, from an office boat moored close by the factories, represented the foreigners before the Hoppo. It was through the linguists that each foreigner or foreign firm obtained its comprador or general manager. It was the comprador who engaged and directed the shroffs or money changers, the clerks, and the other members of the staff.

Above all the hong merchants secured the foreigners; it was the very heart and purpose of their work, at least so far as their own government was concerned. Every foreign vessel that wanted to discharge or load at Whampoa had to be guaranteed by a hong merchant, every foreigner residing at the factories similarly spoken for. From the hong merchants a chain of responsibility passed down the ranks of all Chinese who came in contact with foreigners. Hong merchants secured linguists; linguists secured compradors; compradors went surety for the proper conduct of porters, watchmen, godown men, house coolies, table boys, and cooks. If anything went wrong anywhere, if in particular a foreigner misbehaved, there was sure to be some native Chinese whom an angry government could call to account.

All sorts of regulations—a number of them commercial—hedged the foreigners about. Incoming vessels had to pay measurement duty, *cumsha* (gift), pilotage and other fees, and customs. These payments were made to the Hoppo through the linguists; when it came time for a loaded vessel to sail, it was to the Hoppo, again through a linguist, that the vessel's agent applied for the great three-foot-square grand chop that cleared her for the outer waters. Other regulations directed how and where the foreigners should live. Summers they were to spend at Macao. At Canton, where they might pass the trading season, their quarters had to be in the factories. They were not to employ Chinese body servants, a prohibition regularly evaded. They were not to have their women with them. (In the autumn of 1830 Harriet Low spent three weeks at the factories, passing her days quietly in one of the front houses and in the evenings walking as far as Thirteen Factory Street. Her visit caused a sensation, but it was not repeated or imitated.) They might arm themselves with swords and fowling pieces, but they were not to bring up muskets or cannon or pass warships within the Bogue. They might not leave for Macao without permission; they might not wander out into the country, about the suburbs, or along the city wall; they might not enter the city proper, or take a boat and push at random into the delta. The only excursion officially permitted them was a walk on the island of Honam, just opposite the factories. Above all, foreigners were never to approach a mandarin directly. All communications had to pass through the hong merchants.

Such was the arrangement of life. It might have been expected to sour relations and blight business. How could foreigners deal frankly and easily with merchants who doubled as wardens, how could they put up indefinitely with the indignities that life at Canton promised to bring? Yet they managed.

They managed, in part, because not all the regulations were actually enforced. Foreigners rarely entered the city and never tried to explore the delta or the rest of Kwangtung province; they never hunted for the shortest water passage to Macao or set foot in the Meiling Pass. But they did frequent the alleys in the suburb immediately about the factories. They walked along the city wall and sometimes picnicked in the White Cloud Hills beyond the city, they rowed for pleasure on the river and eventually organized regattas there. To all this the hong merchants, and the mandarins invisible behind them, turned a blind eye—perhaps on the sound Chinese principle that these were simple barbarians who did not know any better: "he who offends unknowingly is not to be blamed."

There was another reason why the foreigners managed. The hong merchants and the linguists did not, in fact, usually behave like wardens. Take, for example, the linguists. Even allowing for the rosy hue Hunter cast over them as over everything else, they seem to have been an engaging and helpful lot. At the height of the trading season, when all was bustle and confusion, Old Tom, Young Tom, Alanci, and the others kept on the go day and night, hurrying from warehouse to warehouse to examine and check out teas, arranging for chop boats, settling various obligations at the Hoppo's yamen. Foreign merchants called relentlessly on their services from one side, the Hoppo chivied them from the other, yet they rarely lost their good humor, rarely failed to make everything smooth with the mandarins and pleasant for the *fan kuei*. As for the hong merchants, in Hunter's opinion a more honorable and amiable class of men was not to be found. In their warehouses, where teas and silks were sorted, weighed, and repacked, where bales of raw cotton and bolts of woolen cloth lay waiting for purchasers on wooden platforms set in paddy husk against the ants, all was order, neatness, and dispatch. Goods moved with very little fuss.

Chops or breaks of tea running as high as six hundred chests each were sold on the basis of a few samples, the buyers having in those days little fear of minced elm leaves, iron filings, or other adulterants. It was the same with silks. Satins, levantines, sarcenets, lustrings, and pongees were bought and shipped on the evidence of a piece or two taken at random from any box the buyer chose to have opened. The buyer signed no contract, expected no receipt, and instructed his comprador to pay by scribbling a note to him on any scrap of paper handy. Nowhere else in the world, said men of business, could goods be bought and sold so easily, so confidently, so well as at Canton.

The money in use made confidence almost obligatory. China possessed a single native coin, the cash. A solitary specimen of these copper and lead pieces was worth, however, nothing at all; it required over two hundred of them, tied in bundles through the square hole in the center of each, to equal one English shilling; it took almost five hundred to equal one Indian rupee, over a thousand to equal one dollar. So the cash was useless in commerce. The silver dollar took its place: Spanish by preference; U.S. if Spanish were not available; Mexican, Peruvian, or other American if no better could be had. Only Spanish dollars, however, were thought well enough of by the Chinese (who distrusted new designs and effigies) to be preserved whole. The rest were examined and stamped by the shroffs, each using his own distinctive mark—were stamped and stamped again, until at last they broke into pieces and could only be weighed. Native *sycee* silver had to be weighed anyway because it came in lumps. So the shroffs employed at the factories passed their time, in the arched passages off which opened the strongrooms, examining by touch and weighing in copper scales enormous heaps of silver pieces of every shape, size, and assay. They worked at great speed and in apparent confusion; a foreigner could not possibly keep tabs on the process and would be lucky even to recognize his shroffs, since they were brought in as needed from shroff shops in the city. So he simply had to trust his comprador. And he had to show that he trusted him. "No man of the character we require," wrote Lancelot Dent in the spring of 1839, "would remain with us if he were disgraced in the eyes of the household by a suspicion of his honesty." Shroffed silver was kept in bags and carried to and from the various treasuries by common coolies. "We rarely or ever examine these bags except to run the eyes over them, and we use no other check over the comprador than occasionally to pay all the money unexpectedly out of the Treasury," continued Dent in a letter explaining for the benefit of the India House that the casualness with which its surviving agents at Canton had been handling company money was entirely normal.[4] These agents had just found themselves short $20,000: to cover his commitments in a private tea speculation, their comprador had substituted cash for broken silver in a number of bags. It was scandalous! But it was also, Dent advised, most unusual, most unexpected. For the China trade was an honest trade, a safe trade, and a participant usually as certain as a man may ever be that his goods and his money were secure.

As also his person. Perched on the edge of a city a full day's journey from the sea, surrounded by people taught to regard him with derision and contempt, protected only by native watchmen armed with staves, lanterns, and conch shells, the foreign merchant at Canton nevertheless felt entirely safe. Pirates made the outer waters dangerous. Villagers about the gulf were not always respectful, especially to *fan kuei* who came ashore to commandeer provisions or steal water buffalo. There were frequent incidents at Whampoa; foreigners were sometimes roughed up at Macao. But to be pelted with mud on a stroll through the suburbs was the limit of the foreigners' peril at Canton, and inside the factories themselves they felt in no danger at all.

Safety was not enough, however. There were moments when the foreigners wanted to be treated as equals—perhaps as a little more than equals. It was a feeling that was stirred immediately whenever anyone mentioned the *Lady Hughes*.

"Has not the Chinese commerce of Great Britain been purchased with the blood of the gunner of the *Lady Hughes*?"[5]

Everyone knew the story: how one autumn afternoon in 1784 dinner guests aboard the country ship *Lady Hughes* at Whampoa were honored as they left with a salute; how the gunner failed to notice a chop boat just beneath the gun port; and how the blast from his gun killed one man and mortally wounded another. The authorities demanded the person of the gunner, a demand at first refused. But when all English trade had been stopped and the *Lady Hughes*'s supercargo seized and held as a hostage, the Factory gave way and instructed the vessel's master to turn the gunner over. The most he could be charged with, it was felt, was accidental homicide. Weeks passed, the *Lady Hughes* weighed and sailed, Christmas came and went. Then one day they learned to their horror that the gunner had been quietly strangled.

In 1821 came the turn of the Americans. A sailor named Terranova from the Baltimore brig *Emily* got into a violent quarrel with a bumboat woman and knocked her into the water, where she drowned. Or that, at least, was what the Chinese averred when they came for Terranova. He and his mates told a somewhat different story.

The trial, held right on board the brig, turned out to be a farce. Witnesses for the prosecution testified to things they could not possibly have seen, and witnesses for the defense were prevented from testifying at all; because the presiding magistrate would not allow an interpreter to be present, the Americans could not even follow properly what was going on. Terranova was found guilty. With reluctance the Americans allowed the Chinese to carry him away. Back came the body some time later, lifeless, the marks of the cord about the neck. Cowardly! disgraceful! cried the English. What the Americans had just done deserved to be held "in eternal execration by every Mortal, honourable, and feeling Mind."[6] But privately they must have reflected that indignation on Terranova's account could not erase the shame of the case of the gunner of the *Lady Hughes*.

Foreigners did not question the willingness of the authorities to deal severely with their fellow Chinese. Thieves caught in the act were flogged through the streets until the blood ran down to their heels. Brigands were publicly beheaded. Hunter once watched fifty-four condemned men arrive in baskets at the place of execution just outside Canton's south wall, kneel there in rows of four, and at a signal from the presiding officer suffer their heads to be severed from their bodies by executioners swinging heavy swords. This severity did not relax when the crimes alleged were at the foreigners' expense. In the spring of 1817 some boatmen happened upon the American *Wabash* lying in Macao Roads half attended with opium exposed upon her deck, swarmed aboard, killed five Americans, and made off with a number of chests. Wilcocks, the American consul, protested the outrage without mentioning the opium—and with little expectation that the pirates, as he thought them, would be caught. Imagine then his surprise when the authorities seized and decapitated five Chinese, explaining publicly that "piratical banditti plundering a foreign ship and murdering the mercantile seamen is the highest possible degree of cruelty and wickedness."[7] When, a dozen years later, the crew of the wrecked French *Navigateur* was set upon near Macao and massacred, the authorities were again indefatigable in hunting down the murderers. Seventeen were tried and beheaded, and their heads displayed in little cages along the shore.

What bothered the English, then, was not any supposed inclination on the part of the Chinese to be easy with their own. Nor was it the tendency (transparent in the Terranova case, they were persuaded) to discriminate against the foreigner. What bothered the English was the very nature of Chinese justice.

It operated, as far as they could see, on the twin principles of collective responsibility and a death for a death. A theft was committed in a village; the entire village was held to account in the person of its headman. A shopkeeper's son assaulted a tax collector; the shopkeeper was arrested to stand surety for his son. The Yellow River burst its banks; the governor of Honan Province begged the emperor to relieve him of his titles. In every case someone was responsible. Where death was concerned, moreover, the distinctions known to English law were (it appeared) largely lacking. To kill in the heat of passion, to kill by accident when only a beating was intended, even perhaps to kill by sheer mishap—these in the Chinese view constituted not manslaughter but murder. When the gunner of the *Lady Hughes* lost his life, English criminal law was still unbelievably fierce. It required the death penalty equally for picking a man's pocket and for taking his life. But this was so only if both were intentional. Accidental death drew a lesser penalty. In 1784 no English judge would have tried the gunner for murder, nor have attempted to hold the vessel's supercargo responsible in his person for what the gunner had done. If he had, no English jury would have sustained him.

Here was another alarming difference. Chinese proceedings were entirely summary. "There is no jury, no pleading," observed Bridgman, the American missionary. "The criminal kneels before the magistrate, who hears the witnesses and passes sentence; he is then remanded to prison or sent to the place of execution. Seldom is he acquitted."[8] Though hardly in a position to know very much about Chinese law—this was 1833, and he had only recently arrived—Bridgman was nevertheless on the right track. To the Chinese the law was not something promptly resorted to in disputes between private parties. These were best settled outside the law, without the help of lawyers. Nor was the law something a man might invoke on behalf of his rights against the state. A man had no rights, only duties. What the law did was little, and that chiefly penal. Persuasion and the example of right conduct were usually sufficient to avert, or at least smooth away, conflicts and disturbances. When they were not, when parties to a dispute had sunk into such bad and vicious ways that they were ready to use violence to gain private ends, then must the law intervene and sternly punish. Punish with an eye to making the punishment fit the crime—which meant, in cases of willful homicide, a life for a life. If the homicide occurred at the height of a riotous disturbance, so that the person striking the fatal blow could not be properly identified, it was even permissible to accuse whom one could, bring him to sentence, and execute him in the real culprit's stead.

Thus to the English, Chinese law seemed largely criminal law; courts appeared to be places where guilt was extracted, often from the innocent, by inquisition and terror. The prospect made a man like James Goddard, the private merchant who put the rhetorical question about the gunner, very uneasy. An Englishman, Goddard felt, deserved to be tried by processes that distinguished action from intent and held no man responsible for another man's offense. An Englishman's trial, he equally felt, should not be an inquisition but a cock fight, a cock fight fought fairly and openly before a special audience, the jury. Moreover, just as an accused person deserved a sporting chance against his adversary, the state, so China herself ought to engage other nations in adversary proceedings—should confront them equal to equal. This she was unwilling to do. Let His Majesty's government, therefore, send a commissioned officer of high rank, an officer not connected with trade (for the mandarins despised merchants and would never respect anyone who mingled with them), an officer empowered to deal directly with Peking; an officer ready and willing, moreover, to use force. So little was needed! A single brig was worth a fleet of China's mightiest war junks, a regiment could master ten thousand of her braves! What an arrogant—and at the same time ridiculous—colossus China was!

"The Tartars in centuries gone by passed the Great Wall of China and seated themselves upon the throne. That wall now remains but an eternal monument of Chinese cowardice and imbecility. Yet the invisible one of prejudice, the wall constructed by a tithe of the people, still towers in all its strength; and the enlightened nations of Europe, the British who pride themselves upon their intellect, who would scorn to be called dupes, crouch nevertheless to its influence, and it may be said worship the edifice they have contributed to erect."

Thus on and on, for more than a dozen pages of rather small print.[9] Goddard was a man with a message.

But messages would not bring on the envoy, the warships, or the men. Whitehall was too far away and too indifferent for that. What was needed was something that would compel England to take notice. And even as Goddard wrote, that something was discernible—in the imminent demise of the Factory, and in the peculiar traffic Harriet Low got a glimpse of when, in the autumn of 1832, she happened to visit Lintin.

4

The Opium Traffic

Lintin is an island in the middle of the gulf twenty-five miles south of the Bogue, or about where the bar of the A should be. Its southeast end—the island is two and a half miles long and lies on a slant—is occupied by a brush-covered hill a thousand feet high. Its northwest end is lower and indented by several small bays, and in one of these there is (or was) a little fishing village. The fishermen work with nets strung from poles driven into the mud, a thing possible because the water is extremely shallow around most of the island. At the very northwest tip, however, there is a fair depth; and it was here that Harriet found the bark belonging to Russell and Company, her uncle's agency house.

The bark was named, appropriately, the *Lintin.* Harriet spent almost a month aboard her as the guest of Macondray, her master. Sometimes she went ashore and explored the island. Once she climbed the hill and ate a picnic lunch at the top—Macondray assured her she was the first western woman to set foot there. For the most part she stayed on board talking to Mrs. Macondray, waging war on the cockroaches, and watching what went on among the other ships.

For there were always ships at the anchorage: her first morning Harriet counted twenty-three. A few of them, like the *Lintin,* did not move from month to month except when bad weather threatened. Most came in, anchored for a few days or weeks, then went away again. Curious native craft came and lay alongside some of them—one day Harriet spent several hours hanging over the rail watching one moored close against the *Lintin.* It was long, low, and narrow, and carried a large crew, a far larger crew than one would have expected for a boat of that size, though Harriet does not seem to have been surprised. "They muster generally about a hundred men," she wrote. While she watched, the crew collected "round five or six little messes of fish and oysters cooked in divers ways. Each man has his bowl of rice in one hand and his chopsticks in the other, which they dip into the public bowl and thence into their mouths . . . and then shovel as much rice into their mouths as they can possibly crowd in."[1] How ugly and dirty they were; and how indolent they seemed, lying about playing cards or dominoes after stuffing themselves so! Only in passing did she mention that the boat was a smuggling boat.

One afternoon after dinner she was rowed over to a neighboring ship, bark-rigged like the *Lintin* but built along cleaner lines, on which a party was in progress. There was a little band, "and we danced a quadrille upon the deck, and the gentlemen waltzed."[2] The name of the ship was *Red Rover.* Harriet failed to add, however, that *Red Rover* was not just another merchant vessel carrying cotton or rattans and pausing momentarily before proceeding up the Canton River. She was an opium clipper—the very first of all opium clippers, being then already three years old—and she had come as close to the Bogue as she was meant to come. Calcutta was her port of origin, Lintin was her destination; of half a dozen vessels anchored within a radius of a quarter of a mile one could probably say the same. As for Macondray's *Lintin,* she was a receiving ship; which is to say she was a permanent floating warehouse, to which clippers and other country ships brought the drug, and from which coasters and small native craft like the one Harriet had watched were systematically supplied.

All about Harriet opium was changing hands in quantities worth hundreds of thousands of dollars. That was what Macondray spent his days doing. From the deck of the *Lintin* he conducted a business that fully equaled what Harriet would have seen aboard any Indiaman at Whampoa. And where was the *Lintin* lying? Off a barren little nothing of an island in the middle of nowhere! How odd, until one remembered that in India opium was legitimate—and in China, contraband.

The first edict prohibiting the drug issued from Peking in 1729. At that time opium was reaching China in very small quantities and was being consumed, in the southern coastal provinces chiefly, as *madak.* So the Chinese government can scarcely have understood how dangerous it was. Very likely Peking pronounced against the drug for the same general reason that, ninety years earlier, it had banned that other pernicious foreign article: tobacco. The emperor, however, had been as little able as the rulers of England, Russia, or the Ottoman Empire to keep his people from smoking the weed. Trying to shut opium out of China was likely to prove equally useless.

For a time consumption rose quite slowly. All through the eighteenth century not China but places short of China took the largest share of India's still trifling production. Penang became an English station explicitly as a convenient Straits outlet for Indian opium; so large was the traffic on Java that when the English occupied the island briefly during the Napoleonic Wars, Raffles, the English governor, actually proposed that the East India Company assume a monopoly of opium distribution there. Fort William refused. Java and its opium trade reverted to the Dutch. At the same time, however, the Dutch share of India's annual export sank to a fraction of the total. By the early 1820s the number of chests leaving India had passed five thousand a year—and almost all of that volume went to China.

As the volume rose and the form in which the opium was consumed shifted inexorably from *madak* with a low morphia content to *chandu* with a high, official declarations against the drug multiplied. There was an edict in 1780, another in 1796, an order from the governor-general at Canton in 1799, and pronouncements thereafter at a rate, counting Canton as well as Peking, of almost one a year. As these emerge in the translations of the time, they seem to show that the Chinese were beginning to discover the damage opium could do. "The Celestial Empire," runs one, "does not forbid you people to make and eat opium, and diffuse the custom in your native place. But that opium should flow into the interior of this country, where vagabonds clandestinely purchase and eat it, and continually become sunk into the most stupid and besotted state . . . is an injury to the manners and minds of men of the greatest magnitude." In fact the injury was to more than vagabonds. Opium smoking was no longer confined to the south coast. It had spread north and west. Well-to-do young men smoked for the novelty of it. They could at least afford the drug; clerks, runners, and other civil service underlings who could not, smoked anyway, and in their efforts to cater to the habit ate badly and sank into miserable little corrupt ways. The emperor discovered that even his eunuchs and the officers of his palace guard were taking the drug. It was alarming. At Canton the authorities exhorted the hong merchants not to let the vile stuff slip by. "Be careful and do not view this document as mere matter of form, and so tread within the net of the law," they warned, "for you will find your escape as impracticable as it is for a man to bite his own navel."[3] The hong merchants took heed. They did not themselves buy or sell opium. They kept the drug out of their warehouses. As for the East India Company, which is to say the Government of India, it too heard the warnings; knew that its opium was being smuggled in growing quantities into China; and knew that Peking knew—the Factory correspondence, still carefully preserved, gives ample evidence of that. But what was the Government of India to do? Should it get out of the opium business altogether?

The answer was not easily yes. Two or three thousand chests of Patna and Benares costing perhaps 300 rupees each to produce, yet bringing in more than three times that amount when sold, were sources of revenue not lightly to be abandoned. The Government of India was anyhow of two minds (if it was of any mind at all) about the effect of the traffic on the Chinese. In 1819 it proposed to raise slightly the quantity of chests it offered. Doing so would not, it told itself, increase the consumption of the "deleterious drug" in China or extend its "baneful effects" there. The only purpose of the increase was "to secure to ourselves the whole supply by preventing foreigners from participating in a trade of which they at present enjoy no inconsiderable share; for it is evident that the Chinese, as well as the Malays, cannot exist without the use of opium, and if we do not supply their necessary wants, foreigners will."[4] Foreigners meant, among others, Indians outside the Bengal agencies; for there was nothing in the laws of horticulture that said the opium poppy could not be cultivated elsewhere than on the Ganges plain. If Patna and Ghazipur did not supply the market, other places would.

Except, however, for one small venture in the 1780s that turned out badly, the Company never itself shipped opium to China. Company officers speculated in consignments sent privately in country ships, but opium was never a part of an Indiaman's regular cargo. Shortly after he came home from Canton to retire, a private merchant named Jardine was asked by a Parliamentary committee whether he and his partners had ever been approached by the Opium Board at Calcutta with proposals for encouraging the sale of opium in China. "Yes," replied Jardine, "we have had musters of opium sent on to us in small quantities, packed in different ways, with a request that we would sell it and ascertain the kind of package that suited the Chinese market best."[5] So the board fussed about how its product was packaged. It did not, however, bother itself with the problem of how to get the product to China or how to sell it there. It left that to the Jardines.

William Jardine was a Scotsman who had come out to China in 1802 as surgeon's mate aboard an Indiaman. Company surgeons were entitled to a certain amount of privilege tonnage in the vessels on which they served, so it was easy for Jardine to acquire over the years a taste for the China trade. In 1817 he made his last voyage for the Company; two years later he left for the East again on free merchant's indentures, settled at Canton (he was now about thirty-five years of age), and began to do business on his own.

At Canton he saw a good deal of another Scot, a man in his twenties named James Matheson. Matheson had attended Edinburgh University, spent two years in a London agency house, and came out to Calcutta in 1815. From Calcutta he made repeated trips to Canton until, at last, like Jardine he settled there. In 1825 Jardine joined the Canton agency house of

Magniac and Company. Two years later Matheson joined also, bringing his nephew Alexander with him. Later still the last Magniac went home, whereupon the house changed its name to Jardine, Matheson and Company. Long before that it had grown into the largest and the most active of the houses of agency at Canton, among the English and the Parsees rivaled only by Dent and Company, among the Americans only by Russell and Company. And one of the things Jardine, Matheson and Company was active in was opium.

Now an agency house, as the name implies, did not ordinarily own the goods it dealt in. Instead it bought (for a commission) what other parties asked it to buy and sold what they asked it to sell. In the case of the opium traffic, the other parties were private merchants at Calcutta. They purchased chests of Patna and Benares at the Tank Square auctions and consigned those chests to agents or agency houses on the coast of China. Naturally they did not do so blindly. Consignors and consignees usually knew each other well; indeed, almost the chief duty of a China agent was to maintain a regular communication with his "correspondents" in India and elsewhere. The fact remains that the parties who bought the drug at Calcutta did not themselves sell the drug at Canton, while the actual sellers there were not the owners. As for the original producer, the Government of India, it turned its back the moment the Tank Square auctions were over. One might almost suppose that to diffuse and dilute responsibility had been the whole intent of the arrangement.

There was a further question, however, When the opium left Calcutta, stored in the holds of country ships and consigned to agents in Canton, it was an entirely legitimate article. It remained an entirely legitimate article all the way up the China Sea. But the instant it reached the coast of China it became something different. It became contraband. This meant that it could not be landed openly, it had to be smuggled. And the question was, who was going to do the smuggling?

Not Russell's men, not Dent's or Jardine's. Not smugglers they! As consignees they had to devise some means for warehousing the opium. So they early hit on the scheme of converting a number of merchantmen into receiving ships, floating depots as it were, and leaving them permanently on the coast. They had also to sell the opium thus warehoused, remitting to consignors the monies received; but the selling could be done while the opium was still afloat. Thus they would stay safely within the letter of the law. "Is it your idea that no one is engaged in smuggling unless he actually conveys the goods on shore?" a member of Parliament asked Thacker, a private merchant, when in 1840 England thought to make inquiries into the war it was about to wage. This was precisely Thacker's idea. "You make smugglers of the Chinese, but you are not smugglers yourselves?"

the M.P. persisted. "We supply the means of their smuggling" was all Thacker would say.[6]

That it was the Chinese who were doing the smuggling was a point of view forced upon the mandarins too. The reason for this was simple. The mandarins had it in their power to make life extremely uncomfortable for a receiving ship. They could harass its servants and scare away its bumboats; they could retaliate against the trade in silks, nankeens, and sugar candy that the agency house in question was also carrying on. But the mandarins had at their command no navy worth the name, whereas even a receiving ship, if armed with a few guns and officered by a few resolute westerners, was formidable. So it was beyond the capacity of the mandarins actually to capture one of these floating warehouses or to drive it clear off. If they wanted to break the opium traffic, they had to turn upon the Chinese end of it. They had to lie in wait to intercept the native smuggling boats or move against the brokers. That was the only way—that or learn to look in the other direction.

As it happened, the habits and circumstances of official life inclined the mandarins to this last. They were poorly paid, so poorly paid that they were obliged as a matter of course to support themselves, their families, and their official establishments out of the perquisites of office. Foreigners did not fully appreciate this. What they *did* see was that in the Canton area extra payments were the normal lubricant of the pilotage, port, and customs systems. Individual Chinese, the hong merchants in particular, might be honest to a fault, yet let a mandarin or a mandarin's underling appear, and "squeeze" appeared too. Squeeze was what civil servants collected for themselves in the process of collecting for the state. It was so rooted, and so ubiquitous, that it was bound (foreigners felt) to make nonsense of edicts against opium. Indeed, were not such edicts simply a device for guaranteeing the mandarins a rake-off! For as the English missionary agent, G. Tradescant Lay, put it a few years after Harriet Low's visit to Lintin, "unless a fisherman has a net, he cannot catch a fish"—by which he meant that without laws against opium, the mandarins would not be able to squeeze so many dollars a chest from the Chinese who dealt in it.

"In China," added Lay, "every man is a smuggler in opium from the Emperor downwards."[7] Now that certainly was not true. But there was no question that very large quantities of the drug flowed from the decks of the receiving ships into the interior of China. And there was no question that they moved there across a thick and almost noiseless cushion of squeeze.

It was not to be expected, however, that the opium traffic would always run with perfect smoothness. From time to time the even surface of

official connivance was bound to be broken by a squabble among the con-
nivers, the arrival of a new mandarin unfamiliar with the system, or an unexpectedly piercing shaft of scrutiny from the yellow-roofed throne halls
of the Forbidden City. Then there would be trouble; opium dens raided;
native smugglers caught and punished; and the traffic interrupted.

In 1821 there occurred a particularly sharp crisis. His attention directed to the problem by the Tao-kuang emperor (who had just ascended
the throne in a reforming frame of mind) and by the circumstance that
opium in the Canton area was fetching the unusual price of $2,000 a chest,
the governor-general of Kwangtung and Kwangsi provinces moved with
unexpected energy against the native dealers. Sixteen of them were arrested. One, sentenced to exile in central Asia, in his bitterness accused
mandarins in the Canton area of receiving so much per smuggled chest. If
Peking got wind of this, there was sure to be an inquiry. Prudently the
governor-general ordered all foreign vessels carrying opium to get out of
the river.

Of itself this order did not mean very much. It was one on the books
all the time, so to speak. On this occasion, however, the hong merchants
were involved. The governor-general was pointing openly at them, accus-
ing them of shirking their responsibilities, threatening to deprive them of
their buttons of rank if the opium traffic did not immediately move out of
the river. They in turn were letting it be known that they would not have
any dealings with ships (they named four) known to contain the drug. This
was serious. Behind it lay the implied threat to stop the trade completely,
not just with opium men but with all foreigners. It was a thing the Chinese
had done before.

One of the named four was the American *Emily*. (She had arrived
with 180 chests of Turkey, had sold only 47, and was waiting at Whampoa
for the market to improve. It was because he did not want to publicize the
nature of his cargo that her master had agreed to let the Chinese try Terranova, but the authorities had found out what she carried anyway.) The
other three were country ships consigned to James Matheson, who used
one to store opium. Matheson asked the Select Committee of senior Company supercargoes—"the Select," as they were sometimes sardonically
called—what he ought to do. This annoyed them. As individuals they
knew all about Matheson's opium activity and even acknowledged its use-
fulness to the tea trade. As Company men, however, they had nothing to
do with the prohibited article and wished to hear nothing about it. So they
turned Matheson a deaf ear. Was he not consul for the king of Denmark? If
he must appeal, let him appeal to Copenhagen!

The fact that Matheson should be met with this response seems odd
until one notices that, by the terms of the Company's charter, private En-

glish had no business being in China at all. Numbers of them were there just the same, of course, and had long been. From time to time, however, the Select tried to drive the more bumptious away; it was to protect themselves from this that some of the private English had taken to obtaining consular commissions from lesser European states: from Prussia, Sardinia, Hamburg, at one time from Poland, and even from the Republic of Genoa. (In 1825 a stubborn Scotsman named James Innes balked at the masquerade and refused to take out consul's papers for Ruritania or any other place. The Select, after huffing and puffing a little, let him stay. But this was still four years away.) Matheson, as it happened, represented Denmark; that was why the Select told him to seek his advice there.

Meanwhile, however, let him do nothing that might embarrass the tea trade. Matheson was only twenty-five, still very new to China. He was ready to risk a brush with the mandarins, he was ready to defy the Select, but he was not ready to do both. So he took his ships out of the river. Other private merchants did the same (Whampoa was uncomfortably confined and public anyway). And after 1821 the drug traffic was conducted entirely at the outer anchorages—particularly at Lintin.

Except for bad weather there was very little to fear at Lintin. Pirates so close to the Bogue were rare, and if they should appear the receiving ships were ready for them with cannon, muskets, cutlasses, and boarding nets well triced up. Of course there were the war junks to consider. A young American visitor describes how they would lie quietly off the island, then suddenly get under way, and sail past the opium ships "with colors and streamers flying, gongs beating, and a vast deal of ridiculous parade; and after a few equally vain manoeuvres, return to their moorings and dispatch a most bombastic letter to Canton announcing the annihilation of the 'foreign thieves' who come to poison the subjects of His Celestial Majesty with this filthy drug."[8] Men like Matheson and Macondray had no opinion whatever of war junks.

So Russell and Company's *Lintin,* Jardine's *Hercules* and *Samarang,* Dent's *Jane,* and other receiving ships that we know existed, but cannot always name, lay month after month—year after year—off Lintin. Into their holds went increasing quantities of Indian opium together with driblets of Turkish brought by the Americans. But though the native smugglers came right to ship's side to take delivery of the stuff, the sales themselves were not arranged on deck. That part of the business was carried on at Canton, just as the buying and selling of teas, silks, and English manufactures were.

This was the beauty of the system. Driven from Whampoa, Matheson had been able to retire to the factories at Canton and dispose of his opium from there. At the factories, consignees like himself committed their chests sight unseen to native brokers acting for the big Chinese wholesale opium houses. These brokers came openly to bargain; they paid immediately, in silver; the consignee received a fixed commission on the sale. When a bargain had been struck, an order to deliver—blank opium orders could be purchased from the Macao printing shops at so much a hundred—was dispatched to the appropriate receiving ship at Lintin, often traveling in the very smuggling craft sent to pick the stuff up. Long narrow vessels beautifully built of bright unpainted wood, these craft were known, from their speed and from the rows of oars that assisted their mat sails, as "scrambling dragons" or "fast crabs." They mounted a swivel or two amidships and another in the bow; their sides bristled with every kind of cut and thrust weapon; they were manned by those superb and fearsome boat people, the Tanka. Once loaded, they made for one of the inlets on the shores of the gulf or pushed boldly into the river, and if the proper palms had been crossed, landed their cargoes without incident. They went prepared to fight, however, being fully a match for the "mandarin boats" they so closely resembled and much too fast for war junks.

The whole business was conducted with the greatest trust and confidence. Native buyers knew that the Patna and Benares they were getting was unadulterated and full weight because it carried the East India Company's mark. Though the traffic was illegal, the mandarins rarely tried to interrupt it. Best of all, what risks there were fell entirely upon the Chinese. It was this splendid feature that moved Jardine to call the opium trade "by far the safest trade in China." It was safe "because you got your money before you gave your order. Whatever the difficulty was in landing it afterwards, you had nothing to do with it. When the cash-keeper reported so much cash paid into the treasury, you gave an order for as much opium as the man wanted, and then you had done with it; it was his affair after that."[9]

Almost anyone could dabble in the traffic. "Dear Sir," began a letter from the Parsee firm of Hukitjee Jimmybhoy to Russell and Company, "we avail of departure of *Cornywallis,* and thanking your favour of April 19 enclosing £2,000 in pamphlets suitable our order. [The writer meant bills of exchange.] Now heavy distress falling upon us through Almighty God taking from bosom of family and friends our worthy father, who died after loitering many days of chronic diarrhoea of guts, much regretted. O grave where is sting! O death where is victory! Nevertheless, resigning to will of Providence, and no change in freights since last advised," let Russell's expect a consignment of opium in eight or ten weeks' time.[10] It would come to exactly twenty chests. That was not an unreasonably small amount; from the Indian end small firms as well as large took their fling at the trade, and at Canton the participants were often equally modest. Hunter remembers visiting an Indian Muslim named Boo-Bull in the Dutch factory one summer day. The fellow sat crosslegged on a mat, smoking a hookah. The only furniture in the room was a large red chest containing papers, account books, pens, an inkstand made from a bamboo joint, rice, dal, ghee, curry powder, a bamboo pillow, a spare turban, and an extra pair of yellow shoes with long points like rats' tails. Out of this chest Boo-Bull lived and did his business; it was his larder, wardrobe, and office; but this did not mean that he was poor or his affairs negligible. Like many other Indians at Canton he handled a great deal of opium, storing it in the receiving ships of the larger firms (for which he paid demurrage), selling it to Chinese opium brokers, and converting the silver into East India Company bills. For all this he needed no clerks, no coolies, no warehouse, no capital even—only his wits. Any private merchant who wanted to could participate in the traffic. And so many did that at last a special kind of vessel had to be developed to bring the drug to China.

The China Sea is dominated by two monsoons, the northeast and the southwest. The northeast begins in October and blows itself out in March; the southwest reaches the Gulf of Canton late in May and dissipates in September. Much the same calendar governs the Indian Ocean, the only difference being that in the Indian Ocean the summer, southwest monsoon is by far the more pronounced of the two. Its onset over the Indian subcontinent, bringing torrents of rain, breaks the terrible dry heat of the Ganges plain and makes the land green again for the indispensable crops of early autumn. In the China Sea it is the other way around. For though Canton's wettest months are the summer ones, it is the winter monsoon that is the more powerful. During almost half the year it blows and blows, not continuously, but often enough and with enough force so that sailing ships find it difficult to move up the coast.

The tubby, bluff-bowed country wallahs of the private trade did not even try. If the best of the European square-riggers, if even the great oceangoing Chinese junks, must think twice before attempting to beat to windward against the northeast monsoon at its height, country ships might as well rest content to roll comfortably up the China Sea before the southwest winds of summer and in the winter roll comfortably down again. By the late 1820s, however, too many chests of opium were trying to reach the China coast to be accommodated in so leisurely a fashion. Opium merchants wanted something faster. They wanted to be able to buy breaks of Patna or Benares at the Company's January sale and put them on the China coast in February. They wanted to be able to load again in May and have the ship back at Calcutta in time to load a third time in July. They wanted, in short, several round trips a year. That meant defying the pattern of the monsoon. In the late summer of 1829 a Calcutta agency house thought it had found a way.

It put three hundred chests into a brig, commissioned the new side-wheel steamer *Forbes* to go along and tow when necessary, and sent the two off down the Hooghly. Partway, however, a serious mishap occurred. The *Forbes* ran upon a shoal. The brig, in tow behind, struck the steamer, had her anchor knocked into the water, and holed herself on one of the flukes. A passing ship helped William Clifton, her master, lift a few of the chests out. Then a gale blew up and pounded the brig and the rest of her valuable cargo to pieces.

Understandably the agency house was in no hurry to repeat the experiment. Clifton, however, persevered. A man of some means and influence, he boldly ordered from certain Calcutta builders a ship closewinded enough, he calculated, so that she would not require a tow but could beat up the China Sea against the full force of the northeast monsoon. Within weeks of the brig's loss the new vessel had been laid down. The Government of India followed and encouraged her construction and on an afternoon in December half the society of Calcutta watched as she slid into the Hooghly. She was narrow, flush-decked with almost no sheer, square in the stern but with a long counter; she claimed 250 tons burden and was in rig a bark—which meant she carried square sails on foremast and mainmast, fore-and-aft sails on the mizzen. She looked less like a merchantman than a privateer, she was in fact said to be modeled after one. And her figurehead was an effigy, as like as the imagination could contrive, of the fierce pirate hero of James Fenimore Cooper's latest novel, *Red Rover*.

Red Rover left Calcutta a few days after Christmas with eight hundred chests from the season's first sale, and Clifton himself in command. On 4 January 1830 she cleared the Sandheads and was off down the Bay of Bengal; on 26 January she touched Singapore. From there it was beat to windward, tack and tack about, until she sighted the coast of China twenty-two days later. Ten days later still she was at sea again, and on 1 April picked up her pilot at the mouth of the Hooghly. Any other vessel would have taken three months simply to reach China and at that time of year would probably have had to get there by a roundabout route through the Java Sea, the Molucca Passage, and the waters east of the Philippines. But *Red Rover* went directly; she made three round trips that year; she was truly the first of the opium clippers, as Harriet Low knew. Her launching suggested that the opium traffic would soon come to dominate the country trade with China.

Perhaps come to dominate the China trade as a whole. It was noticeable that even Company men took a friendly interest in the drug. While
they rarely visited the *Hercules,* the *Jane,* or the *Lintin* and did not cease to
resent the confident manner of the interloping private English, they could
not help welcoming the rising volume of opium. Without opium they
would be hard put to go on doing what they did best and liked best to
do—to buy and ship teas. And how was one to buy teas unless one had
something to buy them with?

5

The End of the Company

To find something the Chinese wanted—that was the problem. For China, it seemed, already possessed everything: "the best food in the world, rice; the best drink, tea; and the best clothing, cotton, silk, fur," as Hart, the Englishman who directed China's customs service later in the nineteenth century, once remarked.[1] To food, drink, and clothing add manufactured articles; for in China, as in India, the industrial arts were so advanced that Europe, before her machine age, could offer almost nothing to compare. What were Birmingham clocks and musical snuffboxes next to the wallpaper, fabrics, lacquer ware, porcelain, *objets d'art*, and bric-a-brac that poured out of the shops and manufactories of China? Even after the passing in the late eighteenth century of the European rage for *chinoiserie*, the superiority of Chinese manufactures continued to be acknowledged. If the new industries of England made anything cheaply and well, it was cotton cloth; yet as late as the 1830s some foreign buyers at Canton held handwoven nankeens to be superior in both cost and quality to what came out of Lancashire. What, then, could the Chinese possibly be induced to take?

It was true there were some things they required. The tea men wanted lead to be hammered into the paper-thin sheets they lined their chests with. Rattans were in demand for beds, chairs, mats, and cordage; pepper, tin, and saltpeter found buyers; and because south China was periodically short of rice, the Chinese authorities systematically encouraged vessels to bring cargoes of that grain from Java or Manila. Best of all was the market for raw Bombay cotton; for while that article could not make the long haul around the Cape and still compete at Liverpool with what the Americas sent, it was in demand at Canton to supplement the Chinese crop or to replace it when it failed. Compacted by a gigantic capstan-operated press into bales each of three to five hundred pounds weight, the stuff reached Whampoa in shiploads sometimes as large as a thousand tons and contri-

53

buted in a normal year from a third to a fourth by value of British imports.

Nevertheless as the quantity of teas taken by the Company and others went up, lead, rattans, rice, and cotton fell further and further short of covering their cost—and the gap in the balance of trade grew wider. To fill the gap ingenious private merchants (led by the Americans) tried to interest the Chinese in a variety of other, more exotic articles. From the South Pacific they brought sandalwood, seal skins, and sea slugs dried stiff and dirty brown, from the Pacific Northwest the pelt of the sea otter. The Appalachians supplied ginseng, a root much valued by the Chinese as a sexual rejuvenator; from the East Indies came birds' nests of swifts' spittle to put into soup. It was no use. The sandalwood gave out, the seals and sea otters were driven to the edge of extinction; and though the Chinese would pay twice its weight in silver for a bird's nest, a bird's nest does not weigh very much. As for the Company, it tried to fill the gap by persuading the Chinese to take England's traditional staple, woolens. Every year the Company shipped out quantities of broadcloths, long ells, camlets, and other woolen fabrics. No one consulted the customer, however. In cold weather a rich Chinese put on silks and furs, a poor Chinese added padding to his cottons. Neither would buy wool, at least not in the quantities necessary to pay for teas.

The obvious way out of this balance-of-payments difficulty was to fill the gap with silver—and this the Company did. For years a very high proportion of its cargoes to China, sometimes almost the whole of them, consisted of silver. It was the same with the Americans. The Chinese were happy to have silver, of course. But silver was hard to get, as well as being something contemporary mercantilist opinion said you ought to hold on to, not lose; and in the early nineteenth century, when mercantilist opinion showed signs of dissolving, the precious metal grew scarcer than ever. Unless some new commodity appeared to take silver's place, and by its ready sale at Canton furnish what was revealingly termed the "investment" for teas, it was going to be impossible to maintain, let alone expand, the flow of the leaf.

Fortunately a new commodity did appear. It was, of course, opium. Private merchants, not the Company, brought it to China, but that made no difference; the Company, with its international reach, could obtain the dollars the drug earned by offering in exchange its bills payable in India or England. When Boo-Bull (he of the red chest and yellow shoes) succeeded in selling a few chests of opium, he took his silver to the New English factory and bought a Company bill. The bill went to his consignor in India—vessels returning there often carried nothing but paper—the silver purchased teas for the Company. London got into the act because each year tens of millions of rupees earned or extracted in India by the Company, or by individual Englishmen, sought ways of returning to England. Had India then produced teas, these rupees could have traveled in that form. Some, indeed, went as indigo and saltpeter; most made a little detour through Canton. Invested in Patna or Benares and consigned to a Canton agency house, they started eastward as opium in the hold of *Red Rover* or another vessel, became silver dollars when a Chinese smug boat took possession of the chests off Lintin, and a day or so later were converted by the consignee into bills payable in London. Again the Company used those dollars to buy teas. So Indian rupees arrived in England concealed, so to speak, inside chests of congou, souchong, and pekoe.

What a marvelous interlocking system it was—and at the bottom of it, opium! Its sale at Calcutta contributed significantly to the revenue of the Government of India. Its sale at Lintin financed the purchase of England's teas, while at the same time making it easier for returning English nabobs and the Government of India to get Indian rupees home. In England, as we have seen, Whitehall depended upon the tea duty for a considerable part of its revenue. How convenient the drug was, how indispensable even— but at the same time how dangerous to the future tranquility of the China trade.

For opium, after all, remained contraband, brought to China by the private English, the Parsees, and the Americans—exactly the most ambitious and ungovernable people in the China trade. (For English read Scots and Irish too.) By the end of the twenties these gentlemen were disposing of goods worth almost four times what the Company's vessels brought to China. Raw cotton accounted for a part of this. Opium made up most. It was opium that drove the volume of the country trade higher and higher each year. It was opium that furnished the Factory with the silver it needed to buy teas. By 1830 enough opium was entering China so that it could have covered, by itself and with a little to spare, the full $9 million that teas cost the Factory. Because the Factory, however, still paid for half its teas out of the proceeds of the woolens, raw cotton, and whatnot that it reluctantly continued to sell, the silver actually remaining after the opium had been sold and the teas bought was far from a little. It was a lot. It came to several million dollars a year. No longer did the foreigners bring silver to China, they took it away. Indiamen often paused at Lintin to load treasure directly from the receiving ships!

Sooner or later this meant trouble. For Peking was accustomed to seeing silver flow in and was sure to make inquiries when it discovered silver flowing the opposite way. It might strike the Dragon Throne, moreover, that foreign mud slipping into the Empire did more than suck silver out. Success at the opium traffic encouraged the private merchants to practice evasions in the legitimate trade too—if you can diddle the law over one thing, you can probably diddle it over another. Already it was notorious that goods were not always loaded and unloaded as they should be. A vessel that entered the river and anchored at Whampoa paid a variety of fees and charges that amounted to a large and not always predictable sum. Customs duties were the unpredictable part. There was no published schedule; it was universally suspected that the Hoppo (superintendent of customs) exacted whatever he felt he could get away with; and as his underlings were generally quite willing to settle for less provided they were cut in on it, foreigners were easily driven, as one American put it, "to seek in the corruptibility of the lower officers a refuge from the cupidity of the higher."[2] Foreigners also resented the measurement duty (officers came on board and literally measured the ship) and the official *cumsha* (gift), which together ran to several thousand dollars and bore more heavily upon small vessels than upon large. Yet it required no special effort to perceive that a ship that went no farther in than Lintin saved her owner customs, measurement, and *cumsha* alike.

Of course you could not trade at the outer anchorages in quite the normal manner, but there were ways to arrange things. Small vessels stopping at Lintin, and learning there that they would pay prohibitive charges if they entered the river, could unload their rattans and bales of cotton into large ships. Or since rice excused a carrier from measurement duty and *cumsha* both, a ship inbound might replace part of its cargo with that grain before heading for the Bogue. "Rice, in quantities for ships to enter the Port free of the Cumsha and measurement dues, may be had at Lintin. Apply to A. S. Keating." That was the way it was openly advertised in the *Canton Register*, the newspaper John Slade published weekly from a press in the Danish factory. This sort of evasion easily suggested others. Why not let goods transshipped at Lintin do the last leg to market in smug boats; not cotton and rattans perhaps, for they were bulky, but lead, saltpeter, that sort of thing? And why not slip goods out the same way? So smuggling in legitimate articles grew up right alongside smuggling in the forbidden drug. That was one reason why Harriet found so many vessels at the island. By the time she paid her visit, fully a third of the more than 150 vessels that reached the Gulf of Canton each year managed to do their business and sail away without ever passing the Bogue.

Finally, why be content with Lintin? The gulf and the river were not the only places where private merchants wanted to trade, and opium not the only article they were anxious to trade in. American merchants, it is true, seemed pretty well satisfied with things as they were. A flow of credit from England to the United States had suddenly made it easy for them to buy teas (like the Company they bought hardly anything else) with bills on London houses. They were beginning, too, to bring a few English manufactures to Canton. But they could do this precisely because the private English could not. As long as the Company kept the legal monopoly of the China trade, private English had to import English goods surreptitiously by way of India or Singapore, which raised the price by almost 10 percent. This was irritating, and the private English were further annoyed by the Factory's acceptance of the traditional Chinese view that international trade may be nice but is hardly necessary. To the private English it was axiomatic that an exchange of goods always benefits both parties. The greater the exchange, the better for everybody. If the Chinese did not see this, it must be because they were obstinate and stupid—a little blind too, inasmuch as they were actually beginning in spite of themselves to welcome some articles (cotton yarn, for example) that they had always made at home. They were even beginning to show a certain interest in cotton piece goods. In India the market for these things had grown tremendously since the Company had lost its monopoly there in 1814. Now Manchester cotton manufacturers were beginning to wonder if it were not their destiny to supply all of China too. As for teas, there was no question at all in the minds of the private English that they could supply the United Kingdom better and more cheaply than did the Factory if only given the chance. What use was the Factory if, instead of leading a general assault upon the closed China market, it simply crouched jealously over the leaf?

Early in 1832 the Factory made as if to respond to this criticism. It permitted an enterprising junior supercargo named Hugh Hamilton Lindsay to charter the country bark *Lord Amherst*, load her with English cottons and woolens, engage Karl Gutzlaff, a German missionary, as interpreter, and sail off to see whether such legitimate articles could be sold up the coast. As an exercise in calculated intrusion, the voyage was a great success. At Amoy, Lindsay and his companions, armed with nothing more substantial than one fowling piece and Gutzlaff's extraordinary self-confidence in the Fukien dialect, went ashore several days in a row and walked now into the town, now out among the villages. Soldiers sometimes followed them, but no one interfered. Off Foochow, when a war junk deliberately anchored so close it ran afoul of the *Lord Amherst*, Thomas Rees, her master, simply sent an officer named Jauncey to cut the junk's cable while her crew fled in panic over the side. When the *Lord Amherst* arrived at the mouth of the Hwangpu, Lindsay, Gutzlaff, and a couple of others got into one of the boats, pushed boldly up the river, landed on the Shanghai waterfront, made their way to the principal yamen, found the gate shut, rushed it, knocked it off its hinges—and were served tea inside. Nowhere were the mandarins able to drive them away, though at every stop they pretended to. So Lindsay coasted the length of China, stopping more or less at will, yet when he got back to Macao it was as if he had never sailed. The senior supercargoes did not applaud his exploits. They pointed instead to his unsold woolens and cottons and observed to each other that this ought to check a little the talk in Parliament about the boundless possibilities of the China market. They had not, after all, wanted him to succeed. Commercial ambition did not excite them to try new articles at new places, commercial ambition did not excite them at all—they had none! Nothing suited them so well as buying teas. Nothing would have pleased them better than to be excused from the necessity of selling anything whatever.

The times, however, were passing them by. For a quarter of a century the political influence of the India House had been declining. And when (in 1830) George IV died, precipitating a general election out of which came the hubbub of the great Reform Bill and two more elections, that influence sank almost to the vanishing point. Monopoly in politics, in religion, in almost everything, was now the object of widespread public suspicion. Opinion held that private merchants should be able to ship manufactures to China and bring teas back. Committees of both houses confirmed this opinion, the merchants of Liverpool and the other outports advertised it with a rain of petitions and deputations, and in the spring of 1833 a bill was introduced into Parliament to relieve the Company not simply of its monopoly of the China trade but of its right to trade there at all.

That meant turning the whole of England's China trade over to the private merchants. Almost to a man they were deeply involved in the opium traffic. And that traffic was booming, bursting its normal limits, spreading beyond the Gulf of Canton, as the number of chests reaching the China coast became suddenly much greater than it had ever been before.

When Clifton launched the *Red Rover* late in 1829, that number had been less than fifteen thousand a year. Four years later it approached twenty thousand. And because this increase was almost entirely the work of chests from a part of India hitherto not represented in the trade, there was every reason to expect that the increase would be permanent. The part in question was Malwa, in west central India, between Ujjain and the border of Rajasthan.

At the time of Waterloo, Malwa opium was little known outside India—the Chinese bought Patna and Benares, and were content. Precisely because they were content, however, the Company (alias the Government of India) was in a position to restrict production in the two Bengal agencies, and thus keep prices high. Year by year, as a swelling demand for the drug pressed more and more strongly against an almost fixed supply, prices at the Calcutta auctions climbed, and with them the Company's profits, until at last a moment came when Malwa fairly cried out to be noticed. Then country merchants, Parsees mostly, began carrying it to China from Bombay side.

Bombay being as much the Company's as Calcutta was, it seems odd that they could manage to carry the stuff if the Company did not want them to. But the Company actually governed no part of west and central India except Bombay itself. Malwa lay in princely India; the Company was not in a position to stop the production of opium there or realize a single rupee from its sale. On the other hand, if the Company did nothing a flood of Malwa was bound sooner or later to force the price of Patna and Benares back down to the point where, at some five thousand chests a year only, its Bengal monopoly would cease to show a profit.

Naturally the Company did not want this to happen, so it tried a number of things. It bought up as much Malwa as it could, for resale at Bombay. The peasants were simply encouraged to grow more. It persuaded some of the Malwa princes to limit poppy acreage within their domains. The others would not be persuaded. It blocked the movement of Malwa through the port of Bombay; whereupon the stuff slipped out through other places, particularly Portuguese Daman, and, when the Company contrived to cut the routes to Daman by negotiating agreements with the states immediately adjacent, reached Karachi by camel across the deserts of Sind. Malwa, it seemed, was irrepressible. Meanwhile the Americans were observed to be bringing increased quantities of Turkey, which the Company could not touch at all.

Two courses were open to the Company. It could make a virtue of necessity and get out of the opium business altogether. It could meet the competition of Malwa and Turkey by increasing production and cutting prices in its Bengal agencies. With no hesitation it chose the second course. The result, measured in chests reaching the China coast, was first a freshet and then a flood. Patna and Benares fell from a high of $2,000 a chest in 1822 to $600 or $700 ten years later, but as the volume from that part of India more than doubled, the Company's revenue (which meant the Government of India's) did not suffer very much. It was threatened, to be sure, by the Company's inability to enforce to the full its monopoly within Bengal itself. "Opium is daily smuggled into the town," observed the Calcutta superintendent of police one year, "and sold to dealers in that drug, shopkeepers and others," some of it then passing by ship to China, some finding its way into "opium smoking places for the lower orders of natives where the morals of our servants are corrupted, the resort of our Calcutta thieves, and the proprietors receivers of stolen property; in fact nurseries of crime, and channels for defrauding the Government of its revenues."[3] But the police were vigilant. At the time of writing agents had been planted, purchases arranged, arrests made. (Did it occur to the superintendent that opium sustained nurseries of crime in Canton too?) Malwa, meanwhile, continued to undersell and outsell the two Bengal brands, though not by a great deal. And since every chest that passed through Bombay (most did now that it was permitted) paid a transit fee, the Company was in pocket by that much extra.

As for the Chinese, they went right on buying all the opium they were offered. How to get it to them was the only problem—and this the private merchants partly solved by laying down more clippers.

Red Rover had been followed by the *Lady Hayes*, the *Sylph*, and the *Water Witch*. (Does Cooper know, wrote Harriet Low, that in the East they are building ships and calling them after his novels?) Several more clipper barks slid into the Hooghly, among them the *Ariel*, the *Rob Roy* (with a nod this time to Sir Walter Scott), and the unusually large and handsome 430-ton *Cowasjee Family*; the Burmese port of Moulmein produced at least one bark and several fast schooners; from Bombay came the *Mahommedie*, the *Ardaseer*, the *Lady Grant* (held by observers to be the very extreme of sharpness), and others.* Bringing the opium from India was only half the problem, however; actually putting it into the hands of the Chinese required attention too. It was hardly practicable to land every chest that arrived about the Gulf of Canton. For a number of years, in fact, Chinese junks had been coming in from points much further east and north to buy chests from the big Chinese brokers or even directly from the receiving ships. In the 1820s Matheson, Bennet Forbes (the American who later brought out the *Lintin*), and one or two others had tried sending their own vessels a little distance to meet these junks and to peddle a bit on their own. Now, in the fall of 1832, Jardine and Matheson decided to see what could be done on a coastal voyage as long as that just completed by the *Lord Amherst*. They hired for the purpose the new clipper bark *Sylph*.

At 350 tons burden the *Sylph* was slightly larger than the *Red Rover*, not so clean and rakish in her lines but just as fast; early in September Harriet saw her enter Macao Roads "seventeen days from Calcutta, shortest passage ever known."[4] After unloading a part of her Patna and Benares into the *Hercules* and taking aboard Gutzlaff (Jardine had asked him to go along as interpreter), she left the gulf and beat steadily east and north against the newly turned monsoon. By the end of November she was off the coast of Manchuria. There she encountered cold so intense it paralyzed her lascar crew. Her rigging iced up; she ran aground on a sandbank, went

---

*The word "clipper" suggests racing lines and a very large spread of sail; it says nothing about rig. The opium clippers of the 1830s were generally barks, brigs, brigantines, and topsail schooners. With two or three exceptions, none were ships—that is to say, vessels with three masts all square-rigged. Most were too small to be. China did not know true clipper ships in any quantity until the 1850s, and then they carried teas.

slowly over on her beam ends, and was on the point of foundering when the Lord "ordered the south wind to blow, thus driving up more water upon the bank"[5] and lifting her off. This at least was Gutzlaff's story. A few weeks later, off the mouth of the Yangtze, he and the captain duly returned Him thanks by refusing to rescue twelve Chinese drifting helplessly on a dismasted junk until they dropped overboard the image of their patron saint and promised to adore the true God. The *Sylph* got back to the Gulf of Canton in the spring of 1833. Though she had not sold an astonishing number of chests, she discharged into the *Hercules* a quarter of a million dollars. The *Lord Amherst* by contrast had shown a loss. Perhaps Innes, himself much involved in the drug traffic, was right when he remarked that "the only chance of pushing English manufactures on this coast is by having them a small item in an opium cargo."[6] And if the drug sold so well on the coast, then surely the time had come to organize the traffic there on a more systematic basis.

In the autumn of 1833, therefore, Jardine gave the bark *Colonel Young* to one of his ablest captains, John Rees, and instructed him to go to Chinchew (Ch'uan-chou) on the Fukien coast and lie there selling opium to such junks as might approach. A brig newly acquired from Liverpool was appointed to shuttle between the *Colonel Young* and the Gulf of Canton, carrying chests, provisions, and mail up, bringing silver back. For a time Rees's was the only vessel continuously on the coast. But others went up for short periods to peddle the drug at Chimmo Bay near Chinchew, at the island of Namoa a good deal farther down, at Tungshan, How-tou-san, and other places. Receiving ships in the gulf and up the coast, couriers between, clippers to bring fresh stocks in bulk from India, and the Canton bill market to sop up the resulting treasure—this was how the thing took shape. And not all the vessels flew the oblique white cross on a blue field of Jardine, Matheson and Company. Some sailed for Dent's (white cross on a blue and red field), some for Russell's or other agency houses; from Macao to the Yangtze the coastal traffic was rapidly becoming routine.

It was certainly an excellent way to run off the extra thousands of chests that buyers at Calcutta and Bombay consigned to the China market. But could the opium traffic go on spreading indefinitely? What would happen when the Act of 1833 came into force and the East India Company's Canton establishment ceased to exist?

For years and years the president of the Select Committee had served, in Chinese eyes at least, as *taipan* or headman for the entire English community. The private merchants had never recognized him as such. Nevertheless they had grown up in his shadow and under his implied protection. His example and his influence had induced them to be circumspect about their opium activities; his presence had encouraged the more hot-headed among them to a certain self-restraint. Now, when his day was almost done—when the Factory was about to withdraw, writers, tea tasters, blazing Christmas raisins, and all—these private merchants were behaving with an exuberance, a downright arrogance, that suggested that in all this time they had in fact learned nothing at all!

In April of 1833, Innes, fresh from a coastal voyage and happening to go one day with Jardine to one of the customs sheds attached to the factories, was attacked there by a kitchen coolie armed with a chopper, and in his anger (though he was not hurt) that evening deliberately fired rockets and "blue lights" from the veranda of his factory, setting the shed on fire. Howqua, the senior hong merchant, protested to the Select; the Select scolded Innes; Innes stuck out his tongue. In June *Red Rover* arrived from Calcutta with chests from the April sale and several bags of mail. Impatient as ever, Innes and Captain Grant of the *Hercules* refused to wait until the Company's steward could distribute the latter in the normal manner, seized the bags, dumped their contents upon a table, and marched off with the letters addressed to themselves and their friends. For this impertinence the Select Committee lifted the *Hercules*'s license, a thing country ships had still to obtain. But Fort William issued a fresh one. Grant waved it contemptuously in their faces.

The worst, however, was reserved for the autumn. As Lintin had come to be considered somewhat unsafe in high winds, vessels this year looked about for other anchorages when the typhoon season came around. One possibility was the roadstead east of Lintin, between the island of Tongku and the peninsula of Castle Peak; another was Capsingmun, at the northeast end of Lantao Island on the inside passage from the gulf to Hongkong. But Tongku was hardly less exposed than Lintin. In 1829 an Indiaman lying there had been caught by a typhoon, dragged both bowers and a sheet anchor, and escaped destruction only by running upon the tail of Lintin. As for Capsingmun, it was if anything too sheltered. High land screened it so effectively that against the troublesome undercurrents known as chow-chow water it was often difficult to get in or out of the place at all. There was a third possibility. Ten miles to the west of Lintin the low western shore of the gulf gathers to a point reaching out towards the island of Keiou. West of the island the waters shoal rapidly away into mud flats, but between the point and the island it is deep enough; and here, at Cumsingmun as it is called, many vessels anchored in the late summer of 1833, among them the *Hercules* and that lesser receiving ship of Jardine's the *Samarang*.

Yet not even Cumsingmun was absolutely safe. A typhoon in August drove the *Samarang* so hard upon Keiou Island that she could not be refloated, and Grant, who from the *Hercules* acted as Jardine's commodore, decided to break her up. His crews worked fast. The Keiou islanders worked faster. Ropes, planks, spars, brass and copper fittings, anchors, a forge even, disappeared from the wreck. Parry, Grant's chief mate, sent parties ashore to recover the lost articles as well as to fetch fresh water and buy or commandeer meat. China being as undergoverned as she was—it was normal for a district magistrate to be responsible for as many as 200,000 people—the islanders had no resident officer to control or direct them. Grant's men acknowledged no authority higher than Jardine; each side regarded the other with suspicion and contempt. So it is not surprising that by the middle of October blood was being spilled.

It was spilled on a Sunday. A farmer working his fields spied sailors from the *Hercules* with a water buffalo in tow and called for help. Some fishermen came running; together they recovered the water buffalo, captured a tindal (or lascar boatswain), and chased the rest of the intruders away. But when they brought the tindal to their village, they did not know what to do with him. His mates, meanwhile, had gone for help. Reinforced and led by Parry himself, they landed, marched towards the village, and met the tindal being escorted they knew not where. Hot words flew, the villagers seized bamboos and other implements and fell upon Parry and his men; and though Parry got the tindal away, a seacunny (lascar steersman) who lagged behind was knocked to the ground and stabbed in the stomach with a knife.

Parry dared not stop. He was glad to get safely back to the boats. On the way he encountered a single Chinese working in the fields and took him hostage, driving several would-be rescuers off with musket shots.

That night the anchorage was in an uproar. Vessels from five nations lay at Cumsingmun. Their masters agreed that something had to be done to rescue the wounded and kidnapped seacunny. Grant happened to be at Macao. Consulted instantly by messenger, he instructed Parry to go after the fellow; so on Monday, Parry went methodically around the anchorage to see what force he could raise. "Every ship here volunteers a boat's crew, and some two, as they can manage, with the exception of the *Mangles*, Captain Cara, who arrived yesterday and is very sickly."[7] Next morning over two hundred seamen and ships' officers assembled near the *Hercules* in eighteen boats, took up a rough formation behind Parry and Captain Hector of Jardine's new clipper bark *Lady Hayes*, and started rowing up the west side of the island towards a small walled town at the head of a bay. Perhaps Parry and Hector meant to storm the place. Certainly they had Grant's authority to land, search for the seacunny, and seize additional hostages if they did not find him. When they came within long musket shot, however, and saw armed men along the walls and a large, hostile crowd collected on the beach, their ardor cooled. Twice they tried to land under a flag of truce. Twice they were fired on and forced to draw off. In the end they gave up trying, allowed their men to bang away at the Chinese for a while from the safety of the boats, and then led the little flotilla back to Cumsingmun.

That was the extent of the fighting. It was not the end of the fuss. News of the affair sped to the district magistrate at Hsiang-shan, and through him to the sub-prefect at Macao and the governor-general at Canton. Mandarins and a war junk appeared at Keiou; soldiers in red jackets occupied the village. Through the hong merchants the Select were commanded to see to the release of the kidnapped field worker and, when one of his would-be rescuers died of gunshot wounds, were commanded to hand over the murderer too. The Select turned to Jardine; Jardine sent Grant up to the anchorage, with Gutzlaff to talk for him; there were meetings aboard the war junk and on shore. In the end Grant let the field worker go, wrote off his losses on the *Samarang*, and accepted the Chinese promise to find and punish the man who had knifed the seacunny—the poor fellow, it turned out, had died on the spot and had been secretly buried. As for punishing the seaman (whoever it might be) who had killed the man coming to the field worker's rescue, a lascar was found who for a sum of money agreed to pose as the seacunny's brother, plead that he had fired while blinded with rage and grief, and throw himself upon the mercy of the authorities. This satisfied the governor-general. By January the noise and fury had pretty well died away.

But not the Select's sense of humiliation and outrage. During the crisis it was to the Select that the governor-general had addressed his inquiries, his protests, and his threats, reminding them that they stood *in loco parentis* to the entire English community, warning them that to attempt to shirk this responsibility would prove useless. Yet the Select knew that it was no longer in their power to compel Grant or Grant's employers, Jardine, Matheson and Company, to behave. They could order the opium vessels to leave Cumsingmun, and they did. But everyone knew that late October was the time of year for vessels to return to Lintin anyway. They could ask Grant for his version of the affair, and they did. What Grant gave them was an unabashed defense of the kidnapping and of the armed demonstration—adding, insolently, that because the Factory would never intervene on the side of the private English, he would be guided in what he did solely by what he owed the owners of the property committed to his care. By property Grant meant, of course, opium.

Always one came back to the drug. From a crutch supporting the legitimate trade it threatened to become powder to blow the entire system of barbarian relations to pieces.

PART TWO

Christ and Opium

6

The Napier Fizzle

It was in the late summer of 1833 that Parliament abolished the China monopoly of the East India Company, effective the following spring. The Chinese had seen this coming and through the hong merchants had urged the Select Committee to get Whitehall to appoint a new *taipan* in the president's place. They entertained, however, no notion of an alteration in their time-tested prescription for the handling of red-haired devils (the English), flowery-flagged devils (the Americans), and barbarians of other descriptions. There could be no question of Peking's receiving a resident English ambassador, no question of Peking's accrediting an envoy of its own to the Court of St. James. But how, then, was the English government to discharge its responsibilities on the China coast?

It might, of course, instruct Fort William to send a Company officer of some sort. Company men already governed Penang, Malacca, and Singapore. The thirteen factories, however, were not English soil. Besides, those who wanted the Company out of China in one capacity could hardly be expected to wish it back in another. So the English government decided to appoint an officer of the crown. The choice fell upon William John, ninth Lord Napier, a Scotsman, a peer, a naval officer, and a direct descendant of the man who invented logarithms. He received his commission in December, his instructions shortly after Christmas, and sailed early in the winter of 1834.

At Canton, on the other side of the world, all anyone knew was that Parliament had fixed the termination of the Factory and had recommended the creation of a Superintendency of Trade to take the Select's place. "31st of January," wrote Robert Morrison, the veteran English missionary who was also translator and interpreter to the Factory. "A fine day for the last Company's ship that will ever visit China to depart for England. . . . My health has been but poorly during the last fortnight, and I am on the point of going with Davis and the Factory to Macao."[1] John Francis Davis was president of the Select. Rather earlier than usual, and for the last time, he led his people down the inner passage to summer quarters. *Red Rover* arrived with chests from the first Calcutta sale, and after her came the *Sylph.* Daniell, the number two man in the Factory, traded insults over something or other with the ever belligerent Innes, was challenged to a duel he would not fight, and when Slade's *Register* gleefully printed the exchange, had the Factory cancel its subscription. March came and went. Jardine sent a ship off for England. (Because she carried no teas, only silks and sundries, Davis looked the other way.) Then it was termination day, 22 April 1834, and three private vessels loaded cargoes of the leaf and cleared for the direct run home.

But it was full summer before Napier arrived. He landed at Macao from the frigate *Andromache* on the afternoon of 15 July and spent the night at Captain Grant's house. Next day he called the onetime Factory together and read to them his commission and the appointments he proposed to make. He himself, of course, was chief superintendent, at a salary of £6,000 a year. Davis became second superintendent, and a supercargo named Robinson third. Another supercargo, Astell, was appointed secretary-treasurer; a young man named Johnston who had come out to China with Napier became private secretary; and Colledge was to continue as surgeon. A certain Captain Charles Elliot, R.N., was made master attendant responsible for supervising English ships and crews in the river. The Chinese secretary and interpreter was Robert Morrison. They were all to pack and prepare to move. Napier meant to go immediately to Canton and stay there, that was how he interpreted his instructions, that was what they seemed to boil down to—though as he read them aloud to Davis and the others on the seventeenth, it must have struck him how very ambiguous these instructions were.

He was, they informed him, to supervise, represent, and protect English merchants and English ships within the port of Canton, which meant from the Bogue to the factories. To this extent his duties were no other than those the president of the Select had been charged with in the days of the Factory's prime. But Napier was to do more. He was to inquire into the possibility of extending English trade to other ports in China and even to Japan. He was to inquire into the possibility of establishing regular diplomatic relations with Peking. Thus in two strokes of the pump, Palmerston, the foreign secretary, swelled and inflated his man from a mere *taipan* into an aggressive resident ambassador—and as quickly collapsed him again! For Napier was to conform to the laws and usages of China and to impress on all his countrymen the necessity of doing the same. He was to refrain from menacing language, expect no additional naval support (though surveying the coast to see where ships might shelter if war did break out), and not pass *Andromache* into the river except in the direst emergency. Finally, he was not, after all, to enter into fresh and unusual relations with the Chinese—what else would relations directly with Peking be?—unless the Chinese evinced an unmistakable disposition to embark on them and unless he had first cleared the matter with London. As for opium, Palmerston had only this to say: "Peculiar caution will be necessary . . . with regard to such ships as may attempt to explore the coast of China for purposes of traffic. It is not desirable that you should encourage such adventures; but you must never lose sight of the fact that you have no authority to interfere with, or to prevent, them."[2]

What was a plain navy man, who had fought as a midshipman at Trafalgar, commanded a frigate on the South American station, and bred sheep in Selkirkshire, to make of instructions like these?

Napier may already have been thinking what soon he was to write in some irritation to Palmerston: "When was it ever known, within the last century, that the Chinese authorities *evinced a disposition* to encourage foreign trade?"[3] He may already have heard that story of Innes, the customs house, and the "blue lights," which later he was to cite as an example of how the Chinese *ought* to be handled. And though he had not yet met Jardine or Matheson—Jardine happened to be at Canton, Matheson on the high seas returning from Bombay—he may already have begun to feel that unless he started out boldly, he would soon find himself as helpless and contemptible as these two had held the Factory to be. "The general opinion here," Jardine had recently written, "is that the Chief Superintendent had better stay at home and leave us to ourselves than come out to this country to negotiate through the Cohong."[4] But how was Napier *not* to negotiate through the hong merchants if his instructions enjoined him to conform to the laws and usages of China?

Fortunately a path through the thicket of these instructions was opened for him by one of the instructions itself. "Your Lordship," Palmerston had written, "will announce your arrival at Canton by letter to the Viceroy."

Placed against the injunction to conform in all ways to Chinese usage, this was hardly a reasonable thing to ask Napier to do. But never mind; at least his doing it would establish, clearly and from the start, that he was not just another *taipan* to be soothed, smothered, and forgotten. Napier settled his wife and his two daughters, bought the Factory's 75-ton cutter *Louisa* complete with three-pounders, side arms, and lascar crew, collected his staff, and boarded the *Andromache* for the Bogue. From the Bogue the *Louisa* carried him on to Whampoa. There he and his party transferred to a small boat belonging to the country ship *Fort William,* pulled slowly through a succession of heavy evening thundershowers, and very early on the morning of Friday, 25 July, stepped ashore at Jackass Point.

It was probably about daybreak, as Napier lay sleeping in the New English factory, that the Hoppo's men brought word to Governor-General Lu that a number of foreign devils had landed and that one of them was obviously a person of some consequence. Lu was startled. Some days earlier the officer responsible for the waters about Macao had reported the arrival of an English vessel of war carrying more than a mere *taipan;* whereupon Lu had sent word that this Barbarian Eye, as he chose to style the intruder, was not to approach Canton without permission. But Lu's edict had reached Macao too late to catch the *Andromache,* and now Barbarian Eye was on his very doorstep—he would have to serve his edict there.

Friday passed, however, without his doing so.

Morrison was ill. The drenching he had received coming up the river had done him no good, and it was with difficulty that he walked the length of the square from his rooms in Number 6 the Danish factory to the New English, where Napier sat drawing up the letter that should announce his arrival to the governor-general and request a personal interview. On Saturday, Morrison and his eldest son, John—only twenty but already competent as a translator and interpreter—remained closeted in Number 6 translating this letter into Chinese. When it was finished, about three, Astell, the younger Morrison, and a dozen others went off with it to the Petition Gate. Meanwhile Howqua and Mowqua tried to serve Napier with the edict that had missed him at Macao. Napier declined to receive it. He meant to get his licks in first and looked with impatience for Astell to return and tell him his letter was safely in the governor-general's hands.

When Astell returned at dusk, however, he brought the letter with him. He and his companions had crossed Carpenters' Square, reached the small opening in the south wall that foreigners called the Petition Gate, and passed through into the alley beyond. There they had stopped—it was the custom to hand over petitions there. A mandarin had indeed appeared. He had refused, however, to take the letter, and other mandarins, arriving, had refused too. It was, thought young Morrison, because the letter did not bear the proper superscription. Yet it is doubtful that a mandarin would have accepted it even if it had. Lu was well aware that Napier wished to circumvent the hong merchants and communicate directly, and Lu was determined that he should not. At the end, then, of three exasperating hours passed in the presence of a crowd sometimes menacing and always derisive, Astell had come away with the letter still in his hand.

The governor-general pursued him with a series of edicts reminding

Napier of the conditions under which foreigners were allowed to trade at Canton and ordering him back to Macao. Even England had its rules. How much more the Celestial Empire. "How flaming bright are its great laws and ordinances! More terrible than the awful thunderbolts! Under this whole bright heaven, none dares to disobey them. . . !" It was up to the hong merchants—the edicts were of course addressed to them—to see to it that Barbarian Eye did as he was told; for was it not their responsibility to open and instruct the understanding of the *fan kuei?* "Tremble hereat— intensely, intensely tremble!"[5]

Language like this made foreigners laugh. "We wait the result," wrote Jardine to a business correspondent in Manchester, "in fear and trembling, as ordered by the Authorities to do."[6] But perhaps the hong merchants really *did* tremble, perhaps they really *were* afraid that inability to tame Barbarian Eye would mean for them imprisonment or worse. Meanwhile the elder Morrison's health was failing completely. On Monday he went twice in a sedan chair to Napier's quarters, but from Tuesday on he was helpless, convulsed by stomach pains for which Colledge and Jardine (the sometime surgeon aboard Indiamen) prescribed opium. On Friday, 1 August, a raging fever seized him. Towards midnight he died.

Young Morrison accompanied his father's body to Macao and did not return for some time; Gutzlaff, who was skillful at interpreting (and would soon, in fact, be added to the Superintendency's payroll), happened to be up the coast in the *Colonel Young;* so the chief superintendent had no one at his side through whom the Chinese could effectively communicate. No matter, he was locked in a battle of wills and cared very little what the Chinese said or thought. What counted was that Lu refused to receive his letter. Very well, he would not receive Lu's edicts—and, when Howqua tried to pass some on, rebuffed the urbane old fellow. With the consequence that when, on 9 August, Napier wrote his first dispatch to Palmerston, all my lord knew of the views and intentions of the Chinese was that they wished he would quit Canton and were nudging him in that direction. His baggage had been broken into at the customs house, and his name was being represented not by the harmless characters the elder Morrison had chosen but by others that appeared to translate "Laboriously Vile." Pinpricks did not bother him, however, he was bound to come out on top. For the governor-general, by refusing to accept his letter, necessarily remained in ignorance of who he was and what his mission, and was therefore quite unable to report properly to the emperor. "Having so far the advantage," noted Napier, "it shall be my duty to hold on."[7]

In less than a week he wrote again. He was in possession of Lu's edicts now (Howqua had taken them to Jardine and Jardine had gotten John Morrison, who was back, to translate them) and knew that four edicts had been loosed against him, that the Canton garrison was said to number forty thousand, and that the authorities were begging him to depart—had, in fact, ordered him to do so. "Yet with all this, and the forty thousand men, and the flaming bright laws and terrible thunderbolts, they have not yet taken me and sent me down the river." What a sham Lu was! Peking must be compelled to open every port in the empire. If this meant war, "three or four frigates and brigs, with a few steady British troops, not sepoys, would settle the thing in a space of time inconceivably short."[8] On 23 August, Napier publicly scolded three mandarins of high rank for being late to an interview of their own arranging at the New English factory. Once more he refused to explain verbally what it was he had been sent to China to do—let the governor-general read his letter! On the twenty-sixth he drew up a short review of the controversy to date. He would publish it and allow the Cantonese to see for themselves what imbeciles their rulers were.

That same evening he gave a dinner in honor of the king's birthday. Sixty English sat down to table in the hall of the New English factory, the Parsees at their own request not coming in till later. With a four times four my lord gave the health of his sovereign William IV. Toasts were drunk to the queen, to Princess Victoria, to the commerce of Canton (Jardine stood up to reply); glasses were raised to the East India Company now that it had been overthrown, as Napier put it, "by the genius of free trade." When Captain Elliot rose to propose His Majesty's chief superintendent, "the hall rang with one universal shout which was heard over the whole range of the foreign factories." After the noise had subsided, the noble lord was heard to say that he "would glory in having his name handed down to posterity as the man who had thrown open the wide field of the Chinese Empire to British spirit and industry."[9] Then they cheered him again and again and again.

It was Napier's finest hour. Confidence in him was complete. He stood, apparently, at the very summit of his powers. Yet the ground beneath him was already beginning to slip.

It was always in the power of the authorities to strike the English in their pocketbooks. Now they were threatening to do so. "Trade is suspended," Jardine had written eight days previously, "but no public notice yet given—and the high tides make a convenient excuse for a temporary refusal of chop boats."[10] Merchantmen were beginning to arrive; if the past season were any guide, there would be more than a hundred English vessels and nearly as many Americans; once they had anchored they would wish to discharge. No one, to be sure, was in a hurry to buy or sell. So many woolens and cotton piece goods remained from the previous year that business must inevitably be sluggish. The first teas could not reach Canton for another six or seven weeks—even the drug market was for the moment dull, with Patna and Benares fetching less than $600 a chest—so a trade stoppage would not do any immediate harm. Besides, the governor-general had very quickly reversed the hong merchants' suspension notice, observing tenderly of distant England that "the tea, the rhubarb, the raw silk of the inner dominions are the sources by which the said nations' people live and maintain life. For the fault of one man, Lord Napier, must the livelihood of the whole nation be precipitately cut off?"[11]

But if Napier stuck to the course he was pursuing, trade was certain to be stopped in earnest. When that happened, Napier might discover that the private English and the Parsees were no longer behind him.

He had his doubts about them anyway. He was sure that Jardine's *Mangles,* sailing direct for London (Davis took dispatches down to her at Macao towards the end of August), would deliberately exaggerate the difficulties at Canton for the express purpose of spreading alarm in London commercial circles and thus pushing up the price of teas. If a trade stoppage went on for very long, he wrote Palmerston, he would retire to Macao "rather than bring the cities of London, Liverpool, and Glasgow upon your lordship's shoulders; many of whose merchants care not one straw about the dignity of the crown or the presence of a superintendent."[12] Privately he mistrusted even Jardine's sense of public spirit. When the hong merchants invited all of the English except himself to a meeting with an undisclosed purpose—trying to drive a wedge, Napier felt sure—he hastily got them together first, reminded them of their duty to England and to the Superintendency, promised them that nothing save the point of a bayonet should drive him from the factories, and finally invited their signatures to a letter declining the hong merchants' invitation. Jardine, Dent, even the Parsees signed. Next Napier proposed (it may actually have been Jardine's suggestion, for the two saw a great deal of each other) a British Chamber of Commerce. It was duly formed, along lines suggested by Goddard, and from the moment of its formation, Napier used it to pass messages to the Cohong; for, he said to himself, if I transmit my own personal determination through these merchant compatriots of mine, perforce they will become determined too.

Canton was full of civil service aspirants sitting for the provincial examinations. It rained and rained, and when it was not raining the air was hot and muggy. The river rose and flooded the factories. Napier felt unwell.

The *Andromache* had been sent away for a while—"to feel the pulse of the Chinese," as the chief superintendent put it. She was back now, and with her was the frigate *Imogene* (Captain Blackwood), recently arrived to take her place. An English merchant happened to pass the two men-of-war lying at the Bogue surrounded by war junks. "The *Imogene* was engaged with ball practise at a buoy with her great guns; immediately above were anchored several heavy stone boats loaded, whose cargoes are destined, on nearer movement of the frigates, to fill up the channel. . . . Now, Sir, as it is half a mile broad, and runs an impetuous tide to the depth of twelve to fifteen fathoms, I leave your readers to imagine what effect a few hundred tons of granite paving stones will have on it."[13] This on the twenty-first. Five days later the chief superintendent was wildly cheered at the king's birthday dinner; and on the thirtieth Napier's own version of how things stood, translated into Chinese by John Morrison and lithographed, was ostentatiously posted up at several places about the factory square. Extra copies of the broadsheet were offered to any Chinese who cared for them. To Napier's delight a number did.

The official reaction, however, was prompt and sobering. Barbarian Eye was trying to appeal to the Cantonese over Lu's head. He was insinuating that Lu cared not at all whether the Cantonese prospered or were ruined; he was suggesting that Lu would find it as easy to check the current of the Canton River as to bend the foreigners to his will. This was intolerable. It was also incredible, for the authorities did not believe there lived a foreigner capable of writing comprehensible Chinese. They had already imprisoned the *Fort William*'s hong merchant for allowing Napier to come up from Whampoa in one of her boats. Now they bambooed and imprisoned a number of Cantonese for allegedly helping Napier with his broadsheet.

The thirtieth, when this broadsheet appeared, was a Saturday. On Sunday a reply was placarded filled with the most extravagant abuse of Napier—dog barbarian, lawless foreign slave—and intimating that he ought to be decapitated. On Tuesday, 2 September, a formal edict commanded him to leave Canton and stopped all trade until he did. On Thursday afternoon, as the chief superintendent sat at dinner with Robinson and others, servants ran into the room crying that soldiers were surrounding the factory. Napier went out on the veranda. Soldiers were indeed drawn up before the garden gate, others were landing from boats; they were armed with swords and spears, and a few carried what looked like manacles. They made no move to occupy the New English factory. Within the hour, however, Napier's entire native staff had vanished. And from the way the soldiers were disposed, from the boats lashed together to block the garden front and the water stairs, the chief superintendent drew the conclusion that he was being put under a sort of house arrest.

Napier's first instinct was to bring the frigates up to Whampoa. A schooner of Jardine's got away early that evening with orders for Captain

Blackwood, the senior of the two commanders, and shortly after midnight Robinson, armed with further instructions, slipped off too. Unfortunately Davis, Elliot, and Astell were all at Macao. Only young Morrison, Johnston, and one or two others remained with the chief superintendent in the otherwise deserted factory. Friday passed without excitement, except that Innes was making trouble again: exasperated by the arrival of a Bombay newspaper with Daniell's version of their quarrel of the previous winter, he had used strong language and a rattan cane on one of Daniell's friends, an outrage now brought unavoidably to Napier's attention. That night Napier thought he heard someone trying to break into the room next his own. Nothing was discovered. Still it was a relief when at dawn Saturday a lieutenant and thirteen marines from the *Andromache* slipped in to join the little band.

While he waited for news of the frigates themselves, surely close behind, Napier drafted a long and firm reply to the closure edict. He announced the imminent arrival of two men-of-war "bearing very heavy guns." He warned the hong merchants that, if they did not pass the paper they were receiving on to the governor-general, they would find copies of it posted about the suburb for the Cantonese to read. He even permitted himself, with a giggle perhaps, a "tremble, Governor Lu, intensely tremble!"[14] Sunday passed and Monday. Napier felt feverish. It was very humid; the temperature in the factory rose frequently to ninety and never dropped below seventy-eight. By Tuesday he was decidedly ill.

Meanwhile Jardine's schooner reached the Bogue too late Friday afternoon for the frigates to get under way that day. Robinson arrived after dark, and as Davis and Elliot were known to be on their way up from Macao in the *Louisa*, he and Blackwood agreed to wait for them. The cutter did not appear until Saturday evening, however; Sunday brought at first a dead calm; it was early afternoon before a light breeze permitted the *Imogene* and the *Andromache* to weigh and begin beating into the channel.

If Blackwood had any doubts about how the Chinese would react, they were dispelled at once by the war junks that for days had been lingering about the entrance. They began firing, first blanks and then shot, at the same time retreating prudently into the shallow bay above Chuenpi. The two frigates came on, and as the range lessened, the several forts on either side took up the fight. For the frigates, and for *Louisa* close behind with Elliot seated imperturbably under an umbrella upon her open deck, it was slow and perilous work. Each time a frigate reached the end of a tack and came about, she exposed her deck to raking fire from the fort nearest. Though she fired back, her thirty-two-pound shot raising clouds of dust along the parapets or plunging clean through the embrasures, the Chinese guns could not easily be silenced. There were not many of them, however, and these poorly served, so that among the English crews only a few men were wounded and only one killed. Beating up in this way consumed two hours. Then the breeze died to a whisper and the three vessels anchored. Early Tuesday afternoon a light wind from the south carried them to Second Bar. Wednesday they gained another five miles. Late Thursday they reached Whampoa.

Once Napier had remarked that, if he had to, he would bring his men-of-war all the way up to the walls of Canton. Of course that was bravado. Vessels as deep of draft as his two frigates would have great trouble negotiating those last dozen miles. At the very least, however, he could expect boatloads of armed men with a cannon or two. At dusk Thursday watchers on the roof of the New English factory spotted, far away across the fields and watercourses and little clumps of trees, spars and canvas just where Whampoa ought to be; and they ran to tell the chief superintendent that the frigates had arrived, that boats would certainly be up on the next tide. But no boats came.

This was not because Napier had instructed them to stay away. He sent no word of any kind—quite probably he could not, for while the frigates dawdled at the entrance, the governor-general had been systematically blocking up the river. Happening to go the previous Saturday from the factories to Whampoa, Hunter had passed through a whole fleet of war boats filled with armed Chinese. When Harriet's brother, Abbot Low, and two other Americans tried to come up to the factories the next day with letters just arrived from London, they were brought to off Howqua's Fort by warning shots and unceremoniously ordered back. Half a mile west of the fort, it later transpired, the Chinese had sunk chop boats weighted with rock. Above the sunken chop boats they had rigged a floating boom of spars lashed end to end, with a thirty-yard gap in the center across which at night a chain was drawn. In the lesser branches of the river they had driven thickets of piles. Napier, they intended, should not be rescued.

This was not all. Lu K'un was a competent and resourceful man who, years before, had organized and sent an army of forty thousand against rebels in Sinkiang province and quite recently had helped direct similar operations in Hunan. Now, besides barring the river halfway between Whampoa and Canton, he was preparing to lay down a second barrier near Second Bar—it was for this that the "stone boats" at the Bogue were almost certainly intended. He had fireboats ready: eight freighted with combustibles floated one day past the factories in what Slade's *Register* thought a "childish parade." He had several thousand soldiers at the factories, in boats along the river, and on the banks overlooking Whampoa. When several British merchantmen at Blackwood's request tried to follow the frigates into the river, the guns of the Bogue forts (they had not been permanently silenced) fired on them and persuaded them to turn back. It was all very well for Slade to be contemptuous of this show of strength after the fact. Davis, Robinson, Elliot, and Blackwood had to size it up at the time from Whampoa, where they were nearly deaf, dumb, and blind. When they tried to slip messages up to Napier by confiding them to Chinese boatmen, the messages came back unopened. They recalled that, though the *Fort William*'s second officer had piloted one of the frigates and a former master of the *Louisa* the other (Chinese pilots were of course unobtainable), both had run aground more than once in negotiating the thirty miles of river. It could easily be worse going back. The two vessels might be harassed by fireboats, peppered with shot, trapped altogether at Second Bar. Unless, therefore, the chief superintendent was in obvious peril or positively commanded them to push a force up, it seemed wisest to stay and to exasperate the Chinese no further.

So the frigates remained at Whampoa, within sight of Canton but not within reach, and for a few days more Napier stuck it out.

He did not know what fresh initiative to seize. Without servants, unable to obtain provisions in the bazaars, he camped uncomfortably in a few rooms and ate mess beef and pork—until some fellow Englishmen began slipping fresh food to him. What defeated him in the end, however, was not the state of his household or table but the state of his health—that and the growing disaffection of people around him. Slade, Goddard, Innes, and Matheson urged him to stand firm, but Dent, Daniell, and others of what one might call the Company frame of mind were already beginning to appeal for a resumption of trade. The Parsees struck him as particularly spineless. The day before the frigates were sighted, they had positively begged him to get goods moving, pointing out that this was the season for raw cotton; if they did not sell, their Indian consignors would be ruined. Now some, apparently anxious for their own personal safety, made plans to slip away to Macao.

It did not surprise Slade. Though these gentlemen were the equal of all the other subjects of His Majesty, they were not, he felt, their equal in all respects. "On the field of Waterloo, for instance, it is doubtful how far the Parsees, however well mounted or accoutred, would have been allowed to take the place of the 42nd, the Blues, or the Scots Greys."[15] Of the likes of Dent and Daniell his *Register* hinted even darker things—cowards they were and traitors, for pressing the chief superintendent to surrender—and in his private letters Jardine made much the same charge. Yet it was Jardine more than anyone else who in the end helped Napier take just that path.

Jardine was not obliged to. Given the earliness of the season (teas were just beginning to reach Canton), given the size of Jardine Matheson's agency business and the proportion of it that was carried on at outer anchorages beyond Lu's reach, Jardine had no particular reason to be excited one way or another by Napier's predicament. Something moved him, however, indignation perhaps or sympathy for the plight of a fellow Scot—for Napier was sick and visibly approaching collapse. At any rate it was with Jardine's foreknowledge and very probably at his urging that on Sunday, the fourteenth, the superintendent at last tossed in the towel. He could discern, he announced, nothing further for him to do at the factories. He would retire to Macao.

And now the terrible weakness of his position was brought fully home to him. He expected to go as he had come, by the river route. He expected to board a frigate at Whampoa, drop comfortably down the river, and pass out by the Bogue as dignity and health alike required. The governor-general would not allow it. The frigates must depart first and Napier follow by the inner passage. Only in this way would it be plain to everyone, and especially to Peking, that Barbarian Eye was leaving not of his own free will but because he had to. If Barbarian Eye did not like these arrangements, he might remain shut up in his factory indefinitely.

Stunned by this cruel and unexpected check, Napier thought of hanging on. He even toyed with the idea of once again appealing to the Cantonese over Lu's head. By 18 September, however—on which day Colledge unobtrusively moved his patient to cooler rooms in the Creek factory, rooms put at his disposal by Innes—the chief superintendent had become so weak it seemed his very life might hang upon his reaching Macao without delay. Together Jardine and Colledge negotiated the retreat. Together they approached Howqua and Mowqua and at last extracted the promise that Napier would receive a departure chop (Barbarian Eye had arrived without a permit, he was not going to leave without one!) the instant the hong merchants held in their hands his order to the frigates to weigh. Reluctantly Napier signed the order. It was the last to which he set his pen.

At six on the evening of Sunday, the twenty-first, Howqua produced the necessary permit. At seven the chief superintendent, leaning heavily on Johnston's arm, walked slowly to the water stairs and was helped aboard a common chop boat. Eight boatloads of soldiers formed his escort, and though Colledge argued and pleaded, and Johnston tried to bribe the boatmen, the pace was maddeningly slow. All Sunday night the little flotilla remained motionless three miles from the factories. For a day and half at mid-week—while the authorities waited to hear that the frigates were out of the river—it stuck fast at Hsiang-shan, Napier constantly disturbed by gongs, crackers, and Chinese thrusting their heads into his cabin. Not until Friday morning was the sick man put ashore at Macao and carried in a litter to a house upon the saddle. There, his wife and daughters about him, he tossed in a fever that never abated; and there, on 11 October, two days before his forty-eighth birthday, he died.

They buried him with all possible attentions, six captains for pall-bearers, minute guns booming from the frigates in the roads, and a Portuguese guard of honor firing three volleys over the grave. Two weeks later, at Canton, Bridgman preached a funeral sermon so affecting (his text was Num. 23:10, "Let me die the death of the righteous, and let my last end be like his!") that Lady Napier, when much later she received a copy in the Lowland home to which she had retired, wrote especially to thank him for it. She had sailed that December. James Matheson followed in March, carrying with him the proceeds of a subscription for a monument to the late peer, to which (among others) Jardine had contributed $100, John Morrison $50, Innes $25, and Daniell nothing at all.

Trade, meanwhile, reopened. The season passed normally. Davis automatically became chief superintendent. To Palmerston, with news of Napier's death, he wrote that unless otherwise instructed he would follow a policy of "silence and quiescence," and when Jardine and others sent a petition home asking for warships to exact reparations for the injuries recently inflicted, advised Palmerston that the paper was "crude and ill-digested"[16] and ought to be ignored. By then, however, Palmerston was no longer at the Foreign Office. Melbourne was out; Peel had taken his place; in January, when the dispatches covering the events of August and September finally reached London, it was the Duke of Wellington who read them. And though the affair made his sovereign, William IV, indignant—so indignant that he actually pressed Wellington for war—the Duke showed no inclination to be led into any course of action at all by what Hunter, among others, was already beginning to call the "Napier fizzle."

7

The Protestant Mission

Early in 1835 Davis went home. His place was taken by Robinson, the former Company man whom Napier had made third superintendent. Robinson filled his letters to London with bombast. Destroy a fort here, occupy an island there, he wrote, and we shall "promptly produce upon this barbarous nation . . . every effect we could desire."[1] In practice he did nothing at all except station himself on board the *Louisa* just off Lintin and, from that floating office, keep an eye on English shipping. It was a routine eye. Robinson inspected manifests, signed port clearances, but thought it not at all his business to regulate, let alone suppress, the opium traffic. From the *Louisa* he surveyed with complete official indifference the opium vessels clustered close by.

In England, meanwhile, the political roundabout turned without any reference to China. Peel was beaten repeatedly in Parliament and resigned; Melbourne became prime minister again; Palmerston replaced the Duke of Wellington at the Foreign Office. Of so little account did the China Superintendency seem that Whitehall took the pruning shears to it: the chief superintendent's salary was cut in half and the office of third superintendent abolished altogether. Astell went home. After a time Robinson went home too. At the end of 1836 Elliot became chief superintendent, with Alexander Johnston his single deputy.

Charles Elliot was then thirty-five. The son of a minor diplomat and sometime governor of Madras, he had risen by continuous service in the Royal Navy to the post of captain and had subsequently been appointed protector of slaves in British Guiana. This office he had found both unpopular and frustrating. On the strength of it, nevertheless, he had been called to London to advise the government as it prepared to abolish slavery in the colonies. Next he had been asked through Davis's good offices to accompany Napier to China. Elliot was an ambitious man. He had friends and relations in high places: Minto at the Admiralty was a first cousin; so was Auckland, the new governor-general of India. It was predictable that when he got authority he would use it.

The first thing he did was to quit the *Louisa*. Canton was where he ought to be. He did not, however, mean to go there like a second Napier, unannounced and unwanted. Perhaps three years in Guiana, trying to remain on speaking terms with planters while at the same time keeping them from flogging their slaves to death, had taught him to be circumspect; for the letter he sent to Teng T'ing-chen, the new governor-general, announcing his appointment to succeed Robinson and asking to be allowed to come up to the factories, was certainly most carefully done. It was inscribed with the character *pin*, for petition. Elliot sent it to Howqua, not to Teng directly. In it he described himself not as a *taipan* (he meant to be more), not as an official representative of William IV (he must pretend to be less), but as an "employee from afar." Teng was puzzled and made inquiries. Elliot handled them so adroitly that early in the spring of 1837 he received permission to settle at the factories. There he immediately hoisted the union jack and wrote Palmerston that at last he was being treated as he ought to be.

His confidence, however, was premature. When an English merchantman lifted seventeen Chinese to safety off a foundering junk, and Elliot drew Teng's attention to "the bonds of peace and goodwill between the two nations" that charitable acts of this sort so notably strengthened, Teng seemed more amused than impressed. Drowning English barbarians would of course be rescued too, he observed. But this was because of "the all-prevading goodness and cherishing kindness of the great Emperor, whose favors are constant and universal." Reciprocity had nothing to do with it, bonds of goodwill or anything else between the Middle Kingdom and little England being quite out of the question. Though Teng, after much struggle on Elliot's part, did permit sealed letters to come to him direct, he went right on addressing his own communications exclusively to the hong merchants, who opened, read, and explained them gently to Elliot. It made Elliot feel like the child who is forced to stand silently by while parents and teacher discuss him over his head. "They speak of me, not to me," he complained to Palmerston.[2]

Palmerston, unfortunately, was not helpful. He was very far away. Letters to and from China still moved more often than not by way of the Cape of Good Hope, and if they went by the Mediterranean and the Red Sea took almost as long; for the overland (as the latter route was called) depended upon a regular service of steamers on both sides of the Egyptian land bridge—and this was as yet hardly to be had. From England steamers ran irregularly to Malta and Alexandria. From India they scarcely ran at all. In the spring of 1830 the *Hugh Lindsay* attempted the first steam passage from India to Suez. She was large and capable of six knots, but she burned such immense quantities of fuel that, though her bunker capacity accounted for half her rated tons burden, she could not steam uninterruptedly for more than five days. Aden, at the mouth of the Red Sea, was 1,900 miles away. So they piled coal in her cabins, in her public rooms, even on her deck, until her transom was under water and the slightest sea threatened to sink her; and away she went in the quiet before the southwest monsoon set in, to creep into Aden eleven days later on the very last sweepings. Any further into the season, with the wind in her teeth, she would never have made it. Thereafter she did the Suez run once or twice a year only, usually going out with the tag end of the northeast monsoon and returning in the lull. And whether Elliot sent his letters overland or by way of the Cape, he continued to expect that seven or eight months would pass before he got advice or instructions back.

There was another difficulty. In those days England's China policy resembled England's Pacific fleet in that, properly speaking, neither existed at all! To the Royal Navy the waters of the Pacific were simply an adjunct to the East Indian Station. Warships assigned to that station based themselves on Trincomalee on the east coast of Ceylon, spent most of their time in the Indian Ocean, and rarely ventured as far even as the recently acquired island of Singapore. It was the same with England's China policy. Since Peking refused to enter into any kind of official relations with the Court of St. James, the Foreign Office had very little incentive to develop a policy towards China. The Colonial Office, then merely a section of the War Office, was even less interested, seeing that the thirteen factories could not by any stretch of the imagination be termed a colony. England was very much interested in India and had decided notions about what should be going on there. She paid attention to the east end of the Mediterranean and to the balance of forces in that quarter that made up the "Eastern question." She had more than a glance to spare for Persia, for Afghanistan (where she would shortly fight a war), for Burma (where she had just fought one), and for the Straits of Malacca. But to places beyond these her attention did not stretch. Year after year Palmerston made do with no opinion about China beyond the vague feeling that she ought not to be catered to, that she ought not to be favored with delicate little exercises in circumspection. China was like any other power and should be treated as such. When, therefore, he learned very late in the day that Elliot was stooping to the use of the *pin*, he told him quite plainly to stop.

In vain Elliot tried to substitute novel and indeterminate modes of address. Teng raised such a fuss that shortly before Christmas of 1837 Elliot was obliged to strike his flag and withdraw altogether from the factories. Thereafter he kept only a clerk at Canton and made Macao his headquarters. (At Macao about this time his wife, a cheerful woman with a red nose, gave birth to a boy whom they christened Frederick.) It was plain that while he had managed to chip away a little at the great granite block of China's insularity, he had not begun to shatter it.

When Bridgman heard that Elliot was leaving the factories and saw Elliot's flag struck, he suggested publicly that the French and Dutch strike theirs too. The way the Chinese treated foreigners made him very angry. "China," he had exclaimed at the time of Napier's discomfiture and death, "is in a position of open violation of the law—*thou shalt love thy neighbor as thyself*." When a year or so later a merchant acquaintance of his got into a dispute with the Hoppo, he appealed for "remonstrance, honest remonstrance, EFFECTUAL GOVERNMENT REMONSTRANCE," until the Chinese learned to look on outsiders as "children of one common Father; and all the rights which nature and nature's God gives us, of free intercourse, can be exercised in a way that does not beggar us of all self-respect."[3] Now he called on the English to go directly to Peking. Nothing was to be gained by approaches at the provincial level, where flags, consuls, and all the other paraphernalia of national equality were routinely ignored.

All this and much more Bridgman delivered himself of in the pages of the *Chinese Repository*, the journal he published monthly from his rooms behind Zion's Corner. The *Repository* was a remarkable work. Printed in small type on native bamboo paper from a press shipped over from New York, it contained beneath covers of common blue silk articles of a length, a seriousness, an impenetrability even, that would have done credit to any reputable European or American review. Most of the English and American missionaries wrote for it. So did a number of merchants, among them Goddard and Innes (though never, for some reason, Jardine). But Bridgman wrote more than any of the others. It was Bridgman who made sure that the journal lived up to its name.

For the *Repository* was just what it said it was, a repository of information about China. From its pages the 200 or so subscribers in the Canton-Lintin-Macao area, the 150 in the United States, and the smaller number scattered from London to Calcutta could discover a great deal about China: about her coasts, her customs, her language and its difficulties; about her government, her commerce, her religion—or the lack thereof. No other periodical anywhere, not even Slade's weekly *Canton Register* or its rival the *Canton Press*, gave so complete a picture of what was taking place not just on the fringes of the Middle Kingdom but deep inside it.

To give a complete picture was exactly Bridgman's intention. "What more effectual way can be devised for benefiting the Chinese," he explained in an early number, "than to learn as accurately as possible their true condition; to exhibit it to themselves; and then to put within their reach the means of improvement?"[4] Once the Chinese had complete their own self-examination—to help them the *Repository* printed accounts of provincial rebellions, of public executions, of young girls sold into prostitution and babies abandoned in the streets— once they had stood before the glass, so to speak, and seen themselves for what they really were, they would be ready, they would be positively eager, to accept what the West had to offer. That was a great deal. A young and pious American merchant named Charles King put the matter very well in another early number of the *Repository*. "Ever since the dispersion of man, the richest stream of human blessings has, in the will of Providence, followed a western course." This certainly left China out. How wrong the emperor had been when he assured Lord Macartney that she possessed all things! How little she had to give, how much to receive! "The earth with its beauty and glory, the laws of nature harmonious and wonderful, the accumulated treasures of western genius and wisdom, the noble, inestimable discoveries of Revelation, how imperfectly known, how perfectly unknown here!"[5] Did King care to descend to particulars, he might have specified (among the things unknown to China) calculus, representative parliamentary government, steam-powered sidewheelers, and nine symphonies of Beethoven. What China stood most in need of, however, was none of these. It was that supreme and saving western commodity, the grace of Christ Our Lord.

Elijah Coleman Bridgman was a Massachusetts boy who, happening to be caught up in the great American religious revival of the early nineteenth century, on a winter morning in 1813 (when he was not yet twelve) joined the Belchertown Congregational Church with 105 other trembling but determined converts and then did most of them one better by deciding to enter the ministry. For this he passed in due course to Andover Theological Seminary. Meanwhile D. W. C. Olyphant, an older man who had experienced his conversion a year after Bridgman but had not on that account left the New York countinghouse of merchants in the China trade, began looking around for someone to go to China to help Robert Morrison, the first English missionary there. The London Missionary Society had sent Morrison out in 1807 and he had remained in China ever since, burying one wife, taking in the course of home leave another, fathering seven children (of whom John was the second and the oldest boy). In the course of several years' business residence at Canton, Olyphant had come to know Morrison well and had developed the highest regard for him, had in fact named a son for him, and would soon name a ship. By the late 1820s, however, Morrison was in a bad way. Time, illness, and the disappointments of mission work had reduced him to a state of almost chronic depression, and he cried out to his American friend for assistance. So Olyphant approached the American Board of Commissioners for Foreign Missions, which already had men in India and Hawaii, and offered free passage out and board and lodging in the American factory to any person the board cared to send. Bridgman was discovered to be willing. After some coming and going between the board in Boston, Olyphant in New York, and Belchertown, the young Andover graduate was hastily ordained, given a public dinner at which his instructions were read aloud amid great enthusiasm, and put aboard one of Olyphant's vessels bound for China. He was then twenty-eight.

With Bridgman went David Abeel, commissioned by the Seaman's Friend Society to work among the American sailors at Whampoa, and Olyphant's sober and intense young nephew, the previously mentioned Charles King. During the voyage, which lasted four and a half months, these three brothers in Christ organized Sunday services, distributed tracts, and penetrated the forecastle. There Abeel faced down one blasphemous but very sick seaman and so influenced him that when he recovered, "though he gave no evidence of regeneration, he was punctual in his attendance on the means of grace"[6] and became quite expert at reproving his shipmates of sins Abeel was sure he had not renounced himself. So the three rounded the Cape, ran down the Indian Ocean, touched Anjer in the Sunda Straits where dusky Malays with filed teeth paddled out to meet them, and on a day in February 1830 anchored among the opium receiving ships off Lintin. King immediately went to work for Olyphant's house. Abeel prepared to raise the Bethel flag among the shipping at Whampoa. Bridgman met Morrison, settled at Number 2 the American factory, and cast about for ways and means of furthering the conversion of China's millions. How was he to proceed?

There could be no question, he was told, of opening a chapel or preaching in the streets. The mandarins would never allow public proselytizing; Morrison had discovered this almost a quarter of a century before. Morrison had discovered, too, that if he wanted a tutor to help him with his Chinese, he must engage him on the sly. The Chinese did not wish foreigners to learn their language. Pidgin was quite enough for them.

Pidgin was a jargon composed of English with a little corrupt Portuguese and Hindustani thrown in, delivered question-and-answer fashion, in monosyllables for the most part, with certain stock changes in suffixes and consonants. First arming himself with such particular terms as *coolie, shroff, junk, joss, chop,* ★ and *pidgin* itself (which means business), the

★The word *chop*, from the Hindi for stamp or brand, had many uses in the China trade. It meant a permit, as with the grand chop of departure; a licensed lighter, as with a chop boat; a consignment of goods all bearing the same mark, as with a chop of silks or teas. First-chop meant first-rate, and for some reason chop-chop signified quickly; hence chopsticks or quick sticks. But chop suey apparently only approximates the Cantonese for "miscellaneous bits."

newcomer to the China coast learned to fill out his sentences with English pronounced in a manner that put it (he was told) within the comprehension of the Chinese. The Chinese did exactly the reverse, relying upon phrase books in which the English sounds of things were as faithfully reproduced as the absence from Chinese of certain English consonants permitted. The results were serviceable though childish. "Chin-chin," the bookbinder might cry as Bridgman entered his shop carrying a book with a torn binding. "How you do? Long time my no have see you. What thing wantchee?" When Bridgman showed him the article, explaining "my no wantchee lever, my wantchee first-chop sileek cofuh," the bookbinder might reply "just now no got," adding he hoped to have some "tomollo" for his "olo flen" the missionary. Every Chinese whose business brought him into contact with the *fan kuei* used pidgin; even the linguists were quite unable to carry on a conversation in true English or to read the simplest document in that language. As for the English, American, and Parsee merchants, with a few exceptions it never occurred to them to learn anything else.

Pidgin being what it was, its universal use practically guaranteed that the *fan kuei* and the Celestials would hold each other in the lowest possible esteem. But it was not to remedy this that the elder Morrison had set himself seriously to the study of Chinese or that the Factory had rewarded his efforts by appointing him (in 1812) Chinese secretary and translator at a salary of £1,000 a year. The Factory had a particular reason for wishing to have somebody at hand with a command of true Chinese. Pidgin was all very well for buying teas, dealing with bookbinders, and handling the servants. At times of crisis, however, when the hong merchants came daily to the factories with edicts enjoining this or that and a stoppage of trade appeared imminent, the senior supercargoes felt the need of communicating in something a little more elevated and substantial. Of course they could always leave things to these same hong merchants. Communications entrusted to hong merchants did not, however, always turn out as the framers intended. This was partly because Howqua, Mowqua, and the others did not understand English and worked on the basis of what they were told in pidgin; and partly, too, because the Chinese language lends itself to the expression of status—and the hong merchants, anxious to save their clients from the possible consequences of impertinence, did not place them very high. Thus the Select often discovered that they were being referred to in terms obviously demeaning or that they were being represented as anxious to obey Peking when what they really meant to convey was their determination to consult Calcutta. This annoyed them. They and the chief superintendents after them wanted to be able to prepare their own papers— wanted to be able to speak for themselves. And as the India House and

Whitehall sent no one who could do so for them, they turned naturally to the missionaries. The missionaries for their part were attracted by the pay. (Missionary societies remitted little, and that often was late.) So a working relationship easily developed; before long it was practically taken for granted that on the China coast the Protestant Mission should be England's official translating and interpreting arm.

Morrison had another and more powerful motive for learning Chinese. On his way to Canton someone had asked him whether he really expected to make an impression on the idolatry of the Chinese Empire. "No, Sir," he had replied, "I expect God will."[7] Neither Morrison nor the London Missionary Society had supposed He would accomplish His task overnight. To prepare His path Morrison had determined to provide the Chinese with the Word of Life; it was a labor Protestants traditionally had the greatest confidence in, and nowhere more so than in a land like China where proselytizing in other ways was so very difficult. To furnish the Word of Life meant, however, translating it first—Morrison knew of no Chinese Bible he could copy or adapt, indeed in the Protestant world none existed—and it was in order to be able to translate that he had bent himself to the formidable work of memorizing those hundreds and hundreds of characters, of imitating those elusive sounds. As a matter of course Abeel and Bridgman followed suit.

Once a certain mastery of Chinese had been obtained and a beginning made at translating the Word of Life, it was necessary to put that Word into print. Here fresh difficulties arose. There was the impossibility of obtaining a proper font of Chinese type in any reasonable time. The making of types required molds, the making of molds required steel punches; a skilled punch cutter working with files, chisels, and counter-punches would be lucky to cut three or four punches a week; so preparing a font of, say, two thousand Chinese characters—you could hardly print with less—might easily take a single punch cutter ten years! Morrison, therefore, had early decided to have his printing done with wood blocks in the Chinese manner. Then a second difficulty presented itself. Whether he put the work out to printing shops in Canton and Macao or hired block cutters and opened his own mission press, printing Christian literature in Chinese aroused (he quickly discovered) the intense suspicion of the mandarins. If the *fan kuei* wished to publish material in their own languages—a *Repository*, a weekly newspaper or two, lists of prices current, bills of lading, blank opium orders—that was their business. But material in Chinese! The mandarins did not care for this. So from an early date the Protestant Mission had found its printing harassed, block cutters arrested or frightened into disappearing, shops broken into and blocks and finished books destroyed, until in the end a large part of the work had had to be moved to the Straits of Malacca.

It so happened that there existed on the southwest fringes of China a very large number of overseas Chinese who preserved their cultural identity but could not be reached by Peking's long arm. Missionaries settled easily among them, proselytized with some success among them, learned Chinese from them; by the time of the Napier fizzle missionary stations could be found at Penang, Malacca, and Singapore, at Batavia and Bangkok. Malacca was a particularly important station. An Anglo-Chinese college had been opened there to train overseas Chinese along western Christian lines. To it was attached a press. It was at Malacca, on the west coast of the Malay Peninsula a hundred miles above Singapore, that a great deal of the work of publishing the Word of Life in Chinese was carried on.

Naturally this work took first the form of a Chinese Bible. Morrison printed his own version of Acts as early as 1810. By the end of 1811 he had turned out a Luke—three-quarters of an inch of soft octavo tied between yellow endpapers with thin silk cord. Twelve years later, with the help of a Scotch missionary named William Milne, the Old and New Testaments stood complete. Thereafter Morrison, Bridgman, a London Missionary Society man named Medhurst, and Gutzlaff continued from time to time to work on improving this indispensable passport to Jesus. But a Chinese Bible, when printed from wood blocks and bound in the Chinese manner (which leaves half the page surfaces uncut and blank), was extraordinarily bulky. Where an ordinary English Luke will rarely occupy more than forty pages, Morrison's ran to one hundred and sixty and would have run to double that had you seized a knife and slit the folds. His quarto New Testament came out in eight parts; the completed duodecimo Bible he did with Milne appeared in twenty-one and weighed five pounds. Distributing it was a bit like peddling Toynbee or the telephone directory. Using it to win converts was like taking up a cannon to shoot quail.

Tracts were another matter. They could be short, they could be written to suit an occasion, and of all the agencies of Christian conversion they seemed the easiest to introduce into China. "Tracts," explained Milne once to the Religious Tract Society, "may penetrate silently even to the Chamber of the Emperor. They easily put on a Chinese coat and may walk without fear through the breadth and length of the land. This we cannot do."[8] Milne himself had composed a number of tracts—on the redemption of the world, on the life of Jesus, on idolatry, "the strait gate," and the sin of lying. When Milne died in 1822 the tracts continued, flowing in ever-increasing volume from the several missionary presses, devouring reams and reams of paper enthusiastically dispatched by the missionary, tract, and Bible societies of England and America. By the middle 1830s the

Malacca press alone had turned out close to half a million. Some of the missionaries had reservations about their use. But as time went on, and they could discover few other outlets for their evangelical energies, many came to feel with the exuberant Gutzlaff that "as the Lord of Hosts is opening doors, there will be Millions of Tracts wanted."[9]

Karl Gutzlaff was a German who had come east for the Netherlands Missionary Society in 1827 at the age of twenty-five, had worked on Java and on the island of Bintang just below Singapore (where he picked up the Fukien dialect from overseas Chinese), and at last had settled at Bangkok. There he ministered to the Chinese of the junk trade. His ambition, however, was to reach China proper, and in the summer of 1831, his young English wife having left him a sum of money at her death, he saw his chance and went to Macao. There he remained for several months, preaching occasionally, overwhelming Harriet Low with his enthusiasm and his apparent command of many languages, impressing Morrison and Bridgman less. Early in 1832 he traveled up the coast in the *Lord Amherst*, as we have seen. That autumn it was the turn of the *Sylph*. Voyages of this sort were becoming a habit with Gutzlaff; as he was a confident interpreter and soon got to know the coast extremely well, he was welcomed aboard opium vessels, particularly Jardine's. "I would give a thousand dollars for three days of Gutzlaff," Innes once remarked.[10]

Gutzlaff, however, did not neglect his missionary work. Everywhere he went he took with him boxes of tracts, cheerfully distributing them from one side of a vessel while opium went over the other. He got rid of so many this way that by the autumn of 1834 he was boasting that all the other missionaries put together did not reach as many Chinese as he was reaching. Christianity, it seemed, was to be floated into the hearts of the Chinese upon a sea of paper—while simultaneously, and from the same vessels, the pipes of the Chinese were to be filled with the choicest Malwa, Patna, and Benares. Christ and opium! It ought to prove an irresistible combination.

Abeel, meanwhile, had gone off to work among the overseas Chinese of the archipelago and returned home sick, so the Seaman's Friend Society sent another missionary named Edwin Stevens. He arrived in 1832 aboard Olyphant's *Morrison*. A year later the same ship brought a young upstate New Yorker, S. Wells Williams, whom the American Board had trained as a printer; a year later still she brought Olyphant himself and (again for the American Board) a Yale-trained doctor and minister named Peter Parker. With Olyphant now physically at Canton, the full resources of Zion's Corner could be thrown into the work of spreading the Word of Life—and without risking contamination from the opium traffic, since Olyphant made it a point never to deal in the drug. When, one year after the Napier fizzle, Walter Medhurst, the London Missionary Society's man at Batavia, came up to Canton anxious to do a coastal voyage on a really grand scale, Olyphant promptly offered him his little brig *Huron*. Stevens agreed to go along, twenty thousand pieces of Christian literature were put aboard, and on a day in September 1835, the two missionaries stepped ashore on the north side of the Shantung Peninsula, a sailor close behind with a basket of tracts.

They were noticed at once, of course. Mandarins of rising rank—gold-button ones, white-button ones, eventually a blue—met and attempted to stop them, but the unexpectedness of their descent upon a part of the coast so little frequented by foreigners seemed to have a paralyzing effect. Besides, Medhurst in particular moved with positively brazen assurance. When a mandarin reminded him that *fan kuei* were not supposed to set foot inside the Celestial Empire, he replied that "if it is truly the celestial empire, it must comprise all born beneath heaven, ourselves [included] of course, and therefore we shall proceed a little distance,"[11] which they did. At the top of a hill several mandarins' attendants caught up with them, puffing and blowing, their white hose spattered with mud, and begged them to pause at a nearby temple for a quiet talk with several of the mandarins. They agreed; but once seated and served tea, Medhurst confounded his would-be interrogators by reviewing for their benefit the principal doctrines of the Christian Gospel. After that they were left to do pretty much as they pleased. In the course of two days' walking about the shores of the bay, they were able to get rid of hundreds of copies of a harmony of the Gospels, a commentary on the Ten Commandments, a life of Christ, and the like. Then the *Huron* moved fifty miles west and the process was repeated.

When they sailed around to the south side of Shantung, however, they found the people distinctly hostile. Indeed, they began to get the feeling that an alarm was out against them. Early in October they left the *Huron* at Woosung and pushed up the Hwangpu in a small boat, as Lindsay and Gutzlaff had done three years before. At Shanghai they were prevented from entering the city proper. An attempt was made to burn some of their books, and though they did what they could, even penetrating the forts at Woosung, after a few days they thought it prudent to sail, tailed by war junks. On the way south they landed on the island of Puto, outermost of the Chusan group and to Buddhists the most sacred place in eastern China. It marvelously restored their evangelical spirits to wander among its dozens of temples, observe its battalions of resident priests, and know that viewed in the light of revelation the place was a colossal fraud. When they reached the Gulf of Canton, however, and the voyage was over, they were not at all sure they should ever have gone. The Chinese who accepted their literature had seemed moved as much by "the bump of acquisitiveness" as by a genuine moral appetite; Stevens remembered villagers grabbing for brown covers because they valued the color over red. The authorities, moreover, seemed now to be thoroughly roused against further ventures of this sort. Within weeks of the *Huron's* return, the hong merchants brought around a recently issued edict on the subject.

The Protestant Mission was not at once deterred. It could not afford to be; Scripture and tracts were spilling from its presses in quantities that drove G. Tradescant Lay to remark, a little desperately, "if the Chinese will not have them, the cockroaches will."[12] Lay was an Englishman who had made a trip through the East Indies as observing naturalist on board a man-of-war and had then been engaged by the British and Foreign Bible Society to work for it in China. He reached Macao in the late summer of 1836 and a few months later set off with Stevens on another tract and Bible voyage—this time in Olyphant's *Himmaleh*, traveling to the East Indies with China to follow. At Singapore, however, Stevens suddenly sickened and died, and as the *Himmaleh's* master was timid and Lay inexperienced, the expedition never reached China at all. The following summer King and his wife, Gutzlaff, Williams, and Parker went off to Japan in the *Morrison*. This time they carried no books or tracts; they went simply to test the wall of Japanese exclusiveness, using as an excuse the necessity of returning seven shipwrecked Japanese sailors who had found their way to Macao. Even so they got nowhere, being driven first from Tokyo Bay and later from Kagoshima on the south side of Kyushu. Thereafter hardly anyone but Gutzlaff persevered with the work of distributing the Word of Life by sea.

As for distributing it by land, about Canton itself, that did not appear at all promising.

Williams, the missionary printer, had not been at the factories a month when he met a certain Liang A-fa, a converted Chinese of remarkable boldness and persistence who composed his own tracts, had them printed right in Canton, and then gave them out to candidates at the periodic provincial examinations. "He got some coolies to take his boxes into the hall," Williams was told, "and there he dealt out the Word of Life as fast as he could handle them."[13] (One of the candidates of these years later got Liang's tracts out again, read them, and became so excited he went out and founded the quasi-Christian movement that turned into the prolonged and immensely destructive Taiping Rebellion.) Liang had already been caught and bambooed for this sort of thing. At the height of the Napier fizzle, when he tried it again, the police pursued him so determinedly that he was obliged, with Bridgman's help, to take refuge on board the *Hercules* and afterward sail away to Singapore. He was there all through the late 1830s, working for American missionaries. If a Chinese could not hand out Christian literature in the Canton area, a conspicuous foreign devil like Williams had better not try.

Something might be possible at Macao. Williams found life at the factories unpleasantly cramped; besides, Bridgman did not need him to turn out the *Repository*, the first number of which had rolled off the press at the rear of the American factory almost a year and a half before Williams reached the coast; so at the end of 1835 Williams left Canton for Macao. There he rented a large house on the side of a hill. "For household J have a porter, a comprador, a coolie, a cook, a printer, and four little boys; in all nine who live in the basement. The printing office is under the parlor."[14] In it Williams began to print a dictionary of the Fukien dialect by Medhurst and a "chrestomathy," or learner's manual, of the Canton dialect by Bridgman and himself.

Sometimes he went up to the factories to visit Bridgman and Parker. Sometimes they came down to visit him. On Wednesday and Sunday evenings there were social gatherings at Mary Gutzlaff's. (Gutzlaff had married again, and again the girl was English.) For the most part, however, Williams stuck close to his language studies, his printing, his students, and the work of bringing Christ to the Macao Chinese. No more than at Canton did he dare open a public chapel or distribute literature through the booksellers. He called his household servants to prayers—behind blank faces their minds, he felt sure, were positively choked by a "luxuriant growth of vicious weeds."[15] He discovered a little colony of beggars on the hillside behind the lazaretto and took to visiting them early Sunday morning before they went out to beg. With Lay he boarded junks in the harbor. The boatmen listened politely but refused to respond even with anger to artful questions touching religion. Occasionally the two would fill a bag with forty copies of the Gospel according to Mark, cross to the Lappa, and spend a morning giving the things away. Again they would be decently received; it was pleasant to walk between fields of ripening rice and reflect "that as the fields, so the mind and heart of the Chinese are whitening to the harvest";[16] but there were few Chinese on the island, and these not of the better sort, so as with the boatmen the harvest promised to be neither large nor choice.

At Canton, meanwhile, the Reverend Peter Parker, M.D., explored the approach of the medical missionary. Colledge, senior surgeon to the Factory at the time of its demise, had shown him the way. When Colledge had reached Macao in the late 1820s, he had noticed with astonishment and pity that large numbers of Chinese walked about with physical complaints that the simplest surgery might have remedied. This was because traditional Chinese medicine concentrated upon acupuncture, diagnosis by pulse-taking, and an elaborate and largely herbal pharmacopoeia. It left surgery to quacks and charlatans. So Colledge had opened a little public clinic to see if he could do for the Macao Chinese what they could not do for themselves.

Many came to him with eye troubles. Barbers had a habit of cleaning the eyes of their customers by rubbing the inner surface of each lid with a bamboo or ivory instrument. If this did not cause inflammation, inversion of the upper eyelid often did; the eyelashes, turning in upon the eye, inflamed it to the point where blood vessels crept across the cornea and the sufferer went blind. Colledge treated this condition by slicing away the edge of the lid just above the lashes. He also operated for cataract, lanced abscesses, and excised tumors—some of a really frightening size.

One day, for example, a man from a distant village walked in carrying with great difficulty, his shoulders thrown back to balance the weight, an immense tumor of the scrotum. Colledge dared not operate. He was moved, however, by the man's courage in coming so far and arranged to have him sent to London. There the fellow was operated upon by Aston Key, pupil and protégé of the celebrated Sir Astley Cooper, before almost seven hundred persons crowded into the anatomical theater at Guy's. While the tumor, which weighed over fifty pounds, was being removed, the Chinese was tied to the operating table and his face covered with a cloth. Twice he fainted from pain, loss of blood, and the foulness of the air at the bottom of the pit. Twice he was revived, and the cutting resumed to no sound but his groans and the gritting of his teeth. Towards the end he fainted a third time, and though everything possible was done to save him, even to injecting watered brandy directly into his stomach, he died on the operating table. But this failure was exceptional. In the course of four or five years Colledge successfully treated hundreds of patients. Then he became senior surgeon to the Factory, which kept him busy, and at the same time married an American girl who happened to be staying with Harriet Low—which kept him busier still. So in 1833, a year before Peter Parker's arrival, he closed his clinic.

Parker did not at once take up the work. Instead he went off to Singapore to learn Chinese and recover from a bowel complaint. In the autumn of 1835, however, he came back, induced Howqua to rent him Number 7 at the Fungtai factory, and opened what he called the Opthalmic Hospital. Through its door, which gave onto Hog Lane, came men, women, and children, first in a trickle and then in a flood, bringing all the troubles Colledge had grown accustomed to. Parker operated on abscesses; he did cataracts; one afternoon in January 1836 he faced his first large tumor, a one-pound growth that hung from a girl's temple down to her mouth.

With Jardine and several other ship's surgeons helping, he gave the girl opium and watered wine, tied and blindfolded her, and removed the thing in eight minutes flat. Gradually his skill increased. He learned to amputate an arm in sixty seconds—speed was essential since ether was still a dozen years away. Though he had some close calls and there were deaths, of course, from other causes, no patient died under his knife.

People of some importance began coming to him. One day he was called on board a splendidly decorated junk to extract the abscessed teeth of the wife of an officer of considerable rank—Manchu, to judge by her unbound feet. To cover his expenses (they ran to a modest $1,500 a year, a third of it rent), he passed the hat among his friends, until at last Jardine, Matheson, King, and others organized a Medical Missionary Society to provide regular support and to recruit additional doctors. Colledge became the society's first president. Later he retired to England, but the society did not falter on that account; it rented a large house at Macao, furnished and equipped it as a hospital, and turned it over to Parker while his own Number 7 was being enlarged and renovated. This Macao hospital had to be closed when, at the end of three months, Parker returned to the factories. By then, however, the society had the promise of a second doctor, a London Missionary Society man named Lockhart, due to arrive early in 1839. With Lockhart on hand it should be possible to practice missionary medicine at Canton and Macao simultaneously the year round.

As the 1830s advanced, the other parts of the Protestant Mission grew larger too. David Abeel was back in America, intermittently but seriously ill. John Morrison was busy filling his father's shoes at the Superintendency; besides, he was not an ordained minister and was suspected of being in some danger spiritually from friends in the agency houses. But there was Bridgman. There was Williams, no minister either but as eager as the rest of them to win Chinese for Christ. From 1836 onward there were two American Baptists, Roberts and Shuck, and Shuck's wife Henrietta, laboring for Christ in her own right. There was Lay. There was a certain Edward Squire, sent out by the Church Missionary Society of London. There were Karl and Mary Gutzlaff, and brothers and sisters in the gospel bonds among the overseas Chinese of Bangkok, Batavia, and the Straits of Malacca. Surveying the whole, perceiving in it clear evidences of God's hand, one could not help feeling that here was "a mighty machinery . . . too powerful to be resisted."[17]

Resisted it was, just the same. The American Board had advised Bridgman to be patient, learn the language, and wait for the "providence of God" to make a way through the seemingly impenetrable wall behind which the Chinese lived. The board had also averred that "the Gospels will some day or other triumph over the Chinese empire, and its vast population be given to Christ."[18] Bridgman wanted to know how.

Perhaps the Word of Life, whether in cumbersome Scripture or nimble tracts, really would do the trick. Unless, however, it brought a significant number of Chinese to the point of actual conversion, it must in the end be counted a failure. For it was not enough to adopt bits and pieces of the Truth, to welcome Our Lord into the pantheon along with the other gods, or acknowledge the peculiar ethical merit of the Golden Rule. A person had to face squarely the fact of his own absolute depravity. A person had to accept that, unaided, there was nothing he could do to escape its consequences, then throw himself upon God's mercy through Jesus Christ His Son. A person had, in short, to dare all, give himself completely, and achieve thereby complete regeneration—as the overwhelming majority of Chinese who accepted tracts and Bibles were *not* doing—as Parker's patients were not doing either.

No one supposed, of course, that medicine alone could overcome sin. What one looked for was a doctor who, in healing the sick, should serve as "an angel of mercy to point to the Lamb of God."[19] Parker, barely thirty, impatient to bring to China's millions the tiding of his Savior's love, wanted a more direct approach. He wanted to scatter tracts about his waiting room. He wanted to make religious instruction a regular part of his treatment. He did not dare; the hong merchants appointed a linguist to watch for just these things. No doubt his patients went away grateful. "Many would knock head on the floor before me," he reported, "and are only prevented by the assurance that if they do so I shall not prescribe for them."[20] No doubt, too, Bridgman was right to maintain that the chief obstacle to missionary work was the stupefying arrogance of the Chinese, for dismantling which there was nothing quite so swift and effective as Parker's minor miracles. It was Bridgman's opinion that Parker had done more for the Protestant Mission in his first two years than Robert Morrison had done in twenty-seven. But Morrison had at least baptized a handful of Chinese, whereas not one of the hundreds who passed through the door of Number 7 showed any sign of being led thereby to the acceptance of Christ.

Liang A-fa was a special and comforting case. "He bears the image of the Lord Jesus," Abeel and Bridgman had reported on first meeting him.[21] Robert Morrison had thought so too and had ordained the fellow, making him the first Chinese Protestant minister. Liang had brought with him into the fold his wife, his children—a son, Atih, studied English with Bridgman—and a few fellow printers. But no one seemed disposed to follow in Liang's footsteps.

Parker lanced abscesses, excised tumors, and restored sight without, as far as he knew, inducing a single Chinese to love Jesus. Bridgman turned out issue after issue of the *Repository*—as a looking glass for the Chinese it was something less than effective, however, because no Chinese with the possible exception of Atih could read it. A Morrison Education Society, organized with the help of a number of merchants, held regular meetings and raised money for a school to train young Chinese along Christian lines, but could find no one in England or America to come out and take charge; for the moment it had to content itself with contributing $15 a month towards an institution for blind and orphaned Chinese girls which Mary Gutzlaff maintained at Macao. As for a Society for the Diffusion of Useful Knowledge in China, again set on foot by merchants and missionaries, it commissioned a number of useful and edifying works in Chinese, among them a translation of Aesop's *Fables* by Jardine's young clerk, Thom. But the Chinese were little interested in these works. Besides, what the missionaries were chiefly anxious to diffuse was a knowledge of Jesus Christ! Over in Burma, Adoniram Judson was diffusing it so widely and so well that hundreds came to him each year to be baptized. In China, after thirty years, you could tick the known converts off on the fingers of two hands. Carefully the *Repository* omitted to name or to enumerate them.

All this did not bother Gutzlaff much. His confidence in his own brand of instant evangelism was proof against shocks and discouragements of any kind. Distributing tracts with him one day near Macao, Lay noticed that before the awful flood of his volubility the faces of the villagers grew "full of terror and amazement."[22] It was Gutzlaff's boast that alone and single-handed he had reached and affected thirty million Chinese. To celebrate this joyous feat he wrote and published (in London) a book modestly called *China Opened*. Williams was annoyed. Magnifying the acceptance of a few tens of thousands of tracts by a few thousand curious Chinese into "China groans to be free" seemed to him quite irresponsible. China was decidedly *not* open; besides, Williams noticed that much of the material for Gutzlaff's book had been lifted without acknowledgement straight from old numbers of the *Repository*. The fact was that the little German was not to be trusted. He was too much the booster, too ambitious, the kind of man (Lay once remarked) whose plans are a secret to everyone but himself.

Up at the factories Bridgman found the daily treatment more and more wearing. Whenever he walked up Hog Lane or into the suburbs, small boys were sure to run after him shrieking, "*Fan kuei! Fan kuei!*" Once he stopped to rebuke one and was told, "If I don't call you a foreign devil, what shall I call you?"[23] What else indeed? An Innes or a Jardine could laugh at the epithet. Bridgman was bothered by it. A missionary, after all, was supposed to establish a special relationship with the people among whom he worked, was supposed so to conduct himself that the heathen positively crowded around him, "hanging on his lips and exulting at the sound of eternal life." The phrase was Milne's, and Milne had added that none of this could be expected "in the present state of China."[24] But that had been twenty years ago! Whose fault was it that this state persisted, whose but the Chinese themselves? How impossible they were; he would have to redouble his efforts; "notwithstanding all their vices, we must love them, we must *love* them, while we *abhor* their evil practices."[25] But this was easier said than done. Meanwhile, would the American Board long continue to support a mission with so little to show?

The others felt depressed too. Williams no longer thought of being ordained; there was talk of leaving the China coast altogether, of withdrawing to Singapore—and a curious attitude developed among the missionaries, a kind of bitterness, a hostility even. It was not that they wished to drag China into the light by brute force. They would not (this is King speaking) "trample down the customs of China with cavalry, nor cut up her prejudices with the sabre."[26] They would not imitate the captain of a certain English frigate who, years before, on being approached by a mandarin demanding to know what cargo he carried, was said to have struck the cabin table with his clenched fist before replying, "Cargo? Cargo did you say? Powder and shot, sir, are the cargo of a British man-of-war!"[27] But did not Scripture itself promise the eventual infliction upon sinners of Heavenly powder and shot? "Sunday morning," the elder Morrison had written one day in the last January of his life. "The dull rainy weather is clearing up a little. . . . I am going to read 2 Kings xviii to my Chinese congregation as the lesson in the New Testament. It is full against idolatry. One would think that as Israel and Judah were both given into the hands of their enemies because of their idolatry, something similar will happen to China . . . for will not like sins produce like punishments?"[28]

It was a grave and somber view, and those who held it felt no lightening of the spirit when they heard—as from time to time they were bound to hear—about the apparently more successful proselytizing activities of the Roman Catholics. For everybody knew that Catholicism was as spurious as it had ever been, and Rome as ever a whore. One had only to look about Macao to see that this was so. One had only to notice St. Paul's.

8

The Catholic Mission

It happened that early in the seventeenth century the Jesuits at
Macao raised a church on the west slope of the Monte hill below the
fort. The body of this church was simple and unpretentious, being constructed of a local aggregate of sand, clay, lime, and molasses. The facade
was something else again. Decorated with four clusters of columns,
pierced and indented with niches and windows at several levels above the
doors, it was elegant and not a little imposing—and built of granite. The
whole was dedicated to St. Paul. Immediately adjoining was a seminary.

In 1762 a decree suppressing the Society of Jesus reached Macao from
Lisbon. Twenty-four Jesuit priests were arrested and deported, and the
church and seminary of St. Paul's closed. The years passed. From time to
time Goanese sepoys of the Macao garrison occupied the abandoned buildings. They were a dirty lot; they piled firewood in great heaps outside the
kitchen door and allowed rubbish and rats to accumulate in the unused
rooms. On a January evening in 1835 a fire broke out in the sepoy guard-
room. It spread rapidly through the refuse, reached the church, ignited the
roof, and brought it crashing to the ground. The sepoys decamped. After
some time the interior of the ruin was cleared out. The walls were torn
back to a uniform height of twenty-five feet. Burial vaults were cut in their
sides, a few cedars planted, and the shell turned into a cemetery. Only the
great granite facade remained. Approaching by the broad flight of steps
that led up to it, one was amazed to discover, through its apertures, open
sky.

To Protestants the facade of St. Paul's—elegant, imposing, and with
nothing behind it—seemed a perfect symbol for the hollowness of
Catholic religious life. What they saw elsewhere about the town
confirmed them in this feeling. His first Lenten season Wells Williams
happened to wander one evening into the cathedral. Hundreds of women
knelt on the floor, talking, while a service was got through "in a chanting
sort of way." The noise was so great Williams could make nothing of the

Latin. "What worship there can be without the understanding and the heart," he wrote his brother, "I cannot imagine. God has declared that in our prayers we are not heard for our much speaking." What bothered him most, however, was the sight of priests moving among the women with clay and wooden images the women prostrated themselves before and kissed. "Surely this must be the mark of the beast."[1]

Harriet Low was not quite so severe. She rather enjoyed the religious processions: men in white satin trousers and loose blue satin gowns bearing on a sort of car an image of Jesus or the Virgin Mary or the particular saint whose day this was; small girls dressed as angels in hooped petticoats and muslin wings and carrying lighted candles; priests in the various robes of their orders; sepoys marching in ragged files with their muskets clasped muzzle up against their chests; governor bemedaled; senators dignified; band playing; church bells ringing; cannon booming from the forts above—it was all, thought Harriet, very chaotic and colorful. But when she remembered Josepha, her aunt's half-breed servant girl, she felt rather differently. Josepha was always mumbling prayers and, when asked why, said the priest made her—"liky or no liky." Studying the girl, comparing these devotions with her own troubled efforts to decide whether she was truly a Unitarian or not, Harriet concluded that there was no more religion in Josepha "than there is in a bamboo."[2] It was a judgment Protestants were inclined to pronounce upon all Catholics.

Pronouncing it, however, had the effect of concealing from Protestants the real extent of Catholic activity in China. Williams knew that Romish missionary orders maintained offices at Macao. He knew that they sent priests deep into the interior of China and kept them there. To the American Board he admitted that, taking China as a whole, "the number of the ostensible adherents to that faith are several tens of thousands, scattered in various provinces of the empire."[3] But he could not forsake that snide little "ostensible," he could not resist the conviction that the Chinese won by his Catholic rivals had been won not for Christ but for the Pope—which was no victory. Besides, he was sure their numbers were not as great as they were alleged to be.

In this last, at least, he was certainly wrong. No one knows, no one can know, exactly how many Catholic communicants there were in China in the early nineteenth century. It is beyond question, however, that they numbered not a few tens but several hundreds of thousands; Chinese who lived a reasonably regular Catholic life; Chinese baptized, married, and confessed by properly ordained priests. Communities of the faithful scattered about a sea of the heathen. But not lost, not forgotten, since Europe still sent to them its missionaries.

Two of these missionaries left Macao at exactly the moment Williams was settling into his rented house. One was a French Lazarist named Jean-Gabriel Perboyre. The other was a French priest of the Missions Etrangères named Louis Delamarre. On the evening of 21 December 1835, the two boarded a Chinese junk bound up the coast. It was a common way to reach the interior. Sometimes missionaries went directly overland, by way of Canton. More often they took ship for Fukien. For there was a large Christian community in that province, the only one on China's seaboard, and it made sense to land a man there on the first leg of the journey to his assigned area—for Perboyre that meant Honan in north central China, for Delamarre Szechwan far to the west.

It being the height of the winter monsoon, and the skipper fearful of pirates and reluctant to sail at night or without the company of others, the junk took nine weeks to beat up the six hundred miles—and Perboyre and Delamarre had plenty of time to reflect on the evidences of Christian influence they found along the way. Of an evening, at anchor close to shore, members of the crew would sit quietly near them telling their beads. A mandarin who paid the junk a visit was said to have a Christian mother and to be well disposed toward missions. (Just the same the missionaries remained hidden while he was aboard.) When the junk paused off "Nan-Goa" to be careened and have her bottom scraped, Perboyre and Delamarre were told that there were a number of Christians living on the island. The most impressive evidence of the church's presence awaited them, however, at the end of the nine weeks. On landing, again under cover of darkness, they were met and led inland by a Spanish Dominican named Carpena who (it appeared) had been in China uninterruptedly for almost fifty years. Carpena carried the Pope's commission as vicar apostolic of Fukien and the adjoining provinces of Chekiang and Kiangsi. He lived in a village called Thing-Theou; it had fifteen hundred inhabitants, two-thirds of them Christian; in all Fukien there were forty thousand Christians, Carpena said, most concentrated in this northeast corner about the town of Fuan. There they were served by seven or eight European Dominicans and an equal number of native priests. They walked about with their heads high; the mandarins looked the other way. "It is wonderful," wrote Perboyre, "they have no idea of all this in Europe."[4]

Perboyre and Delamarre spent three weeks with Carpena and then set off on foot for Kiangsi Province. Four Fukienese Christians hurried them across hill and mountain at the rate of fifteen to twenty miles a day, taking them through towns at a trot to avoid the curious and, when the curious could not be avoided, letting it be supposed that the two men with their foreign features and Chinese dress were tea merchants unfamiliar with the local dialect. (Perboyre was careful to keep his blond hair, and its point of junction with his long black false queue, covered.) At the edge of Kiangsi fresh guides took over. A little distance into the province they met a French Lazarist named Laribe, with whom they passed Easter. By boat now they moved north to the Yangtze and up that river to Wuchang. At Wuchang they separated. Delamarre kept to the main stream. Perboyre followed the Han and early in May encountered two more French Lazarists, Baldus and Rameaux, whose people guided and took care of him. Days of travel were punctuated by weeks of immobility; at last he left the river, turned due north into the hills, and reached his appointed station of Nanyang, eight months after leaving Macao, sixteen months after leaving France.

The details of Perboyre's immense journey halfway around the world were soon known in Catholic missionary circles because several of his letters appeared in the *Annales de la propagation de la foi,* the international missionary journal published every other month in Lyon. Delamarre was not thus favored, or perhaps he did not write so copiously. Somehow he reached Szechwan, however, and put himself at the disposal of Fontana, Bishop of Sinita and vicar apostolic for Szechwan, Kweichow, and Yunnan. (Sinita is not a Chinese town; it lies in Armenia; but Fontana, as a bishop *in partibus infidelium,* had no cathedral of his own to draw a name from and was obliged to style himself by a defunct see.) Fontana had been in China for thirty years. Six other Missions Etrangères priests worked under him in Szechwan. Delamarre took up his share of that work. What it consisted of is suggested in a letter one of the six, Julien Bertrand, wrote a few years later.[5]

Fontana had assigned Bertrand to a district about eighty by eighty miles and consisting of one continuous mountain cut by monstrous ravines. It was Bertrand's custom to begin a tour of this district each year towards the end of September, after the worst of the hot weather, taking with him a native catechist and the few articles necessary for the administration of the sacraments. Arrived at a town, he settled unobtrusively in the house of a known communicant and let the faithful come quietly to him. A lesson of perhaps half an hour was followed by the celebration of the mass. While he stood at his makeshift altar the congregation sang prayers appropriate to the season or the saint's day—singing because, as Bertrand explained, "these people do not know how to pray in a low voice and are even less capable of meditating in silence." After the mass Bertrand led those who wished to confess into another room, examined them one by one, and confessed them. The rest of the day he spent preparing newly converted adults, giving the resident catechist (if there was one) instructions, and settling disputes. Often several days passed in this way. Just before leaving, small children not yet baptized were brought to him; these, together with the newly converted, he not only baptized but confirmed. "With us even the little children are thus treated, such is the constant danger of persecution." Then Bertrand struggled on to the next Christian community.

Many of these were in the countryside, where Bertrand's ministrations could be much more open; there his coming and going was less noticeable, and the people less suspicious. In the countryside a major religious holiday sometimes brought together four or five hundred of the faithful. They came boldly, bearing religious images; the room in which the mass was said was handsomely decorated with religious ornaments; the day might end with fireworks. Such occasions excited Bertrand and tantalized him too—so much to do, so much more that might be done— "oh! if our Church was free to display the full splendor of its ceremonial before the eyes of the Chinese, if the harmonious sound of the organ could reach their ears, fountains of water would not suffice to baptize all the converts there would be." Of course the church was not free to do so. Should Bertrand attempt to preach outside the little Christian communities that knew and expected him, he would immediately be arrested, brought before a magistrate, and interrogated. Then his flock would almost certainly be dispersed, and he himself might suffer the fate that, a quarter of a century before, had overtaken Fontana's predecessor, the martyred Dufresse.

Not that martyrdom was something Bertrand and the other Catholic missionaries in China consciously shrank from. Quite the contrary. Unlike their Protestant rivals, they did not have wives and children, official positions, or salaries. They did not even have the prospect of retiring from China at the end of their working lives. Unencumbered they walked to meet their Savior, and other things being equal, they might as well meet him sooner as later. When still a young seminarian, Perboyre had positively hungered for the martyr's palm. At the Lazarist mother house in the Rue de Sèvres he had been shown the blood-stained gown and the cord used for strangling Francis Clet, put to death at Wuchang in 1820, and this had actually strengthened his resolve to become a missionary. His younger brother, also a Lazarist, had set off for China but had died en route. Perboyre had applied for permission to follow. Over the protracted objections of his superiors, who thought him sickly and noticed he was past thirty years of age, he had finally had his way and sailed. If now he should confront Clet's fate, he would advance towards it gaily, for was it not in his willingness to die that a Catholic perceived the full truth of his own faith and the proud emptiness of Protestantism?

But Perboyre was a special sort. The threat of persecution and the other difficulties of missionary work deep inside China seemingly purified and ennobled him. To judge by the tone of the letters, these difficulties merely upset Bertrand. Indeed, in spite of Perboyre and others like him, in spite of a missionary apparatus that quite dwarfed what the Protestants possessed, the dominant note in the Catholic Mission as the 1830s drew towards a close was a note of discouragement.

It was partly a matter of contrast. The Protestants had little to show but had begun with nothing, whereas the Catholics had the great days of the seventeenth and early eighteenth centuries to look back upon—the great days of the Jesuits at Peking.

Then Jesuit priests lived openly in the imperial capital. Then they prescribed medicines, cast cannon, reformed and directed the calendar (a thing the Son of Heaven had a special responsibility for and was always having trouble with), gave advice on how to handle the Russians, and in return were allowed to celebrate the Mass publicly, to preach, and to baptize. Through their good services China and Europe touched and mingled at the highest level of culture and with an astonishing degree of mutual respect—even Protestants grudgingly admitted this—while in the provinces the number of the converted approached a third of a million.

But the Jesuits paid a price. To get themselves accepted, they deliberately accommodated themselves and their religion to Chinese life. They dressed as mandarins dressed; they avoided unnecessary display of the crucifix; they took pains to learn Chinese, to become familiar with the Chinese classics, and were quick to point out passages in the latter that seemed to teach of God (whom they denoted by characters suggesting a prior Chinese acquaintance). Above all they permitted their communicants to observe the rites and ceremonies by which Confucius and one's ancestors are honored. Thus they soothed the apprehensions of the magistrates at the same time that they won the adherence of a respectable number of ordinary Chinese—Rome permitting what, after all, Rome did not hear very much about. Eventually, however, critics of accommodation, from conviction or from jealousy, brought this compromising behavior so insistently to Rome's attention that she was obliged to act. As the seventeenth century gave way to the eighteenth she commanded the Jesuits, at first tentatively, at length categorically, to stop.

That the expansion of Christianity in China would someday be checked was probable; that the rites controversy should check it was a shame. The injunction to all missionaries to wear their Christianity on their sleeves led to bitter quarrels and recriminations between the Jesuits and the priests of the other missionary houses now active in China. First bored by the controversy, later annoyed by the papal pressures and pretensions to which the controversy exposed it, Peking became more and more suspicious of missionary work in general. Local persecutions had always punctuated that work. Now they multiplied and began to undo it.

In Europe, meanwhile, the Jesuits for other reasons were expelled from country after country (it was now that St. Paul's at Macao was closed) until at last the society itself was dissolved. Rome asked the French Lazarists to take the Jesuits' place at Peking. Three reached that city as the Revolution broke upon France. On the day before the Bastille fell, a mob broke into the Lazarist mother house and sacked it. Napoleon suppressed the French Lazarists outright. The Missions Etrangères (whose home was also in Paris) and the Roman Propaganda suffered the same fate. The European reinforcements upon which the church in China depended dwindled from a stream to a trickle. Those who still came found it harder and harder to remain, let alone to pursue effectively their mission work, and Macao began to be less a port of entry than a refuge for the expelled. At Peking the survivors abandoned those high standards of learning and of expertise that had made their predecessors so much respected. They squabbled among themselves, each dragging behind him a little congregation of Chinese, until death gradually put an end to the scandal of their behavior. At the time of Waterloo there were fewer than a dozen Catholic missionaries remaining in the imperial capital. By the middle 1820s there were only three. The last, a Portuguese Lazarist named Pereira, died in the fall of 1838, and the Catholic Mission at Peking was ended.

Elsewhere in China, however, the church survived. Though the number of its communicants fell from three to perhaps two hundred thousand, it did not go any lower, and with the defeat of Napoleon and the gradual revival of missionary enthusiasm in Catholic Europe, recruits began to move east again.

Once more you found at Macao the *procures* or mission agencies of the five groups that interested themselves in China: the French and the Portuguese Lazarists (as Europe calls Vincentians or members of the Congregation of the Mission), the Spanish Dominicans, the priests of the Missions Etrangères, and the priests of the Propaganda. A procurator headed each *procure*. It was his task, from a rented house he never left (*procures* did not make the seasonal move to Canton), to receive new missionaries from Europe and to prepare them for the interior. Preparation meant learning a smattering of Chinese, if not the dialect of the province of destination (that was rarely possible), then at least some Mandarin (Peking dialect) or Cantonese. It meant learning how to pass for Chinese in manners and in dress. By the late 1830s the five procurators were handling among them four or five entrants a year—enough, balanced against natural deaths, expulsions, and an occasional martyrdom, to keep the number of European missionaries inside the Celestial Empire above thirty. Indeed, if you judged the Catholic Mission in China by the ecclesiastical map, it was more than holding its own, for between 1838 and the end of 1840 Gregory XVI created six additional vicariates apostolic to place beside the three already there.

Appearances, however, were deceptive. The multiplying of jurisdictions as much reflected the rivalries and jealousies of the various missionary groups, so loosely directed from Rome or not directed at all, as it was evidence of renewed missionary vigor. The Portuguese were the most troublesome of the lot. Lisbon had always claimed the *padroado* or patronage of the church in China. Priests who came to China were supposed to be named by Lisbon or at least to receive Lisbon's approval; it was because Lisbon and Rome could not agree on a successor to the late bishop that the diocese of Macao, which nominally covered south China but in practice meant the town, was being administered by a temporary deputy. During the Napoleonic War the *padroado* had been ignored. It had not lapsed, however, and with the revival of Catholic missionary activity after Waterloo—a thing the French were particularly conspicuous in—the Portuguese seemed inclined to reassert it. In the early 1830s the accident of a civil war in Portugal ending in a victory for the anticlericals provided an opportunity. A decree reached Macao from Lisbon closing the *procures* and all religious houses and expelling any priests not born in Portugal. Several churches were converted into barracks, as St. Paul's long before had been. Jean-Baptiste Torrette, the Lazarist procurator, had to take refuge at the factories. Pierre-Louis Legrégeois, procurator for the Missions Etrangères, felt obliged to go all the way to Goa to plead his congregation's case. In the end both were permitted to return to Macao. But Portuguese jealousy of the French—both Torrette and Legrégeois were Frenchmen, and Theodore Joset, the new procurator of the Propaganda, was a French Swiss—did not abate. And the Lazarists as a whole, both French and Portuguese, were vigilant to see that the Society of Jesus (which had been reconstituted at Napoleon's defeat) should never again send its priests to China. One would have thought that after the shocks and disasters of the French Revolution the missionary houses and the several Catholic monarchs would pull together. They did not. If Catholic mission work in China faltered, the cause lay partly with the church itself.

Meanwhile the Christian communities—in northeast Fukien, in Szechwan way to the west, in the middle and lower Yangtze valley, and astride the Yellow River in Shensi and Shansi—had been weakened in other ways. Half abandoned for many years by Europe, harassed by persecutions now proclaimed from the imperial throne itself, without anyone at Peking to intercede for them or give them direction, they had been left very much to their own devices, and they were beginning to show it. Some conducted themselves bravely and well, as Carpena's flock seemed to Perboyre to be doing. Others shrank in upon themselves. Where formerly they had contained Chinese of means, education, and station, they now numbered only the poor and the illiterate. The surviving European missionaries seemed to take their cue from this; they did not study Chinese as once they had—after thirty years in a district many still could not carry on a quarter of an hour's conversation in the local dialect. Their deficiencies were not made good by their native, and sometimes female, catechists.

All might have been well had there been a proper Chinese clergy. Native priests there were, and more were in training at the Lazarist seminary of St. Joseph at Macao, which Torrette directed (the Portuguese *procure* being practically moribund). St. Joseph's was a fine place. It was not large, however, and its only equivalents were far away: the Missions Etrangères college at Penang on the Straits of Malacca and the College of the Holy Family at vastly more distant Naples. Of the seminaries inside China itself, some had been shut, others forced into hiding; the rest were precariously situated—it is a question, indeed, how substantial any of them can have been in the first place. Their graduates, together with the graduates of St. Joseph's, Penang, and Naples, outnumbered Europeans in the China Mission by more than two to one. They baptized and confessed; they kept the church alive in many places where otherwise it would have died. By themselves, however, they could not enlarge it or even perhaps prevent its gradual erosion. For that matter, though one ordained Chinese had become a bishop at the end of the seventeenth century, none had since been consecrated—or would be until early in the twentieth. It was Rome's way of saying that in her opinion, at least, the church in China was far from capable of standing on its own.

But neither could she be adequately reached and supported from the outside. So the little communities of the faithful muddled along, each not above a few hundred families in size, linked by a handful of peripatetic priests to a shadowy Chinese Christendom of a couple of hundred thousand. And a man like Bertrand tended to feel discouraged. Moving always on foot, baked by the sun and drenched by the rain, devoured by mosquitos, forced to sleep on straw, given nothing to eat but pork or fowl with vegetables (because the country produced neither bread nor wine), without the diversion of friends or books even, Bertrand sometimes allowed himself observations of a surprising darkness. "How deep and awful are God's designs upon the peoples of the East," he once wrote. "One would say that some sort of terrible judgment has already been passed upon these unhappy lands."[6]

Another Frenchman, a Lazarist named Jean-Ferdinand Faivre, came to look at the situation in much the same way.

Faivre reached Macao in the autumn of 1836, one year after Perboyre, bringing with him (as so many new arrivals did) vestiges of the conception of China common in Europe two generations before. Faivre half expected to see a land of verdant plains sprinkled with stately cities and laced by rivers and canals along which drifted fleets of graceful junks bearing porcelain, jade, silks, and delicately scented teas; a land of small, neat, peace-loving people directed by mandarins chosen for the excellence of their verse and presided over by a wise and virtuous philosopher-king. This was how Europe used to view Cathay.

A closer look changed Faivre's opinion, however. At Macao, where he passed eighteen months preparing for his inland station, he heard stories of how cowardly, idle, dirty, and immodest the Chinese were; how they fished naked, allowed corpses to lie in the streets, and in their temples smeared the blood of freshly killed domestic animals upon the eyes, nose, and mouth of monstrous great-bellied stone Buddhas. Walking one day on an island in the gulf, he met a woman who actually tried to sell him her baby! These people, he was told, liked to imagine *they* were the civilized ones. Looking north from one of Macao's hills, it seemed to Faivre that it was *he* who stood at "the outer limit of civilization . . . face to face with barbarism."[7]

What had happened that the Chinese did less and less with those mechanical arts in which they had once led the world? Why had their literature dried up, their moral fibre loosened; why had a stinking rottenness spread through every nook and cranny of their public life? The answer must be that they had taken, at some point, a wrong turning—or rather, had failed to take a right one. They must have become what they had become because they were pagan. Nothing now could save this "body without a soul," this "giant's carcass," Faivre decided, save immersion "in those Baptismal waters from which peoples, like individuals, emerge regenerated."[8] China must undergo a complete rebirth in Christ.

That was exactly what the Protestant missionaries thought.

They and the Catholics were not on this account drawn into partnership. Catholic missionaries were alternately amused and disgusted by Protestant reliance on the printed word. "These Protestants," protested Pupier, one of the directors of the Missions Etrangères seminary at Penang, "simply will not see that Scripture by itself . . . can no more develop true faith and check error than a code of laws without judges can preserve order in the body politic."[9] What happened, after all, to the heaps of literature flung about by Gutzlaff and his fellows? From Bangkok, Malacca, and Penang, from all the places where Catholics watched the process, came the same report. Tracts and Bibles were having no spiritual effect at all; when they were not put to a use one "dare not specify," they served as cigar ends or came back from the bazaars wrapped around candy. "How many houses are there in Singapore alone in which the interior partitions as well as the ceiling are papered with pages from dozens and dozens of Bibles?"[10] As for the Protestant missionaries, they simply turned their backs upon the Catholics. Lazarists and Missions Etrangères men, titular bishops and vicars apostolic, entire communities of Christians with their own churches and priests—there was hardly a mention of them in the pages of the *Repository*. When the Church Missionary Society asked Squire, its newly appointed China agent, whether Romish priests managed to work in the interior of China in any numbers, he replied that this was not the main question. "The main question is, do they preach the gospel, do they distribute the word of God and Christian books, do they even propagate Christianity?"[11] Squire was certain they did not. The deceits they practiced simply to be able to live and move among the Chinese—washing their faces with tea to render the complexion yellow, dressing in thick-soled shoes and robes with long sleeves, eating with chopsticks, wearing false queues—seemed to him all of a piece with the accommodations they were so ready to make in matters of doctrine and ritual. "Teach me the way and lead me in a plain path" was what the true penitent required, and received instead an invitation to adjust slightly his customary rites and ceremonies, to amend a little his old and vicious ways. It was very sad.

But though the Protestants had no use for the Catholics, they looked at China much as the Catholics did, perceiving clearly (behind the size, the numbers, and the abundance of material wealth) her essentially beggarly condition. China was not, of course, savage and uncivilized like the peoples the elder Morrison would have encountered had he gone to Africa with Mungo Park. Over the course of centuries she had climbed to quite surprising heights. But she had done so while all the time remaining ignorant of her Maker, and her alienation from Him had at last begun to exact its price. Risen just so far, China was now on an unmistakably retrograde course. Daily she sickened and was borne backward. The signs of this were observable in the character and behavior of her people.

John Chinaman was industrious. John Chinaman respected his elders. John Chinaman, being largely free from that "sullen notion of honor" that so easily drove Europeans like Innes to violence, would stand and reason with a man (as the elder Morrison once put it) "when an Englishman would knock him down or an Italian stab him."[12] But here John Chinaman's virtues ceased. He was frivolous. He was avaricious. He bullied, stole, and fornicated. Above all he lied—Protestant missionaries did not encounter John Chinaman in his commercial capacity and so did not see him as a Hunter or a Jardine did—continuously, systematically, and on purpose. How contrary he was too, seeing that he mourned in white instead of in black and wrote from top to bottom of the page instead of across it. And how barbarously he lived! He ate dogs and cats; you came across the poor creatures being poked and examined in the markets just like rabbits or fowl. To public charity he seemed an utter stranger. Morrison had noticed how, after the disastrous Canton fire of 1822 when the factories and most of the waterfront went up in flames, suspected incendiaries were beheaded, wretches caught plundering the ruins flogged, but for the homeless (whom one Chinese informant estimated at fifty thousand) nothing at all was arranged, not even a public subscription. As for John Chinaman's religious life, it appeared to consist of theatrical performances, colored-paper images with movable heads and goggle eyes, fireworks, temples, gongs, roast pig, the continual burning of joss sticks—these and the most extravagant idolatry. "Will not like sins produce like punishments?" Morrison had asked.

It might be that God's punishing hand was already discernible in the rapid expansion of the opium traffic and its appearance at new and unexpected places along China's coast. Faivre himself was about to see something of this traffic. The letter in which he laid bare the corrupt condition of the Celestial Empire was written on board a receiving ship off Lintin. (It was on Lintin that he had met the woman with the baby.) The junk that usually carried missionaries having failed to appear, Faivre was preparing to travel by an English vessel instead. She was an opium clipper, just in from Calcutta with chests from the first sale of the year; every day mandarin boats came openly to her to pick up consignments of the forbidden drug. "If others want to do the same," observed Faivre with disgust, "they are forced to pay a levy of a hundred francs a chest to the mandarin."[13] Soon, however, she would sail for Fukien Province and beyond that to Chekiang, where Faivre hoped to land. Thanks to the generosity of the "rich Canton merchant" who owned her, he was to be carried up free. How amiable, how full of delicate attentions, these English gentlemen were!

The receiving ship was Parry's *Hercules,* the merchant Jardine, and the clipper the *Corsaire Rouge*—or *Red Rover.*

9

A Rising Tide

Faivre joined the *Red Rover* off Lintin early one March day and left her in the Chusan Archipelago five weeks later. From Kiangsi much later still he wrote home an immense letter, half of which is devoted to those five weeks.[1] It is a curious fact that from no principal in the trade—certainly not from Harry Wright, the *Red Rover's* master (Clifton had retired to England)—have we anything like so full an account of what a coast run on an opium clipper was like.

Faivre was never obliged to hide below deck as Perboyre and Delamarre had been. He enjoyed the freedom of the ship and was as comfortable aboard her as any of the officers. But Wright pushed his bark as no Chinese master pushed a junk, and in the strong monsoon winds of this time of year that meant misery for a landlubber. A sailor told Faivre that of all the seas there are the China Sea is the worst because, the water being shallow, the waves are steep and take a ship sharply. "Every wave she strikes brings her up short and fairly tears your guts out." Faivre could not remember being as sick on any part of the much longer voyage out from France. His two Chinese couriers were sure they were going to die, and he himself was much relieved when, after eight days of constant beating to windward, sometimes gaining as little as twenty miles between dawn and dusk, once gaining only five, *Red Rover* dropped anchor off an unusually large island and remained there.

The island was Namoa, the "Nan-goa" near which Perboyre and Delamarre had paused, lying on the Kwangtung-Fukien line two hundred miles northeast of Macao. Twelve to fifteen miles long, Namoa boasted a tiny town on a bay defended by forts but was otherwise almost empty of people. Faivre roamed the hilly barren interior. Once he ventured into one of the forts. Fishermen occupied it: the walls were fifteen feet high and correspondingly thick, and there were six guns. These were of such light caliber, however, and so clumsily mounted (if mounted at all, for some did not seem to have any sort of carriage) that they struck one as utterly harmless. From time to time Wright and his officers wandered over the island too, shooting wild fowl. At the anchorage *Red Rover* lay beside four other ships, "three of them English, one American, all loaded with opium."

Almost certainly Wright discharged chests and received silver (he had stopped at Macao to take aboard a shroff), but Faivre does not mention it. By his own admission he did not watch the shooting either, preferring instead to withdraw to a quiet spot, recite his breviary, and pray for the poor fishermen-gunners, not because their guns were useless but because they would die without knowing their Savior. What *did* invariably draw Faivre's attention (or command, later, his pen) were the ship, her course, and the weather encountered. He was astonished when, at the end of five days, Wright insisted on taking the *Red Rover* to sea again though there was (for a change) no wind. The venture nearly ended in disaster. *Red Rover* had oarsmen to spare (she carried a crew of forty-five), so two longboats were put to towing while the bark set every sail she possessed. Suddenly the sky darkened and a squall struck, so swift and furious that Wright had no time to reef but was forced to let everything go to avoid capsizing. One longboat lost her towing line, the other cut and went to the rescue, and it was hours before the two little craft, struggling through heavy seas, rejoined the bark at the Namoa anchorage.

Two days later *Red Rover* finally got away, but bad weather plagued her the rest of the way up the coast. Once she met an offshore wind so persistent and so powerful that, though several miles from shore, the helmsman could hardly see for flying sand. Another time it turned hot, cold, thundered, rained, hailed, dropped to a dead calm, then blew furiously again, all in the space of twenty-four hours. Above Formosa there was a heavy fog. At last she fetched the outer Chusan group and dropped anchor off Puto—the same Puto that Medhurst and Stevens had visited—and there Faivre left her. First, however, Wright gave a small supper for the officers of a neighboring ship. Wild duck was the fare, shot that very morning on Puto by sportsmen of the party; there were popular and patriotic songs until the singers grew hoarse and exhausted; and at last Faivre rose and rendered two little religious canticles so clearly and so sweetly that at their close one of *Red Rover*'s officers sprang to his feet and rushed madly about the cabin shouting his delight. "I was sure he would crack his head against the ceiling," remarks Faivre. "Who will say now that the English are a phlegmatic people!"

A fonder parting it would be hard to imagine. After reading Faivre's long letter we are almost persuaded that to assist French missionaries and enjoy a little rough shooting were Jardine, Matheson and Company's chief concerns. Almost persuaded—not quite—for though Faivre chose to direct his gaze almost anywhere than at the thing Wright was defying wind and weather to pursue, he could not ignore it altogether. "You probably want me to say something," he writes, "about the drug the Chinese pay so much to obtain." There follows a brief, inaccurate description of poppy cultivation—Faivre has the grower incising the *stalk* and attaching cups for all the world like a Vermont farmer tapping sugar maples—and he is on to the damage the drug inflicts. Nothing is more pitiful than a confirmed opium smoker. "Resembling neither the dead nor the living, he seems rather a member of some brutalized and degenerate race apart." Faivre does not reproach Jardine or Wright (though he names them both). It is the Chinese love of gain, it is mandarin rapacity, he blames. Yet this one paragraph, midway in the narrative of that five weeks' voyage, quite demolishes any notion we may have unwittingly begun to entertain that the *Red Rover* and her sisters were coasting China's shores for cottons, Christ, and simple manly pleasures. "They tell me," adds Faivre, "that the sale of this attractive poison will soon reach one hundred million francs a year." It was in fact approaching thirty thousand chests.

To carry this growing volume the agency houses continued to order clippers from Indian shipyards, and when Indian construction lagged bought fast vessels wherever they could find them. Many, like the brig *Ann* and the schooner *Psyche*, had once been slavers. In Boston, Bennet Forbes, a veteran China merchant who had brought the *Lintin* out in 1830, commissioned the clipper brigantine *Rose* and sent her out to work the coast for Russell and Company. From England, Grant, formerly skipper of the *Hercules*, dispatched the onetime slaving brigantine *Kelpie* and the Mediterranean fruit schooner *Hellas*. Grant did more. He ordered from a Thames shipyard a full-rigged clipper ship. She was to be owned jointly by Jardine and his principal Bombay business correspondent, the Parsee Jamsetjee Jeejeebhoy (Jamshedji Jijibhai); she was to reach India early in 1840; and she was to be named after the peacock that adorned Jamsetjee's personal crest—in Hindustani, *mor*.

Not all the opium vessels were clippers. At Bombay country ships like the *Fort William* and *Good Success* and former Indiamen like the *Scaleby Castle* and *Vansittart* regularly loaded Malwa. Since a chest of Malwa weighed only 150 pounds and took up no more space than a footlocker, such vessels were theoretically capable of stowing an immense number: the unusually large 1,400-ton *Earl of Balcarras*, for example, could easily have swallowed 6,000 or 7,000. But because such a cargo, worth at least $2 million (or forty times the value of the ship), would never find insurers and might knock the bottom right out of the market, Malwa generally traveled in company with much larger quantities of raw cotton. Bengal, by contrast, had very little cotton to offer. Most of her drug moved in the newer, smaller clipper ships designed for nothing else.

A typical season went something like this. At eleven o'clock of a Monday morning shortly after Christmas, between 4,000 and 6,000 chests of Patna and Benares would be put up for auction at the Exchange Rooms on Tank Square, in breaks of five or ten, terms a small sum down and three months to pay. A few days later the *Ariel*, the *Sylph*, perhaps the *Water Witch*, would have loaded from the opium warehouses at the edge of the river and be off for Singapore. A short layover there (every winter seagoing junks came down to Singapore to buy the drug and carry it back to China with the first breath of the new monsoon), then up the China Sea they would go, racing to see which should first sight the islands that mask the Gulf of Canton. At Lintin they would discharge into receiving ships, consignees who did not have their own placing their chests with consignees who did. Some, however, would go right on up the coast, for supplies of opium had to be got to Namoa, Chinchew, and points beyond, and the little schooners that ran back and forth were not large or numerous enough to handle all the work. If a clipper turned right around, she could count on passing the Sandheads and regaining Calcutta sometime in March. By then, however, a second flotilla—say the *Cowasjee Family*, the *Rob Roy*, the clipper bark *Sir Edward Ryan*—would be off and racing for China with consignments from the second or February sale. There would be consignments to be moved after the third sale in April, after the fourth sale in May, and even (as the volume grew) after a fifth sometime in June or July.

It was a relentless business. Spectacular runs of three or four hundred miles a day, made under a tremendous press of canvas with decks constantly awash, were things of later years, when full-rigged tea clippers as large as Indiamen sailed the roaring forties and sometimes disappeared there. Opium skippers did not drive their ships so hard, nor were their ships built quite so shrewdly and so single-mindedly for speed. Still they were uncomfortable enough, with very small forecastles because of their lines. Beating to windward, their decks were sure to be smothered in spray.

And as Faivre had discovered, they paid no regard to weather or the time of year; to move opium was their only object, so they suffered more than a little from accidents of the sea. On her maiden voyage a typhoon struck the *Ariel*, dismasted her, and forced her back to Singapore. Running up the China Sea one June, *Water Witch* was similarly caught and saved herself only by cutting away her main and mizzen masts; then turned for Calcutta that November, met a cyclone in the Bay of Bengal, and lost all three. You could buy charts of the local waters prepared by the English hydrographer Horsburgh. They were regularly on sale at the factories at Canton.

But there remained plenty of unmarked rocks and dead lee shores, and it was easy to get off course. Once the *Sylph* ran full on a reef just a few hours east of Singapore and lay there for a week with eight feet of water in her hold before she could be floated. They got her cargo out first, however, eleven hundred chests, and though some of the chests had been entirely under water, so tough were the poppy-petal casings of the opium balls and so relatively imperishable the drug that the whole lot eventually found buyers.

So year after year, more and more opium came to China. Sometimes the quantity reaching the coast leveled off, or even dropped a little. But always it resumed its upward climb, and always the drug remained contraband—foreign mud introduced into the Middle Kingdom in defiance of reason, right relations, and the imperial will. The most generous applications of squeeze could not be expected to disguise indefinitely so offensive a thing.

In the summer of 1836 a Calcutta journalist paid a visit to Cumsingmun. As usual a number of western vessels lay at anchor between the point and the island of Keiou. Among them could be seen the fast crabs and scrambling dragons of the Chinese. Some rested motionless beside receiving ships, loading opium; others approached, "foaming along under sail as if they would dash their stems against the vessel"; still others, their cargoes complete, pulled away for points about the gulf or up the river. Everywhere was bustle and confusion. "For while the depot vessels are supplying the smuggling boats, the clippers and other vessels importing the drug are supplying them; and launches, cutters, and even jolly boats are engaged in the work of transhipment of opium and cotton, which last article is often unloaded here from vessels of comparatively small burden, and sent up in large ships."[2] Our visitor from Calcutta had himself rowed over to one of the receiving ships. "On one side of the deck you see ranges of chests of Patna and Benares; the other strewed with the contents of Malwa, which is not packed in balls like Patna but in loose cakes, every one of which the opium dealer examines, rejecting many chests perhaps before he takes one."* What struck the journalist most forcibly, however, was the quan-

*The cakes were shaped without a mold, and varied in size and weight—the average was perhaps four inches in diameter, two inches thick, and weighed a little over half a pound—so that a chest of Malwa, though slightly smaller than a chest of Patna or Benares, contained not forty cakes but several hundred.

One such cake, fresh and unadulterated (Malwa was notoriously suspect in this regard), possessed beneath its deep chestnut exterior the consistency, says Impey, of good cream cheese. Because it was not encased in petal sheets, merely rolled in poppy trash, there was little, however, to prevent its gradually drying out, until even its insides became "as hard and brittle as coal." How, then, it reached China in a marketable state is a bit of a puzzle. Yet it managed.

tity of silver. Bags of it lay everywhere; the contents of some had been emptied out upon the planking; shroffs moved among the heaps, passing the silver with a clicking noise across their thumbs and weighing it just as one saw them doing in the arched passageways up at the factories. A part of this silver was coin. The rest was *sycee*. "The large *sycee* lumps are like small pigs of lead in form and size; but the brightness of the pure silver, of course, prevents your mistaking one for the other." What our man saw before him was an absolute fortune in precious metal, a fortune repeated on the deck of the next ship and the next and the next. At any given moment literally millions of dollars were tied up in the opium traffic.

Some of this treasure eventually found its way back into the interior to pay for teas, but by now the balance of trade had turned decisively against the Celestial Empire. The *fan kuei* sold a great deal more than they bought; every year more and more silver dollars and *sycee* left the Gulf of Canton for Calcutta, Bombay, and London, never to return. Informed Chinese knew this and knew, too, that given how little silver China mined herself, such an outflow threatened the entire monetary system. While day-to-day business was conducted in copper cash—huge quantities of it—major transactions were always made in silver; taxes, for example, could not be remitted to Peking in any other form. Thus there were always a great many Chinese who needed the precious metal. For centuries they had bought a tael of it (one ounce and a third) for a thousand cash; through most of the eighteenth century, in fact, they had bought a tael for less. Lately, however, the rate had shifted. Salt merchants, buying salt at the government depots for silver and selling it to the general public for cash, found when they came to convert their cash back into silver that it took a full thousand of the one to purchase one tael of the other—after a while that it took more than a thousand. Naturally they grumbled loudly. Much more cautiously but more ominously, China's taxpaying heads of households grumbled too. The Tao-kuang emperor already had plenty of domestic worries. Floods, famines, and insurrections so marked his reign that it seemed to the *Repository* that not a year passed without a major calamity somewhere. Now the emperor faced a deepening money crisis as well. By the middle 1830s the relentless outflow of silver, and its rising price in terms of copper cash, had driven his principal civil servants to distraction; and to a man they blamed the crisis on opium.

They blamed opium for other things too: for brigandage, for corrupting the army and the civil service, for ruining increasing numbers of ordinary Chinese. No systematic census of users was attempted or was, of course, possible. No one knew exactly how many people smoked or precisely what smoking was doing to them. By the early 1830s, however, a number of serious investigations of drug use had been made, at least one of them inside the imperial household itself. The results were terrifying. Soldiers indulged in the drug and, in the provincial insurrections that tormented the empire, were sometimes defeated because of it. (When troops from certain coastal garrisons were sent against rebels in the area where Kwangtung, Kwangsi, and Hunan meet, a proportion of regular smokers among them simply refused to fight at all.) Among governors-general, governors, and their immediate subordinates, it was estimated, those who did not smoke were fewer than those who did. The habit grew rarer as one descended the ranks. In the countryside the poor as yet hardly touched the stuff. But in town coolies, chair bearers, and boatmen were beginning to discover that opium made life more bearable. They found it no great matter to obtain a supply.

Chinese brokerage houses bought the raw drug from the receiving ships in the Gulf of Canton and sent it overland into Kwangsi, Kweichow, and Hunan. Agents of these houses, men with names like Affoon and Tom the Birdman, traveled up the coast on the vessels dispatched by Jardine, the Rustomjees, Dent, and others and at the various opium stations put chests ashore for Fukien, Chekiang, and the immediate interior. Junks rendez-voused with them or else came all the way down to Canton to load; these junks carried the drug to places the *fan kuei* did not as yet dare approach; so opium flowed up the Yangtze, penetrated Shantung, and could be found as far north as the Peiho. At Canton, meanwhile, the apparatus for smoking—pipe, lamp, iron stillets, and scraper—was hawked openly about the streets. (The lamp was of glass and burned oil. One stillet, long and thick, was used to clean the inside of the pipe; the others were for taking up the opium and heating it. The scraper was for removing the deposits that formed on the bowl.) As more and more people took to the drug, its effect became a popular subject not simply for the moralist but for the artist as well.

From a shop in New China Street, for example, you could buy a set of rice paintings depicting the six stages in an addict's life. In the first he appears in the bosom of his family, young, vigorous, an elegant foreign clock on the table beside him, a chest full of silver nearby. In the second he reclines upon a sofa, opium pipe in hand, attended by courtesans. The third finds him on an ordinary couch; the drug has already cost him wealth and appetite; "emaciated, shoulders high, teeth naked, face black"—the *Repository* translates the captions but does not reproduce the paintings[3]— he dozes from morning to night, the treasure chest empty beside him. In the fourth he sits upon a ragged mattress, "his face half awry, breathing with great difficulty," while his wife angrily dashes his apparatus for smoking upon the floor. In the fifth he is reduced to buying the scrapings from other smokers' pipes. And in the last he is seated upon a bamboo chair "continually swallowing the faeces of the drug, so foul that tea is required to wash them down his throat. His wife and child are seated near him with skeins of silk stretched on bamboo reels, from which they are winding it off into balls, thus earning a mere pittance for his and their own support, and dragging out from day to day a miserable existence."

Perhaps Sunqua, the artist, was imitating Hogarth. At Canton there was an entire school of Chinese painters who copied the West. Nevertheless the degrading effects of opium were real—and plain for all to see. Faivre observed them, as we have noted. A fellow Lazarist, François Danicourt, observed them too. Danicourt taught seminarians at St. Joseph's, Macao, and continuous residence in that predominantly Chinese town had given him a firsthand acquaintance with opium use. "You can easily recognize a smoker from the paleness of his skin and the emaciation of his frame," he wrote a Sister in his native France.[4] "Once they have got the habit they cannot rid themselves of it, and every day they have to smoke as often as they smoked before; because if they don't have a pipe at the usual hour their eyes begin to run, their mouths fill with saliva, and eventually they faint dead away." Year by year there were more of these "walking skeletons" about. Indeed, to Danicourt it seemed that opium might be becoming more truly China's sorrow than ever the Yellow River could be.

A number of high Chinese civil servants saw things the same way. About a year and a half after the Napier fizzle they began casting about for a remedy.

Some suggested making opium legal. Smoking, they reasoned, is widespread; the drug traffic is already in the hands of criminal elements who do not shrink from blackmail and extortion. (The writer of this particular memorial had recently served as a judge at Canton and knew what he was talking about.) Simply to prohibit opium is therefore quite useless. If, however, it is admitted as a medicine, subject to duty, and with the stipulation that it be purchased only with teas, the silver drain will immediately stop. Of course scholars, soldiers, and yamen attendants must give up the pipe, but others who continue smoking, being idle and frivolous, need not be accounted society's loss.

The memorial in question reaching Peking in May 1836. The Taokuang emperor studied it carefully—unlike William IV, his English counterpart, he saw and studied everything. In June he referred the memorial to Governor-General Teng at Canton. At once the English knew that legalization was in the air, for what the Peking gazettes did not tell them, or the newssheets based thereon (and printed right at Canton from wax blocks), the hong merchants very quickly did.

They were not particularly surprised. As Elliot explained to Palmerston (he was not yet chief superintendent, but this did not prevent a vigorous correspondence), it was a confusion of terms to call the opium traffic smuggling. It was formally prohibited, of course, but no part of China's external trade had the more active support of the local mandarins, it bringing them revenue—a thing Elliot entirely understood. At Penang, Malacca, and Singapore the opium farm (or sale to the highest bidder of the right to resell the drug at retail) had for years been the largest single source of local government revenue, exceeding even that produced by the farm of native liquor. If the mandarins wished to substitute a system like this for the prevailing practice of nominal prohibition and actual squeeze, Elliot could only applaud. For the prevailing practice simply encouraged smugglers to greater and greater boldness, and that, in turn, increased the probability of violent clashes like the one on Keiou Island three years before.

It was Elliot's opinion, too, that making opium legal would draw it to Whampoa. For this Jardine, to be truthful, was something less than enthusiastic. The rights and wrongs of the drug did not much excite him—his own comprador smoked constantly, though the fellow was afraid of its making him black in the face—but from a purely business point of view the change was unattractive. Up the coast Jardine had the jump on competitors. Making opium legal and bringing it back to the river could hardly advantage the house.

Jardine need not have worried. Though the hong merchants were enthusiastic for legalization and Teng was cautiously disposed that way, at Peking memorials in favor quickly encountered a more powerful current against. These argued that to barter teas for the drug would never work because the *fan kuei* already sold more of the one than they bought of the other (which was true); that it would prove impossible to limit smoking to ne'er-do-wells (which was probable); that lifting a prohibition just because it was not working was immoral anyhow. "Opium is nothing else but a flowing poison; that it leads to extravagant expenditure is a small evil, but as it utterly ruins the minds and morals of the people, it is a dreadful calamity."[5] One of the memorials accused nine foreign merchants of selling the vile stuff right in Canton.

The emperor listened. In September 1836 he ordered Teng to investigate the allegation and move against the drug. Teng had no confidence that opium smoking could be stopped. He was said to have remarked to an associate that to ban it would be like prohibiting tea. Nevertheless he turned without hesitation upon the hong merchants, brushed aside their efforts to pretend that smuggling outside the river was beyond their ken, and towards the end of November served them with a number of emphatic public notices. One admonished them not to feed the lascivious appetites of the *fan kuei* with Chinese women or boys. (This particular warning was posted every autumn, and made the foreigners furious. To be denied the company of your wife was bad enough; to be accused of searching out prostitutes was worse; to have it insinuated that you resorted to buggery was unspeakable.) The others were directed at the opium trade. No foreign vessels were to anchor at Cumsingmun or Lintin. Opium brokers, proprietors of opium dens, and sailors of the coastal preventive service conniving in the vile traffic were to be arrested and punished. Nine named foreign merchants—Dent, Innes, Jardine, Turner, one other Englishman, one American, and three Parsees—were given two weeks to pack and get out of Canton. Peking, it seemed, meant business.

Nothing happened to the nine, it is true. "At a distance all this fulmination may look terrific," observed Bridgman; close up it was just "a shower of rockets in a mild summer's evening."[6] Two of the nine had already left China. Iron-headed Old Rat, as the Chinese called Jardine—because once, standing at the Petition Gate, he had borne without flinching a terrific blow on the head—sent his nephew Andrew down to Macao in place of himself. The others pleaded press of business, obtained extensions, and in the end never left the factories at all.

This did not mean, however, that the opium traffic went ahead untouched. It had always been susceptible to certain prescribed punishments, and now these began to be administered. A linguist, caught smuggling *sycee*, was marched around the factories wearing the cangue, a sort of wooden door with a hole through the middle which Chinese justice fastened upon a man's neck in the manner of portable stocks. Other arrests were made, opium dens raided, and after a time Teng was able to render an impressive public accounting: so many smugglers and brokers apprehended, so many cakes seized, all offenders tried and sentenced—and the opium destroyed by burning. Of course hardly a foreigner believed this last. More likely the authorities were simply reselling the stuff. But no one doubted the strangling of a broker just outside the St. Antonio Gate at Macao. Several mandarins escorted by police runners and soldiers brought the poor wretch there late one afternoon in April. Tumbled out of his bamboo cage, filthy, emaciated, stupefied from fright or the effects of imprisonment, the fellow was lashed to a six-foot wooden cross. A cord was thrown about his neck, slipped through a hole in the upright, and looped over a stick. Three cannon boomed; the executioner took a few twists of the stick; the official procession moved away. For two days the corpse remained hanging. It was a warning to all, and not least to the *fan kuei*.

They were beginning to feel Peking's determination in other ways. Early in 1837 the authorities built a battery overlooking Cumsingmun so that the receiving ships dared not anchor there. Things grew so hot for the fast crabs and scrambling dragons that at one point their owners deliberately destroyed them. New ones were soon bought or built—the local mandarins did not want the traffic to shift entirely to the coast where others would profit from it—but the new ones ran under a heavy charge. By late July it was costing native brokers $75 a chest to get opium from the receiving ships into the river. Only $20 of this went to the boat people, Jardine estimated. The mandarins pocketed the rest.

In August the pressure grew worse still. Jardine sent his receiving ships out to the very edge of the gulf, hoping that in their absence the governor-general (whose views on the impracticality of suppressing the traffic were well known) might report to Peking that they had been driven away, but no relief came. Late in the month there was a second burning of smug boats, and after that very little opium could be landed anywhere in the vicinity of Canton. Prices declined just the same—by year's end Malwa had fallen from $600 to less than $500—because so many Chinese were being driven off the drug that demand did not meet even a reduced supply.

Yet not for a moment did Jardine, Dent, or any of the others contemplate getting out of the traffic. Opium was the only ready money article sold in China. Nothing else could be counted on to produce the dollars needed for buying teas. And even the tea trade was not what it was supposed to be. Merchants who turned their backs on the drug faced the prospect of having no business at all! The fact was that, against all expectation, the China trade did not flourish.

It was not for want of trying.

With the abolition of the Company's monopoly a little army of private merchants had descended on Canton. Two years after the Napier fizzle there were more than 150 Englishmen doing business at the factories. The newcomers imagined that the entire cotton crop of the United States would soon be passing, by way of Manchester, onto the backs of the Chinese. They imagined that tea, since it was no longer a privileged article, would immediately be drunk in double quantity by every loyal subject of His Majesty. With great energy they set about fulfilling these prophecies. They pushed cotton yarn and piece goods, at first smuggling them from the outer anchorages, later discovering that the hong merchants would take them openly at the duty price. They bought teas at such a rate that the quantity moving from Canton to London leaped from thirty million pounds a year to fifty. But the Chinese tea men naturally allowed their prices to rise, while in England (loyal subjects declining to double their consumption) prices steadily declined. By 1837 a boom in the leaf had turned to bust, the volume entering England was back to thirty million pounds, and several of the newer Canton agency houses had gone to the wall.

Cottons did almost as badly. English merchants discovered that the American product undercut their own. They discovered, too, that such piece goods as they did sell were often taken up, for the ready money that could be got for them, at a loss. In 1836 a hong merchant named Hengtai went bankrupt on this account, owing Jardine's $1,600,000 and other private English less. Hong failures were nothing new. Getting one's money back took time, however. Jardine had wanted to retire to England; now he would have to put off going; besides, the failure of one hong always shook the others, which was bad for trade—and by the autumn of 1837 trade was in a bad way. Only twenty-five vessels lay at Whampoa instead of the usual hundred. Some private merchants wondered whether getting rid of the Company had brought any advantages at all.

In England, however, hardly anyone shared their doubts. Confidence in the immense promise of English manufactures mounted higher than ever. It appeared likely that the export of cotton piece goods would rise from half a billion yards at the beginning of the decade to one billion by the end of it. In this expansion the China market was certain to share—were not the private merchants in that quarter a determined and enterprising lot? Though Jardine had not been home for twenty years, at Liverpool they were naming a vessel for him. Matheson, when he landed to commission the monument to Napier, was equally well received. Indeed, so infectious was the enthusiasm he met with in the outports that, before he sailed for Canton again, he sat down and wrote a little book about the China trade, its state and prospects. "It has pleased Providence," he began, "to assign to the Chinese—a people characterized by a marvelous degree of imbecility, avarice, conceit, and obstinacy—the possession of a vast portion of the most desirable parts of the earth, and a population estimated as amounting to nearly a third of the whole human race." Yet from these riches foreigners were deliberately excluded. It was unconscionable; had not Vattel, the celebrated Swiss jurist, demonstrated for all to see that nations are obligated by the laws of nature to mingle openly and freely with each other! Matheson advised His Majesty's government to intervene in China, using force if necessary, and to pay no attention to Peking's blusterings. With them it was always "a flourish of trumpets, and enter Tom Thumb."[7] His message found ready takers at Canton, and when the official campaign against opium grew hot and heavy, the factory community showed no inclination at all to lie low. Quite the contrary.

There were exceptions, of course. From Zion's Corner, Charles King urged his fellow Americans to get out of the drug traffic—Olyphant and Company did not handle opium, though Jardine was pretty sure they smuggled in everything else—and early in 1837 announced a prize of $400 for the best essay on the dirty business. So few were the entries, however, that when the deadline arrived the award had to be put off, then put off again. In the *Repository*, meanwhile, the whole question of opium and its effects was thoroughly aired. One contributor condemned the drug without reservation. Nonsense! protested Innes (though, of course, he did not actually try a pipe—one gathers that none of the resident merchants ever did). Opium is no more harmful than strong drink. Are we to lay waste the barley fields of Norfolk and the vineyards of the Rhine simply because a few fools grow sodden on gin and wine? Reverse the analogy, rejoined Keating. Imagine junks lying regularly in St. George's Channel; imagine them making side trips to the Severn or Southampton Water to peddle "so harmless a thing as arsenic or corrosive sublimate." What would Englishmen think then? Keating added a comment that struck to the very heart of the opium traffic, carried on as it was so shamelessly on such a very large scale. "Sales are made in thousands of dollars' worth. The amount is gentlemanly. Single balls would be low."[8]

Even as the debate proceeded, however, events overtook it and left it behind. For by the beginning of 1838 it was clear that Dent, Innes, Jardine, all of them except King (Olyphant had gone home), were pushing opium more obstinately and with greater daring than it had ever been pushed before.

Things being so sticky in the Canton area, agency houses with chests to unload turned more and more to the coast. Russell and Company sent the *Rose* there and were looking for a schooner. Dent had the bark *Lord Amherst* (Thomas Rees) and two schooners, the *Aurelia* and the *Psyche*. The Parsees worked several vessels. But Jardine's was by far the largest single fleet. John Rees, Thomas's elder brother, lay off Chinchew in the *Austin*; Jauncey commanded the *Governor Findlay* at Namoa; the *Colonel Young* covered a variety of stations; and three schooners, the *Harriet*, *Omega*, and *Jardine*, did courier service and sold chests besides. Sales were arranged at the house's offices in the Creek factory. Skippers loaded in the gulf, sailed up to the designated point of delivery, and made contact by—for example—flying a red flag at the mainmast while watching for a junk with red at the fore; they then compared delivery orders (a duplicate usually came overland), turned over the chests, and received the silver due. At Namoa the activity was so intense and regular that a pleasant little ritual developed to adorn it. William Hunter describes it: the new arrival dropping anchor close by a little piece of land called Brig Island; a suitable wait; then up comes a mandarin seated on an armchair in a sort of open scow; he climbs gravely aboard, walks to a clear space on the deck, draws from his boot an edict ordering the barbarian vessel away, reads it, and steps into the cabin for a glass of wine and a cheroot; after which merchant junks stand out from the mainland to receive the new arrival's chests. This was the way the coast opium business went, with rarely any dangers other than those of wind and weather—though occasionally it was otherwise, as two French missionaries discovered when they tried to land where Faivre had landed.

Faivre had made it all right. He had left the *Red Rover* on Palm Sunday, marked time for a couple of days while his couriers made arrangements, then passed by a succession of hired junks to Ningpo and beyond. His success had persuaded the French *procures* that they should move missionaries up the coast in no other way. When, therefore, a Lazarist newcomer named Guillet and a Missions Etrangères recruit named Callery had finished their Macao apprenticeship—when they could dress like a Chinese, eat like a Chinese, and even speak a little like a Chinese—Torrette and Legrégeois arranged to have them travel aboard Jardine Matheson's *Lady Grant*, just in from Bombay.

The *Lady Grant* sold a few house chests without incident off Namoa; she sold a few more at Chimmo, where the two Frenchmen went ashore for a walk; but when she reached the Chekiang coast and approached her appointed rendezvous, six war junks appeared. They hung about and hung about until Jeffrey, her master, thought it prudent to take her off to the eastward. When he came back there were the war junks again, more attentive than ever. One night they crowded in so close that Jeffrey got jumpy and sent a charge of grapeshot flying in the general direction of the nearest. The junks simply doused their lights. Next morning there were fifteen of them. One larger than the rest turned out to be an admiral's flagship. They made no move to attack; indeed, visits were exchanged, and Callery (who knew a bit of Mandarin and served as interpreter) discovered that a Chinese man-of-war had no bulwarks and no gun ports and that her deck was almost impassible for the mats, cordage, firewood, and kitchen gear that littered it. It gradually dawned on everybody, moreover, that the squadron had been collected at this particular spot not to watch for opium trafficking but to catch pirates. Just the same its presence was extremely inhibiting. No vessel dared approach the *fan kuei*, not even bumboats, so Jeffrey sold no opium at all, and so intense was the alarm on land that the couriers who had come up with Callery and Guillet refused to lead them ashore. The two missionaries had to go back to Macao aboard the brig.

But checks like this were rare. And should a Jeffrey feel a bit nervous when surrounded in the dark off a strange shore by vessels he could neither identify nor count, his nervousness was not likely to last. Once, a couple of years before, as the *Lady Grant* lay becalmed at night off the Sembilans in the Straits of Malacca with four hundred chests in her hold, five proas moving at great speed had come down upon her from dead ahead where her guns could not bear; and Jeffrey had kept his head, had coolly let go a kedge, pulled the brig broadside with a spring line, and met the little outrigger craft with such a blast of grape and canister that they sheered away disabled. Malay pirates were as fearsome as any in the world, and alarms like this common over the whole fifteen hundred miles from Penang to Palawan; if the *Lady Grant* could survive these waters, she did not have much to fear from the pirates up China's coast. As for war junks of the several provincial flotillas, Keating had taken their measure pretty convincingly in a piece Bridgman put into the *Repository*. "Large unwieldy-looking masses of timber," he had written, "with mat sails, wooden anchors, rattan cables, a considerable sheer, flat upright stems, no stern posts, enormously high sterns ornamented with gold and paintings, considerably weakened too by a large hole in which the monstrous rudder can be hoisted up and housed in bad weather; immense quarter galleries, and look-out houses on the deck; generally drawing but little water, flat floored, painted red and black, with large goggle eyes in the bows. . . ."[9] War junks ran generally under three hundred tons burden, only a third the tonnage of many oceangoing merchant junks and not a fifth that of an English frigate. They were armed, in the waist only, with two, four, or at the most six guns lashed clumsily to heavy blocks of wood. They holed easily; once, off Chinchew, when Dent's *Lord Amherst* chose to send a few warning rounds over the heads of several anchored rather too close, a gun happened to hang fire until the ship rolled, and she accidentally put a ball smack into one and saw her fill and go down. It was impossible to respect such vessels.

So as 1837 gave way to 1838 and Peking's campaign entered its second year, not edicts or squeeze, not pirates or war junks (or conscience either, it might be added) could deter or more than temporarily interrupt the flow of foreign mud.

By now the bigger agency houses were working the west coast as well as the east. More ominous, in the Gulf of Canton foreigners were beginning to put opium ashore right in their own passage boats. With the fast crabs and scrambling dragons burned or scared away, with the difficulty of getting the drug up to Canton so great that servants secreted the stuff in wine bottles and pickle jars, it was the most natural thing in the world to look to the small, decked sailing vessels that normally carried passengers between Macao, the outer anchorages, and the factories—you found their schedules advertised in the *Register* and *Press* alongside bottled ale and bills on London at six months' sight. The police were on to them quickly, to be sure. In January they searched the *Swift* as she lay near the factories, took three chests out of her, and compelled Just, her owner, to pay several thousand dollars in hush money. In February they seized twenty-three chests from the *Alpha*. The practice continued just the same. There was money in it, so much money that sloops and schooners grew hard to find, and the Chamber of Commerce had to drop plans for a postal service between Macao and the factories—it could not engage any boats. By June of 1838 the number of European craft putting opium ashore about the gulf and up the river had risen to somewhere between thirty and forty.

This was asking for trouble, and no one appreciated it better than Captain Elliot. Receiving ships and opium clippers were well able to take care of themselves. Passage boats were not. They mounted popguns; their crews were usually a single European and half a dozen lascars; they positively invited attack. Sooner or later there was going to be a serious incident, Englishmen killed or Englishmen kidnapped, and the legitimate trade interrupted or shut down. Then Her Majesty's government (Victoria was sovereign now) would be obliged to intervene. Elliot hoped that the request he had made some time ago for a visit from ships on the East Indian Station would soon be honored.

Summer came, hotter and muggier than usual. A floating hospital for seamen at Whampoa had to be broken up because the hong merchants were sure it stored opium. At Macao, Lay felt sick and discouraged. For almost a year, ever since the abortive voyage of the *Himmaleh*, he had been trying to get Jardine Matheson to take him, his Bibles, and his tracts up the coast in one of its vessels. In February he had at last been invited aboard one. She carried opium, however, and he had declined—he was no Gutzlaff, he would not deceive Bible House. In the spring another vessel had prepared for Formosa, and this time he had swallowed his scruples, only to withdraw again at the very last minute. What does he expect? inquired Jardine sharply. Are we to excuse our vessels from the drug traffic just for him? Though the house had recently added a brig and a schooner and was expecting the *Hellas* from England, it felt pressed for tonnage. Jardine kept his namesake up the coast though she was leaking badly and wished he had not sent the *Lady Hayes* off to New South Wales with teas.

In July the 74-gun ship-of-the-line *Wellesley*, accompanied by the corvette *Larne* and the brig *Algerine*, passed through Macao Roads and anchored at Tongku. The *Wellesley* carried Rear Admiral Sir Frederick Maitland, commanding the East Indian Station; Palmerston had at last honored Elliot's suggestion and sent a warship to the coast. Her appearance produced a crisis of sorts, for the Chinese insisted on knowing what brought her. When Elliot would not tell them—the paper conveying the governor-general's inquiry bore the superscription for "command," and Elliot refused to open it—they stopped the passage boat *Bombay* as she was entering the river and searched her. It was not opium they expected to find, it was Maitland or one of his officers; the Napier affair was still much on their minds, and they did not propose to have a new barbarian headman slipping up to the factories undetected. But Elliot cried outrage, Maitland was persuaded to see it the same way, and the squadron moved up to the Bogue. There, for forty-eight hours, the big two-decker, the corvette, and the brig lay over against the three war junks of Admiral Kuan, the *Wellesley*'s loom and bulk—from stem to stern she measured almost two hundred feet, with thirty feet of freeboard, towering masts, and a bowsprit immensely extended by jibbooms—quite overwhelming the clumsy halfmoons of the Chinese. Then Kuan made what the English took to be apologetic noises, and Sir Frederick dropped back to Tongku. His instructions were simply to show the flag; when the monsoon turned (seventy-fours were not clippers and waited where possible for favoring winds), he would sail away; in October it turned and he sailed, though not until he had presented Kuan with several bottles of sweet South African wine. His visit produced only one lasting consequence. When he departed he left the *Larne* behind, with instructions to take up station on the coast.

But Blake, the *Larne*'s master, did not pay any attention to the opium traffic. He did not nose his way about Namoa or lie off Lintin, and Elliot did not ask him to. Palmerston had made it plain, as much by what he did not say as by what he did, that the ground rules Napier had operated under still held. Officers of the crown were neither to protect nor to discipline private merchants dealing in the drug. Elliot was of two minds about those private merchants anyway. What a pity it was that their contraband produced the ready money needed for the purchase of teas! "It cannot be good that the conduct of a great trade should be dependent upon the steady continuance of a vast prohibited traffic in an article of vicious luxury, high in price, and liable to frequent and prodigious fluctuation."[10] Just the same the chief superintendent did not know what legitimate commodity could possibly take opium's place.

So the traffic rolled on. As regular as clockwork the clippers and the country ships sailed in, unloaded their chests into receiving ships or coasters, and sailed away again. Neither Elliot's misgivings nor Peking's anathemas could easily interrupt such a relentless rhythm as this.

King made one last try. He announced a public meeting at which the foreign community was to rediscover its conscience and take a pledge to drop the drug. No one came, and when he circulated a paper on the subject, the only signature he collected was his own. The other merchants were one with Slade of the *Register* and Moller of the *Press*, who went right on reporting (for the benefit of subscribers) when consignments of the drug arrived, to whom consigned, and the prices current. Business, after all, was business. Besides, no one could forget that the Bengal opium reaching China was the provision (as it was called) of 1836/37. It was almost *two years* since those poppies had been sown, almost one since the cakes had traveled in dammared chests down to Calcutta; at this very moment a fresh provision lay in the airing sheds at Patna and Ghazipur, ready to enter the pipeline. It was a long pipeline. It was a full pipeline. China was easily its principal outlet. It would have been the height of irresponsibility had consignees at the China end failed to make every effort to sell what they were sent.

Yet selling, in this summer of 1838, was becoming decidedly difficult. Even Jardine's felt the strain. For though the foreigners could not know it, the situation was almost certain to grow worse shortly, for Peking was about to take a decisive step.

10

Peking in Earnest

For some time the wind in the imperial capital had been blowing more strongly in the direction of suppressing opium outright—not simply the traffic in it, but its use. In June a mandarin of high rank had formally recommended that real and effective pressure be brought to bear upon the people who smoked. As things stood they were punished, if they were punished at all, by being flogged or made to wear the cangue. These punishments, however, were often easier to bear than the want of opium itself. Would it not be wiser to offer the smoker a certain period of time in which to shake off his habit, and if he failed serve him with the garrote or the axe? This recommendation was put to the Tao-Kuang emperor; the emperor was interested and asked governors-general and others to comment; all through the summer of 1838 the answering memorials flowed in. Though a majority of these memorials stuck to the traditional view that foreign mud could and should be intercepted before ever it reached the consumer—by driving the receiving ships away or by withholding silks, teas, and rhubarb root until they voluntarily withdrew—eight out of the twenty-eight took the new line. Among the eight the most persuasive was Lin Tse-hsü's.

Lin Tse-hsü had been governor of the province astride the lower reaches of the Yangtze when Lindsay and Gutzlaff blustered their way up to Shanghai in 1832. By that time he had already earned the sobriquet "Blue Sky," meaning that his reputation bore comparison with the clear and untarnished heavens—and in fact his career had been exceptional. The second son of an aspiring but needy teacher, he had passed out seventh in a field of 237 in the metropolitan examinations for the *chin-shih* degree and has risen steadily thereafter. In 1837 he was made governor-general of Hupeh and Hunan. Teng T'ing-chen, governor-general at Canton and ten years Lin's senior, had reached the same eminence only two years before. On one occasion the emperor told Teng quite frankly that between him and Lin there could be no question as to where the greater talent lay.

Lin's qualities showed themselves in the thoroughness with which he examined the whole question of opium, how it entered China, how it was distributed and consumed, and what effect it had; in the care and detail he lavished, too, upon the apparatus for smoking, who made the porcelain bowls and the wood or bamboo stems for the pipes, which pipes the smokers valued most and why. He even reviewed the drugs helpful to an addict trying to withdraw. But the most impressive thing about his memorial was its recommendations. They amounted to a comprehensive assault upon the Chinese end of the opium traffic, an assault based not on exhortation and anathema but on real consequences for the violator. The emperor paid close attention, marking with vermilion the parts that particularly pleased him. In October he ordered a joint session of the Grand Secretariat and the Grand Council for the purpose of framing a campaign for the entire empire. At the end of the month Lin was summoned to Peking for the first of nineteen personal interviews. The emperor was in earnest; he was said to have demanded, weeping, how he could face the shades of his ancestors while his people ruined themselves with the vile drug; now he closeted himself with a civil servant who was in earnest too.

At Canton, meanwhile, tension mounted. Peter Parker estimated that in and about the city tens of thousands used the drug. With such a market to cater to, traffickers in opium gave no sign of drawing back; Squire, the Church Missionary Society man, was much struck by the fierce determination with which the business was conducted. "Even those deeply engaged in it stand amazed at the rapidly increasing demand, the intense eagerness with which it is sought, the risk and adventure willingly incurred by the native dealer to escape the punishment to which a breach of the law lays him open, and the bribery and corruption by which he defeats the ends of justice."[1] Perhaps in the interior of Kwangtung Province the dealer did, indeed, defeat it; for Peschaud, the French Lazarist, making his way toward his station in Kiangsi, reports that though several times taken for an opium peddler, nothing at all happened to him. About the delta and the gulf, however, Chinese were being arrested for opium offenses almost every day. Once a group of more than twenty were brought into Canton in chains. At Whampoa villagers fought a pitched battle with soldiers sent to confiscate the drug, with the consequence that for several weeks Jardine could not land a chest anywhere in the river. Russell and Company was expecting a new schooner but they entertained no great hopes for the coastal trade; even at $350 a chest, Turkey opium refused to move. "It appears to be going wholly out of use. Malwa has fallen to about $600 and Patna to $590."[2]

In October matters improved slightly. "A little more doing on the river," wrote Jardine,[3] hoping to get rid of the unsold balance of the fifteen hundred chests that Jamsetjee Jeejeebhoy had sent him in the spring. The governor-general was about to visit his adjacent province (governors-general were entrusted with two), leaving behind him a governor thought to be a good deal more complaisant on opium matters, and Jardine meant to seize this opportunity to force sales all he could. In November, however, rumors of Peking's hard new line abounded, and prices declined still further. Jardine sold cotton off the *Fort William* and the *Earl of Balcarras* and waited for the tea market to open. He kept more vessels than ever at the opium business, having added one schooner on the west coast and two on the east. He went right ahead with plans for the clipper ship *Peacock* (or *Mor*) to be built in England for Jamsetjee and himself. Yet even he was anxious, sending word to his coasters to make sales at the going prices whatever they might be—below $500 even! For with next season's supplies only six to eight weeks away, "sell you must, it is our only chance of saving ourselves from a most serious loss."[4]

It was time for the sailing buffs of the foreign community to hold their annual autumn race in the Macao Passage. Hunter's *Ferret* came in first with Bennet Forbes at the helm, and that evening bumpers were raised to next year's meet—no one suspecting that it would never be held. One of Peter Parker's patients, a hong merchant named Tingqua who had come to the Hog Lane hospital with a badly diseased foot but then had left because he was impatient with the treatment, was reported dead of his complaint, the ginseng his native practitioner prescribed having proved useless against gangrene. The ranks of the Protestant Mission swelled with the arrival of a young Cambridge University divinity student named Stanton, brought out by the English merchant Turner to be tutor to his children. In Macao Roads lay another new arrival, the French heavy frigate *Artemise,* sent (Legrégeois was told) to help the French Catholic mission. Her captain visited both *procures* and gave the priests a shipboard dinner to which were invited a number of English and Americans; indeed, it was none other than Captain Elliot who, at the proper moment, proposed the toast to all French missionaries in China. Danicourt, the French Lazarist, tells us about this (characteristically the *Repository* does not mention it at all), adding that he later took his Chinese seminarians through the *Artemise*'s gun decks and that they were much impressed—as of course they should have been. "A single frigate could sink their entire fleet."[5] Whether the frigate (let alone the toast) could actually be of assistance Legrégeois rather doubted, unless just possibly it served to humble the Portuguese a little. As usual he and Torrette were much occupied with the problem of getting their men into the interior. The last thing they wanted was a confrontation with the Chinese.

It was the last thing Perboyre, deep in the interior, wanted either. At the beginning of the year he had moved from Honan Province down to a mountainous corner of Hupeh on the slopes of the Tapa Shan. There he led a life not unlike that of a country curé. "As for my church, you must imagine an earth floor, mud walls, a roof of straw, and for an altar a plain table with above it a hanging like the canopy of a bed. This is our sanctuary; it will hardly stand comparison with an ordinary barn at home." His flock, in number a couple of thousand, was poor and starving, yet on Sundays and saints' days the communicants among them came to mass so eagerly "you would think yourself in the middle of the thirsting crowd that followed Jesus Christ into the desert."[6] Ministering to them, Perboyre felt ennobled by their constancy and overwhelmed with pity for their miserable condition. But if he was to be called to some extraordinary sacrifice on their behalf, it would not be yet.

Away to the south the weather became cold and gloomy. Governor-General Teng returned to Canton. Opium offenders were being picked up now in very large numbers—Jardine was told that the Canton prisons held no fewer than two thousand, three or four of whom died daily for want of their accustomed pipes. "Buy cheap if you buy at all," he warned Jamsetjee in Bombay. "We know similar storms have blown over, and so may this; but appearances are at present unfavorable, probably more so than ever we saw them."[7] Then it was December, and before the month was out the factory community and the local authorities had had their first collision.

It involved, naturally, James Innes.

Innes was by now a thorough old-timer, and time had not dissolved his bumptiousness, nor impaired his talent for getting into trouble with the mandarins. You will remember that on first reaching China thirteen years before, at a time when English private merchants still showed their respect for the Company's legal monopoly by taking out commissions as consuls for Denmark and other minor European powers, Innes had refused to act out the charade. He had openly advertised himself as an interloper, defied the Select Committee, and stayed on. There had been plenty of alarms and skirmishes since, some with the Company, some with fellow merchants (particularly if, like Daniell, they were former Company men), many with the Chinese. No one could forget the affair of the coolie with a chopper, the customs shed, and the ship's signal lights. On another occasion Innes had forced the mandarins at the Petition Gate to accept a certain paper by sending for a bed and a lamp and preparing to spend the night there. Commercially Innes was pretty much of a loner. He worked often with Jardine, Matheson and Company, had in fact helped them pioneer the coastal traffic, and was their neighbor in the Creek factory—he occupied Number 1, they Number 4. But he was never their partner or anyone else's, did not even belong to the Chamber of Commerce, and preferred to do his agency business all by himself. A large part of that business was in opium.

On Monday, 3 December, two coolies were caught unloading raw opium from a boat in front of the Creek factory. Questioned closely, perhaps threatened with torture, they admitted they were bringing the stuff for Innes and named a vessel at Whampoa that the authorities took to be the *Thomas Perkins*. Talbot, an American merchant, was her consignee, and Punhoyqua her security. On Tuesday all eleven hong merchants were summoned before the governor-general. That evening Punhoyqua went down to Whampoa with the cangue about his neck to be publicly exhibited there. Innes and Talbot were given three days in which to leave China—if they procrastinated, the hong merchants from whom they leased their factory houses would be cangued too. The *Thomas Perkins* was to sail at once, and no other vessel was to be worked until she weighed.

For an offense that cannot have been particularly rare, this was swift and decisive action. The hong merchants followed it up by placarding the factories with Innes's name and by threatening—in Innes's own best manner—to burn the Creek factory down if the offender did not leave at once. He, of course, denied everything, doing so in a written statement that he asked Robert Thom, the Jardine Matheson clerk and amateur Sinologist, to translate into Chinese. Thom refused, explaining apologetically to his employers that "though I make no pretensions to having an unusually tender conscience, I cannot bear to serve so rascally a cause."[8] It was an uncommon attitude.★ When Howqua approached Hugh Hamilton Lindsay, chairman of the Chamber of Commerce, Lindsay took the more usual tack, explaining that his chamber could not discipline Innes because Innes was not a member, could not regulate the passage boats because commercial associations lacked that power, could not in fact do anything at all—really, Howqua must have told himself, dealing with these *fan kuei* is like punching into a paper bag!

Talbot, however, was not evasive. Talbot was genuinely upset, for the authorities, in their language difficulties, had fastened upon the wrong vessel. The *Thomas Perkins* carried rice and rice only; she had had no dealings with Innes, who must have gotten the opium from a passage boat or a receiving ship—if Talbot knew the exact source, common sense and a cer-

---

★Thom was an uncommon young man. Only one other Englishman in the merchant community, Samuel Fearon (who translated and interpreted for the Chamber of Commerce), had an equal knowledge of Chinese, and only King was equally determined to promote good feeling between the Chinese and the *fan kuei*.

tain loyalty made him keep silent, and of course Innes was not saying. Talbot petitioned the governor-general to be allowed to stay and the *Perkins* to work, and though Teng (always through the hong merchants) stuck to his original order, he extended Talbot's period of grace from three days to eight—a sign, perhaps, that he was about to take a second look. Before he could do so there was a riot.

Again both Innes and opium were involved. About eleven on the morning of Wednesday, 12 December, foreigners walking in the factory square, which was crowded as usual with beggars, boatmen, sailors up from Whampoa, peddlers, pimps, and peepshow men, noticed something unusual going on. Close in front of the Swedish factory, just beneath the windows of old Peter Snow, the American consul, preparations of some sort were being made. A wooden cross lay on the ground; coolies had unrolled a large tent and were getting ready to raise it; two men, obviously jailers, held a third with a chain about his neck, while nearby stood an officer. By asking questions and putting two and two together the foreigners discovered that a convicted opium dealer named Ho Lao-chin was about to be strangled, publicly, before their very eyes, with the express purpose of advertising their complicity in the pernicious opium traffic.

The prospect made them furious. It was one thing to offer an insult like this outside the St. Antonio Gate at Macao, which foreigners need not visit. It was quite another to arrange one for the factories, particularly when the imminent opening of the tea and silk markets obliged everyone to be present. Hunter led the protesters—Innes, Lindsay, and (a little surprisingly) King were close behind—and as more and more merchants came piling out of the back houses to see what was going on, a sizable group collected before Peter Snow's. Some argued hotly with the Chinese officer. Others seized the cross and began rolling up the tent. In a minute or two the officer would have nothing left to do his awful business with; by signs he indicated his willingness to move to another place. But when the second place turned out to be the water's edge opposite Old China Street, Hunter and the others insisted that tent, cross, prisoner, and all be loaded into boats and carried out of sight. This done—no one much cared if the wretched Ho were put to death somewhere else—the foreigners stood about talking a little before preparing to go back to work.

Meanwhile, however, a great many curious Cantonese had gathered in the square. They did not seem unfriendly; every witness testifies that if anything they appeared to sympathize with the driving away of the executioner and his dreadful apparatus. But there were a great many of them, they pressed very closely about the foreigners, and some of the latter, growing annoyed, cried out to clear the square. Others, to the dismay of cooler heads like Jardine's, began laying about them with sticks. The

Chinese replied by throwing anything that came to hand. Innes and some of the younger men (among them an energetic little American named Gideon Nye) made a rush and momentarily drove the crowd back, but it thickened remarkably, stones and earth clods flew in showers, and suddenly the foreigners were running for the shelter of the factories. It was everyone for himself, wrote Slade (who ran too); "the door of the Imperial hong was choked like the pit-door of a theatre."[9] Nye and Matheson plunged together through Snow's entrance. Others got safely into the Lungshun and the Fungtai, where they barricaded themselves with furniture and casks of coal accumulated against the approaching winter. Hunter and his friends even spread broken bottles up and down the passage leading to their particular house, in case the rioters (who went barefoot) should break in and come their way.

Break in they very nearly did. Shrieking and yelling, climbing the walls to throw brickbats through upper windows (Nye remembers that at every crash of glass old Snow, who suffered from rheumatism, clasped his left arm with his right and groaned, "Oh, my pains!"), using the rails of the factory fences as battering rams, the rioters threatened to storm several of the front houses. About two o'clock someone got word off in a boat to Captain Elliot, who happened to be at Whampoa. But Whampoa was several hours distant, and by three o'clock things looked so bad inside several of the factories that fowling pieces and other weapons were collected and preparations made to break out, if possible, to the river. Still the authorities gave no sign of intervening—the guards stationed about the square had long since disappeared. In desperation Nye and Hunter climbed out onto the roof of Number 4 the Swedish factory, worked their way over the Lungshun and the Fungtai, dropped into Hog Lane, and ran through the suburbs to Howqua's house. That old gentleman seemed unaware of the extent of the disturbance. Nevertheless he sent a runner to the magistrate of the Nanhai district, in which the factories lay, and half an hour later, just as the rioters were at last actually breaking into the Lungshun and bloodshed seemed inevitable, soldiers rushed into the square with staves at the ready. That was sufficient; the rioters turned and fled; in another quarter of an hour the foreigners were out surveying the damage.

It was hard to say how serious the affair had been. No one had been badly injured, and the servants had not melted away as they certainly would have had they smelled real trouble. The whole thing, moreover, had been surprisingly localized. At the height of the noise and fury Peter Parker had been busy removing a right arm—typical instance of advanced neglect, sarcoma of the lower arm nineteen inches in circumference—in his Hog Lane hospital just around the corner. All was quiet, he had later reported, and except that the woman overate and had to be dosed with castor oil, the operation a complete success. Parker did not seem at all rattled.

Just the same, the tension did not subside but continued to mount. Innes took a chop boat down to Macao, meaning to slip back later. Talbot was exonerated. Trade remained closed, however, and the search for opium grew if anything more intense. It was unprecedented, this tenacity in the service of the imperial will, and Jardine was sure Innes's behavior had nothing to do with it. More likely seizures of the drug at the Peiho, close to the Tao-kuang emperor's own person, were to blame. To Jamsetjee he wrote that the campaign against the drug "pervades every province throughout the Empire, a circumstance never before known to have occurred."[10] All that could be done was to lie low and wait for something to come up. Perhaps the Cantonese would revolt!

Captain Elliot looked at things differently. His eye was on the river, on Innes and others scrambling recklessly there for gain. He believed the hong merchants when they told him, with great bitterness, that if opium continued to move openly upon the inner waters, they would be ruined and disgraced. It was no good expecting big houses like Jardine Matheson to do anything about the matter. Big houses were not much involved in the river traffic anyway, they had outlets up the coast that little agents like Innes could not easily afford; besides, Jardine had made it plain he did not intend to play policeman to his fellow countrymen. Lindsay had said the same thing for the Chamber of Commerce.

It was up to Elliot to act. If he did not, if he let things drift on as they were, "the refuse of all the countries in our neighborhood"—adventurers from Manila, Singapore, and God knows where else—would swarm into Canton,[11] and a legitimate commerce conducted in confidence and safety would become a thing of the past.

Accordingly he called his fellow countrymen together and gave them three days to get their small craft out of the river. When the three days were up, he notified Governor-General Teng—through the hong merchants, using the *pin*; it meant, he explained to Palmerston, not "petition" at all but simply "respectful report"—that English boats taken inside the Bogue with opium on board would receive no assistance from him. He even asked to be present in the *Louisa* when they were chased and caught. Otherwise their skippers might elect to stand and fight.

Jardine was disgusted. The chief superintendent and his friends ("if he has any") were fools to suppose that the governor-general could be conciliated in this way. By what authority did he act? Let him publish the instructions he carried from Her Majesty, *then* it would be seen whether he had any business meddling. But Teng was pleased, or else the tea men were ready to begin selling, for on the first day of 1839 the trade reopened.

With the new year came a ship from England bringing two orphaned daughters of a Staffordshire ironmaster named Parkes to join their cousin, Mary Gutzlaff, and bringing also William Lockhart, the medical missionary promised some time before by the London Missionary Society. Lockhart went at once to join Peter Parker at the factories.

Since the remodeling of the Hog Lane hospital the previous summer, Parker had been busier than ever. One recent patient had been Lu, the Nanhai magistrate, the man who had dispersed the rioters the day of the attempted strangulation. Twelve days after the riot Parker had been called to Howqua's house to see Lu. "His tongue was coated, his eyes turgid, and his appetite indifferent," as well they might be in someone suffering from nephritis and chronic constipation. Strong medicines and plasters had soon brought a marked improvement, however. By early January "the lively expression of his countenance and the sparkling of his eyes" had made it plain that Lu was cured. When the Chinese New Year came around Lu had expressed his gratitude by sending Parker some porcelain, several pieces of silk, two boxes of tea, and a brace of wethers.[12] Now Parker had a helper, and so did Bridgman—for Abeel was back.

Abeel, you will remember, had come out to China in 1830 with Bridgman and King. Illness had very quickly driven him home, however; in the intervals of lying at death's door he had been able to do no more than preach the Protestant Mission; not until the autumn of 1838 had he felt strong enough to practice it. Given the usual free passage on Olyphant's *Morrison*, he reached the factories just after the Chinese New Year, moved in with Bridgman, and began studying Chinese. Parker, Lockhart, Bridgman, and Abeel—that was the extent of the mission at Canton. At Macao, however, there were the Gutzlaffs and Wells Williams; there was Squire, young Vincent Stanton tutoring Turner's children, Issachar Roberts, Lewis and Henrietta Shuck; and there was Samuel Brown, a Yale graduate just arrived for the Morrison Education Society (it had taken that body two years to find someone willing to start a school). As Lay, still sick and even more discouraged, departed about this time for England, Brown and his wife moved into Lay's rooms in the large house that Williams rented.

The house stood close to the ruins of St. Paul's. Not far away was the *procure* of the Missions Etrangères—no doubt Williams and Brown would have mingled with Legrégeois and his priests, did oil mix with water. Keeping Legrégeois company at the moment were only Libois (his assistant procurator), Callery, and several young Koreans and Cochinchinese in training for the priesthood. Then on 2 January three new recruits landed, fresh from the mother house in the Rue de Bac. Forewarned of their coming, Legrégeois had tried to prepare Silveira Pinto, the Portuguese governor. "How many of you are there?" Pinto had inquired. "Only three," Legrégeois had replied, "and the three who are about to arrive make six. But I shall do my best to send the latter on as fast as I can."[13] Galy was intended for Singapore, Renou for Szechwan; Legrégeois would have to see about Desflèches.

It was not with the Portuguese, however, that the French Catholic Mission's chief difficulties were going to lie. On 12 December, the day of the factory riot—though people at Macao knew nothing of that—Legrégeois had remarked in a letter to Paris that "there is occurring a fearful revival of severity at Canton against the smugglers and smokers. The prisons are full of these unhappy fellows."[14] A little later he reported: "Nothing passes the customs without being most thoroughly searched. They go so far as to feel about in the trousers of the Chinese, something previously unheard of."[15] Though the Hoppo's men might uncover missals or other missionary articles, Legrégeois knew very well it was not these they were looking for. They were after foreign mud—it was the side effects of the emperor's campaign against opium that the mission had to fear. As the winter of 1839 advanced, it became clear this campaign had not been abandoned.

"Not a chest can be disposed of," wrote Bennet Forbes on 1 January, the day he became a full partner in Russell and Company.[16] Six vessels consigned to the house lay at Whampoa, two empty, one half loaded with outgoing cargo, three still carrying the rice they had franked themselves in with. The tea men were asking extremely high prices and showed no signs of coming down; cottons and woolens sold poorly (Russell's found the market so depressed it sent some off to Manila). The fact was, decided Forbes, that the entire fabric of legitimate trade suffered from the uncertainty surrounding the opium traffic. The bill market was particularly affected: Russell's could get no one to take its paper at the usual 4s. 7d. to the dollar because, as less opium got sold, less treasure reached the gulf, and anyone with silver to spare found he could hold out for 5s. What if the worst happened? What if sales of the drug ceased altogether? "If we are to be permanently cut off from some twelve to fourteen millions of dollars heretofore received for opium, and a considerable proportion of it returned in Bills on England, it will be necessary to provide for half to two thirds of a cargo in specie."[17] It was a long time since Americans had brought their own treasure to China. It might not be easy to start doing so again.

Any way you looked at it, everything turned on the opium traffic. Nobody knew what would happen to that, not even well-informed Cantonese; they are as much in the dark as we are, observed Jardine. Of one thing he was certain, however. Sales this season would not be half what they normally were.

January went by. In the river hardly a chest moved. Off Namoa, where the *Jardine* and the *Colonel Young* lay, little more was doing. Further up the coast, from the *Austin* stationary at Chinchew and the *Governor Findlay* cruising above Chimmo, Rees and Jauncey sold chests with tolerable regularity. But they sold them on such a diminished scale that when the *Lady Hayes*, back from her tea run to New South Wales, came up in the middle of the month to take the *Austin's* place, she did not need to bring a fresh supply of chests; the *Harriet*, following at the end of the month, brought only thirty.

At the factories Jardine packed. He was going home at last; on the twenty-third over 130 persons representing every house but Daniell's and Dent's sat down to dinner in his honor. There were toasts and speeches; Parker thanked Jardine for his help at the hospital; Bridgman painted in glowing colors the domestic happiness (for Jardine, it was thought, meant to marry) that awaited him in the company of the loveliest of women—to which Jardine replied that he would settle for fat, fair, and forty. Jardine said more. He denied that he or any other foreign merchant smuggled. "We are not smugglers, gentlemen! It is the Chinese government, it is the Chinese officers, who smuggle, and who connive at and encourage smuggling, not we."[18] Applause and much cheering followed, and while the younger men sat to their wine, Old Rat slipped away to bed. A week later he was on board ship.

He left behind two nephews, Andrew and David, but James Matheson, who had his nephews, Alexander and Donald, on the coast too, was now the senior partner and the house's guiding hand. Matheson thought he saw signs, just before Jardine sailed, that the campaign against opium was beginning to falter. The governor-general was said to be having trouble with the Cantonese. They lampooned him publicly and obstructed the house-to-house searches of his police; already the persecution of offenders had somewhat abated. "Affairs will no doubt in due time return to the old system of venality and connivance; though we have the report," Matheson added, "of an officer being on his way from Peking to fill a newly created situation for the express purpose of enforcing the prohibitory laws."[19] Matheson was referring to a piece of news Morrison had picked out of a Peking gazette on the twenty-first. The officer in question was Lin Tse-hsü.

On the last day of the old year the emperor, in a brief but emphatic edict, had appointed Lin a *ch'in-ch'ai ta-ch'en*, or special high commissioner with plenipotentiary powers, and had ordered him to Canton to cope with the opium problem. Lin had set out on 8 January accompanied by a small household staff; at the moment Matheson wrote he was south of the Yangtze, pushing by boat up the rivers of Kiangsi. Informed of his appointment, his purpose, and his powers, Governor-General Teng in the meanwhile attempted to alert the *fan kuei* by means of a proclamation addressed (against all precedent) directly to them. Morrison translated it, the two weeklies printed it, Howqua got offprints made and saw that every house in the factories had several. By the first week in February, therefore, the foreigners knew in some detail what the high commissioner was coming to do. While he lingered in Kiangsi's provincial capital, held there by snowstorms and then struggled southward towards the Meiling Pass, each merchant prepared in his own way for the high commissioner's arrival.

Russell and Company wondered whether to drop opium altogether as Howqua advised and, while it wondered, raised the demurrage rate on the *Lintin* to discourage additions to the thousand chests she already contained. Dent's friends urged him to leave Canton for Macao. As senior China hand now that Old Rat had gone and head of the house that in the opium traffic stood second only to Jardine's, he might be in some danger when the *ch'in-ch'ai* arrived. But Dent declined to go, and there were others who refused to alter by one jot or tittle their plans.

One of these—we know a good deal about him because he testified later before a Parliamentary committee—was a certain John Thacker who had left England in the spring of 1838, possessing a considerable familiarity with the opium trade (he had had dealings with Jardine), a sum of money accumulated in the London agency business, and an honest appetite for speculation. Thacker had stopped at Bombay to acquire Malwa, at Singapore to get rid of some (he learned there of the execution riot); he had reached Canton in February with eighty-six chests, half his own and half on consignment from a group of Bombay Parsees. The approach of the *ch'in-ch'ai* did not alarm him at all. Perhaps it was because he lodged near Innes in the Creek factory, perhaps it was because he *had* to be sanguine to have come out to China in the first place—whatever the reason, Thacker refused to take seriously a special officer so determined to "strip bare and root up" the opium habit (Teng's proclamation lost none of its turgidity in the translating) that "though the axe should break in his hand or the boat sink beneath him, yet will he not stay his efforts till the work of purification be accomplished." This officer was said to be on the point of reaching Canton. "From morn to eve his arrival may hourly be looked for."[20] Yet day followed day and he did not appear. Even were he in earnest—with relish Thacker repeated the story then current that Teng, on learning of Lin's appointment, had fainted dead away—he would find the system more than he could overcome.

As February advanced, however, the more experienced among the foreign merchants began to feel uneasy. Business was not what it should be. Teas moved at last, but languidly, not much was doing in silks, exchange on England was sluggish at 4s. 11d. A Jardine Matheson schooner came in from the east coast with $15,000 in treasure, the proceeds of hardly more than forty chests, and there seemed nothing better to do than send her to join others on the west coast, for it was thought some opium might still be disposed of at Tinpak and other stations between Saint John Island (Shangch'uan) and Hainan. Tiny quantities still moved in the Canton area, but though passage boats were once more active on the river, they did not risk carrying opium—the police were everywhere.

Early in February they seized sixty cakes in circumstances that pointed the finger at Just, the watchmaker. Then on the twenty-sixth a much more dramatic demonstration of official zeal took place. Late in the afternoon, at an hour when many of the foreigners were out rowing or walking in the Honam gardens, a file of soldiers carrying a man in a basket came suddenly down Old China Street. Lockhart, strolling with a friend along the river bank, saw them emerge into the square, turn left, and stop in front of the American factory—saw them raise a pole, lash their prisoner to it, loop a cord about his neck, and draw it tight. There was hardly time to interfere, the thing was over in an instant, the most Lockhart and the others could do was insist that the body be carried away. Later it was learned that the dead man had been a ringleader in the September opium fracas at Whampoa. The foreigners were furious. That evening seventy-two English and Parsees petitioned the chief superintendent to strike his flag until satisfaction for the insult had been received. The flag was struck, and so were the American, Dutch, and French; no one foresaw that none would fly again save briefly for over three years.

Next morning, 27 February, Russell and Company took the plunge and formally withdrew from the opium business. It would handle consignments already on the way, John Green, the senior partner, told his Indian correspondents, but it would accept no new ones. The measures being pursued by Peking and the approach of a high commissioner deemed incorruptible (Russell's listened to Howqua as no other firm did) threatened to make the traffic not just disreputable but downright dangerous. By a Jardine Matheson ship Green sent word to the *Rose* to stop selling along the coast and come in.

A few merchants had already quit handling the drug. Now a few more followed. Green's announcement was not widely copied, however; most of the merchants still preferred to wait and see, and some were too busy being annoyed with the chief superintendent to care. It happened that Elliot was once more enjoining Her Majesty's subjects to keep their opium schooners out of the river. "I thought it very hard," protested Thacker later, "when I arrived in China, having paid for this opium, which was a trade perfectly understood in this country, and perfectly recognized by the

Government of India, and fostered by it, that when I came to the only market which it was grown for the express purpose of being sent to, I should be met by any obstruction in selling it on the part of the representative of the British Government."²¹ At a purchase price of approximately $400, with interest and expenses added, his forty-five chests represented an investment of something like $20,000. How could he possibly think of doing as Russell and Company were doing and turn his back on the traffic?

At Number 4, Matheson and his partners took a less melodramatic view. Theirs was too large a house, with a business too varied, to fear anything but the most prolonged depression in the opium trade. At Howqua's "earnest solicitation" they were busy moving their receiving ships from Hongkong to the south side of Lantao. All the houses were doing the same, even Russell's; Lantao was about as remote and inconspicuous an anchorage as it was possible to find. There the opium fleet would be well out of sight when the *ch'in-ch'ai* reached Canton—out of sight, too, while it struggled with a problem that quite dwarfed Thacker's: what to do with the huge quantities of fresh opium about to descend on it from India?

The depressed state of the China market and the warnings conveyed by Jardine and others had had no effect at all on the Indian end of the trade. Before ever a clipper arrived, Bennet Forbes had heard that seven thousand chests would be offered at the first Calcutta sale. He was right, they were, on the other side of the subcontinent there was an equal absence of restraint, with the consequence that when, in the last days of February, the *Ardaseer*, *Mahommedie*, and *Lady Grant* came in from Bombay, they brought among them nearly five thousand chests. On 2 March the *Good Success* arrived with another twelve hundred. Then it was the turn of the Bengal clippers, on the fourth the *Red Rover*, on the eighth Dent's *Ariel*, a day or so later the *Syed Khan*. If the rest of the season went to pattern, the agency houses could expect a total of forty-five to fifty thousand chests. Added to the stocks already in hand, which quite swallowed Thacker's eighty-six, this constituted an absolutely fearful impediment to the abandonment of the opium trade.

So no one thought of abandoning it—not in the Creek factory, at least. Thacker, with Innes's help, made a deal to deliver thirty chests a day's sail from Macao at a miserable $250 a chest. (The deal fell through.) Matheson dispatched a vessel to Tinpak with a small quantity on Chinese account and some on his own. To a correspondent in Bombay he reported cheerfully on the progress being made with the new clipper ship *Mor*. "The future course of the opium trade," he wrote, "will in all probability render such vessels more necessary than ever."²²

That was on 9 March. Next day Lin entered Canton, prepared to prove Matheson wrong.

11

Lin and the Twenty Thousand Chests

Lin's arrival was known at once to the foreigners. Hunter, lounging that Sunday morning aboard the *Ferret*, saw him pass the factories in formal water procession, debark at the nearby water stairs, enter a palanquin, and disappear into the city. Matheson asked Mowqua was it really he, and Mowqua said it was, adding his opinion that the high commissioner would probably act more with an eye to impressing Peking than anything else. Just the same Matheson thought it prudent to send his nephew, Alexander, down to Lantao to talk to Parry about the disposition of the opium fleet there. Perhaps it should shift to some more distant anchorage, Lark's Bay, Saint John Island even. "How would it answer to cruise about at sea within sixty or a hundred miles of the coast for a week?"[1] But Matheson was wrong if he supposed that the mischief of Lin's coming would be over in a week. Methodical as ever, Lin meant to look about him before he moved.

From the memorials he had read he already knew something about the local situation—he had in fact brought with him a list of sixty-two known opium offenders, some of them men who had arranged the fast crabs and scrambling dragons of past years, others conniving officers in this yamen or that. In Canton he took up quarters in the Yueh-hua Academy close to the Consoo House (the hong merchants' guild hall). There he received the governor-general and the lesser provincial authorities, began making inquiries, and started laying plans. He moved the hong merchants into houses close by. He issued a number of public notices: to the people of Kwangtung, advising them to surrender their pipes; to the men of the water forces (Lin had no illusions about the dependability of that service), warning them to stop appropriating to their own use the

142

opium they seized from smugglers. He even drafted a letter to Queen Victoria which, in its mixture of candor and cant, of nobility of spirit and a sort of vain ignorance, shows us perhaps what Lin himself was like.

"The Way of Heaven is fairness to all," the letter begins. "It does not suffer us to harm others in order to benefit ourselves. Men are alike in this all the world over: that they cherish life and hate what endangers life. Your country lies twenty thousand leagues away; but for all that the Way of Heaven holds good for you as for us, and your instincts are not different from ours." Over many, many years Englishmen have traded peacefully and profitably at Canton. Lately, however, some of them have taken to introducing opium. This poison, it appears, "is manufactured by certain devilish persons in places subject to your rule. It is not, of course, either made or sold at your bidding, nor do all the countries you rule produce it, but only certain of them. I am told that in your own country opium smoking is forbidden under severe penalties." (This, of course, was not true, but Lin was persuaded by it that Victoria must be aware how harmful the drug was.) Why, then, do you permit it to be produced and carried to China? Perhaps it is because you have never been clearly and formally warned. "I now give my assurance that we mean to cut off this harmful drug for ever. What is here forbidden to consume, your dependencies must be forbidden to manufacture, and what has already been manufactured Your Majesty must immediately search out and throw to the bottom of the sea." The letter ends with a truly Confucian estimate of the happy consequences to Victoria if she does as she is told. "Calamities will not be sent down on you from above; you will be acting in accordance with decent feeling, which may also influence the course of nature in your favor."

It is a marvelous letter, made so partly by its substance, partly by the grace of Arthur Waley's translation;[2] had we only Morrison's or Thom's to depend on, we might not feel so good about it. Queen Victoria, however, had no opportunity to feel good or bad or anything else. She never saw the letter; Lin could not hit on a satisfactory way of getting it to her; as for the foreigners, they did not even know it was being prepared.

Indeed they knew very little about what the *ch'in-ch'ai* was up to. He was interrogating, they could see, all sorts of people: hong merchants' clerks, linguists, the compradors of several of the leading agency houses. He was serious, they were beginning to suspect, about suppressing the opium traffic. But how did he propose to do it? It was Howqua who gave an intimation. If the opium fleet did not sail away to Singapore (he told his American friends) or alternatively give up its opium to be destroyed by burning, the legitimate trade would be closed indefinitely and the hong merchants ferociously punished.

Green and his partners were impressed. "Although we are under no fears for our personal safety," wrote Bennet Forbes, "we cannot but fear that the hong merchants will suffer unless we join heart and hand to get the opium ships out of the way."[3] Had Forbes realized just how angry and determined Lin actually was, he might have worried a bit about himself too; for Lin knew better than the foreigners supposed who among the *fan kuei* handled the drug, whose vessels were involved, how many chests they carried, and where they were lying. He knew that Russell and Company was still very much in the business in spite of its announced withdrawal. He knew about Jardine and had intended to arrest him. Now Jardine had skipped. But Dent was still around, Dent who handled as much opium as ever Jardine had and maintained contacts fully as numerous with the Cantonese—teaching them English, reading their newssheets. When the time came, Lin meant to arrest and try Dent. Green, Matheson, and Forbes did not know this, however. If they had they would certainly have warned Dent. And Dent did not know it either.

So the foreigners waited. On the afternoon of Monday, 18 March, eight days after reaching Canton, the high commissioner struck.

Lin summoned the hong merchants to the Yueh-hua Academy and read them two edicts. One, which they were to pass on, ordered the foreigners to surrender all the opium aboard their vessels and undertake to bring no more. The other was addressed directly to the hong merchants. These twelve unfortunates, facing the high commissioner (if Bridgman gets the matter right) upon their knees, were treated to a long, carefully studied account of their complicity in the opium traffic, an account into which Lin threw all his accumulated disgust for them and their ways. For twenty years, he pointed out, it had been the law that foreign vessels entering the river not carry opium. For twenty years the hong merchants had been accepting bonds and securing vessels. Never had they turned one away, yet the foreign mud flowed in—to say that these vessels all unloaded at Lintin first was to advance a transparent subterfuge. At the factories, which the hong merchants owned, servants, shroffs, and outside shopmen went openly about the business of moving and dealing in the drug; they wrote letters, took orders, passed bills, and arranged for smug boats. Did the hong merchants pretend to know nothing of this too? They connived at the export of silver, even to supplying the wooden boxes in which the stuff was shipped; they rose to the foreigners' defense (here Lin named Jardine). In short they behaved like traitors—"truly I burn with shame for you"—and if they did not instantly arrange the opium surrender (they should have three days to do it in), Lin would ask the emperor for permission to execute one or two of the more notorious among them and to confiscate their property.

Within hours of this painful audience Howqua and Mowqua had passed the texts of both edicts on to the foreigners, and Morrison and Thom had begun translating them. Next day, Tuesday, 19 March, the Hoppo forbad the further departure of any foreigners for Macao. This order Howqua transmitted verbally to half a dozen of the leading foreign merchants—Dent, Matheson, Green, Daniell, Dadabhoy Rustomjee, and the American, Wetmore—at the same time having Thom read aloud to them the high commissioner's order to surrender all opium. Did the foreigners mean to comply? They would not answer but promised a general meeting of the Chamber of Commerce for Thursday, the twenty-first, the day Lin's time limit was up.

Thursday morning the chamber duly met, forty strong, Wetmore in the chair (Lindsay was on his way home in the *Ardaseer*, which had unloaded her opium and was returning to Bombay), and at once it was apparent that hardly anyone was willing to accede fully to Lin's request. Some sort of gesture would have to be made, no doubt, but even the most conciliatory of the merchants could not see the agency houses surrendering millions of dollars worth of opium just because a special officer sent from Peking asked them to. Most of it was not theirs anyhow—here was the rub! Russell and Company had over fourteen hundred chests in Chinese waters. Two-thirds belonged to constituents in Bombay, not quite one-third was on consignment from Calcutta, the balance (a tiny quantity of Turkey) lay to accounts in London; not a chest was owned by the partners. That, no doubt, was one reason why Russell's had found it comparatively easy to follow Howqua's advice and announce its withdrawal from the traffic. Dent's and Jardine's had by contrast a good many chests on house account, but less by a great deal than they held for others. "What we do not own we cannot in conscience surrender!" ran a sentiment so powerful, so convenient, that even King (who of course neither owned nor held any) did not try to meet it head on. As for the hong merchants being personally in danger, there was nothing to it! In vain King protested that their fears were genuine and well founded, that it would be shameful "to put the pocket of a constituent in competition with the neck of a neighbor."[4] By a vote of twenty-five to fourteen the intransigents had their way. The high commissioner was to be informed that, though the foreign community received his edict with the greatest attention and respect, no answer would be forthcoming until a committee of the chamber had studied it carefully—a matter of at least six days.

With this message the hong merchants disappeared into the city. At dusk they were back with word that the *ch'in-ch'ai* was angrier than ever. Could not the foreigners surrender at least a token quantity at once?

So a second meeting of the chamber was called for ten that night.

Again Dent argued the case for firmness. This time, however, the hong merchants were brought in and questioned. Had they actually seen the high commissioner, not just some lesser mandarin? They had, and he was adamant. "Seriously and solemnly, are you in fear of your lives?" One by one each replied that he was. That did it. Dent gave way, a token surrender was agreed upon, and a little over a thousand chests (a quarter of them Jardine Matheson's) were subscribed on the spot. By daybreak the high commissioner knew that the foreign community was prepared to feed his righteousness—or would it be his private coffers?—with property worth at least a third of a million dollars.

Lin's reaction was not what Dent and the others expected. Already there had been signs he meant to use instruments more powerful than exhortation. A day or so before, a newly licensed passage boat, the *Snipe*, had been stopped at the Bogue, her cargo confiscated, and she herself sent to Canton to be broken up. Now other things began to happen. Merchantmen lying at Whampoa, loaded and ready for sea, discovered that they could not obtain their grand chops of departure. The captain and boat's crew of one, a Philadelphia vessel consigned to Nye, were actually turned back when they tried to leave the factories. Soldiers appeared in Thirteen Factory Street and in the alleys leading down to the square. On the afternoon of Friday, 22 March, Lin commanded Dent to come into the city to be questioned.

Dent was inclined to go. Doing so would exactly suit his feelings, which were a mixture of indifference, scepticism, and contempt, but his colleagues reminded him of the gunner of the *Lady Hughes* and of a certain James Flint held prisoner once for two and a half years (though that had been eighty years ago), and in the end he told Howqua that he would not leave the factories unless he had a safe-conduct from the high commissioner himself.

This Howqua, of course, could not obtain. Saturday morning he and Mowqua appeared at the factories, visibly depressed and wearing iron chains about their necks, to say that if Dent did not obey Lin without delay they would certainly be strangled. Some thought them genuinely desperate. Matheson judged their performance "the most complete exhibition of humbug ever witnessed in China."[5] Whether one or the other was no matter, however, Dent had his mind made up and would not budge. All day the tug-of-war went on. Dent's partner, Robert Inglis, ventured up to the Consoo House with Morrison and argued in vain with the Canton prefect. Three mandarins, one of them Lu, the Nanhai magistrate, entered Dent's house at the back of the Paoushun factory, settled themselves in the ground-floor office, and made it plain they would not leave unless Dent left with them. The afternoon passed, night fell, Dent (who was upstairs and came down from time to time) sarcastically offered them supper and beds. At this they went away. But several hong merchants took their places; it was past midnight before they too gave up and departed, and a sort of twenty-four-hour truce began in honor of the barbarians' Sabbath.

Yet all along it had been in Lin's power to resolve the contest with one simple order. Dent's friends mounted nothing resembling a guard over the Paoushun factory; Johnston, the second superintendent, remained entirely passive; Dent himself kept saying that he would not resist if Lin tried to take him by force. Lin, however, did not want to use force. He did not want an open rupture, he certainly did not want war; he meant, in the best Ch'ing tradition, to handle these border barbarians without provoking them to violence. So he gave no order to seize Dent. At this point Captain Elliot arrived.

The chief superintendent, it happens, had been at Canton the day of Lin's arrival. He had gone to Macao, however, expecting the high commissioner to strike first at the outer anchorages—there, after all, was where the opium lay. Consequently he was not at the factories when Lin broke silence on the Monday; indeed, he did not learn what was happening until Friday and might not have learned then had not someone slipped a note off to him in a hired Chinese boat. The note enclosed Morrison's translations of the two edicts and warned Elliot that the factories were probably going to be cut off. Elliot decided to go up at once.

First, however, he wrote to Palmerston, enclosing the Morrison translations and taking care to get his dispatch aboard a vessel cleared for England. "I have no doubt," he assured the foreign secretary, "that a firm tone and attitude will check the rash spirit of the provincial authorities."[6] Privately he instructed Blake of the *Larne* to wait six days and, if he heard nothing from Canton in that time, to act as he thought best, but he did not suggest that this should include trying to enter the river. If Canton became a prison, it would take more than an 18-gun corvette to force the lock. In a public notice he asked all the English merchantmen at the outer anchorages to assemble at Hongkong under Parry of the *Hercules*, the senior ship's master. Then he started off in the *Louisa*—it was Saturday afternoon—taking with him the gig of the *Larne* (his own had been stolen) and four of her crew. Reaching Whampoa the next day and learning from vessels there that all communication with Canton had been broken, he changed into full uniform, told the highest mandarin he could find that he was going up willy-nilly, pushed on to Howqua's Fort, transferred to his gig, and sometimes sailing, sometimes rowing, hastened the last four miles to the factories. There he was expected, for his notice to shipping had somehow come up that morning, but no one knew when he would arrive or how. Daniell, walking in the garden of the New English factory, saw a small boat flying the English colors approaching, saw a mandarin boat trying to head it off, guessed who it contained, and ran to meet it. Others saw it too. Someone cried that boats from the merchant fleet were forcing their way to the rescue, there was a general shout, in the middle of the uproar the gig came smartly up to the landing, and Captain Elliot stepped ashore. It was five-thirty on the afternoon of Sunday, 24 March.

The chief superintendent's first act was to run up the English flag. "For I well know," he wrote Palmerston, "that there is a sense of support in the sight of that honored flag, fly where it will, that none can feel but men who look upon it in some such dismal strait as ours."[7] As it had been struck after February's execution, and the upper half of the flagpole with it, and neither could be found, there was a bit of a pause in the execution of this invigorating gesture until someone thought of the gig's ensign and made it fast to the stump. Then Elliot walked briskly into the Paoushun, took Dent by the arm, and brought him through an excited crowd of Chinese to the Superintendency's own rooms in the Lungshun. There Dent must remain. For Elliot was determined that come what may he should be found standing resolutely between his countrymen and the Chinese.

The rest of his plan of action, such as it was, he revealed at a meeting convened that very evening in the hall of the New English factory. Speaking to most of the English and Parsees, many of the Americans, and Howqua and Mowqua sitting quietly and without embarrassment among the rest, Elliot advised all British subjects to move their property out of the river and get ready to follow themselves. The execution in front of the factories, the appearance of soldiers at the Barrier and fireboats at the Bogue (Elliot had seen, or thought he had seen, both), the announcement that foreigners were not to go down to Macao, and the generally threatening attitude of the local authorities made it impossible for foreigners to remain longer at Canton with safety, honor, or advantage. He would demand passports for all who wished them. If passports were not produced, he would take this as an indication that the authorities meant to hold the British hostage, and meant by doing so, by perhaps offering actual injury to them or to the hong merchants, to wring from them "unsuitable concessions and terms."

This completed the formal part of the notice, but Elliot felt it necessary to reassure the community (and possibly himself) with a few additional remarks. The situation, he observed, was an anxious but not desperate one. "Thank God we have a British man-of-war—small indeed she is!—outside." He offered all present the protection of her flag. (As his instructions to the *Larne* had been private, his listeners could hardly know that they were not likely to see her on their side of the Bogue.) He was delighted to observe a number of Americans in the hall. Two of their warships, the *Columbia* and the *John Adams*, were hourly expected at Macao. He was sure he could count on their assistance and support. ("That you may surely do!" someone cried.) Meanwhile it was imperative that the English and the Americans stand united before the dark and menacing gestures of the Chinese.[8]

Applause, a few scattered cheers, and Matheson rose to express thanks for a brave and heartening speech. The effect outside the hall was not, however, what Elliot intended. By taking Dent into protective custody and demanding passports, the chief superintendent hoped to give Lin and the provincial authorities pause. Instead he simply persuaded them that he planned to whisk Dent and the other opium criminals out of the river and out of their reach. This they were determined to prevent; that very evening the factories took on the aspects of a place besieged.

A few of the servants had already quietly decamped. Thacker had noticed his removing their clothes from the Creek factory during the middle of the week; Daniell's comprador had disappeared on Friday. Now Old Tom, Young Tom, and the other linguists went from house to house ordering the rest away. For half an hour the factories were a wild confusion of porters, cooks, house boys, and compradors hurrying off, each with bed, bundle, or box. "It looked," wrote Hunter in the journal he began that night, "as if they were running from the plague."[9] Then quiet returned. In the Lungshun factory Elliot sat with Morrison preparing the letter demanding passports. Outside a scratch guard of coolies occupied the square. Lanterns, blazing a little unnecessarily in the light of a full moon, illuminated a multitude of tea boats and chop boats moored in a great arc from one end of the factory waterfront to the other. Soldiers scattered about in them made the night noisy with the beating of gongs and the blowing of conch shells.

About midnight the demand for passports went up to the Consoo House. It was addressed not to Lin but to Teng, for Elliot, though fully aware who Lin was and what his errand, wished to avoid an open collision with him if possible. It set a time limit too. If passports were not forthcoming within three days, the chief superintendent would know himself detained "and act accordingly."[10]

Morning would surely reveal that this threat was having its effect. It revealed, instead, the extent of the foreigners' predicament. During the night Hog Lane, New China Street, and the alley to the west of the Danish factory had been closed off. Old China Street remained open, but soldiers let no one pass save those who carried, attached to the waist by a piece of red string, a wooden permit. The square itself was occupied by the coolie

who? Teng?
is Teng?

guard, now fully organized and perhaps five hundred strong. Its members wore loose coolie trousers and jackets, sandals of twisted grass, and conical rattan hats bearing in large characters the names of the factories from which they were drawn. They were armed with pikes or heavy staves and carried rattan shields able to deflect a cutlass blow. During the day they drilled (like boys at a mock training, Bridgman thought) or took shelter from the sun in mat sheds placed about the square. At night they patrolled the factory frontage and Old China Street while the hong merchants, their masters, slept by turns in large chairs at the command post under the arch of the New English factory. At the back of the factories along Thirteen Factory Street were stationed regular soldiers with matchlocks. Officers tethered their ponies outside the Consoo House; other officers occupied the customs posts at the water's edge and supervised the soldiers in the arc of boats. Except that no watch was set inside the houses and no obstacles placed in the way of visiting or moving about the square, surveillance was complete. The factories had become a cage.

Foreigners felt certain inconveniences at once. Abeel's Chinese teacher did not show up that Monday morning, neither did the cook at Zion's Corner, neither did the pressmen at Bridgman's *Repository*, Slade's *Register*, or Moller's *Press*; it was the same everywhere. The foreigners, who numbered at this moment well over two hundred, were normally cared for by a small army of Chinese. These had been driven away the previous evening, and when morning came they did not reappear. At Number 2, the Swedish factory, the eight Americans of Russell and Company, and Peter Snow (who came in from next door), discovered where the kitchen was (none had ever set foot in it before) and set about getting breakfast. Bennet Forbes served up ham and eggs the consistency and color of shoe leather. Warren Delano, Abbot Low, and Green, hastily appointed to replace him, produced hardboiled eggs that resembled grapeshot and rice indistinguishable from glue. Meanwhile Hunter trimmed the lamps and old Snow swept the floors. The Parsees had their own Indian servants (Matheson managed to borrow a few). Some merchants were able to command the services of sailors trapped by the cutting of communications with Whampoa. In most of the houses, however, the cooking, the drawing of water from the river for washing (drinking water came at long intervals from a spring in the suburb and was stored in huge jars), the laundering, bedmaking, and general cleaning were done by the foreigners themselves or not done at all.

Provisions were a problem too. Factory residents usually brought with them biscuits in puncheons, butter in tubs, wines, beer, ale, salt beef, hams, coffee, jams and jellies, pickles, candles, and soap, but for perishables, especially fresh meat, they depended on what their cooks purchased locally. Now these cooks had vanished; the foreigners could not leave the square, and anyhow knew not the first thing about where to shop. During that last frantic half hour on Sunday, Green had managed, with Howqua's help, to bring in sugar, cooking oil, fifteen tubs of water, and a few other things. Several days later two of Howqua's coolies slipped Hunter some capons and three loaves of bread. Not many of the foreigners were as lucky, however, or as well connected. Had the siege continued as it began, most would soon have been reduced to pretty dreary fare.

What saved them was the quick collapse of the chief superintendent's position. His request for passports, sent up late Sunday night, produced a refusal so abrupt, so peremptory, that early Monday afternoon Elliot wrote again apologizing for the tone he had used and asking for an interview with a mandarin—any mandarin! But he repeated his request for passports; if he had any thought of abandoning his general stance, he gave no sign of it in a conversation that evening with Inglis. Then on Tuesday, Lin himself took a hand.

The day dawned hot and still. "New China Street still closed," Hunter wrote in his journal, "with bars of wood nailed across the gates and police stationed to guard them. The Chinese houses in all directions filled with people looking from the roofs and out of the windows, but none daring to attempt an entrance into the square, which is perfectly clear except the police force."[11] No one had come up the river since the day before when two Englishmen somehow contrived to slip in under Dutch passports. Abeel read his Bible. The 121st Psalm gave him particular comfort; it was "quite enough for personal safety, and the security and increase of the church are equally promised."[12]

Elliot stayed in his quarters. He did not go up to the Consoo House even though he was told he would find a mandarin there. It was beginning to dawn on him that talking to mandarins, talking to hong merchants, talking to the Nanhai magistrate, or even to Teng, would get him nowhere. Lin was his real antagonist; he could not continue avoiding the fact.

That very morning a public notice, five feet square and lettered in one-inch characters, had been discovered posted at several places about the factories. Morrison had translated it. It was addressed to the *fan kuei*, came from the high commissioner, and it repeated (in language most patient, for Lin, it said, would rather "weary his mouth" than resort to harsh measures) the order to surrender the opium. Elliot had still been at Macao when the surrender order was first issued. So far he had managed to ignore it; he had, for example, said nothing about it when addressing the factory community the evening of his arrival; here it was again, placarded under his very nose! Impossible to ignore it now.

And the notice, for all that it laid out so patiently, so kindly even, why the foreigners must swiftly obey and turn in their pernicious cargoes, breathed a kind of menace that Elliot could hardly mistake. "By reason of the necessity of the case," it explained, and Elliot saw with his mind's eye the triple line of guard boats rocking gently against the water stairs. "By virtue of that reason which heaven hath implanted in all of us," it continued, and Elliot was sure that by this Lin meant more than an appeal to his head and heart. Indeed the notice itself made it plain that Lin meant more. Napier, it reminded the reader, had died *within weeks* of his impudent assault upon the proprieties and with him the elder Morrison, "who had been darkly deceiving him." If Elliot persisted in his present contumacious course, heaven might serve him the very same way![13]

It was not that the chief superintendent actually feared heavenly retribution. His temporal difficulties were what troubled him. Like Napier he was trapped at Canton. Unlike Napier he could not simply humble himself, ask for a passport, and leave. For the object of the authorities' pressure was not he alone but the entire foreign community, and that community would not be permitted to make its usual spring move to Macao or the two dozen merchantmen at Whampoa to sail simply upon Elliot's undertaking to quit Canton. Besides, it was precisely to put himself between his countrymen and the authorities that he had come up in the first place. "I will remain with you," he had promised, "to my last gasp."

Already he suspected a number of the merchants of belittling him behind his back. As for the Chinese, they openly jeered; here, for example, was a paper from the high commissioner himself, a paper containing the most unflattering estimate of his position and powers. Since the chief superintendent, it ran, cannot stop the English from bringing opium to China and selling it there, "I would ask what is it that Elliot superintends?"[14]

It was a good question and one that Elliot was about to answer with a display of authority in a quite unexpected direction. He was about to order the surrender of the opium.

He did not arrive at this decision by consulting his fellow countrymen. Some of them later complained that they had had no inkling at all of what he meant to do. About three o'clock Tuesday afternoon, however, he did tell Dent; Dent passed the word to his partner, Inglis; Inglis hurried over to the superintendent's quarters and asked Elliot exactly what he had in mind. To whom was the opium to be surrendered? Who would pay?

It was to be surrendered to the Superintendency, Elliot said. Her Majesty's government would pay. Inglis got him to repeat this once or twice, but that was as far as the discussion went. About ten that evening, while the Chinese were hauling the foreigners' small boats up into the square to render them unusable and Hunter was confiding to his journal that "tomorrow is Captain Elliot's last day, when I am quite sure the passports required will not be granted,"[15] Inglis happened to pass Elliot's open door. The chief superintendent saw him and asked him in. Would Inglis glance over the order he was drawing up? Inglis complied and at the same time took the opportunity to inquire whether Elliot was quite sure he was acting within his powers in asking for the opium. Elliot replied that he was. Except that he got Elliot to put off publishing the order until the morning, Inglis had no influence at all on the serious step the chief superintendent was about to take.

At the Creek factory next morning, Wednesday, 27 March, James Matheson woke Thacker a little after six and told him that Johnston, the second superintendent, would be around shortly to read the formal text of the order. Five houses to the west Edward Elmslie, secretary to the Superintendency, brought another copy to Green, Hunter, and the others in Russell and Company. "Constrained by paramount motives affecting the safety of the lives and liberty of all the foreigners here present in Canton, and by other very weighty causes," the document ran in language heavy with the sense of someone acting for Whitehall across thirteen thousand miles of ocean, "I, Charles Elliot, Chief Superintendent of the Trade of British Subjects in China . . . do hereby in the name and on behalf of Her Britannic Majesty's government enjoin and require all Her Majesty's subjects now present in Canton forthwith to make a surrender to me for the service of Her said Majesty's government, to be delivered over to the government of China, of all the opium belonging to them, or British opium under their respective control; and to hold the British ships and vessels engaged in the trade of opium subject to my immediate direction."[16] Agency houses were to furnish lists of the opium they held. Upon receipt of these lists, the chief superintendent would assume responsibility on behalf of Her Majesty's government for the full value of the chests. Failure to include all the opium in a house's possession would free Her Majesty's government of responsibility or liability for any part of it. What the opium was worth would have to be determined later.

Elliot did not give the merchants much time in which to mull this order over. The lists were to be brought to Elmslie by six that evening. Little deliberation was needed, however, to comply with something essentially so attractive. Already several of the smaller agency houses had tried to entrust their chests to the Superintendency—Thacker had offered his to Johnston on Saturday—and now it did not take the rest long to decide to do as the chief superintendent wanted. Later, a whole year later, before a Select Committee of the House of Commons, some of the merchants tried

154 The Opium War, 1840–1842

to cultivate the impression that they had wished to weather Lin's assault alone and unassisted, that they would have preferred to offer the high commissioner at most three or four thousand chests, for then he would surely have told his emperor that the barbarian smuggling vessels were quite driven away and their contents destroyed. Elliot, by ordering the surrender of *all* the opium, had cut the ground from beneath their feet; he would have done better to remain at Macao; never, suggested Jardine, had the English community shown so little spirit as it did from the moment the chief superintendent put his foot upon the water stairs! But Jardine, of course, had been on the high seas homeward bound when the whole affair took place. As for the others who talked this way in London in the spring of 1840, anxiety very probably colored their recollections. They had yet to be compensated for the chests they had surrendered. Not a penny had been paid. So it behooved them to act as though they had obeyed the chief superintendent at least somewhat against their will.

That was decidedly not the way they felt on this Wednesday morning in March 1839. Immense quantities of a commodity for which China offered the only practicable market pressed upon them from Calcutta and Bombay. Lin threatened to bar access to that market. Even if he did not touch their persons, even if he relaxed the cordon he had thrown about the factories and allowed them to leave, it was most unlikely in the present state of affairs that they would be able to sell more than a fraction of the chests they were responsible for. And at this moment of commercial crisis, when there seemed to be nothing to do but send the chests back to India with all that such a move entailed, the chief superintendent did not simply invite them to turn the chests over to him, he positively commanded them to! Whitehall, he said, *would* pay. As he gave the impression that he was governed by powers and instructions that he was not at liberty to divulge, the merchants cheerfully assumed that he knew what he was doing and that Whitehall indeed would pay. Pay handsomely, too; Matheson planned to ask for Calcutta's January prices plus interest and carrying charges. How many chests should a merchant turn over? Every chest he could lay his hands on! As Matheson's nephew, Alexander, later put it, before that same Parliamentary committee, "the opium was deposited in our hands to dispose of it, and the money of the British government was as good as any other money we could get."[17] What the merchants required were customers. Here was the chief superintendent gallantly offering himself.

So the opium passed promptly to the Superintendency. Thacker came around with his eighty-six in the middle of the morning; the big fellows took a little longer; but there was no need to extend the 6:00 P.M. deadline. Well before dark Elliot stood possessed (on paper at least) of 20,283 chests.

"What for he pay so large?" the hong merchants are reported to have exclaimed. "No wantee so much!" Elliot, however, had made up his mind. Next morning he passed the full figure on to Lin.

Lin's response was somewhat disconcerting. There was no relaxation of the pressure upon the foreigners, if anything the screws appeared to tighten. Workmen came and carefully bricked up the outer entrances to Hog Lane, New China Street, and the alley in front of the Danish factory. As the back doors into Thirteen Factory Street had already been blocked in this way, it was now physically impossible to enter or leave the enclave except through Old China Street, where soldiers stood guard day and night. Patients from the city could no longer reach the Opthalmic Hospital, and Parker moved his much reduced practice to private quarters in the American factory. Communication with Whampoa and the gulf remained difficult. For $50 Matheson got a note through to his nephew, Alexander, rolled up inside a cigar. A merchant at Whampoa managed to write twice to Blake of the *Larne* on slips of paper inserted between the thick parts of the soles of a messenger's shoes. But these ruses were expensive and undependable, particularly after the rumor began to circulate that a boatman caught with a foreign-devil letter in his clothes had been tortured to death. Elliot continued to prepare dispatches for the Foreign Office. He kept them by him, however, until he could be sure they would get safely out.

Getting them out might be some time away, for in Lin's mind the order to surrender the opium was only a beginning. He counted twenty-two English and Parsee opium vessels in China's waters; he was willing to concede that twenty thousand chests was probably all they held; but the other nations represented at Canton must be heavily involved too. Where were *their* chests?

In truth they had none. The handful of Dutch did not deal in the drug; there were no Frenchmen at all at Canton, though there were a few French Swiss; the opium in the possession of the Americans actually belonged to other people—Russell and Company had hardly a chest, as we have seen, that was not on consignment from Englishmen or Parsees somewhere. So Green carried his list to Elliot, who made the 1,400 a part of his 20,000. Wetmore, with 104, did the same. And in the end the flowery-flag devils had nothing at all of their own to give up.

It made no difference; Lin pursued them just the same, insisting that they surrender a quantity of opium not less than what the red-haired devils were surrendering and dismissing Snow's protestations as "mere tissue of senseless prattle."[18] As for those same English, they were told that they were not to be trusted, that intent to give up the vile dirt was no surrogate for doing so. The restraints laid upon the factory community would be lifted, Lin decreed, by stages only, as the stuff actually flowed in. When a fourth had been delivered, the foreigners might have their servants back. Passage boats would run when they had delivered half; at the three-quarters mark normal trading would resume; when the whole was surrendered, "everything to proceed as usual" (whatever that might mean). In vain Charles King pleaded that he ought to be excused from these restraints, that in all his years at Canton he had never bought, sold, or handled so much as a catty of opium. Why then, inquired Lin, had he not persuaded the others to surrender their opium at once? It was too bad if foreign devils doing wrong dragged down foreign devils who did right, but carefully laid plans could not be altered just for the sake of one man. King must suffer with the rest. When Van Basel, the Dutch consul, insisted upon the innocence of the single Dutch ship at Whampoa, he was served the same way.

Lin meant to have his own officers carry the individual delivery orders down to the opium ships. They might then accompany the ships to the point of delivery, a tiny spit of an island five miles below the Bogue called Lankit, and see the chests turned over. Elliot balked at this arrangement. He had managed, by his surrender order, to place himself between the ch'in-ch'ai and the English merchants, and he was determined to keep things that way. The less Lin's people saw of the Hercules and her sort, the better. Let Johnston go down to the gulf and organize the business.

To Lin this seemed to be simply "multiplying the twists and turns of the transaction."[19] Nevertheless on 3 April he reluctantly allowed Johnston to start for Macao by the inner passage. Johnston took Thom as interpreter, Elliot's accumulated dispatches, and letters from Dent and other private merchants; at Macao he boarded the Louisa and disappeared into the gulf. Chop boats began to gather at Lankit. On the tenth Lin and the governor-general set off together for the Bogue. Near Whampoa they passed right through the two dozen vessels of the merchant fleet. Except that the men on board were cut off from the factories and the gulf, they were perfectly comfortable and secure. Bumboats brought provisions to them daily, no one molested them; they let the high commissioner go by without lifting a finger. So Lin reached the Bogue and on the eleventh wrote in his diary that fifty chests of opium were received that day. The physical surrender of the foreign mud was at last beginning.

At Lin's request the clippers and receiving ships came to Lankit two by two, like animals to the Ark, and unloaded there into chop boats. First to arrive were the Austin and the Hercules—it was an appropriate choice,

for Jardine Matheson had more opium to surrender than any other house.★
Not all the opium these two ships delivered was actually Jardine's, however, Many persons stored chests aboard the *Hercules*, and she and the
Austin brought chests from other vessels too. At Johnston's bidding the
opium fleet had quietly collected in Macao Roads. There the skippers con-
certed the mechanics of the surrender, sending some ships up again and
again and others not at all, until in the end, of the more than forty receiving
ships, country ships, and clippers on the coast with opium in their holds,
only a score actually delivered—the *Lintin*, for example, sent a thousand
chests by another Russell and Company schooner and never appeared herself at all.

Early in the business rough water at Lankit forced a removal to
Chuenpi, at the edge of the Bogue. Johnston lay there in the *Louisa*, issuing
receipts for the chests as they came in. Lin lay there too, making sure the
work was properly done: whole chests moved intact, loose cakes placed in
sealed bags, boatmen watched lest they overturn a boat meaning to retrieve its contents later. Fifty chests arrived on the eleventh, six hundred on
the twelfth, more than a thousand on the thirteenth, and thereafter, for
nine straight days, the figure was rarely less than a thousand a day.

At the factories, meanwhile, the constraints and discomforts of daily
life lifted a little. Fruit, bread, drinking water, and hay for the cows began
to slip in; the authorities made occasional presents of pigs and poultry. Lin
more than held to his schedule and on the twelfth, long before a quarter of
the opium had been delivered, sent word that the servants might return.
Since many were occupied with guard duty and many others were frightened, there were even now not nearly enough—not enough, for one thing,
to carry the enormous quantities of washing water needed, from the river,
through the passages to the houses at the rear, and up the many flights of
stairs. Forbes and Low tried to rig a whip with which to hoist pails to their
veranda. They failed, and their floors grew filthy and their sanitary
facilities indescribable. The boredom, however, was worse.

The prisoners played ball and leapfrog, arranged footraces, organized
rat hunts. A sailor from the *Larne* got everybody laughing, and the Chinese
gaping, by shinnying up the American flagpole and pretending to signal
Whampoa. Once, when soldiers with horses came into the square and half

★There were 7,000 chests to Jardine's name, 2,000 of them the property of the house. Dent
and Heerjeebhoy Rustomjee shared second place with more than 1,700 each; Daniell and
Company and Russell and Company came third with a little over 1,400. One other house,
Macvicar's, had over 1,000; the firm of Dadabhoy and Maneckjee Rustomjee claimed almost
that many; the remaining eighty-odd houses and individuals (a third of them Parsee) turned
in amounts ranging from Thacker's 86 to 3 for a certain Bomanjee Hossongjee. Two-thirds
of the total were Malwa. Of Turkish there were only 53 chests.

seriously offered their mounts, one man leapt into the saddle and to the infinite delight of his fellows galloped madly round and round, basket stirrups flapping, hallooing at the top of his voice. But ten minutes later ennui, like the fog, settled again over everyone and everything. It was time for the annual migration to Macao—it was past time—and the foreigners were more than usually anxious to go.

So when, at the end of the third week in April, the opium deliveries passed the halfway mark and still the passage boats did not run (though Lin had promised they would), a gust of anger swept the factories. Even the mild-mannered Hunter cried treachery. Elliot instructed Johnston to stop deliveries; for three days not a chest moved; the high commissioner, however, was obdurate. Of the opium vessels he knew to be on the coast, only half had come to Chuenpi, and some of these were riding high in the water as though not fully loaded. Were the foreigners trying to hold chests back?

They were not, as it happened; commercially it made no sense to— there were such numbers where these twenty thousand had come from. Besides, as Matheson pointed out later to Jamsetjee, had a house withheld chests, Whitehall could have used this as an excuse for not paying. It was essential that Whitehall pay. "We think ourselves entitled to coast prices,"[20] Matheson advised Parry in a letter discussing ways and means of getting the house's seven thousand to Chuenpi. Getting them there, not withholding them, was the problem. How could you deliver at the rate Lin expected when so many of your chests were not in the gulf at all? To bring coasters in took time. In the case of Jardine Matheson it took an especially long time because, early in the crisis, Matheson had advised his skippers not to pay any attention to his instructions but to consult only his nephew, Alexander—he hoped in this way to insulate the fleet from any pressure that might be put upon him personally—and it was the middle of April before he issued a convincing order to the contrary. Even then some of his skippers read between the lines, or thought they did, and paused on the way down to sell a few chests. It was early May before the *Colonel Young* reached the gulf, mid-May before certain others came in, and at month's end the *Governor Findlay* and the *Lady Hayes* had still not appeared at all.

When, therefore, the deliveries resumed—for Elliot quickly got over his annoyance and told Johnston to get on with the work—the delivery ships brought far less than a thousand chests a day to Chuenpi. At one point they moved nothing for five days. Elliot wondered whether he would ever meet the promised figure; Matheson wondered too and in a strained interview reproached the chief superintendent for having pledged a fixed quantity. Some merchants repacked their chests to make a hundred stretch to a hundred and fifty. What principally saved them all, however, were fresh arrivals from India. Matheson bought seven hundred chests from this source to replace what the *Findlay* and the *Hayes* ought to have contributed. When several Parsees ran short, Elliot plugged the hole with a consignment just in for Dent. And so at last, very early on 21 May, Johnston was able to report the final shipment unloaded at Chuenpi and the full twenty thousand chests in the hands of the high commissioner.

Long before that, however, life at the factories had returned to something like normal. The compradors, cooks, and house boys were back, and with them came enough coolies to do the worst of the carrying and cleaning. Surveillance remained close; but curious Cantonese no longer peered down from the roof tops, and at night the coolie guards in the square and the soldiers in the boats beat their gongs and blew their conch horns less loudly, as if they too were bored. Very early in May, Hunter had word from Chuenpi that nearly fourteen thousand chests had been delivered and that the *Mahommedie* and the *Lady Grant* were in sight. "It is said they have on board near two thousand chests, and when they are discharged we shall see if the Commissioner intends to break his word again."[21] On Sunday, 5 May, six weeks to the day after Elliot's arrival and the beginning of the blockade, Hunter had his answer. Officers rode into the square and ordered the line of boats broken up. The soldiers withdrew, the mat sheds of the guards came down, the hong merchants left their station under the arch of the New English factory and went away into the city. Rudders were shipped and sails bent once more on the four passage schooners deliberately disabled when the blockade began. On Monday morning fifty foreigners set off down the river, most of them sailors anxious to rejoin their ships.

Not everybody followed immediately. Sixteen alleged opium traffickers of long and infamous standing, among them Dent, Matheson, the two Matheson nephews, and Andrew Jardine, were commanded to remain at the factories as hostages against the completion of the opium deliveries—and then to leave China forever! A number of other foreigners stayed with them. On the twenty-fourth, however, three days after the last chest had passed hands, Elliot led Dent, Matheson, and such others of the proscribed sixteen as were actually present, out by way of Whampoa. Abeel, Bridgman, and Snow had already departed. The life-size portrait of George IV had been crated and was on its way. Five days later Hunter left by the inner passage, in a chop boat sparely loaded with ledgers, clothes, candles, cheroots, and forty dozen bottles of wine. A whole fleet sailed; many of the English took their furniture; the *Repository*, the *Register*, and the *Press* picked up and moved, though Parker and his hospital did not. By the end of May the foreign community at Canton was down to fifteen or twenty Americans, half a dozen Englishmen, and not a single Parsee. It was an exodus on much more than a normal scale, and Lin began to wonder what it all meant.

In June the twenty thousand chests were destroyed. Five or six miles above Chuenpi, at a point where a creek flows into the river from the east, the high commissioner had three shallow basins dug, each roughly fifty yards by twenty-five, with timbered sides and flagstoned bottoms. Fresh water was let into the basins. Across each ran wooden platforms; to these coolies brought the balls and cakes, broke them there by stamping upon them, and pushed the fragments into the water with their feet. Lime and salt were scattered on the surface, other coolies waded in and stirred vigorously with hoes and shovels, and at last the watery mess, stinking horribly, was allowed to run into the creek and out to sea with the tide.

The work began on June 3 and proceeded without interruption for three weeks. Part way through King and Bridgman went up to Chuenpi on the *Morrison* and obtained permission to see for themselves how swiftly and efficiently it was being carried on. Sixteen hundred chests were destroyed the day of their visit. Officers were everywhere, making certain that not a cake escaped. After a time the high commissioner invited the two Americans to an interview in a pavilion overlooking the basin. Picking their way to him through piles of broken chests and torn coverings, many with the East India Company's mark upon them, bowing low (for they had made sure in advance that the kowtow would not be required), they attempted through the official interpreters to present two petitions.* One urged fundamental changes in the way China met the West. The other requested compensation for the losses Olyphant and Company had sustained through the interruption of trade. (King's hands, after all, were clean, *he* had never dabbled in opium!) Lin would not touch either petition; they were not, he pointed out, in Chinese; instead he plied King and Bridgman with questions of his own. Why were the English all leaving the river? How could he best communicate with England's queen?

---

*Lin had at least four interpreters. One, known to the foreigners as "Shautih" (actually Yuan Te-hui), was an overseas Chinese who had studied with the English Protestants at Malacca and with the French Catholics at Penang and had subsequently been employed at Peking as a sort of general interpreter—one barbarian language being, after all, much like another. He was considered Lin's senior interpreter; Morrison, who met him at Canton in 1837, thought him rather stupid and ill-informed. A second interpreter had spent several years with the Baptist mission at Serampore near Calcutta, helping Marshman with his Chinese Bible. A third had acquired a certain competence in English at a school for "heathen youth'" in Cornwall, Connecticut—a school abruptly closed in 1827 when two Cherokee Indian pupils made the mistake of marrying Cornwall girls. The fourth was Atih, Liang A-fa's eldest son, now nineteen and recently taken into Lin's service on the strength of the English he had learned from Bridgman and Brown.

The two Americans did not allow themselves to be put out by the *ch'in-ch'ai*'s refusal to meet them on their own ground. They had just seen the deliberate destruction of property worth millions, by officers deemed corrupt beyond redemption, and they were impressed. "Have we anywhere on record a finer rebuke administered by Pagan integrity to Christian degeneracy?"[22] Lin, for his part, was pleased by their visit. They had been respectful and attentive. As far as he could tell, the English were displaying the same qualities. "Judged by their manners," he wrote the emperor, "it appears that they feel a sense of shame." This was due, of course, to the penetrating virtue of the Lord of Ten Thousand Years, which taught barbarians and Chinese alike how to fear and obey. "Henceforth," Lin added, "it seems that all will reform themselves and be greatly improved."[23]

The crisis was over; the opium had been confiscated and in a few more days would all be washed out to sea; relations with the foreign merchants could go back to what they had been. There was only one difficulty. To go back required that, when the new trading season opened, the English be once more at Canton and their vessels at Whampoa. But to Canton and Whampoa the English now refused to return.

12

We Won't Go Back!

At the very beginning of the crisis the chief superintendent, you will remember, had demanded passports for himself and for his countrymen. The river, he had warned, is no longer safe; merchants must put themselves and their ships beyond the Bogue. Almost immediately had come the exodus of servants and the triple line of boats. Far from getting passports, Elliot had had to surrender twenty thousand chests, and for six weeks the question in everyone's mind had been not "Do we go back?" but "Do we get out?" Nevertheless, during all this time the chief superintendent had never swerved from his original purpose, conceived at Macao when the news of Lin's blow reached him there and turned over in his mind as the gig of the *Larne* hurried him towards the factories. Once the merchant community had been extricated and led safely into the outer waters, it must not return.

Just as the merchants fell in with Elliot's surrender order, executing it with all the energy of self-interest, so they listened when the chief superintendent asked them not to reenter the river. They even began to talk the language he talked, the language of danger and durance vile—they had actually faced nothing more menacing than dirt, discomfort, and boredom, yet you would have thought, to hear them, that they had barely escaped with their lives. They had reasons for sounding this way. One was the bond—the famous, or infamous, bond.

For twenty years it had been the practice for a hong merchant who secured a ship to join with the ship's captain and the ship's consignee in a guarantee that she carried no opium. Obtaining this bond, as it was called, had become as much a part of port routine as obtaining the grand chop of departure or paying *cumsha*. Just the same the practice bothered Elliot. He was sure some merchantmen carried chests and did not relish the scandal if they were discovered. As for Lin, he found the bond business infuriating for the opposite reason: in all these years no hong merchant had ever reported a violation! He pointed this out to the hong merchants in the course of the tongue-lashing he gave them on 18 March. A week later all the foreigners, even Dent and Matheson, signed a solemn pledge not to deal in the drug in the future. Lin, however, was not satisfied. He wanted an undertaking that could be repeated each time a ship entered the river; he wanted one that could be enforced too. On 4 April he announced a new version of the bond.

According to this version, a merchantman entering the river and found to contain opium was immediately to be confiscated, both vessel and cargo, "and the parties left to suffer death at the hands of the Celestial Court."[1] What Lin had in mind was the arrest and execution of the person or persons actually doing the smuggling. The foreigners, however, thought they sensed here the old Chinese principles of collective responsibility and a life for a life. Everyone remembered Terranova and the gunner of the *Lady Hughes*; Parker predicted that the authorities would muddle names (as they had in the case of Talbot and the *Thomas Perkins*) and seize the wrong persons; Hunter and Snow were sure they would try to strangle entire crews. When, therefore, Howqua and Mowqua brought the bond to Elliot, he declined to accept it. When they brought it to the general committee of the Chamber of Commerce, it hastily dissolved itself. Snow would not touch it, Van Basel would not touch it, and when, on 21 April, the hong merchants tried the chief superintendent again, "I tore it up," he wrote Palmerston, "and desired them to tell their officers that they might take my life as soon as they saw fit, but that it was a vain thing to trouble themselves or me any further upon the subject of the bond."[2]

The bond was not the only bar to normal relations, however. Twenty thousand chests of opium had been most rudely extorted. What these chests were worth varied as you calculated their cost in India or tried to estimate what they would have fetched in China (which, given the state of the market, was certainly a good deal less). Any way you worked the sum, however, it approached $6 million, it could easily run to $8, it might even top $10. That was almost two and a half million sterling! Was it reasonable to expect Her Majesty's government to budget such an amount simply for the purpose of buying off a Chinese high commissioner? Palmerston was much more likely to insist on placing the burden on Peking—and if Peking declined? "No one doubts," observed Legrégeois from his Macao *procure*, "that if the Chinese do not pay, the English will come with arms in their hands and make them."[3] Ten days earlier Matheson had arrived at the same conclusion. "I suppose war with China will be the next step."[4]

It was not that Matheson was particularly eager for war. Reading his letters now to Jamsetjee or Jardine, now to other commercial correspondents in India or England, one gets the feeling that his house was large enough and adroit enough to do quite well in peace or in war—with legitimate goods or with contraband. Matheson was certainly not forgetting the legitimate side. By late May outbound cargoes of teas stood complete, inbound cargoes of Indian cotton were largely sold, and the trading season was nearly over. If war came, actual hostilities could not possibly begin until an expeditionary force had reached the coast. Long before that another season would be under way, and Matheson meant to do his share of it from the outer anchorages. He was bringing the firm's entire establishment down from Canton, clerks, ledgers, the lot, putting it on board the *Hercules*. As for opium, he no longer felt bound by the pledge he had given in March. The inclusion of himself and his nephews in the list of sixteen who must leave China forever seemed to him an open violation of Lin's implied promise to let bygones be bygones, and he considered himself free to return to the drug. "I strongly recommend your losing no time in sending back the *Mahommedie* with a full cargo," he wrote Bombay towards the end of May.[5] A number of ships bound for China with opium in their holds had stopped at Singapore or had turned back to India. Now Matheson urged them to come on again; if the traffic picked up as expected, he would put a few tens of thousands of dollars of the firm's own money into the drug.

So Jardine, Matheson and Company got ready to work either side of the street. War or peace, opium banned or opium legal, it was all the same to them. Most of their countrymen took a less dispassionate view. "The English," wrote Abbot Low to his sister Harriet (married now and living in London), "are full of fight and threaten to clear out, one and all."[6] Late in May, Dent, twelve of his fellow countrymen, and twice that number of Parsees sent Whitehall a memorial protesting in the strongest possible terms the "spoliation" just inflicted upon them and begging for prompt and effective armed intervention. As for the chief superintendent, he was more unwilling than anyone to go back to things as they had been.

His measures, he had confided to Matheson shortly after the surrender order, would make Canton "too hot to hold any European, even the Americans."[7] For Elliot was tired of being half merchant *taipan* and half harbor master, poised uncertainly between a contraband traffic he could not control and a legitimate trade he could not protect. Now at last he saw a chance to do something about his situation. Lin had held the English prisoners for six or seven weeks. That gave them an injury to brandish. Lin, instead of requiring that each Englishman surrender his chests individually, had fallen into the snare of allowing them to turn the things over to Elliot. But Elliot was England's official representative. The consequence of this, and of the injury done the merchants, was that Palmerston simply *had* to pay attention whether he wanted to or not. All Elliot need do was keep the merchants outside the Bogue—lest they drift back into the old arrangements or get themselves trapped again—until Palmerston took notice. When Palmerston took notice, saw what a sum of money was involved, and realized that such a sum could never be recovered by talk, he would be bound and certain to send a squadron and a regiment or two. Elliot was so sure of this that in April he had written India asking for the immediate dispatch of all the warships that could be spared from that station.

He did not actually want war. He wanted it no more than Matheson did. (Some of the merchants did not believe this and paid Elliot the grudging compliment of supposing that he deliberately lured the Chinese down a collision course.) He was confident he understood the Chinese well enough and, in particular, appreciated keenly enough their preoccupation with preserving appearances, to avoid formal and prolonged hostilities. But he was absolutely set upon changing things—for which simple negotiation, even negotiation backed by the threat of force, would not be enough. The Chinese must first be knocked about a little. That was why he needed ships and men. When they arrived, he would get down to the business of it.

There was, in fact, a little splutter of hostilities before the month was out. The queen's birthday happened to be on 24 May, the very day Elliot quit the factories, and Parry arranged a little jollification on board the *Hercules* in Macao Roads. A good deal was drunk, and after dinner and the usual toasts nothing would satisfy the company but to see whether a certain long eighteen-pounder would carry all the way to the Nine Islands. She carried all right; the shot struck a war junk anchored off Sandy Bay. But the junk weighed and moved quietly away. If serious fighting had to come, it was not going to come quite yet.

The summer of 1839 was one of the pleasantest in years, cool and relatively dry, so that the Protestant missionaries later remembered it as almost delightful. Except for Parker they were all at Macao. Abeel shared a house with the Squires and their small children and resumed his study of the Fukien dialect. Bridgman and Williams put together the *Repository*, writing much of it themselves and sending the printed pages up to Parker at Canton to be bound. Mary Gutzlaff, assisted by her young cousins Catherine and Isabella Parkes, took care of orphaned Chinese girls in the house overlooking the inner harbor. The Browns kept a school for Chinese boys; Lockhart opened a Macao hospital on the model of the one in Hog Lane; Stanton tutored the Turner children and served the Superintendency as acting chaplain, the appointed fellow having gone home mortally ill. Things, in short, were much as before. Here they all were, safe, comfortable, and perched as always upon the outer rim of the Celestial Empire with no prospect at all of getting in.

Of course one had to be grateful for the "check" administered to the opium traffic—thus Williams to the American Board, further explaining that opium destroys the bodies of the Chinese, renders them insensible to the tidings of Christ's saving grace, and drags a dozen other evils in its train. Some people thought England would resent the forced surrender of the twenty thousand chests. Williams thought that when the news got through and mingled with the natural moral sense of the English people, "they will rather applaud the firmness of the Chinese."[8] But if all that the English did was to applaud, how on earth was Williams ever to find an adequate outlet for his evangelical energies? Possibly Parker took a more realistic view. All decent people, he wrote the board, deplore the opium traffic. Opium, however, is not the real issue, "it is the whole system which per se is wrong, and requires to be changed."[9] Parker did *not* find things exactly as they had been. He was still in the American factory, unable to go back to Hog Lane. As for Roberts and Shuck, though they were at Macao they too found things rather different. They had been used to distributing tracts and Bibles pretty freely about the town. Now, when they tried to resume the practice, Governor Pinto told them warmly to stop.

Pinto was apprehensive. He did not know what Lin intended for Macao. In a quiet way the Macaists had always done a considerable business in opium, bringing it ashore and selling it from godowns just as other foreigners did from ships. Lin had soon discovered this, of course. By the middle of March he knew that there were between two and four thousand chests in the town. Naturally he demanded their surrender, at which the Macaists hastily put them on board ship and sent them off to Manila. The job was carelessly done, however. Legrégeois noticed that some of the chests were carried through the town in broad daylight. Then came the affair of Innes's eight.

Since the execution riot of the previous December, Innes had stayed clear of Canton. He had not, however, quit handling opium and, when the delivery of the twenty thousand began, deliberately lifted eight chests out of the *Hercules*, intending apparently to sell them on the sly. By a series of mischances, however, the eight were stolen by some drunken English tars and recovered by the Macao police, who declined (on Pinto's instructions) to release them. Innes hurried to Macao and made a terrible row. In the end he was allowed to turn the chests in at Chuenpi—the eight drove the total of surrendered chests to 20,291, which became the final official figure. Nevertheless the row drew everyone's attention to the town. Lin wanted to know why such a notorious smuggler still lingered in the outer waters, and Elliot, who was sick and tired of being betrayed from the rear while facing the Chinese in front, ordered Innes to leave China. Innes refused. Elliot threatened to throw him out bodily. Innes withdrew to the *Austin*, dared Elliot to lay a finger on him there, and fired off a letter to Queen Victoria protesting that since the Government of India (which Her Majesty appointed) grew opium explicitly for the China market, the chief superintendent had no power to interfere with its sale. For weeks the uproar continued, in the letter columns of the two English papers and wherever Englishmen met. Pinto wished it would stop. Several war junks, including the one momentarily discomfitted by Parry's ranging practice, lay within sight of the town. Soldiers camped on the sandy neck just beyond the Barrier. How long, Pinto wondered, before the Chinese authorities attempted at Macao what they were executing so smartly at Canton?

He might, of course, turn for help to these very English. Early in April, Elliot had written from Canton, offering to join forces and promising immediate facilities on the British treasury to equip gunboats—for Macao had no navy of any kind. Pinto, however, was leery of such overtures. The English had taken Macao briefly in the Napoleonic Wars and were bound to think of it again; he preferred to defend the town himself. For this he had his forts. He had four hundred Goanese sepoys and could easily arm an equal number of Kaffir slaves, fine, big fellows from Portugal's African possessions with a natural contempt for the Chinese. The sepoys were rather a seedy bunch. Nevertheless on 30 May they made quite a decent showing as they marched to the Senate House in the Corpus Christi procession. Out in the roads lay the American frigate *Columbia* and the sloop *John Adams*, arrived at last from Singapore and so openly disposed towards the Portuguese that the rumor was they had landed fifty barrels of gunpowder for the governor's use.

The two French procurators, Legrégeois and Torrette, and their French-Swiss colleague, Joset, were anxious too. The long slump in opium sales made it difficult for them to sell the bills on London and Calcutta that the mother houses regularly sent them. They did not trust Governor Pinto, fearing that if their presence embarrassed him he would expel them without a qualm. They did not trust the mandarins either. Just outside the St. Lazarus Gate lay a little village of native converts, about six hundred of them—the only Christian Chinese that Macao could boast of (though the church had been active there for three hundred years). Many of these villagers were now quietly decamping. They were afraid of Lin; he was said to have spies everywhere; the rumor spread that he would shortly order all foreigners' servants away. Suppose he ordered the European priests away too? At a loss what else to do, Legrégeois put Libois, Callery, and Desflèches on a Spanish ship for Manila. "If I am surprised," he wrote as soon as he was alone, "I can always hide in some Portuguese house. To that end I have gotten together some lay clothes, and have put our money with the priests of St. Anthony's." Oh, if only some good would come of all this turmoil and anxiety! Legrégeois was not at all sure any would. The high commissioner was clever; no doubt he had dealt opium a heavy blow;

but the strength of the habit among smokers, the venality of most government clerks, and the "frightful thirst for gold" of many mandarins all conspired to guarantee the "dreadful traffic" a long, long life.[10]

It was certainly reviving smartly for Jardine, Matheson and Company. By the end of June the house was well settled at Macao, and its opium fleet active again. The *Governor Findlay*, in from the coast at last and found to be too unsound for further service, had become an auxiliary receiving ship. The *Colonel Young*, old and tender too, had been sold to Innes for $6,000. John Rees had taken the *Lady Hayes* and her unsold cargo back up the coast. The *Hellas*, with Jauncey in command, and the clipper brigantine *Kelpie* (recently arrived from England) were sent to join the *Lady Hayes*. The *Harriet, Jardine, Omega*, and *Snarley Yow* ran back and forth between the gulf and these three, taking instructions up to Rees (who served as commodore) and bringing treasure down. All was as before— with certain differences.

Manila now became an intermediate point of supply. Ships on the India run went there to unload opium, coastal schooners went there to replenish. The Manila government was agreeable—it even promised warehouses—and Matheson made an arrangement with an agent in the city until he should be able to send over Andrew Jardine. Indian correspondents were informed of the change by means of a circular printed at Macao on the house's own little lithographic press.

Along the China coast itself the traffic was conducted with a guardedness that was little short of stealth. The word "opium" disappeared from the instructions Matheson sent his skippers. When he absolutely had to specify types and quantities, he clothed them in the nomenclature of the cotton textile trade, Patna becoming "whites," Benares "greys," and Malwa "chintzes." Correspondents in England were advised that the whole subject was "under the rose," and the vessels that brought treasure down to the *Hercules* and the *Governor Findlay* passed it to them at night only, afterwards anchoring some distance away. To keep the traffic as quiet as possible was what Matheson and his partners wanted. "Because," as an English merchant named Hughes explained in a letter home, "they want neither the Commissioner to know, nor the people at Bombay or Calcutta, else the drug there would soon recover from its present very low prices—nor the parties in England who are the opponents, and have been so, of the opium trade all along."[11] Of course quiet could not always be obtained. Working the Tinpak station in a flat calm one July day, the *Ann* was set upon by war junks using sweeps, fought for four and a half hours, lost seven of her crew when a gun burst, and was lucky to get away at all. Other vessels had trouble in that quarter too; for a time the entire west coast was effectively shut to the traffic by the energy and ingenuity of the local mandarins. Matheson, however, was only confirmed in his feeling that the less noise the better. When Innes asked for chests to sell off the *Colonel Young*, he obliged him with some but privately urged Rees to restrain the irascible old fellow, "and prevent his committing acts of violence on the Chinese, to which he is much inclined."[12] Violence would not sell opium. Sober, steady application would. Buyers that summer were few and easily frightened—Matheson estimated total Chinese consumption at a fifteenth to a tenth of what it had been, "say two hundred to three hundred chests a month"—[13]but the destruction of the twenty thousand and the brief spring interruption in the normal flow from India had driven prices up. Before the summer was half over, good whites were fetching $700 a chest, greys and chintzes almost as much.

Dent too worked through Manila, in fact stayed there briefly himself, and put two vessels on the coast—first, however, changing their names, a thing Matheson did not think necessary. Failure to resume the traffic, he wrote a friend, would be tantamount to abandoning it to really desperate types, some of whom were fitting up ships at Singapore and other places and arming them heavily. Russell and Company did not follow Dent's example. The *Lintin* accepted only legitimate goods now. As for the smaller Canton houses, many of them tried to get back into opium, but with Lin so close, peddling in the gulf was out of the question, and they lacked the ships and resources to work the coast effectively. For a while the three or four big houses were going to dominate the traffic. The little fellows would have to content themselves with watching.

So that was how things stood. The last English merchant had left the factories, the last English ship had cleared the Bogue. In a series of meetings organized principally by Dent, the English community had agreed to abide by Captain Elliot's injunction not to reenter the river until the certain and powerful intervention of Her Majesty's government should put everything on a new and proper footing. That left only a few Americans in Canton. No other foreigners were present when early in July the *ch'in-ch'ai* paid a visit to the factories.

Lin came partly out of curiosity, partly to oversee certain physical changes. Already the square had been fenced into sections. The shops in Hog Lane and New China Street had been boarded up, and in the tangle of alleys behind Thirteen Factory Street the foreigner no longer discovered signs in crudely lettered pidgin inviting him to buy. Now workmen began to tear down certain terraces at the back of the factories from which the *fan kuei*, it was alleged, used to slip into the suburbs. Lin was purifying the area. When the English returned, they would find the arrangements and the atmosphere much more conducive to correct conduct and true filial subordination than they had been before.

The visit took place on 7 July. That same day, eighty miles to the southeast, a Chinese was fatally injured in circumstances that made an English return to Canton less likely, in fact, than ever.

On the east side of the Gulf of Canton, among the crowd of islands opposite Macao, are two conspicuously larger than the rest. The first, Lantao, stretches from Capsingmun southwestward fifteen miles into the gulf and, by its presence, blocks easy access to the Canton River from that side. A few miles east of Lantao is the second and smaller of the two, an oval ten miles long and up to four miles wide, lying lengthwise against the mainland. This is the island of Hongkong.

Hongkong is nearly all steep hillside, some of it eroded and barren, some of it grass-covered, rising in places to a height of not quite two thousand feet. From a half dozen gaunt granite peaks, gullies clothed in light jungle growth fall abruptly to the narrow beaches and rocky coves of a much-indented shore. On the south side there are a number of bays, among them "Heungkong" or "fragrant water"—later Aberdeen Bay, after Palmerston's successor at the Foreign Office. But these bays offer little shelter. For an all-weather anchorage you must go to the north side of the island, to the point where the peninsula of Kowloon pushes towards but does not quite reach the island's concave northern shore. Here there is a magnificent roadstead, deep, U-shaped, not much over a mile across, and so locked in by Lantao to the west and an extension of the mainland to the east that the sea traveler from distant parts, coming on deck the morning after his arrival, wonders how his ship got in at all.

When foreigners spoke of Hongkong it was this roadstead they had in mind, not any part of the island itself. There was little to draw them to the island, no town, only a few villages that lived on fishing and a touch of piracy. The emptiness and isolation of the area—forty miles from Macao and more than forty from the Bogue—suited the opium traffic very well, however, and by the late thirties the roadstead was as much used as Lintin. So when the typhoon season of 1839 approached and opium ships and merchant vessels had to leave Macao Roads, a great many moved to Hongkong as a matter of course, anchoring a few miles west of Kowloon off a promontory later called Possession Point.

To protect this fleet through what seemed likely to be a troubled summer— the *Larne*, in commission for several years and badly in need of caulking and a refit, had sailed for Trincomalee at the end of May—Elliot hired two little opium craft, the *Pearl* and the *Psyche*. Then early in June a former Indiaman with a remarkable broadside came into the gulf. She was the *Cambridge*, out of Bombay with a cargo of raw cotton and opium. She had spoken the *Good Success* off Malacca, learned that the English were held prisoners at Canton, and had then stopped at Singapore, where Douglas (her owner and captain) bought twenty-six eighteen-pounders and four long twelves to add to the six carronades she already carried. Douglas had been a master in the Royal Navy. His crew was European, a thing rare for vessels east of the Cape, and trained to fight. He offered the *Cambridge* to Elliot with such enthusiasm and such persistence that Elliot engaged him at a handsome fee until a proper warship should turn up.

Douglas and the *Cambridge*, however, could not prevent little brushes between the English and the Chinese. Ships at Hongkong regularly watered from springs on the Kowloon side and sent their compradors there to buy rice, meat, and other provisions. The Chinese authorities did nothing to interfere with this practice. Still, there were several war junks in the vicinity, particularly about a small Chinese shore battery at Kowloon point, and it was obvious they meant the foreigners no good. Towards the end of June men from one of these junks seized the comprador of the *Carnatic*. Her master was with difficulty dissuaded from sending a raiding party to retaliate. A really serious clash seemed only a matter of time—and on Sunday, 7 July, it came. All sorts of people were ashore on the Kowloon side that day, among them sailors from the *Carnatic*, from another English ship, and from several American ships. No doubt they were looking for women and alcohol. Perhaps they found the first; certainly they found the second; for towards midday, in the little village of Chien-sha-tsui (about where the Kowloon railroad terminal now stands), they came across a quantity of *samshu*, the powerful native rice liquor, got drunk, fought the villagers, half wrecked a temple, and did not withdraw to their ships until dusk. Next day one of the villagers was dead.

The news alarmed Elliot. He had never liked the way some skippers let their men wander about unsupervised. What was done, was done, however, and it remained only to hurry over from Macao and hush the matter up. He did not succeed. Though he spent almost $2,000 in and about Chien-sha-tsui, word reached Lin before the week was out—and Lin demanded the person of the murderer.

With the best will in the world he would have been hard to identify. The villager was dead all right, but no one could be sure it was the beating that had killed him, and if it was the beating, which blow. Besides, the sailors from the two English ships insisted that their buddies of the moment, the Americans, had been drunker than they and had hit harder. But Lin *would* have a life for a life! Was it to be Terranova or the gunner of the *Lady Hughes* all over again? Elliot convened a special court, with himself the judge and merchants for a jury, and charged five English sailors with riot and assault. He was not going to turn anyone over to the Chinese, however. He made that perfectly clear.

The refusal annoyed Lin. He could not simply ignore it, and it threatened to divert him from the work of winding up the opium business—a matter of more, much more, than simply seizing the chests in the possession of the foreigners and arranging that no more came in. There was the whole domestic side of the traffic to be dealt with: from the farmers who grew the poppy (some opium was already grown in China), to the police officers who took bribes, to the brokers who bought and sold the partly refined drug, to the proprietors of the opium dens. There were the addicts themselves, in the Canton area tens of thousands of them, to be somehow cleansed of their vice. For this formidable work the various organs of the imperial government had begun, the previous autumn, to draw up a comprehensive statute, but Lin had not waited for this statute to appear. From the moment of his arrival in Canton he had pursued opium offenders, cunningly, relentlessly, using the old *pao-chia* system of mutual incrimination where he could, developing his own sources of information where he could not. Once, for example, he asked six hundred students assembled for a mock provincial examination to write down all that they knew about the traffic and, at the end of the day, when the eight-legged essays on the usual topics had been collected and the doors of the examination hall unlocked, had quite a number of fresh suspects to add to his list. By the middle of May he had arrested over fifteen hundred persons and confiscated forty thousand pipes. Such quantities of the drug were coming into his hands that he had a special destruction basin built right in Canton. When the new thirty-nine-article statute finally appeared in July, Lin was simply encouraged to greater efforts. Death was now the penalty for every variety of opium offense. Even the smoker had only eighteen months in which to give up the habit. (To help him Lin opened a sanitarium just outside the city wall.) A supplementary statute, placing the same penalty on foreigners, seemed to make the bond superfluous, for the western merchant who stayed outside the river was, from this moment, just as liable to be executed as the merchant who signed and went in.

Every weapon the law could give Lin was his. Yet now, suddenly, he was told that the English roamed the Kowloon shore, that some of them plundered and murdered, and that Elliot, their *taipan*, refused to turn the culprits over so that life should pay for life. It was insufferable! If the red-haired devils would not reenter the river and behave as they ought to behave, they must be harried—wherever they could be reached.

On 12 August the trial of the Chien-sha-tsui rioters began on board the *Fort William*, which Elliot had rented to supplement the *Louisa*. Lin was invited to send observers. None came. On the fifteenth an edict reached Macao prohibiting the sale of provisions to Englishmen on land or on sea. A day or so later the Chinese servants in the English households began to disappear. Some Portuguese halfbreeds, hired hastily to take their places, got the message and stayed away too. In the coves and inlets about Hongkong there were suddenly more war junks than there had been before, and when watering parties went ashore to fill their casks, they found above each spring a sign in Chinese saying it was poisoned. One was dragged. Up came a stone-weighted bag, filled with leaves "and something else mixed, but no one could say what it was."[14] Other springs yielded the same strange objects. Perhaps it was bluff. Just the same no one cared to call the bluff by drinking.

Meanwhile the *ch'en-ch'ai* left Canton and moved by the inner passage to Hsiang-shan, only forty miles above Macao. It began to look as if he planned a descent upon the town. Matheson boarded a schooner. Elliot sent his wife and two-year-old son, Frederick, over to the *Fort William* at Hongkong and on 23 August started for that place himself. This was on a Friday. Saturday passed without incident, but Sunday morning Governor Pinto let it be known that he had just received an edict directing him to expel the English immediately. At almost the same moment Jardine Matheson's *Harriet* came into the outer harbor towing the passage schooner *Black Joke*, crewless, the marks of blood upon her deck. It seemed that off Lantao the night before, seven boatloads of Chinese had attacked the schooner, killed every man of her lascar crew except the serang (who had jumped into the water and clung to the rudder), and savagely knocked about the single passenger, an Englishman named Moss, finally cutting off his left ear, stuffing it in his mouth, and leaving him for dead. Then they had plundered the boat and would have burned her, but the *Harriet* came up. Moss was alive and likely to survive, Matheson wrote Elliot by the *Ann*, adding he felt sure the attackers had been common pirates. But the general opinion was that they were mandarins' men; so when, that afternoon, a second chop reached Pinto, he decided he could answer no longer for the safety of the English. They must all leave on the morrow.

Meanwhile there were the next twenty-four hours to be got through. To this day the traveler feels exposed and vulnerable when first he sets foot on Macao. The peninsula is so diminutive, the Lappa to the west and the hills to the north so much higher than the elevations on which the forts sit—even the islands to the southeast, among which lies the Typa, seem threatening in their closeness. But that afternoon there were better reasons to be afraid. Soldiers were known to be camped just beyond the Barrier. More soldiers were thought to be on the islands, and towards sunset the rumor spread that they were coming to take the red-haired devils in their beds. Under a brilliant moon large numbers of Chinese hurriedly deserted the town. The English packed, fowling pieces and other arms laid handy. Pinto stayed awake too, seeing to the posting of his sepoys, for honor required that he fight if the Chinese tried to enter before the English left. Nothing in fact happened. The morning dawned without incident, but Abeel, looking up at the Monte Fort from his house below, saw in the embrasures the muzzles of cannon and knew that "the guns had been ready to perform their awful work."[15]

Abeel himself had nothing to worry about, nor did the Catholic procurators as it turned out. The order to leave affected only the English and the Parsees. Except for Caroline Squire (her baby's wet nurse would, she knew, refuse to set foot on a foreign devil ship), one other woman too sick to be moved, and old Thomas Beale (who could not be separated from his birds and, anyway, passed for Prussian consul), they all went: Chinnery, the painter, in a pitiable state of nerves; Medhurst's young son, Walter, fresh from England; Lockhart, Slade, Stanton, and Stanton's pupils; dozens of merchants and their families—all that Monday morning the lanes and alleys leading down to the Praia Grande were filled with men, women, and children moving to the boats. By the middle of the afternoon the thing was done. Almost 250 English rested safely aboard eighteen merchantmen collected for the purpose in the Typa. On Tuesday, Gutzlaff and his household slipped out too, friends having convinced him that, though nominally a German, he was pretty well tarred with the English brush. Wind and rain held the merchantmen motionless. On Thursday, to everyone's joy, the 26-gun *Volage* came in from the Indian Ocean with the news that another of Her Majesty's warships, the 18-gun *Hyacinth*, was not far behind. Next day the weather cleared, and with the frigate for escort, the little fleet sailed for Hongkong.

At Hsiang-shan, Lin received with delight the news that the English had fled. "No doubt they have on their ships," he wrote the emperor, "a certain stock of dried provisions; but they will very soon find themselves without the heavy, greasy meat dishes for which they have such a passion."[16] Besides, he meant to deny them fresh water, and without water it was impossible to live. It occurred to him that this would be an opportune time to visit Macao. Pinto, forewarned, sent a deputy to meet him at the Barrier, and Lin was carried ceremoniously about the town, sepoys and band in front, Chinese soldiers trailing behind. To the few Americans out watching, these soldiers with their bows and arrows, their pikes and halberds and matchlocks, seemed straight out of the sixteenth century. What Lin noticed, however, was that in several places the local

Chinese had erected arches decorated with flowers and festoons of silk to express their gratitude for the struggle he was waging against the foreign mud.

So the English were driven from Macao and lived now at Hongkong. The arrival of the merchantmen from the Typa had brought the number of vessels there to nearly seventy. That meant, if you included the seamen (many of whom were lascar), several thousand men, some armed and all restless, cooped aboard ship in the most trying season of the year. Elliot did not think he could control them indefinitely.

To relieve their feelings, and perhaps his own, he ordered three war junks suspected of directing the embargo on provisions and the poisoning of springs to leave the vicinity of the Kowloon battery and, when they would not, went at them in the cutter *Louisa*, with the hired opium brigantine *Pearl* and the pinnace of the *Volage* in support. To his surprise the three did not run but stood and replied with everything they had. Fortunately their fire was high. "Nineteen of their guns we received in our mainsail," wrote a young Superintendency clerk who happened to be present, "the first broadside I can assure you was not pleasant."[17] In half an hour the *Louisa* had run out of cartridges and was forced to draw away. Boldly the junks gave chase. They were twice the size of the brigantine and four times the size of the cutter, the pinnace had gone for help, but a few cartridges were hastily made and, when the junks caught up, "we hove the vessel in stays on their starboard beam, and the *Pearl* on the larboard bow of the van junk, and gave them three such broadsides that it made every rope in the vessel grin again. We loaded with grape the fourth time, and gave them gun for gun. The shrieking on board was dreadful." Help, meanwhile, was arriving. The wind was too light for the *Cambridge* or the *Volage*, but a number of boats came up, among them the barge of the *Cambridge* commanded by Douglas himself and manned by eighteen sturdy English seamen in white shirts and blue trousers. Then the wind died completely, and Elliot allowed the junks to regain the shelter of their battery.

Lin accepted the account concocted by the local naval commander, claiming many red-haired devils killed and a two-masted vessel sunk, and forwarded it to Peking. Elliot for his part worked hard to dissuade Captain Smith of the *Volage* from going back, sinking the three junks, and blowing up the battery. Palmerston might overlook a skirmish fought in the heat of exasperation from a 75-ton cutter; he would not forgive a formal assault mounted from a frigate—besides, fighting seemed suddenly unnecessary. Within days of the encounter ships' compradors were obtaining everything they wanted. Knocking the three junks about had apparently taken the heart out of the embargo on provisions. Watering parties noticed that the signs at the springs were gone.

A few English slipped back to Macao. Squire was one; coming into the Typa aboard a French merchantman early one morning, he was astonished to see a large vessel burning fiercely. She was the Spanish brig *Bilbaino*, taken it was said for an English opium carrier—indeed an English carrier *had* anchored in the Typa, sold some of her drug to men masquerading as brokers' agents, then sailed at dusk just as the *Bilbaino* entered; Lin's raiding party, attacking at midnight, had got the wrong ship!—and for a moment Macao was once more in an uproar. Pinto armed a vessel, Elliot offered powder and shot to any merchantmen that needed them, but no further incidents occurred, there or at Hongkong, and as September drew to a close an uneasy quiet settled over the gulf.

For the Americans, unexpectedly, it was a time of intense activity. Though John Bull was gone from the river, his cargoes had still to be gotten up, and who but the Americans should carry them? All that was needed was to accept Lin's bond. In July, after some hesitation, they had accepted it—in a version whose English, which alone they could read, made no mention of capital punishment. The commander of the *Columbia* was surprised, old Peter Snow was disgusted, but as Bennet Forbes put it to Elliot himself, it was not for health or pleasure that he and his countrymen had come to China. Green was gone. Forbes was head of Russell and Company now. From rented quarters aboard an English merchantman at Hongkong he supervised the loading of the *Lintin*, the *Rose*, and such other vessels as he could lay his hands on. The trick, he discovered, was to fill every inch of the hold, pile the deck right up to the leading blocks, take out the upper spars to lessen the danger of capsizing, and send the vessel into the river under nearly bare poles. In this way huge quantities of cotton went up to Whampoa, and rattans and other cargo too. Not that the English enjoyed seeing the Yankees so busy. "While we hold the horns," observed one drily, "they milk the cow."[18] But how else were goods to be moved?

Lockhart went off to Batavia. Mary Gutzlaff took the Parkes girls to Manila. Legrégeois, on the other hand, felt confident enough to write his people to return. In Canton, where a dozen Americans did agency for the English and for themselves, Peter Parker practiced medicine with such skill and tact that his list of patients lengthened to include the *ch'in-ch'ai* himself. Lin suffered, it seemed, from a hernia. He sent to Parker for medicine; Parker recommended a truss; when the great man declined to come in person to be fitted, Parker passed along six he had in stock. Later he learned that one of the six suited Lin tolerably, "excepting that when he coughs the contents of the abdomen are liable to descend."[19] A new medical missionary named Diver reached Macao for the American Board.

If Lin was not always at the provincial capital, it was because he liked to spend time with Admiral Kuan at the Bogue. There he watched drills and exercises—a matter of war junks and fireboats arranged in neat lines, of marines shooting arrows, hurling lances, nimbly slashing and striking. Lin did not expect the early employment of this finely honed instrument of war. Without saying anything about it, he had pretty much given up the idea of trying to make the English enter the river or leave the coast. They might stay where they were until Peking, by sign or signal, suggested a fresh approach or until instructions from the English Queen moved them to a more obedient course. But when would these instructions arrive? Bridgman, invited to the Bogue and questioned, could not tell him, and he did not care to ask the red-haired devils themselves.

At Hongkong, Elliot slipped into a similar acceptance of things. The corvette *Hyacinth* arrived, giving him two warships and permitting him to drop the hire of the *Cambridge*. Provisioning was adequate, water safe; he felt so comfortable that he let his old mistrust of the opium traffic revive—and requested all English and Parsee opium vessels to quit the anchorage. Few moved, of course, and these not far, but it was a gesture of conciliation, and the Chinese, in their way, replied. The five sailors charged with riot and assault in the Chien-sha-tsui affray had been convicted and shipped to England (where their sentences to short terms at hard labor were revoked the moment they landed), but this had not put an end to the demands for the person of the murderer. Now, when a sailor from Jardine Matheson's *Snarley Yow* was found drowned near Hongkong, the Chinese intimated that *his* body might do. Perhaps in this way the painful issue should at last be put to rest.

It was in the matter of trade, however, that the rapprochement seemed most promising. As the weeks passed and the opening of the tea market drew near, only Dent and his friends took pleasure in the prospect of the English being denied access to it. (Their London correspondents wanted to keep the price of tea high, to which end the less leaving China the better.) Matheson and the rest were eager to buy and ship; it bothered them that as things stood they must put their business entirely in the hands of the Americans; Lin on his side was no doubt pressed by the Canton tea men, who cannot have relished selling to so narrow a ring. So the chief superintendent and the high commissioner were driven almost in spite of themselves to negotiate a resumption of trade. They did not negotiate face-to-face. The taboo upon that sort of thing was far too strong. But they exchanged views through the hong merchants, Elliot went to Macao to explore the subject, and an agreement took shape that would allow English merchantmen into the river upon inspection for signs of the drug—but without the bond.

Carrying the agreement through hung, however, upon preserving a united front. And this, as it happened, the English could not manage. For towards the middle of October a former Indiaman, the *Thomas Coutts*, out of London and Bombay with a mixed cargo of cottons and rattans (but no opium), entered the gulf, moved quietly to the Bogue, executed the bond, and went up.

Lin was astounded. For months the barbarian headman had represented his countrymen as being quite unable to accept the bond. Now here was one that arrived, looked briefly around, and signed without the least hesitation. Another, he heard, was willing. Away then with the tentative agreement! Let the English turn over the Chien-sha-tsui murderer, do as the *Thomas Coutts* had done, and come promptly to Whampoa—or he would drive them all from the coast! With a fresh confidence, or it may be a last desperate hope, the high commissioner marshaled his forces for the decisive test.

Cursing the *Thomas Coutts* and Daniell, the unregenerate former Company man to whom she was consigned, Elliot boarded the *Volage* and set sail for the Bogue, the *Hyacinth* close behind. The common front he had struggled so long to maintain was broken. A potential hostage lay within Lin's grasp. Worse, Lin threatened the rest of the merchant fleet, for it was collected just below the Bogue, ready to enter the river the moment the agreement should be final, and where it lay it was vulnerable to attack. Elliot would have to come to its aid.

So the two men-of-war beat slowly up the gulf. On Saturday morning, 2 November, they reached the vicinity of Chuenpi. There they found Admiral Kuan with sixteen war junks and a dozen fireboats. For twenty-four hours each side tried to discover, by means of notes and deputations, what the other side was up to and, across the barriers of language and dignity jealously guarded, got nowhere. Early on Sunday, Kuan led his junks toward the anchored English merchantmen. Simultaneously a second English vessel, the *Royal Saxon*, appeared from the south and made as if to enter the river. Captain Smith brought her up with a shot across her bows and at the same time sent a warning to the admiral to turn back, but he, instead of withdrawing, anchored close to the Chuenpi shore in such a position that his junks and fireboats could easily pass inside the two men-of-war and drive down upon the merchantmen during the night. To prevent this Smith must either force the junks to retire or himself fall back and cover the merchantmen. The second course seemed to him consistent neither with his own character as an English officer nor with the known inclination of the Chinese to read prudence for weakness, so he determined to take the first course. Elliot had misgivings. Smith jogged his elbow.

Towards noon on the third the two gave the order to attack.

The frigate and the corvette had been lying hove to. Now they bore away smartly on the starboard tack (the wind was from the northeast) and ran up the Chinese line, delivering broadsides as they ran. The junks and fireboats slipped or cut and fired back, but the contest was terribly unequal. Very early a fireboat sank. A junk, hit in the magazine, blew up showering the *Volage* with burning fragments. When the two English vessels reached the top of the Chinese line, they came about and ran down again with their port broadsides bearing. By this time the Chinese were in desperate confusion, and the *Hyacinth*, getting well in among them, banged happily away at very short range. Where were the arrows and the lances now, the marines nimbly slashing and striking? Three more junks went down. Several others were deserted by their terrified crews. The rest tried to run—all except the admiral's flagship which, mounting the unusual total of twelve guns, and with the admiral himself erect before the single, immense mast, continued to stand against the English though she had been holed repeatedly and was on the point of foundering. Before the *Hyacinth* could finish her off, Smith flew the signal to break action. He had accomplished his purpose. He had removed the immediate threat to the merchantmen. So he let the remnants of the Chinese squadron limp back to the Bogue. His own damage came to sails, spars, and rigging a good deal knocked about (as usual the Chinese fired high), a twelve-pound ball in the *Hyacinth*'s mizzenmast, and one sailor slightly wounded.

Born swiftly on a following wind, Elliot reached Macao late that afternoon and invited those few of his countrymen who had slipped back to the town to come on board the *Volage*. He had no illusions about what was going to happen next, and in Canton, where Nye and the other Americans had heard the faint but ominous sound of cannonading, they had no illusions either. War was going to happen next. The only question was, when would an expedition arrive to fight it?

13

India and England Take Notice

On 25 May 1839 George Eden Baron Auckland, governor-general of India, sat down to his desk at Simla in the foothills of the Himalayas and wrote a letter to John Cam Hobhouse.

Hobhouse was president of the Board of Control, or what a later age would call secretary of state for India. Although the East India Company retained the administration of British India, a Board of Control nominated by the Queen's ministers oversaw that administration and made policy in all matters of importance—which meant above all matters of war and peace. To the senior presidency of Bengal with its seat at Calcutta, and thence to the subordinate presidencies of Bombay and Madras, the board regularly sent its directions, using as a channel the Secret Committee of the Company's Court of Directors. This Secret Committee met behind green baize doors at the India House in Leadenhall Street, London. There it frequently initiated business of its own. The last word, however, rested always with the president of the Board of Control, who as a matter of course was a member of the cabinet, so it was perfectly proper for Lord Auckland to write directly to Hobhouse. He did it all the time.

Auckland and Hobhouse were on intimate terms with Lord Melbourne, the prime minister. Indeed, Auckland had served Melbourne as first lord of the Admiralty until Hobhouse tapped him for India. The two were in their middle fifties, Palmerston was the same age, Melbourne was only a little older—and there were reasons why three out of the four should know each other particularly well. For a time it had seemed likely that Melbourne and Auckland's sister Emily would marry, and though they had not, and Emily had accompanied her brother to India, the two still corresponded. Between the prime minister and his foreign secretary the link was closer still, since Palmerston was in love with—was reputedly the lover of—Melbourne's sister Lady Cowper and waited only for a decent interval (Cowper had just died) to make her his wife. Then there were the Elliot connections. Auckland's successor at the Admiralty was Gilbert Elliot, Earl of Minto, one of whose daughters would soon marry Melbourne's chief lieutenant in the House of Commons, Lord John Russell. Minto was first cousin to Auckland; both were first cousins to the considerably younger Charles Elliot, our chief superintendent of trade; Minto's brother, George, was commander-in-chief on the South African station; and there were other Elliots scattered about the navy as far as the eye could see. But one may play this little game indefinitely. In politics and the services, as in so many other areas of English life, ties of blood and marriage reinforced the cementing influence of privilege and property and gave to the direction of England's affairs something of the atmosphere of a club.

Where foreign policy was concerned, what the club had on its mind in the spring of 1839 were the French and the Russians. Though the French had been beaten decisively not many years before and should consequently be free of imperial ambitions, it was clear enough that they were not. In size and design of ship they possessed a navy second to none and might expect to rival the English even in numbers, once they had solved the problem of crews (seamen came from the merchant marine, and the French merchant marine was tiny). They had designs upon the north coast of Africa. They were making a beginning with Algiers. It was at the eastern end of the Mediterranean, however, that their presence was most seriously felt. Though the Suez Canal was not yet dug or even seriously contemplated, Egypt was already held to be a vital station on the route to India, and Egypt was in the hands of Mehemet Ali, an Albanian adventurer and soldier of genius who for years had looked naturally to Paris. French instructors trained Mehemet's excellent army. An obelisk from Luxor adorned the Place de la Concorde. What if, in Egypt, French patronage entirely replaced the nominal suzerainty of the Turks?

A year or so before the Napier fizzle, Mehemet Ali had invaded Syria and beaten the Turks so badly that only the arrival of a Russian fleet and Russian regiments had deterred him from advancing on Constantinople. After a while the Russians had withdrawn. Now, early in the spring of 1839, the Turks, blinded by a passion for revenge and unwisely confident that a handful of Prussian advisers (among them the youthful von Moltke) had succeeded in transforming their army, were about to attempt the reconquest of Syria. If Mehemet beat them again the Russians would certainly return to Constantinople, this time perhaps for good. That was bad news for Palmerston. For if the English distrusted France in Egypt, they distrusted Russia at the Bosporus even more.

In fact they distrusted Russia all the way across Asia. Kipling was yet unborn, the Russians had only recently pushed around the top of the Caspian, Company rule in India still stopped short of the Indus River—but from Tabriz to the Hindu Kush the "great game" was already on. In the late 1830s it centered upon Afghanistan. In the summer of 1837 the Shah of Persia sent an army against the western Afghan city of Herat. Persia was then much under Russian influence. If Herat fell Afghanistan (which was in an unusually disturbed state) might yield to Russian influence too, and from Afghanistan a number of passes led by easy steps down to the Indus valley. The Russians themselves were still far away. They had not yet occupied Khiva, on the north edge of the Kara Kum desert. From Khiva you mounted the Oxus River for nearly five hundred miles before turning due south towards those Afghan passes, and even then you had two hundred miles of very difficult ground before you reached the first, the Khyber Pass. Nevertheless there were men in high places who, looking solemnly ahead, saw (or thought they saw) Russian horsemen at the heads of those passes with all India at their feet. Somehow Auckland must manage to bar the door before the Russians could get into Afghanistan at all.

A way came to hand. It happened that Ranjit Singh, the ruler of the independent Sikh state that stretched from the Sutlej to Peshawar, was on very bad terms with Dost Muhammad, the prince who held Kabul. It also happened that there was an alternative to the Dost, a certain Shah Shuja who had been forced from Kabul many years before. Auckland brought Shah Shuja and Ranjit Singh together. An agreement was reached. English soldiers with Sikh assistance would restore Shah Shuja to Kabul. Once restored, Shah Shuja would confirm Ranjit Singh in the possession of certain places the Dost coveted—and for England's sake hold the Russians at arm's length. Early in 1839, accordingly, European and sepoy regiments of the Bengal army crossed the middle Indus. Units of the Bombay army set off by ship to join them (to secure the mouths of the Indus the 74-gun *Wellesley* went to Karachi, demolished the unresisting fort on Manora Head, and accepted the surrender of the city). In March the Bengal column climbed the Bolan Pass. Early in April the Bombay column followed. By the end of the month both had reached Kandahar, well inside Afghanistan, and there, on 24 May, the Army of the Indus celebrated the Queen's birthday with a double issue of liquor. The first Afghan War, as it would later be called, was off to a satisfying start.

All this is not irrelevant to our story. The Afghan campaign preoccupied Auckland. It claimed a major share of Palmerston's attention, it stirred the English public as much as any foreign development could in that summer of the Chartist petition and the Birmingham riots, and when Afghanistan was not in the news, the Near East was. In June the Turkish army, attempting to recover Syria, was utterly routed by Mehemet Ali's son, Ibrahim. In July the entire Turkish fleet, on the urging it was suspected of a French admiral, turned itself over to the Egyptians. Next to these rousing developments what had China to offer? What could she show that would attract more than a glance from Whitehall or the newspaper offices along Fleet Street?

When, therefore, Auckland went to his desk on the twenty-fifth, one day after Elliot had left Canton, one day after Parry and his drunken friends had ranged their eighteen-pounder on the unsuspecting junk near Macao, it was not to tell Hobhouse the bad news from Canton, it was to tell him the good news from Kandahar. The Army of the Indus was safely over the frontier. Shah Shuja was with it. In a few months he would be king again in Kabul, and the door firmly locked against the Russians. "Yesterday was Her Majesty's birthday," Auckland continued, "and all that are white in Simla dined with me in our most beautiful valley, and all that are black sat on their heels amidst bazars of sweetmeats and rejoiced in the fireworks, and Victoria and Kandahar blazed in letters of lamps amidst the fir trees, and there were cheers for the Queen, and never was loyalty better displayed than it has been in the Himalayas." Then, without a pause, "as I was about to finish my letter, the news from China came in, and here is a new source of trouble and anxiety."[1]

Just how troublesome the China question would turn out to be, how much more troublesome and decisive for England and the world than anything that could possibly come out of Afghanistan, the governor-general was hardly in a position to see.

It was Jamsetjee Jeejeebhoy's country ship *Good Success* that brought the news. She had reached the Gulf of Canton with Malwa early in March; she had sailed the second week in April, carrying the dispatches brought downriver by Johnston; she had touched Singapore, spoken Douglas's *Cambridge* a few days later off Malacca, and dropped anchor in the roadstead of Madras on 13 May. Although Simla was a very great distance away and the summer heat at its fiercest, *dak* runners had carried the news to Auckland by the twenty-fifth.

The information that Elliot was a prisoner and that his ransom must consist of twenty thousand chests did not send Auckland hurrying south. He had been at Simla a year and a half and at Simla he meant to stay, partly because it was vastly preferable to Calcutta in climate, partly because it was much closer to Afghanistan and the army there. What to do about China he knew not. There would have to be a show of force, of course—but war? "The decision must be with you in England," he wrote Hobhouse early in June. The only thing certain was that the opium trade could never be the same again. "As regards India, we must for the present look upon the opium revenue as annihilated. It will probably be determined that the disconnection of the Government from the cultivation of the poppy shall gradually take place."[2] To do without the opium revenue would of course be difficult. But if the Chinese were not going to permit the drug to be sold on their shores, its price on the Calcutta market was certain to fall disastrously and with it the government's profit. In that case there was hardly any point in going on with the agencies. Salt and land taxes must take up the slack.

These, however, were the reflections of a governor-general far from the scene and not particularly familiar with the matter. Bombay and Calcutta merchants actually dealing in opium looked at things rather differently. Many were small-time speculators—"men of straw" Matheson once contemptuously called them[3]—with consignments on the China coast or headed there, and if these consignments did not sell they would be in serious trouble. Even the large and established Indian houses of agencies like Jamsetjee Jeejeebhoy and Sons of Bombay, or Lyall Matheson and Company of Calcutta (in which another James Matheson nephew, Hugh, was a partner), looked at the swift decline in the China market with dismay. Before ever news of Lin's arrival in Canton had reached Calcutta, a number of houses in that city were petitioning Fort William to postpone the third opium sale until the stock accumulated on the China coast could be worked off. Fort William refused. It had, after all, given public notice of the year's sales long in advance, seven thousand chests at the first sale (duly sold the first Monday in January at excellent prices), twenty-five hundred chests at the second sale (duly sold late in February at reasonable prices). That left thirty-four hundred to be put up in April, with another twenty-five hundred in May, and an odd but substantial balance in July. Such was the schedule drawn up by the Board of Customs, Salt, and Opium. The thing could not reasonably be done in any other way. For the board knew to the cake exactly how much opium it had in hand, knew too exactly how many acres of the poppy were even then ripening across the Ganges plain. To slow the disposing of the 1839 crop when the 1840 was already visible in the fields would be the height of folly. Each sale must proceed on schedule. And at the third sale late in April (an auction being after all an auction) every chest was sold—but at what prices!

In January, Patna had fetched over 800 rupees a chest, about $330. In February it had fetched nearly Rs. 700. Now, in April, when Calcutta knew that Commissioner Lin had reached Canton, the figure sank below Rs. 400! Came the "momentous intelligence" that the factory community was being held for a ransom of twenty thousand chests, and again the agency houses begged Fort William to postpone a sale. Again Fort William refused. The fourth sale was held on the last Monday in May, three days after the queen's birthday. Patna dropped below Rs. 250, Benares below Rs. 200 (or $80). At such prices the board did not even cover its costs!

Yet it kept right on selling. And though it closed five of the smaller and less productive subagencies and instructed the rest to contract for no additional acreage in the coming growing season, it went bravely ahead with arrangements for disposing of the provision of 1838/39 (which, fortunately, was a little less than normal because of unusual winter winds and rain), stipulating only that there would be at each sale an "upset price" below which the auctioneer need not go. Continued volume at low prices conferred, it was beginning to be seen, its own distinct advantages. It promised to drive Malwa, which cost more to produce than Patna and Benares, clean out of the market. Even at depressed China coast prices it left the consignee plenty of silver to bribe mandarins with—a thing more likely than anything else to move Peking to legalize the traffic. Suppose, moreover, that English public opinion compelled the Whig ministry to order the Government of India out of the opium business? Private poppy cultivation on the Ganges plain was sure to continue; the government would wish to draw revenue from it; unless it wanted to risk repeating its previous experience with Malwa, it must draw that revenue by applying modest duties to a substantial volume. Any way you looked at the matter, concluded the board's senior member in a carefully constructed minute, the government would be well advised to stick to an annual provision of twenty thousand chests.

What if opium was debilitating? Twenty years earlier the board, contemplating a slight increase in production, had admitted that it was. Now the junior member, in a minute following his senior's, argued that it was not. "During the nearly nine years I was attached to the Benares Agency," he wrote, "I never knew one solitary instance of impaired health amongst natives resulting from the use of the drug, not even in the factories, where the people passed twelve hours a day in an opium atmosphere and ate as much as they could consume."[4] No doubt the emperor and his ministers were truly anxious to check the flow into China, but why? From the frigate *Conway*, lying in the Hooghly, Captain Bethune wrote privately to Sir Frederick Maitland (commanding the East Indian Station) that the explanation was simple—and well known to everybody. The Chinese hated losing silver! "I do not think they care two pence about the immorality of using opium."[5]

Was the traffic Calcutta's concern in any case? When, somewhat later, Captain Elliot's April dispatches reached the Foreign Office and were in due course passed on to the Board of Control, somebody there penciled: "India, as India, appears to be only concerned in the China question inasmuch as there can be no doubt that if the Chinese will not eat opium, the Indian Revenue must materially suffer; but it is presumed that it is quite out of the question to suppose that the British Government would be justified in compelling the Chinese to eat opium. The question, therefore, of the propriety of listening to Captain Elliot's suggestions seems entirely one for the consideration departmentally of the Foreign Office, with which the President of this Board has nothing to do except in his capacity of a Cabinet Minister."[6] You may read that twice, you may read it three times, and not be certain what it says—except this: *China policy is not India's business*. If this was how they felt in Leadenhall Street, could one expect more of Fort William?

So the Board of Customs, Salt, and Opium went its own way and as the summer advanced was modestly rewarded for its perseverance. At the fifth and final July sale over three thousand chests changed hands at an average approaching Rs. 300. For the season as a whole the board was actually in the black!* Malwa, as the senior member had predicted, recovered much more slowly, yet a few vessels had loaded it in the spring. Now the *Good Success* (which came around from Madras) did the same; the *Mahommedie*, which had brought Matheson's London-bound nephew, carried very little else when she left Bombay for Manila in August; in September the *Lady Grant* weighed for the same port with seven hundred chests. While in the Hooghly vessels came and went with all their accustomed intentness and dispatch—in August, for example, the *Red Rover* and the *Sir Edward Ryan* sighted the Sandheads the same day, loaded eighteen hundred chests between them, and raced for China just hours apart.

Matheson's men of straw did not, of course, recover *their* spirits so easily. They had sunk everything into their speculation and were ruined if Whitehall repudiated Captain Elliot; in Bombay the thought drove a number to the very edge of suicide, and two (it is said) quite over. Nevertheless the traffic was clearly fated to continue. Nobody close to it, not even the suicides, expected otherwise, and as Auckland began a leisurely descent that autumn from Simla, he more and more looked at the matter in the very same way. Indeed, when he finally reached Calcutta in February of 1840 and saw before him the mass of accumulated business, his calendar crowded with councils and audiences, worst of all the expenses of the Afghan venture, all thought of abolishing the two Bengal agencies went out of his head. What to do about smuggling on the China coast remained a question—a question, he wrote Hobhouse, "of much difficulty and embarrassment, and I cannot bring myself to a satisfactory opinion upon it." Meanwhile, however, opium prices were recovering nicely.

---

*But barely so. In the late 1830s the yield of the Bengal monopoly, after expenses, had regularly approached Rs. 10 million annually in a net revenue for the Bengal government of Rs. 70 million or more. In 1839 the opium net was just a little over Rs. 3 million.

Chests in the first sale of the year had fetched well over the Rs. 400 upset price; in February, Patna topped Rs. 600. "One small cruizer came in last week with seven lakhs' worth of sycee silver."[7] Things, it seemed, were moving back to normal.

So India weathered her opium crisis. Auckland's task now—a task explicitly assigned him in a letter that had reached him at Agra in January and sent him hurrying in his palanquin towards Calcutta—was to put a naval and military force on the coast of China. Afghanistan was quiet. Shah Shuja sat in apparent security upon the throne at Kabul. As February gave way to March and the torrid heat of a Bengal summer began to fasten upon Calcutta, Auckland turned his attention eastward. But though he and his government had the immediate work of dispatching an expedition to China, the order creating that expedition, the instructions governing its use, even a part of the expedition itself, must come from England. This being the case, it is time to ask when England learned about Commissioner Lin and the twenty thousand chests, and what she made of it.

In the years since the *Hugh Lindsay* had first tried to steam from Bombay to Suez, the movement of people and mail by the overland route to India had considerably improved. From Falmouth steam packets regularly sailed for Lisbon, Gibraltar, Malta, and Alexandria (though travelers and letters often made their own way across France to embark on the swifter steamers of the French). From Alexandria you took a verminous canal boat to Cairo; at Cairo you engaged a camel or donkey litter to carry you across the desert to Suez; and at Suez, an unspeakably desolate and dreary spot, you boarded a sidewheeler (if the timing was right) for the voyage down the Red Sea, through the Bab el Mandeb Strait, and over to Bombay. This Suez-to-Bombay leg was the responsibility of the Indian navy, alias the navy of the East India Company, which by 1839 had made considerable progress in conquering the winds of the Arabian Sea. Thus when the old *Hugh Lindsay* was forced back to Bombay on 4 May of that year by the unusually early onset of the monsoon, the *Berenice* steamed out four days later on her more powerful engines, reached Aden on 20 May, touched Mocha on the twenty-first and Cosseir on the twenty-seventh, anchored at Suez on the twenty-ninth, weighed for the return trip on 11 June, and was back at Bombay on 27 June—by which time the *Atalanta* was well along the same circuit. When the *Atalanta* caught fire and had to be laid up for repairs, there was the *Zenobia* (which had begun her career carrying swine from Waterford to Bristol), and early in 1840 the *Victoria* and the *Cleopatra*. The fact was that a regular overland to the orient—comfortable, dependable as clockwork, the English mail made up and dispatched from London on the fourth of every month, the Indian mail made up and dispatched from Bombay on the first of every month, and each coming to its destination in five to seven weeks—was a thing nearly within reach.

Nearly, but not quite. Though the *Berenice* was bigger and faster than the *Hugh Lindsay*, there was nothing "posh" about her, nor any occasion for the word: travelers departing London did not know what steamer they would board at Suez and took accommodations as they found them. The *Berenice*'s cabins were tiny, her saloon doubled for a dining room, coal dust was everywhere and got into everything. Worse, even the newer steamers still had trouble with the southwest monsoon at its height. Passengers and mail leaving Bombay between May and August stood a good chance of being divided between an Indian navy schooner for the Red Sea and a steamer for the Persian Gulf. East of Bombay, moreover, there was hardly any system at all. The mails went on to the other two presidencies by *dak* runner; passengers shifted for themselves, often going by sailing ship the long route around Ceylon. As for communicating with Singapore, Manila, or Canton, that was a matter of obtaining passage (or access to the letter bag) in whatever vessel happened to be bound that way. Seasonal variations of wind and commerce made a difference: it was unlikely, for example, that anything but an opium clipper would run up the south China coast in the late autumn or run down it in July. The consequence of all this was that mail from the foreigners in Canton traveled to Europe in a number of ways and by a variety of conveyances—when Matheson wrote Jardine the full story of the opium crisis at the beginning of May, he committed seven copies of his letter to seven different ships! Communication was swifter than it had been when everything went by the Cape. But private correspondence at the best of times took three months to reach London, and official dispatches (for some reason) often took four.

So England learned about Lin and the twenty thousand chests slowly, in little spurts and rushes, with the official information always a step behind the private. In April, Palmerston had Elliot's account of the strangulation riot. In May he knew that the new year had opened in an atmosphere of surface calm. At the end of May he was informed that a special high commissioner approached Canton. But this was the news of early February, what happened during the rest of February and all through March was delayed for want of suitable sailings—and in July, Palmerston knew no more than he had known two months before.

The *Good Success*, it is true, carried a full budget of accounts and papers when she left for India in the middle of April. By her Fort William quickly became aware of what was going on—and Auckland too, as we have seen. But the express that left Madras the day after the *Good Success*'s arrival reached Bombay too late to catch the *Atalanta*; the China news, in consequence, did not start for England until the next overland on 4 June, which was divided between the schooner *Constance* to Suez and the *Hugh Lindsay* to the Persian Gulf; the two parts of this overland did not reach London until 31 July and 5 August; and when they got there, Elliot's most recent dispatches were for some reason not in them. On 1 August the *Times* carried the "important intelligence" that the English merchants at Canton "had been put in prison and summoned to deliver up all the opium in their possession," that Elliot (who shared their hardships) had advised them to comply, that the opium was duly surrendered, but that the merchants were still in prison "and treated with great harshness." The same evening questions were asked in both houses of Parliament. In the Lords no less a person than Ellenborough, president of the Board of Control ten years before (and certain to have a hand in Indian affairs when the Tories returned to power), rose to recite what he had read in the papers and to inquire whether the government could add to his stock of information. Melbourne replied that it could not. He had read only what the noble lord had read. He knew only what *he* knew. The government had nothing from the chief superintendent later than 22 March, the day before that gentleman left Macao for the factories. It awaited further dispatches and until it received them had nothing to say.

Nothing to say! All through the summer and autumn, as information about the enormities at Canton gradually accumulated, this remained the official attitude. A high Chinese officer confiscated property worth perhaps £2 million—and Britannia had nothing to say!

Appearances, however, were deceptive. China would never occupy Parliament and the public as the "eastern question" (meaning Mehemet Ali and the French) did, as Afghanistan did. Yet the China crisis had nevertheless its own imperative; and though Parliament and the public knew very little about the matter, and possibly cared less, Her Majesty's government was obliged to listen to that imperative and to formulate a plan to satisfy it long before the old year was out.

The imperative was money. A great many men would suffer in their pocketbooks if England persisted in ignoring what had happened in Canton. English merchants doing business in Bombay had been distressed that winter and spring, as opium sales steadily declined along the coast of China, by the gradual contraction of credit and the drying up of silver. They had conveyed their distress loudly to their friends in England. Then had come the two weeks of waiting between the receipt of the crisis news by way of the *Good Success* and the departure of the *Constance* and the *Hugh*

Lindsay. They had used those two weeks well. When the overland left for England on 4 June, it was the fatter for a petition from the Bombay Chamber of Commerce to the queen in council begging for a cash advance against full compensation for the confiscated chests; the fatter, too, for a sheaf of letters from the Bombay chamber to the East India and China Associations of London, Liverpool, Manchester, Glasgow, Newcastle, and Hull, urging them to press Whitehall not just for cash but for action that would put the whole of the China trade "on a more secure and permanent basis."[8] If Bombay had its wish, a campaign as powerful as that which had forced the abolition of the East India Company's monopoly six years before would soon be under way.

Calcutta made her contribution too. Her Chamber of Commerce drew up a petition that observed, among other things, that the foreigners in Canton had been threatened with "rapine and massacre" on the model of the Black Hole of recent fame and the Amboyna affair two centuries before. (At Amboyna, in 1623, the Dutch had dissuaded interlopers from trying to break into their spice trade by torturing and killing several Englishmen.) Fort William, the petition continued, ought to pay the merchants at once for their confiscated chests and let the British treasury reimburse it later. When, early in July, Dent's *Water Witch* came in from Canton, the chamber chartered her to carry the paper directly to Suez.

Another of Dent's opium vessels was headed for Suez too. Captain Elliot had advertised for a fast clipper to carry dispatches, Dent had offered the *Ariel* (terms $8,000 for seven months), and on 30 May she sailed. Of course Elliot might have sent his dispatches by the *Larne*, which weighed the same day. But the *Larne* was bound only for Trincomalee; besides, with blunter lines and a bottom foul from two years at sea, she was much slower than the *Ariel*. So the chief superintendent turned easily and naturally to the smuggling fleet. He did more, he gave the dispatches to Inglis, Dent's partner, who agreed to travel on the little coal-black vessel and to deliver the papers in person. The voyage took longer than expected. Powerful headwinds kept the *Ariel* twenty-four days between Aden and Suez. Inglis did not reach London until October, weeks after copies of Elliot's dispatches had arrived by other means, but not too late for Inglis to lend a hand with the China lobby.

A lobby had been agreed upon while everyone was still shut up in the factories. Dues had been levied, several thousand pounds raised, and three gentlemen named to go to London to undertake the work. One was Inglis; another was Hugh Hamilton Lindsay, who had already left in the *Ardaseer*; the third was Alexander Matheson, sailing in June. In London these three could count on Jardine; on Alexander Grant, late of the *Hercules* and busy now with the launching of the new clipper ship *Mor*; on John Abel Smith, a young Liberal M.P. and partner in the agency house of Magniac Smith and Company, which did Jardine Matheson's London business; and on a man from the house that took care of Dent. "You may find it expedient," wrote Matheson to Jardine and Smith, "to secure the services of some leading newspaper to advocate the cause" and perhaps even to engage "literary men" to draw up "the requisite memorials in the most concise and clear shape."⁹ For Matheson was not happy with some of the things his Canton acquaintants had produced along this line. He had, in fact, refused to sign the Dent memorial of May. It mixed insistence upon compensation with a defense of the opium traffic in general, and the second seemed to Matheson unwise. ("Quite irrelevant," agreed Jardine, "opening up questions and vindicating things that require no vindication."¹⁰) Of course some thought the opium traffic *was* the central issue. This, Matheson had to admit, was how Lin looked at the matter; Lin really *did* desire the annihilation of the traffic, desired it so intensely that he was in the process of staking everything he had upon it, his reputation, "most probably his life. And he perhaps knows enough," added Matheson in a letter to Smith, "of what I must be excused for terming the senseless clamour of the High Church party against the traffic, to hope for the cooperation of our Government in his designs." What a pity it was that pious gentlemen in England had no firsthand acquaintance with China's use of the pipe. He, Matheson, could honestly affirm that in twenty-one years on the coast he had never seen a Chinese "in the least bestialized" by smoking. Opium simply did for the upper levels of Chinese society what brandy and champagne did for the same levels in England. It was essential that Palmerston be made aware of this fact.¹¹

Matheson need not have worried. Palmerston was not the sort to pay much attention to high churchmen or evangelicals either. He was a comfortable, plainspoken pagan, a survival (like Melbourne) of the previous century; low church despite his Tory origins; distrustful of cant and prompt to find it in the arguments being raised against opium. By the autumn of 1839 there were a number of these circulating. One was a piece Charles King of Olyphant and Company had written during the spring incarceration as a letter to Captain Elliot (angrily Slade pointed out that it was not delivered and was never meant to be). King's tone was moderate. Though he prayed that England would disassociate itself from the opium traffic, he acknowledged that the owners of the confiscated chests would have to be paid. A Church of England curate named Algernon Thelwall was a good deal less indulgent. His *Iniquities of the Opium Trade with China* was just what its title suggested, a detailed, remorseless illumination of the darkest sides of the business, based convincingly on materials from the *Repository*. The *Times* ran Thelwall's polemic in installments. Palmerston, however, was immune to the proddings of the Kings, the Thelwalls, and the other men of conscience. He found their memorials and letters tiresome. (A number are preserved in the Public Record Office. In the margins of several is the comment "tirade," and on the back of one the penciled observation "most probably the work of anti-slavery agitators whose occupation is in a great measure gone.") The lobby's problem was not how to prevent the foreign secretary from taking Lin's side but how to get him to pay any attention to China at all.

John Abel Smith went to see him. George Gerard de Hochepied Larpent, chairman of the London East India and China Association, went to see him. Sir Alexander Johnston, father of Elliot's young deputy superintendent and a veteran of years of service in Ceylon, took him letters recently received from Canton. After some delay Jardine and Grant were admitted to see him too, and straightway laid out charts of the China coast "in order that his Lordship might have a clear idea of the country with which we must cope" should war be intended.[12] Then, as the news from China grew fuller and was more widely grasped, the merchant memorials began to flow, not the moralizing material of the antiopium enthusiasts, but serious commercial stuff. If trade interruptions are to become a commonplace, what will happen to the half million pounds' worth of cottons sent annually to China? Is the foreign secretary aware that English consignors are directing their goods to American agency houses because they cannot see how else to get them sold? From Blackburn came a paper bearing the names of thirty-four firms, from Manchester one with thirty-nine, from Liverpool fifty-two, from Leeds seventy-two, from London almost a hundred. Not all the memorialists talked the unequivocal language of the Blackburn merchants—"atrocious transactions at Canton . . . wanton seizure of British property"—or thought the business a simple affair of honor to be settled by the sword. Larpent's London Association was of the opinion that if the Chinese really wished to prohibit opium, England must find some other way of financing its purchases of tea. But what other way was there except the wider sale of English manufactures? That meant opening additional ports and placing the trade under the close protection of Her Majesty's government—things not likely to be secured merely through the asking.

So the consensus of opinion was that armed intervention of some sort would have to be arranged. From the pile of Captain Elliot's dispatches it was not difficult to extract the same advice. "It appears to me, my Lord," the chief superintendent had written Palmerston early in April, "that the response to all these unjust violences should be made in the form of a swift and heavy blow unprefaced by one word of written communication."[13] This suggestion reached the Foreign Office at the end of August; dispatches to the end of May came in on 21 September; on the twenty-seventh Palmerston saw Grant and Jardine, studied their charts, and asked if he might keep several. Three days later "we had an early Cabinet," remembers Hobhouse, "and discussed the China question."[14] Palmerston read portions of Elliot's dispatches and explained, with the help of Jardine's charts, "how one line-of-battleship, with two frigates and two or three steamers and some small armed vessels, might blockade the whole coast from the river of Pekin down to . . . Canton." Macaulay was "eloquent against the Chinese" and argued at length for "hostile measures." What finally dominated the discussion, however, was not the war-or-peace aspect of the China question, but the pounds, shillings, and pence of it.

For Baring insisted on knowing "what was to be done in regard to the two millions of money which the merchants had lost by giving up their opium." Baring was chancellor of the exchequer and a grandson of the man who had founded Baring Brothers, the London financial house on which so many American bills sold in Canton were drawn, so that he must have been quite familiar with the workings of the China trade; £2 million was not a terribly formidable sum. Still, if the opium merchants were to be repaid out of the British treasury—and the lobby, the memorials, the piercing sounds of distress from Calcutta and Bombay all combined to persuade the cabinet that they must—Baring would have to find the money. That was next to impossible, given how weak Melbourne had become.

Only a handful of votes separated Melbourne's government from defeat in the House of Commons. Indeed, it had been beaten there in May and had resigned in favor of Peel, only to resume office when Queen Victoria (who was young and inexperienced) insisted on keeping her Whig ladies about her. After the Bedchamber Crisis, as this was called, the government was weaker than ever. And its most vulnerable point was its budgets. They did not balance. In 1837 the deficit had exceeded £1 million. In 1838 it had mercifully been less. For 1839, however, it was estimated at close to a million again; and by the autumn the Chartist riots and the introduction of cheap postage threatened to drive it well over a million. In such circumstances it was madness to think of extra expenditure of any sort. So when Baring asked where the £2 million were to come from, Melbourne gave the only possible answer: they were not to be had from Parliament.

The sum of £2 million was not to be had from the Government of India either. Auckland faced the expenses of the triumphant Army of the Indus and did not enjoy his usual revenue from opium; he would find it as impossible as Baring to furnish such a sum. There was, however, another potential source, a source incalculably more attractive than the other two. Macaulay spotted it at once. "Macaulay was for seizing Chinese property," remembers Hobhouse. "And so was Palmerston." For why, after all, should not the Chinese pay? Why not bill them for the value of the confiscated chests and for any expenses that might be incurred in the process of collection? Why not take them to war, and at its victorious conclusion make them pay for the opium and for the war too?

It was agreed. The cabinet, without thinking it necessary to wait for further news from China (its latest reached only into June), without consulting Parliament, set England's course for war. Several weeks later Palmerston decided to alert Elliot and, when Jardine offered the newly completed *Mor*, hurried a secret letter down to her at Plymouth. She sailed on 23 October; on the same day the *Times* ran a leading article describing how the Government of India managed its opium business. Patna and Benares, it observed, were put up specifically to suit the tastes of the Chinese. "This is going very coolly to work, we must confess. It almost suggests the idea of a joint stock company for furnishing the most approved means of committing suicide." But the leader came to no conclusion. Palmerston would have paid no attention if it had. Though the *Times* was influential and proportionately much larger in circulation than it is today, he had ignored it before and would ignore it again. Early in November he sent off preliminary instructions for the necessary expeditionary force. One set traveled aboard the *Ariel*, held in the Red Sea for just that purpose.

What, exactly, would England be fighting for? Not to open China to English manufactures, though there were great hopes in some quarters that ports of entry besides Canton could be obtained. Not to win China for Christ, though that might follow too. Certainly not to force opium down the throats of the Chinese—Palmerston was quite emphatic upon this point. "Her Majesty's government," he wrote in his November instructions[15] (which mingled what was to be done with the whys and wherefores), "by no means dispute the right of the government of China to prohibit the importation of opium into China" and to confiscate any that foreigners or Chinese might bring in. But the prohibition ought to be bona fide. It ought to be enforced, impartially, consistently, unremittingly. "Traps ought not to be laid for foreigners"—and traps, alas, *had* been laid. The authorities (it is Palmerston speaking) had allowed the prohibition to lie dormant; they had let opium be smuggled in very large quantities and had even participated in the smuggling themselves; then quite suddenly they had turned upon the traffic and, unable to reach the outer anchorages, had laid violent hands on the English at Canton—though many of these, Palmerston was sure, had never dealt in the drug.

They had made the English prisoners, Elliot with them, intending to bring about their deaths "by the cruel process of starvation" and would have effected that dreadful object had not the prisoners purchased their lives with twenty thousand chests. This, then, and not the prohibition was the abominable aspect of the case, and for it England must have satisfaction.

So Her Majesty's government prepared to go to war to efface an unjust and humiliating act, to recover the value of certain property plus expenses (to the twenty thousand chests Palmerston added the hong debts due English merchants), and almost by the by to put England's relations with the Middle Kingdom on a new and proper footing. Jardine and his friends were content enough. They harbored no grand designs and would have felt uncomfortable with a government that did. When, however, they attempted to persuade Whitehall to anticipate its victory a little by paying at once for the confiscated opium, they got nowhere. Palmerston listened perfectly readily when they had anything useful to provide—as when Larpent, for example, brought letters with the story of the Chien-sha-tsui riot. Jardine laid out in great detail exactly what kind of naval force ought to be sent to China and what it ought to do when it got there, and Palmerston not only passed the paper on to the Admiralty but, when the war was over, thanked Jardine for contributing materially to England's success. But whenever the subject of money came up, the foreign secretary was suddenly distant. Her Majesty's government, he explained to Magniac Smith and Company, could not buy up the scrip that represented the confiscated twenty thousand chests because Parliament had not voted the money. (He had not the slightest intention, it was apparent, of asking for a vote.) In vain Smith pleaded that this posture, when it became known to the native merchants in India, would produce the most intense distress. Could not Palmerston hint at the *possibility*, at least, of immediate partial compensation? Palmerston could not and, when Smith's importunities continued, had his clerks pencil them "returned by Lord P. without observation."

Thus the parties for whose property the war was to be fought would have to wait for their money until the fighting was over. Commercially, some might not survive the test. Deep inside China, meanwhile, Jean-Gabriel Perboyre faced an equally severe test of another sort—and it was a question whether he would survive it either.

14

The Coming of the War

It was early in 1838, you will remember, that Perboyre had moved from Honan Province to a mountainous part of Hupeh close to the Tapa Shan. There he labored for more than a year, as quietly and as little interrupted as if he had been at home in his native Lot. He kept in contact with Baldus and Rameaux. After a time Baldus came to stay with him. In September of 1839 an Italian named Rizzolati appeared at his cottage. Rome had recently created the new vicariat apostolic of Hupeh and Hunan, confiding it to the Propaganda and shifting the French Lazarists eastward into Kiangsi and Chekiang (where Carpena, old and tired, made them welcome). Rizzolati, a veteran of eleven years' service in China, had come down from Shensi to arrange the transfer. Before he could get well into his work, however, disaster struck.

He, Baldus, and Perboyre were celebrating mass together one morning when a young convert burst in crying that the local prefect was approaching with mandarins and soldiers. The three priests had no time to collect anything, to lay any sort of plan; they fled in the clothes they stood in. Baldus and Rizzolati got away into the high country and wandered for days before finally escaping the area altogether. Perboyre was not so lucky. Twenty-four hours after his flight he was betrayed by one of his own catechumens—for thirty pieces of silver, some accounts say. (The reported dialogue between him and his captors closely follows Matt. 26:15.) Brought first to Kucheng on the edge of the hills, later to Hsiangyang on the Han River, he was eventually put into a prison at Wuchang. There, after a time, a number of native Christians managed to get access to him by bribing his jailers. (They spoke to Rizzolati, who had made his way to the same place to lose himself briefly in the city's faceless crowds, and it was Rizzolati who sent out the first full account.) Perboyre, it seemed, was interrogated repeatedly and mercilessly. He was asked how he had reached Hupeh from the coast and who had been his guides. He was asked where Baldus and Rizzolati were hiding—and about Rameaux, of whom something seemed to be known. He was challenged to admit how many small children he had robbed of their eyes.* He was slapped, beaten with rattans, made to kneel upon chains, hung from his hands and hair with his knees on a brick edge and weights upon his lower legs; towards the end of his ordeal he was tattooed on the face with characters denoting that here was a truly evil man. Yet through all this and a physical weakness so great that for weeks he could not stand unaided, he maintained a marvelous constancy, betraying neither his God nor his fellows, preparing to earn the martyr's palm as Clet had earned it in this same place twenty years before.

At Macao, meanwhile, Legrégeois was occupied with the ordinary business of the *procure*. His principal courier Paul and another courier named Joseph returned from leading Renou part way to Szechwan. They brought with them three young Szechwanese who were to be trained for the priesthood at the Missions Etrangères seminary at Penang. Libois, Callery, and Desflèches returned from Manila; Desflèches started for Szechwan; Christmas came and went. "Today we are sending off our eight Cochinchinese pupils and the three from Szechwan for Singapore," wrote Legrégeois on 6 January, "from whence they will pass to Penang."[1] Paul and Joseph were in charge of the party. And suddenly Legrégeois met trouble right on his own doorstep.

When customs men began a routine check of the oceangoing junk Paul and Joseph had boarded, Paul (who was Cochinchinese by birth and probably felt ill at ease among the Cantonese) became extremely nervous, could not keep still, paced up and down with his hands tucked into his armpits, trembled violently whenever anyone approached him, and at last tumbled letters and two Latin missals out upon the deck. He and the junk's captain were immediately hurried before a magistrate. The junk was searched, jars of sacramental wine and several thousand dollars in silver uncovered, and though Joseph and a servant managed to talk their way free, Paul, the three novices, and the Cochinchinese pupils were taken to Canton and thrown into prison.

Poor Legrégeois did not know what to do. He noticed that his ser-

---

*Catholic missionaries made it a point to find and baptize infants on the point of death. This practice gave the perishing unfortunates the immediate and automatic promise of eternal joy, on which account alone it could not in conscience be neglected. It also added impressively to the statistics of the Catholic Mission: in a single year Bertrand in Szechwan was able to report 484 adults baptized by himself, against 16,000 children baptized *in articulo mortis* by native catechists! Many of these were the victims of famine or deliberate abandonment, and almost all died shortly after receiving divine grace. But since their parents (when there were any) did not understand what was being done or why, infant baptism easily aroused the most intense suspicion. Might it not be that what the foreign devils *really* wanted, as they muttered their abracadabra over the poor little innocents, was fresh black eyes to make magic potions of, to extract silver from lead by?

vants stayed away, a sure sign the affair was serious. Suppose the authorities managed to translate the letters Paul had dropped! Many of them were from priests deep inside China and contained information that, if translated and put into the wrong hands, would almost certainly lead to the priests' arrest. To whom could Legrégeois turn? He was on friendly enough terms with Captain Elliot, but at the moment the chief superintendent was hardly in a position to exert influence at Canton. How, then, was Paul to be freed and the letters recovered?

Help came from an unexpected quarter. "This morning," wrote Legrégeois four days after Paul's arrest, "an American Protestant minister came around to tell me that my letters for Cochinchina were in the hands of one of his countrymen, who was supposed to translate them and wished to warn me."[2] The minister was Bridgman, the countryman Hunter. It turned out that Hunter had been near the customs barrier during the search, had heard the commotion, made inquiries, and discovered what was happening. That was not all. In due course the letters, twenty-two in number, had been laid before Lin Tse-Hsü. Lin had sensed their importance and had instructed the hong merchants to get them translated; Howqua had brought them to Hunter; Hunter, seeing at once how dangerous they might be, had determined to alert Legrégeois.

Legrégeois's response was to beg Hunter to keep their contents from the high commissioner. He need not have worried, Hunter had already told Howqua he would not do the translation and doubted whether any other foreigner would. The refusal alarmed Howqua. The *ch'in-ch'ai,* he pointed out, knew Hunter by name and knew that he understood Chinese. If Hunter refused to translate, there would be "muchee trub." But Hunter was obdurate, and as a few of the letters were written in romanized Cochinchinese, which in fact neither he nor any other foreigner *could* make sense of, it was decided to represent to the high commissioner that *all* of them were.

"Hae yah, Kin Chae too muchee foolo," Hunter remembers Howqua exclaiming to him over a cozy cup of tea.[3] (Some Englishmen, Gilbertian in spirit though Gilbert was only three, already called Lin the "Yum Chae.") So the letters went unread, at least by the authorities, though Legrégeois was pretty sure Hunter had looked them over. Uneasily he wondered whether one by himself to a Missions Etrangères man near Hué had contained anything that might give offense to the Americans. In the end he decided that it had not. "Without being a friend of any of them," he wrote his superiors, "I do not think I am regarded by any in an unfriendly way."[4] Indeed, everyone was most kind. Elliot offered shelter aboard an English ship. Pinto, who only a few months before had been openly annoyed with Joset over the arrival of an Italian priest and two Chinese trained at Naples, now summoned Legrégeois and told him that though the mandarins were pressing hard to obtain the identity of the person responsible for dispatching Paul, his name had so far been kept from them; he need not go into hiding.

The attention was warming. Just the same Paul and his companions remained behind bars—and now this business of Perboyre! Shortly after Christmas, Torrette had learned the bare fact of the Lazarist's arrest. Later another courier had brought details of the interrogation and torture. The news did not bother the Protestants particularly, they may even not have heard it, but over the Catholics it cast a pall.

In fact Perboyre's sufferings were by this time pretty well over. The authorities had given up trying to extract a recantation or to discover from him the whereabouts of his colleagues. They had sentenced him to death, and while they waited for the sentence to reach Peking and be reviewed there, they were letting him lie among the common prisoners. It was no great trick for a few of the bolder native Christians to bribe their way past the jailers and bring him clothing and food, comfort him, tend his hurts, and confess him. At Macao, however, everyone supposed him to be in desperate straits. Even Rameaux, in Kiangsi, thought so. "It is probable that he has already received the martyr's crown," he wrote Torrette early in March. With Baldus's help Rameaux was hard at work organizing the new Lazarist vicariat apostolic of Chekiang-Kiangsi and paused only to slip briefly over the border into Fukien to be consecrated bishop of Myra (a defunct see on the south coast of Asia Minor) by Carpena. "They say here," he continued in his letter to Torrette, "that war is declared between the English and the Chinese. God knows what the consequences will be, but we may all suffer for it."[5]

Three more Missions Etrangères recruits arrived from France. Joseph set off with one of them for Hinghwa in southern Fukien, where the *procure* kept a man. Legrégeois felt harassed and tired. He was selling bills again, but money troubles bothered him; Thomas Beale, the old fellow with the birds, owed a considerable sum and repaid slowly, probably because his opium speculations did not do well. From time to time, too, Legrégeois was overcome with a terrible sense of personal helplessness and futility. "The only spiritual advantage I can discover in China," the martyred Clet was once said to have remarked, "is that if I stayed at home I would be able to think I was good for something, whereas here all the evidence suggests that I am good for nothing at all."[6] Clet had derived profit from his uselessness. Legrégeois was simply depressed by it.

Still the affair of Paul and the letters dragged on. Towards the middle of March, Pinto sent a second warning. The mandarins had finally identified Legrégeois and wanted him shipped up to Canton, which of course Pinto would not do, but might it not be prudent of the procurator to shift his place of residence? Legrégeois took the hint and went into hiding at Torrette's. "Let us hope," he wrote his directors in Paris, "that the war, which we understand has finally been decided upon, will alter things a little."[7]

War was certainly in the air. "Chances are five to one that we are all out of Canton in three months," Bennet Forbes had remarked in January.[8] In February there was a bit of a scare at Macao. Some time previously a number of Englishmen, among them Elliot and his family, had quietly returned to the town. Now suddenly placards appeared saying that Chinese soldiers were on their way to expel once more the red-haired devils. Nothing came of the threat, perhaps because Captain Smith moved the *Hyacinth* into the inner harbor, but Elliot sent his wife and his little son, Frederick, off to Singapore by the *Scaleby Castle*. With relations worsening as they were, it seemed the only thing to do.

Yet it was not until now that Elliot learned of England's plans. Jardine's and Jamsetjee's new clipper ship *Mor,* full-rigged, 280 tons, and commanded by the brother of a sometime member of Parliament (which suggests something about the standing of the opium traffic), had left Plymouth towards the end of October. She entered the Gulf of Canton on 15 February after an excellent passage of 114 days, and her canvas bag brought an important private letter to Captain Elliot. It was Palmerston's of 18 October, informing the chief superintendent that a naval and military expedition was collecting to descend upon the coast. Elliot was to keep mum about the matter—Matheson noticed that he seemed "beyond measure delighted" with the letter but could only guess why[9]—for merchants and manufacturers concerned with China did not want anything done that might disrupt the legitimate trade of the year.

The legitimate trade stood, in fact, pretty well complete. Teas for England had departed the gulf in the usual volume and at the usual times: three sailings in November, two in December, six in January, one early in February, with a score of vessels almost ready to sail the day the *Mor* came in. This was not because the chief superintendent and the Yum Chae had buried the hatchet. Elliot's injunction to stay out of the river held firm; save for the *Thomas Coutts* and the *Royal Saxon* (the latter had slipped in unobserved at Christmas time), no English merchantmen lay north of the Bogue. Lin, for his part, declared the commerce with England forever at an end. But that commerce was not easily stopped. The Americans in particular went vigorously ahead with their transshipping business, carrying raw cotton, rattans, and English cloth up to Whampoa, bringing teas, silks, and tubs of sugar candy back; and when they discovered they did not have enough bottoms for the work, went right out and purchased more.

The *Hercules,* too old and too notorious, Matheson felt, to continue in the drug traffic, passed to Bennet Forbes for $25,000. The country ship *Sir Charles Malcolm* became the *Kosciusko,* after the American patriotic hero of that name; the *Cambridge,* no longer in demand as an auxiliary warship, became the *Chesapeake.* Peter Snow obligingly supplied American papers. Matheson, who still kept his consular commission from Denmark's Indian colony of Tranquebar, supplied Danish. In this way Jardine's *General Wood* became the *Syden,* Heerjeebhoy Rustomjee was overnight possessed of a *Norden,* and the former Indiaman *Vansittart* reappeared as the *Danske Konge.* French, Prussian, and Swedish flags were suddenly to be seen, and from Manila came a number of bona fide Spaniards to claim their share of the freight. Lin's feelings about all this were probably mixed. He did not actually forbid transshipping, yet he put such obstacles in its path that many skippers found it expedient to carry English goods to Manila and obtain fresh bills of lading there before actually entering the river. Some Englishmen too were annoyed—with the Americans especially, because they made so much money out of the practice. Nevertheless Elliot, though he had begun the season by begging the Americans to withdraw from the river, ended it by congratulating them for staying. "My dear Forbes," he told Bennet, "the Queen owes you many thanks for not taking my advice as to leaving Canton. We have got in all our goods, and got out a full supply of teas and silk"[10]—something impossible without "Black Ben" and his sort. Perhaps the Chinese tea men and silk merchants were grateful too.

The consequence was that on the other side of the world the London tea market, though shaken by what was occurring in China, was not shaken for long. Congou had by this time replaced bohea as the variety most commonly drunk. In the summer of 1839 it fetched, wholesale, a little over a shilling a pound. The news of the opium surrender and the events immediately following produced a general alarm. Imports, it was felt, must fall short this season; if a blockade was imposed they might fail altogether. Speculators came into the market and bought teas against the prospect of selling them soon at higher prices. Prices did rise; in October congou approached two shillings; in February it passed three. By February, however, nine million pounds of the leaf were on their way to England. Ships carrying the first of it were very near the Channel; when they docked, with the intelligence that in China the season (thanks to neutral bottoms) was proceeding much as usual, some of the speculators sold and congou fell. It recovered, of course. The battle at Chuenpi and the news that the high commissioner had declared trade with England forever at an end drove it above three shillings again—but not for long. In March came fresh news of teas leaving the Canton River. There was near panic, congou touched two and threepence, one large speculator failed. A recovery in

April, another collapse in May, and as the summer began, the price steadied at a little under two shillings; for by then it was clear that England was going to receive at least twenty-five million pounds this season—only five million fewer than normal.

So the tea trade settled down. As for concern in England for the other aspects of the China question, it was a long time stirring at all.

Right through the Christmas season, which Jardine and Alexander Matheson spent together in Dumfriesshire, Melbourne's government continued to say as little as possible about the matter. When Parliament reopened in January, the speech from the throne observed simply that events in China must soon receive the queen's attention. Merchants anxious to know whether Her Majesty intended to blockade the coast were told by the Foreign Office that they would have to estimate the probability for themselves. In the House of Commons, Palmerston openly affirmed that he had no intention of asking for money to pay for the twenty thousand confiscated chests and, when badgered a little on the subject, replied in so peremptory a manner that the *Times* could not make out what it was he said.

There was, to be sure, a request for papers. This the government could not very well refuse. Late in January it promised the China correspondence for the past six years, but its sheer bulk was considerable—Palmerston complained that the weight of the type required for its printing broke through a floor at the Foreign Office—and when it finally appeared, it had still to be read and digested. Meanwhile the public learned that at Calcutta preparations were being made to send an expedition eastward. "War Declared on China," the *Times* announced in March, citing intelligence just received from Bombay. It occurred to some people that China might become a vast dependency of England, like India. "Only imagine the brother to the Sun and Moon a pensioner on our Government for half a million a year," suggested the *Bombay Gazette,* "with a British Ministry to manage his affairs."[11] Then it was April; and on the seventh there opened at last a full-scale Parliamentary debate.

Sir James Graham began it, with a motion condemning the Melbourne government's handling of the China question—but not because the government proposed to go to war. That was not the issue Graham wished to raise. At a party meeting at Peel's house it had been agreed that to make the coming war an issue would only divide the Tories. What was needed was something to unite upon, which meant attacking not the war but the ministerial bungling that had brought England to the verge of it.

Graham set out to do this by reviewing the China question all the way back to Napier. The correspondence just printed, which he made the basis of his case, was voluminous and badly organized (it had, for example, no index); if printing it had nearly crushed to death the clerks in the Foreign Office, perusing it had nearly killed himself. What Graham particularly wanted members to observe, however, was the indolence, the apathy, of the Foreign Office. Month after month Captain Elliot had been left without instructions. He had tried to check his countrymen's involvement in the opium traffic, only to be warned repeatedly by the foreign secretary to mind his own business. He had behaved honorably enough during the surrender crisis but had perforce reverted afterwards to the lame and ineffective course of action dictated by Palmerston's inattentiveness; a course of half measures, including forbidding the English to enter the river while permitting Americans and the *Thomas Coutts* to go up; until drift was king, and a trade worth millions of dollars (a trade indispensable, too, for the large sums it brought the treasury) was threatened with extinction. It was astonishing, it was unforgivable, and Graham proposed to fix the responsibility squarely upon the ministerial bench, where it belonged.

In this vein the Tory attack proceeded for three consecutive nights. Alone among Graham's supporters, William Gladstone tried to face the question of opium itself: its use, its effects, and England's involvement with it. Then only thirty years of age, Gladstone had nevertheless been an M.P. longer than Elliot had been in China, and his oratorical powers (exercised thus far in oddly conservative causes) were well known. Speaking now with great earnestness and at considerable length, he demanded to know why the efforts made by the Chinese authorities to check the opium traffic had invariably been discounted. Did not everyone recognize that opium was a thoroughly pernicious drug? The Chinese were right to be alarmed by it; "a war more unjust in its origin, a war more calculated in its progress to cover this country with permanent disgrace," he knew not of.[12] Warming to his work, Gladstone allowed himself the remark that *of course* the Chinese had poisoned the springs at Kowloon—how else were they to drive the drug dealers away? Shouts and jeers from the Whig benches. The next speaker estimated that the member for Newark had carried the "anti-opium mania" about as far as it could be carried. But even Gladstone had not proposed that the expedition now fitting out should be dismantled and the war called off. And when at last it was Peel's turn, not opium but Palmerston's mismanagement at the Foreign Office became more clearly than ever the issue upon which the success or failure of the opposition motion would turn.

Alas for Peel and his friends, the Whigs still held a narrow Parliamentary lead—which Palmerston knew very well how to preserve. Rising directly after Peel and speaking with a gay and infectious assurance, Palmerston exposed the motion for exactly what it was: a transparent maneuver to shift political power from one side of the House to the other. What, exactly, was it that he ought to have done? The mandarins allowed opium to be cultivated right inside China itself and objected to its importation only because it cost them silver. Would Parliament have welcomed his proposing "a large naval estimate for a number of revenue cruisers to be employed in the preventive service from the river at Canton to the Yellow Sea, for the purpose of preserving the morals of the Chinese people, who were disposed to buy what other people were disposed to sell them?"[13] Graham tried to reply; but it was nearly dawn on the third night of debate, members were weary, there were cries for the question, and the House divided. Graham's motion lost by nine votes.

That did it. In the Lords the eccentric Lord Stanhope tried to get the government's China policy condemned on the moral grounds advanced by Gladstone. Melbourne easily parried the attempt, remarking that opium was probably not as dangerous an article as spirits (being a good deal less palatable), that the Chinese *would* smoke it, and that perhaps the most that could be expected was some rearrangement of the Indian end of the traffic that would have "less the appearance of connecting it with the Government of this country."[14] As for making China a party issue (the Tories had a majority in the upper house), the Duke of Wellington quite dashed any hope of that. He was past seventy, had recently suffered a stroke, and was thought by some to be the very ruin of a man, yet he managed to answer Stanhope with a long and vigorous speech in the course of which he praised Elliot to the skies and insisted that in fifty years of public service he had not seen insults and injuries to equal those heaped upon the English at Canton. Any man of spirit could now desire but one thing: to see the Chinese punished! There was not a word about ministerial bungling. Graham's motion had received its most complete and mortifying answer.

Very little more argument followed. The *Times* called it an "opium war"[15] but agreed it had to be fought. De Quincey, living sick and solitary in Edinburgh—and making spasmodic efforts to cut his daily dose of laudanum from eight thousand drops (six or seven wine glasses) to two or three hundred—did not so far as we know give China's numberless addicts a thought. Opium was entering England at the rate of almost three hundred chests a year. Temperance circles noted with dismay that the slight decrease in general drunkenness was fully matched by the increased consumption of the drug. In the manufacturing towns rows of penny and twopenny packets waited on druggists' counters of a Saturday evening to give the working man the means of stupefying himself over the Sunday. Harriet Martineau, who observed and deplored this interesting phenomenon, took opium herself to relieve the misery of a retroverted uterus and was to be saved from total dependence on the drug only by the discovery that mesmerism was for her quite as effective. The English did not believe they had an opium problem.

Opium was not a problem in India either, as we have seen—except, perhaps, in that part of the subcontinent that lies in the angle between the Himalayas and Burma and is drained by the Brahmaputra, the part known as Assam. In Assam there *was* a problem, and for a moment an alarm was sounded there.

The Assamese did not eat opium. They smoked it, not as the Chinese smoked it, but mixed with chopped betel leaves. This of itself would probably not have bothered anybody, but it happened that in the middle 1830s the Government of India had begun casting about for an alternative to haughty and exclusive China as a supplier of England's teas. It had sent a tea expert to Fukien to bring back the seeds of the Chinese tea bush, meaning to attempt plantations in the Nilgiris and other hill districts,* and though the experiment had failed (the seeds, each a little larger than a hazel nut, germinated nicely in the Botanical Gardens at Calcutta but did not survive transplanting), Fort William had gone ahead anyhow and begun to gather tea from the wild tea bush native to Assam. In 1838, 450 pounds of the leaf were sent to London. For 1840 the yield was expected to pass 10,000 pounds. Obtaining tea in this fashion required, however, a great deal of labor—the bushes, which grew wild to a height of thirty to forty feet, had to be pruned to picking level, and the dense growth around them cut back or grubbed out before production could begin—and it was at this point that opium threatened the entire enterprise. Too many of the hill people had been made almost useless for hard physical work by reason of their smoking.

Or so, at least, thought C. S. Bruce, a naval officer who had once commanded gunboats on the Brahmaputra and now superintended tea production for the newly formed Assam Company. Speaking at Calcutta in August 1839 before the Agricultural and Horticultural Society of India, Bruce declared that if steps were not taken to curb the cultivation of the poppy (it was grown in a small way right in the tea districts), the plains people who were being brought up to work on the new plantations

---

*The expert, a man named Gordon, traveled from Calcutta to the Gulf of Canton aboard the *Water Witch,* and from that point made two expeditions to Fukien Province, one in the early autumn of 1834 (during the Napier affair), the other the following spring. Gutzlaff guided him on the first, Gutzlaff and Stevens on the second; they were put ashore on the Fukien coast by the *Colonel Young* and the *Governor Findlay* in that order; and while the two parties made their way inland to the tea country, distributing tracts as they went, Jardine Matheson's men sold chests over the side and waited for them to come back. Thus tea, opium, and the Word of Life walked hand in hand without discomfort.

would pick up the opium habit too; and that would render the production of tea impossible on any scale.

Here, perhaps, was the opium smoking question come home to the English at last. Assam was governed by the English, the Assam Company was an English company with an English address, and Bruce was English. If opium taken in this peculiar oriental fashion really had ruinous consequences, England must soon learn about it. Parliament, after all, was familiar with the Assam experiment. Temperance societies regularly urged both houses to encourage tea there.

And Bruce's opinion did reach England. At the Assam Company's first annual meeting in London, a meeting chaired by the same G. G. de Hochepied Larpent whom we saw cooperating warmly with Jardine and John Abel Smith in the autumn of 1839 (so that in his person the opium question in China and the opium question in Assam met), the formal hope was registered that Fort William would suppress outright the cultivation of the poppy in the province. But this was as far as the matter went. Though Bruce's dire prediction was taken seriously by the Assam Company, it was apparently not known in Parliament when Graham's motion came up for debate. Had it been, just imagine what Gladstone would have made of it!

Then again, it would probably have made no difference. Perhaps it is foolish of us to wish that the English, or anybody else, should have perceived how destructive opium smoking in the orient was going to be. Or perceiving, have cared.

Lin kept trying to make the English aware. By the *Thomas Coutts,* sailing early in February, he sent a second letter to Victoria, and though the letter was never actually delivered—Palmerston remembered what the *Coutts* had done the previous autumn and categorically refused to talk to her master or to transmit anything he bore—it was printed in the *Times.* But a piece containing such extravagant conceits (including the old one about foreigners not being able to exist without China's rhubarb), a letter couched moreover in such stilted language, was not likely to be taken any more seriously than the "naval serio comic sketch" of the "Chinese War" then showing at one London theater. It included the fight between the *Volage,* the *Hyacinth,* and the sixteen war junks; when English Canton merchants needed to be introduced, they carried enormous pistols and looked as fierce as pirates. That was about the level at which London looked at Anglo-Chinese relations. Lin by his letter can have done little to elevate it.

From Peking, Lin learned that his term as *ch'in-ch'ai* was coming to an end but that instead of moving to a fresh appointment he was to remain at Canton as governor-general in Teng's place. This being so, it behooved him to redouble his efforts to inform himself about the westerners. "Only by knowing their strengths and their weaknesses can we find the right means to restrain them."[16] Through Liang A-fa's son, Atih, he had already obtained (in translation) extracts from Vattel's *Law of Nations,* Thelwall's piece about the opium traffic, and some issues of local English-language journals—particularly the *Canton Press.* Now he arranged to buy the *Cambridge,* alias the *Chesapeake,* for his water forces. He could not get her armament, Elliot having insisted when Douglas first sold her that her guns be shipped to India, and he could not sail her because he did not have men capable of managing her exotic rigging and strange sails, but he could moor her in the river, just above First Bar. There he equipped her with a heterogeneous collection of cannon, some of them western, painted two great eyes upon her bows, and hoped she would keep the foreign devils from Canton. So Lin made his preparations. The English did likewise.

Some of the needed men-of-war were already on or near the East Indian Station. The *Wellesley,* Maitland's flagship, had been struck by illness at Bombay the previous autumn and had put to sea to shake it off—in which endeavor she had failed, Maitland and many others aboard her dying—but that January she sailed down to Trincomalee and in February moved to the mouth of the Hooghly. The *Druid,* a 44-gun frigate, was able to leave Sydney for China shortly after Christmas. A 26-gun frigate, the *Alligator,* came up to Trincomalee from Sydney too; another, the *Conway,* was already at Calcutta; and there were a few lesser sailing craft available, among them the *Larne* (with her bottom scraped and caulked and a new suit of sails). As for steamers, the Indian navy agreed to lend the *Atalanta;* the brand new *Queen* and the elderly *Enterprize* were already working for Fort William in the Bay of Bengal; and a fourth, the *Madagascar,* was hastily purchased.

There would have to be more vessels than this, however—at the Admiralty no one had ever taken seriously the suggestion that the job could be done by a handful of frigates—and they must come principally from home waters. So broadsides in green, yellow, blue, and red appeared in the streets of Portsmouth to advertise the 74-gun *Blenheim,* the 42-gun *Blonde,* and the corvettes *Pylades* and *Nimrod.* Crews were hard to come by, in part because the fleet as a whole was expanding; it was because of this that the *Blonde* did not complete her complement until she shifted down channel to Plymouth. China, moreover, was a good deal less important in the Admiralty's eye than the eastern Mediterranean, where it seemed that naval operations against Mehemet Ali and the French could not much longer be avoided and where, in consequence, a dozen ships of the line must regularly be kept. Nevertheless the China expedition would receive three seventy-fours: the *Wellesley,* the *Blenheim,* and the *Melville*—the last recently gone out to the Cape. For the Admiralty, when it learned that Maitland was dead, named Rear Admiral Sir George Elliot (then commanding the South African Station) to take Maitland's place, and instructed him to bring with him his flagship as well as a corvette and a 10-gun brig.

About the middle of February, accordingly, the *Blenheim* and the *Blonde* lifted anchor and were off down the Atlantic carrying a party of artillery and a larger than normal complement of Royal Marines. At Cape Town the *Melville* loaded missing guns, filled out her crew, and departed at the end of April. In India, meanwhile, regiments were alerted, vessels engaged, and preparations made to dispatch the land forces of the expedition. Towards the end of March, the 26th (Cameronians) left Fort William nine hundred strong and marched aboard five transports lying in the Hooghly. Down from Patna came another European line regiment, the 49th, with 670 officers and men. A volunteer battalion of Bengal sepoys embarked at Calcutta too—because the sepoys of the Bengal army were mostly high-caste Hindus who could not eat food prepared over salt water and so could not be sent overseas, it was the custom in these circumstances to attract low-caste Hindus and Muslims from the ranks of the regular regiments by the offer of extra pay. Two companies of native sappers and miners and two companies of European artillery with nine- and twelve-pounders boarded transports at Madras. From Trincomalee sailed a third European regiment, the 18th or Royal Irish.

With the men went drinking water for two months and salt meat, flour, biscuits, sugar, rum, lime juice, tea, and tobacco for six; also rice, dal, and ghee, for besides the Bengal volunteers and the sappers and miners there were Indian servants and followers to feed—the 49th alone had over two hundred. Three small merchantmen were fitted with stalls for bullocks so that the expedition might for a time enjoy fresh beef; coal, upwards of six thousand tons of it, was required to fuel the steamers; and there were munitions of course: hundreds of barrels of gunpowder, thousands of rounds of shot, canister, and shell, tens of thousands of musket cartridges and balls with flints to match. In numbers this would not be a very large force, not half the sixteen thousand men that one English provincial newspaper was sure were being prepared "to compel those besotted Celestials to listen to a little reason."[17] Yet it would be a force such as had never before been seen in the China Sea.

And as it began to move east, in merchant vessels hired locally at ten to twelve rupees per ton per month, opium moved with it—not in the same bottoms, of course, but in the clippers and country ships accustomed to the trade. Six thousand chests changed hands at the Calcutta January sale; twenty-four hundred were sold in February, an equal number in April; from Bombay came Malwa, though in a far from normal flow. Practiced vessels with familiar names carried the drug directly to the coast (the detour to Manila was abandoned), and though the quantity on hand gradually pushed prices down and the big houses once more encountered the competition of the small, prospects were bright and the approach of the expedition no cause for worry. "I am glad to say our Chief Superintendent seems completely weaned of his hostility to the drug traffic," wrote Matheson to Jamsetjee.[18] Indeed, it was hard to see how war with China could trouble the opium business at all.

In the Gulf of Canton winter turned to spring. The *Mor* sailed for Bombay to fetch her first cargo of Malwa. *Red Rover* arrived with a consignment of Patna and Benares and the December overland containing the first reliable public news of the expedition forming in England and India. From the coastal stations, from the fringes of the gulf even, came reports of violent clashes between opium craft and war junks or pirate boats. (Skippers rarely distinguished between the two, and underwriters insured against neither.) Jardine Matheson made plans to resume landing the drug right inside the gulf. "The *fast crab boats* are going to run again," reported John Rees from the *Governor Findlay* (Parry was sick and Rees now in charge), "first five, and if they succeed five more."[19] H.M.S. *Druid* came in from Sydney. Elliot himself piloted her up to Tongku.

Elliot decided it would be a good idea to reconnoiter the approaches to the Yangtze—take soundings, establish channel marks, that sort of thing—and asked Matheson for an opium clipper with a captain who knew the coast; he had recently treated the Scotsman to a private reading of a part of his confidential correspondence with Palmerston and expected the favor to be returned. So Matheson sent Jauncey in the *Hellas,* with instructions to sell a little Malwa on the way. On 22 May, however, as the big schooner lay becalmed a little to the east of Namoa among what Jauncey took to be ordinary merchant junks, eight of them suddenly attacked, approaching cannily from the stern, so that what with no wind and the fishing stakes she was entangled with the *Hellas* could not bring her broadsides to bear. For four hours the Chinese poured in musket and gingal fire, tossed pots of flaming pitch, and tried to board. At last a breeze came up and the *Hellas* broke away. All fifteen of Jauncey's Europeans and ten of his lascars were injured, however, and Jauncey himself had had his jaw broken and one eye nearly put out, so he gave up the venture and turned south.

The *Hellas* reached Macao on the twenty-eighth and put Jauncey ashore to be doctored. By this time only a handful of Americans remained at the factories; with few English merchantmen still waiting for cargoes, there was little left for them to do. Williams made a quick trip up the river to fetch the printing office and the more valuable of his books. Even Parker thought of leaving—except for him, the entire Protestant Mission was concentrated at Macao. The Squires had gone home, Lockhart was not yet back from Batavia nor Mary Gutzlaff from Manila, but there were two new London Missionary Society men, William Milne, Jr. (the eldest son of the Milne who had started the Malacca press), and a doctor named Hobson. Milne lived with Brown and helped him teach English to the six Chinese boys in his school (for which the Morrison Education Society continued to raise money). Hobson got ready to reopen the Macao hospital with Diver when Lockhart should return. Both Milne and Hobson studied Chinese, and both assumed quite easily and naturally that attitude of mingled hope and exasperation which impelled Bridgman to begin an issue of the *Repository* upon the theme "the time has come when China must BEND or BREAK."[20] Of course everyone knew who would be doing the breaking. "We are daily looking towards the sea in expectation of a force from England," wrote Milne. It was said the Chinese were building a number of armed light craft along western lines— "fine boats of thirty tons each, cutter rigged, and with a nine-pounder on a carriage in the bow," one American described them—as well as some sidewheelers worked mechanically by treadmills. Just the same Milne was not sure they grasped the full and awful truth of the approaching onslaught. "So it was," he observed for the benefit of his Society, "with the sottish Belshazzar and his court."[21]

Legrégeois, in his own house again but keeping very quiet, had a letter from a Catholic lieutenant aboard the *Wellesley* informing him that the expedition was collected and almost ready to start. A week went by. Then on the night of 8 June the Chinese sent a score of junks loaded with gunpowder and combustibles down among the fleet at Capsingmun. Carried by wind and tide, they drifted in among the anchored ships, which hastily slipped or cut, but boats from the *Druid*, the *Volage*, and the *Hyacinth* boldly grappled them and towed them aside, and little damage was done.

At the height of the confusion, fireboats blazing and exploding, ships blundering here and there, the frigate *Alligator* slipped quietly into the anchorage. She had left Singapore on 18 May, and she reported the main force of the expedition not far behind.

PART THREE

The War

15

The First Expedition

Singapore had been appointed the expedition's place of rendezvous. The ships from England and South Africa, the men and ships from India, were to assemble there under the direction of Sir Gordon Bremer, senior naval officer on the station now that Maitland was dead. When Rear Admiral Sir George Elliot arrived from the Cape, Bremer was to surrender the command to him. In April or at the latest early May—by which time the northeast monsoon should have ceased and the southwest monsoon be stirring—the expedition was to set off for China, confident of a good four or five months in which to do its business on the coast.

This assumed, however, prompt sailings from Portsmouth and Cape Town. In fact Sir George and the *Melville* did not leave the Cape until the end of April, the *Blenheim* (which touched there) not until the middle of May. Then there was the Bay of Bengal to reckon with. The *Wellesley* came down to Singapore without incident early in April, the five transports with the 26th arrived safely a couple of weeks later—and at that point the weather changed. The *Madagascar* steamer (with Bremer aboard) made such heavy work of it that she reached Penang, where coal was available, only by burning yards and studding sail booms. High winds drove a number of transports all the way back to Calcutta; two never left the Hooghly at all, but collided with each other on the way down and were forced into dock for repairs. At the very end of April a cyclone caught the *Marion* near the Andaman Islands, snapped her topmasts like matchsticks, and left her drifting helplessly for days while her crew struggled with a jury-rig. Besides medical stores for the entire expedition and barrels of silver with which to pay the troops, she carried headquarters for the combined land forces and Lieutenant Colonel Oglander of the 26th (commanding). The expedition could not very well set off for China without it and him.

Gradually the transports straggled in, received large painted numerals on their bows and quarters, and if necessary had their loads redistributed. Singapore was a pretty place, approached through wooded islands that gave her waters the appearance of an inland sea, with the governor's bungalow on a grassy hill and merchants' houses below. Evenings the *Wellesley*'s band played on the esplanade, while officers from the ships and regiments mingled with the local white residents.* Most of the troops were kept aboard ship, there being (it was alleged) insufficient cleared ground for a camp, but marines from the men-of-war practiced landings on a nearby beach, approaching in neat files of longboats, splashing ashore, forming line, and advancing. Sailors armed with the new percussion muskets skirmished ahead and on their flanks.

The *Atalanta* arrived from Bombay. She was armed with pivot guns and brought the March overland mail from England—Bremer sent the *Alligator* on with it at once, as we have seen. He would have liked to follow himself, but Admiral Elliot and Oglander and his headquarters were still missing. In the roadstead scores of great oceangoing Chinese junks watched the barbarian fleet accumulate and felt perhaps a certain apprehension, for though it was a little early to be starting for China again and their opium purchasing was still brisk at $325 to $350 a chest, most of them had weighed and disappeared by the third week in May. On the twenty-ninth the *Marion* crept in. Some of the other transports were yet to be heard from, only half the 18th had arrived, but the monsoon was turning and Bremer waited no longer. Headquarters was ordered bag and baggage to the *Queen* steamer; at noon on the thirtieth the *Wellesley* with a part of the warships and transports moved into open water; next day the rest came out, and the whole fleet sailed.

In the upper reaches of the China Sea the southwest monsoon was not yet blowing, and the *Madagascar*, pushing ahead alone with the help of her paddle wheels, steamed into the Gulf of Canton on 16 June. Four days later the rest of the fleet sighted the Great Ladrone. It hove to, however, only the *Atalanta* moving in close enough so that Elliot could see her smoke. On the twenty-first the *Wellesley* entered Macao Roads. Elliot came aboard and conferred with Bremer. On the twenty-second the *Larne* (with the April overland) and several overdue transports arrived and entered the roads too. Meanwhile the *Conway* and most of the fleet remained invisible beyond the islands, and on the twenty-third took up course again for the eastward, Bremer and the *Wellesley* following the

*One young officer of the Madras artillery met in this way "a Captain Brooke, formerly of our Service; but having a large fortune left him, retired, and is now moving about in this part of the world in his yacht, exploring islands along the coast of Java which have never before been visited by Europeans" (Wyndham Baker, "An Artillery Officer in China, 1840-1842," *Blackwood's Magazine* 296 [1964]: 75). It was James Brooke, soon to become rajah of Sarawak.

next day. For Palmerston did not mean to waste his ships and regiments on the Gulf of Canton. It was not there that he meant to bring the Chinese to terms. Peking was the goal.

In fixing his eye thus upon Peking, the foreign secretary was certainly guided in part by his recollection of the Napier fizzle. Napier had tried to negotiate at the provincial level and had gotten nowhere at all. Palmerston was clearly not forgetting, too, the advice given him by William Jardine. Blockade the coast from Hainan in the south to the Great Wall in the north, Jardine had urged. Seize as hostages the island of Chusan and one or two other places. Present your demands at the mouth of the Peiho and compel the Chinese to discuss them there aboard a warship. For this you will re- quire a first-rate of 120 guns or so, a third-rate carrying 74, a few frigates and lesser craft, with sailors and marines enough to make a landing force of a few thousand men. These were Jardine's suggestions of October. Except that Palmerston sent no first-rate but three thirds, raised the landing force by several regiments, and limited the blockade to only a few of China's ports and rivers, this is what he laid down provisionally in November and in February in full and final form. This is what Elliot was apprised of when the *Ariel* returned from the Red Sea early in April. This is what Bremer and he discussed in the great cabin of the *Wellesley* as she lay in Macao Roads in June.

Not everyone concurred with these plans. Sir John Barrow, second secretary at the Admiralty and a plainspoken man of much experience and influence (he was older even than Wellington), thought Jardine's propos- als "extraordinary" and said so.[1] Negotiating at Peking had been tried be- fore, by Macartney and others, without success. The city was more than a hundred miles from the Gulf of Chihli, where the waters shoal for such a distance that Jardine's first-rate would be compelled to anchor beyond sight of land. Finally, seizing Chusan and menacing the coast would only infuriate the imperial court and so disincline it further to accept free inter- course with England. Barrow admitted that negotiations not backed by force were bound to prove fruitless. The wise thing, it seemed to him, was to apply that force in the Gulf of Canton—to occupy the island of Hong- kong (where a handful of guns and one man-of-war could guarantee the safety of a fleet of merchantmen), to penetrate the Bogue and perhaps send a few light craft to throw shells and rockets into Canton itself. Auckland too wanted more activity in the Canton area than just a blockade. And though Elliot had at first thought of action along the whole length of the coast, by May he had come quite independently to the conclusion that the first thing the expedition must do was to show clearly that it could com- mand the river. If it did not do this, if it moved north without delivering a smashing blow, the Chinese would think it possessed of "the fear and trembling of which they admonish us so often"[2] and would certainly not listen when it reached the Peiho.

Another possible theater of operations attracted the chief superintendent. From opium skippers who regularly visited Shanghai (already a port of consequence in the Chinese coasting trade) and from French missionaries who knew the Yangtze River and the delta country towards its mouth, he had learned a good deal about the Grand Canal and the traffic it carried. Every year quantities of rice moved north along this stupendous man-made waterway towards the tribute granaries of Peking. The canal began at Hangchow, at the head of the gulf of that name some distance below Shanghai. It crossed the Yangtze at Chinkiang, 150 miles up the river. Elliot was sure that a very modest flotilla—a couple of frigates with corvettes and steamers in support—could cut it there and bring most of the grain to a halt. Here was something calculated to unsettle the Dragon Throne! If the frigates pushed on another fifty miles, they might dictate terms to the Chinese before the former capital of Nanking itself.

Elliot had another reason for wishing to see a Yangtze campaign. Warships in that river, while capable of applying effective pressure and applying it cheaply, remained distant from Peking and therefore out of Peking's sight. None of these things could be said of warships at the Peiho. Experience had taught the chief superintendent that the Chinese recognized reality when they had to but that they were determined, even in the most desperate of times, to save face. They would not simply be persuaded. They had to be frightened. But it was as necessary to leave them the means of salvaging appearances as it was to awaken their fears; otherwise all you got was shock, unreasoning anger, and a withdrawal to fresh levels of hauteur. England's expedition, then, had first by act or threat to "incite the needful yieldingness of spirit."[3] It had next to give the Chinese the opportunity actually to yield something while preserving the appearance of yielding nothing at all. It was the *pin* all over again, and for this skillful double operation the Peiho was ill suited: for on the one hand warships there could not *do* much—a landing was no part of the plan, and the river not navigable by vessels of any size—and on the other, even if the sight of an English fleet inclined the authorities to make an accommodation, Peking was too close and the general visibility too high for them to make it.

Elliot, then, would have preferred something further south. In Palmerston's dispatches he could discover, however, no room for maneuver, nothing that would permit him to substitute Canton or the Yangtze for a diplomatic confrontation at the Peiho. What he received from the Foreign Office instead were inquiries and admonitions both out-of-date and carping. Had the Yum Chae actually destroyed the twenty thousand chests? *More probably he had sold them*. What, pray, induced the chief superintendent to suppose he had the authority to prevent English merchantmen from entering the river? Elliot was named plenipotentiary jointly with his cousin, Admiral Sir George Elliot, who ought to arrive any day now in the *Melville*, but their commission was simply for the purpose of negotiating a treaty with the Chinese, and even here the discretion allowed was small. Palmerston sent along a complete draft of a treaty, stipulating that the two plenipotentiaries must make Peking agree to all but one of the points it contained—they were not to call off the war till they had. (A few days after dispatching this sine-qua-nonical injunction, it must suddenly have occurred to Palmerston that Elliot might already have made some arrangement with the Chinese, for he dashed off the warning that if such was the case he should jolly well scrap it.) As for the fighting itself, its direction lay entirely with Admiral Elliot as naval commander-in-chief. The most the chief superintendent could hope was that his cousin's inexperience in Chinese matters would make him a good listener.

So in spite of Captain Elliot the expedition did not linger long in the vicinity of Canton. Palmerston's instructions, the lateness of the hour (the campaign was at least a month behind schedule), and the imminence of the typhoon season combined to hurry it north. A blockade of the river was announced. (Just before it took effect the *Kosciusko* and a bona fide American, the *Panama*, slipped up to Whampoa.) On the twenty-eighth the *Melville*, the 42-gun *Blonde*, and the 18-gun *Pylades* reached the gulf and anchored in the Lamma Passage. Early on the thirtieth they sailed again, with the two Elliots aboard. The *Druid*, the *Madagascar*, and three other men-of-war were left behind to protect the shipping and to enforce the blockade.

Matheson and his friends were disappointed. The failure to make a demonstration in the gulf would, they feared, encourage Peking to suppose it could avoid a showdown indefinitely. Still, they were pleased to see the ships and men, and Bridgman was pleased too—without their reservations. "The Rubicon is passed," he wrote in the *Repository*. "A force has entered that cannot be expelled and will not pay homage."

And added, a little gratuitously, "All the world must rejoice that such a force is here."[4]

Chusan, eight hundred miles up the coast, was the first objective of the force. To pilot it there Bremer engaged the Rees brothers, Thomas from Dent's opium fleet and John from Jardine Matheson's. The interpreters were John Morrison, Gutzlaff, a newly recruited Chinese Christian named Rodriguez, and Jardine Matheson's clerk, Robert Thom.

Thom saw service first. On their way up the coast the two Elliots decided to try to deliver a letter from Palmerston to the emperor—or more exactly, to "the Minister of the Emperor" (whoever that might be). This letter, which had come with the February instructions, reviewed in general terms England's past relations with China, narrated for the emperor's benefit the harrowing tale of the English merchants held to ransom at Canton, cast the opium question in what Palmerston hoped would prove a useful and instructive form—if the Chinese wished to check the spread of the drug, let them begin by disciplining themselves!—and announced the arrival of an expeditionary force resolved to blockade the emperor's principal ports, occupy "some convenient part" of his dominions, and bring his ministers to the negotiating table aboard a warship off the Peiho.[5] It was supposed to have been delivered at Canton, but there had been no opportunity to deliver it there. So the two plenipotentiaries determined to make the effort on the way to Chusan. When not quite halfway to that place, they sent Captain Bourchier and the *Blonde* into Amoy, with Thom to interpret.

Amoy lies on the south side of the island of that name, in the middle of a great shallow bay dotted with smaller islands and sheltered to the east by the large island of Quemoy. Half a mile off the city's waterfront is the little oval of Kulangsu. Between its lower end and Amoy proper the *Blonde* anchored about noon on 2 July.

Very soon several men with an official air about them, magistrates' runners probably, came by in a small boat, and Thom took the opportunity to explain carefully to them what the white flag means among civilized nations, writing down his explanation, and appending to it a warning (in the language of menace the Celestials themselves used) that if *his* white flag were fired upon the English would return "a most fearful vengeance! beware, beware!"[6] Then he got into the frigate's cutter and set off to deliver the letter. His explanation apparently did not precede him, however, for when he got close to shore and pointed to the white flag fluttering above his head, the small crowd collected there made such menacing noises that he thought it prudent to withdraw without landing.

Next morning Bourchier prepared to bring the *Blonde* in closer and try again. While he waited for the breeze to freshen, he observed the Chinese dragging guns into a small fort and mounting others on junks towed down from the inner harbor. By noon the frigate was anchored a few hundred yards from a beach, and off went Thom, this time in the jolly boat. Approaching within hailing distance, he had his crew turn the boat around and scull slowly stern first; then, when only five or six yards of water remained, he held up a piece of calico on which he had painted in large, bold characters the reason for his coming and the awful consequences should his white flag once again be held in contempt. There were more people than there had been the day before, there were soldiers among them, and their anger when they read the calico was great. Thom tried to speak, but his voice was drowned in the hubbub, and some of the crowd made the well-known gesture of cutting off the head. Meanwhile the boat had drifted on until she was almost aground. Suddenly a few Chinese started to wade out. Thom called for a stroke or two, stood up, and shouted for the last time would they take the letter? "No!" roared the crowd. "Pull!" cried Thom. The frightened oarsmen pulled, the jolly boat shot forward, Thom lost his balance and fell into the stern sheets, and an arrow whirred over the spot he had just occupied. Bullets followed, two cannon were discharged, the soldiers appeared on the point of delivering a murderous volley, when a couple of thirty-two-pound shot came bounding and skipping in among them, felling half a dozen and putting the rest to flight. Bourchier had been watching.

After that there seemed nothing to do but visit a few of the promised consequences on these people. As soon as Thom had regained the *Blonde*, she trained her broadside on the anchored junks and fort and pounded them methodically. Thousands of Chinese watched from the rocky hills above. Next Bourchier had Thom compose a message protesting the violence shown the jolly boat and pointing out that the English had no quarrel with the Chinese, only with their rulers. The boat he sent the message by was met with determined musket fire and obliged to withdraw, so Bourchier slipped the message into a bottle, corked it, dropped it over the side, and saw a fisherman pick it up. Then he set fire to a merchant junk that had the imprudence to be lying near, weighed with the evening tide, and resumed his voyage towards Chusan.

The Chusan archipelago lies about that part of the coast a hundred miles below the Yangtze where the mainland of China pushes as far east as it is going to push—the Cape Hatteras, as it were, of the seaboard. Some of the islands in the archipelago (the map shows hundreds) are pinnacle rocks rising unexpectedly from deep water, and some are smooth round pebbles a couple of hundred acres in extent. A few run to a square mile or more—Puto, famous for its Buddhist temples and resident priests, is one of these—but Chusan itself is twenty-five miles long, six to ten miles wide, and upwards of fifty miles around.

It lies on a slant above and very near the mainland's easternmost extremity, the long finger of high land called by foreigners Keeto Point. Midway along Chusan's south side, and only seven or eight miles from Keeto Point, is the town of Tinghai. In the old days, before the English had resigned themselves to living and doing business only at Canton, Tinghai had frequently seen barbarian merchants, and its waters occasionally saw them still. Barrow had gone that way with the Macartney embassy and

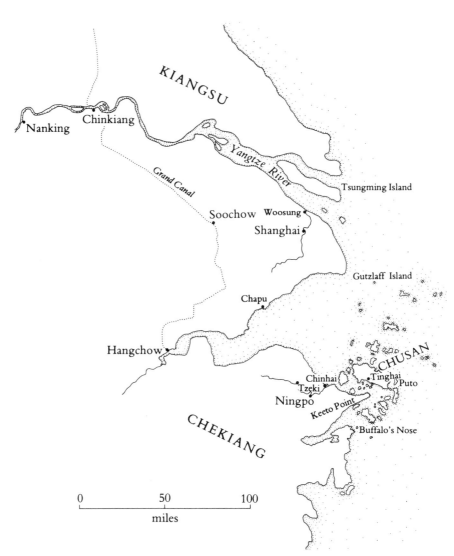

Chusan and the Yangtze

had written a description that Bridgman (now the subject was once more current and choice) resurrected for the June issue of the *Repository*. Lindsay, Gutzlaff, and Thomas Rees had taken the *Lord Amherst* past Keeto Point in 1832. Opium skippers knew the area well and called many of its ins and outs by names of their own devising. So it was with no particular difficulty that the *Wellesley* and the rest of the advance squadron of the fleet, sailing a comfortable distance out from the coast, turned west below the archipelago, passed Starboard Jack and the Corkers, and rendezvoused off Buffalo's Nose twenty-five miles below Chusan. Indeed, the only untoward event of the 800-mile voyage was the death of Oglander. He was old, had chronic dysentery, the ordeal aboard the *Marion* had exhausted him, and on the way up from Canton he died. Thereupon the command of the brigade devolved upon Lieutenant Colonel Burrell of the 18th—at sixty-three, even older than Oglander. For the moment the change seemed unimportant. Time was to put another face on the matter.

The rendezvous off Buffalo's Nose was accomplished on Wednesday, 1 July. Next day the squadron moved northward past Keeto Point towards the little islands that cover the harbor of Tinghai. Just short of them they anchored; the tidal currents in this area were known to be strong, there seemed to be rocks everywhere, and not even Thomas Rees cared to take a ship as large as the *Wellesley* through without a reconnoiter. On Friday morning, therefore, the *Atalanta* steamed off alone making soundings. That afternoon she was back with what appeared to be a feasible route and early Saturday took the *Wellesley* in tow, starting in by the south passage. Part way the set of the tide forced her suddenly onto an underwater obstruction of some sort, and for a moment it looked as if the seventy-four, bearing irresistibly down upon the fragile little craft, would crush and sink her. But the larger vessel caught the bottom too, was checked in her rush, and only grazed the steamer, smashing gig, cutter, and starboard paddle box and knocking the funnel askew. Her captain backed her off, made full sail, and took her the rest of the way himself. Before the tide turned that afternoon, the *Conway*, the *Alligator*, and three transports had joined her in Tinghai's harbor.

Their coming was watched by a dozen war junks. From the flutter of pennons upon the stern of one Bremer concluded that here was a naval officer of considerable rank and had himself rowed over with Gutzlaff to do the talking. Thom's experience at Amoy was not repeated. The party was allowed on board, and after a time an officer appeared wearing a red button. He was not, however, an admiral but the commander of the military garrison, though the English did not appreciate this fact, and he showed no inclination to do Bremer's bidding. So he and his staff were invited to the *Wellesley*, where they were served sweet wine and shown about the gun decks. "It is very true you are strong and I am weak," Gutz-laff has this officer remark when the tour of the seventy-four was over. "Still I must fight."[7] Gutzlaff thought the man rather stupid. Viscount Jocelyn, a young officer with excellent connections whom Auckland had sent out from Calcutta to be military secretary to the plenipotentiaries, was impressed by his resolution and wondered how there could be any talk of Chinese officers deserting their "Tartar" rulers. Bremer again demanded surrender, gave Red Button until two the following afternoon to arrange it, and saw him off in the gathering dusk.

From the *Wellesley* Tinghai itself could not be seen. It lay a little dis-tance inland, masked by a low hill on whose southern slope stood a "joss-house" or temple. At the base of this hill was a straggling village and a stone sea wall. Men had been observed building a rampart of grain sacks along the wall; there were guns among the sacks, more visible on the hill, and a few mounted in a round Martello tower at the water's edge. All night the Chinese struggled by lamp light to strengthen their defenses, while merchant junks loaded to capsizing stole to safety through the English fleet.

Early Sunday morning Bremer moved his flagship closer to the shore. Burrell had as yet few men to make a landing with, but towards noon a flood tide brought several lesser men-of-war through the islands and with them the rest of the transports, the *Atalanta* towing several. The men-of-war mustered to quarters, cleared for action, and took up line about two hundred yards from the sea wall, port broadsides bearing. A part of the Cameronians, the grenadiers of the Royal Irish, the Royal Marines, and some Madras artillerymen with two nine-pounders waited in longboats behind them. Right along the sea wall lay the war junks of the Chinese. Armine Mountain, a veteran officer serving on Burrell's staff, thought these vessels "with their huge mat sails, their eyes and tiger heads, and high, elaborately painted sterns and bluff prows" like something out of Froissart—"exactly as if the subjects of his old prints had assumed life and substance and colour, and were moving and acting before me unconscious of the march of the world through centuries, and of all modern usage, in-vention, or improvement."[8] By the glass they appeared to carry among them some three dozen guns, in number practically the same as the *Wellesley*'s broadside, but capable of delivering (in weight of metal) no-thing like her more than half a ton.

Two o'clock came, and not a sign the Chinese intended to surrender. At twenty minutes past the hour Bremer called for a single round upon the Martello tower. The shot was answered from the Chinese flagship. At once Bremer hoisted the signal to engage, and the whole English line began to fire. For eight or nine minutes upwards of seventy guns hammered and thundered, building clouds of smoke that the breeze struggled to dissipate. Then the *Wellesley* flew the signal to desist and the troops went in, Burrell and his staff in the lead boat, the gun crews cheering wildly through open ports as they rowed by. The English ships had been struck repeatedly and one sailor aboard the *Conway* wounded, but the Chinese guns were silent now. Four of the war junks were shot to pieces and the others very much damaged. The Martello tower lay in ruins; the sea wall, with its smashed guns and its litter of burst and scattered grain sacks, was deserted except for the dead and dying; and there were not many of these because Bremer had deliberately ordered round shot instead of canister—besides, at the very first broadside most of the Chinese had turned and run. Red Button, it was said, had been carried away on a litter with a serious injury to one leg. The boats unloaded their men without incident, and while they went back for more, the grenadiers of the Royal Irish climbed Joss-House Hill. Sixty-five summers before the same grenadier company (though not of course the same men) had climbed Bunker Hill—or Breed's, as it actually was—and found the going difficult. They reached the top of this one with no trouble at all and immediately planted their flag, "the first European banner," Jocelyn was confident, "that has floated as conqueror over the Flowery Land."9 It was not yet three o'clock.

Less than a mile away across the flooded rice fields lay Tinghai itself. A party of Cameronians and the little detachment of Madras artillery skirted the hill and started towards it, moving with difficulty along raised paths and a single modest causeway. At four or five hundred yards distance the artillerymen laid their two nine-pounders and threw a few shells* into the town. From the walls, gay with banners and noisy with the sound of gongs, came a smart returning fire, and Burrell decided to postpone the assault. So the day drew towards a close without further fighting. Soldiers searching for billets in the half-wrecked village came across quantities of *samshu* (Chusan, it seemed, manufactured the "brutalizing poison" for export to the mainland), and began to help themselves, and though their officers smashed all the jars they could lay their hands on and let the stuff run out into the streets, by nightfall many of the men were stupefied or roaring drunk. Towards midnight a fire broke out, fed by powder in abandoned Chinese ammunition tubs, and proved so difficult to extinguish (of course the seamen sent to fight it got at the *samshu* too) that the 49th, landing very early Monday morning, had to avoid the village altogether lest burning embers ignite the cartridges each man carried in his pouch.

This, however, did not delay the taking of Tinghai. At first light the

*Hollow iron balls filled with gunpowder and ignited by means of a fuse inserted in a hole left for the purpose. The fuse caught fire when the gun was fired, burned throughout flight, and hopefully touched off the powder as the ball came to earth.

English on Joss-House Hill saw streams of Chinese hurrying out the north gate into the hills and guessed the city would not be defended. Jocelyn, Mountain, Bethune of the *Conway*, and several other young officers ventured towards the south wall, drew no fire, got across the canal that ran along its base, threw a ladder against the angle of the gate, climbed over (the wall was less than twenty feet high and quite deserted though banners still waved), cleared away some grain sacks piled in the archway, and let their compatriots in. Then everyone fanned out to explore what might, after all, become England's first permanent possession in China.

It was a fair-sized town, perhaps three-quarters of a mile on a side, not completely built up but capable of containing (the English estimated) twenty-five to thirty thousand persons. The houses were low and windowless and built of bluish brick, the streets mere alleys with a covered sewer down the middle. There were no squares or public gardens; the only open spaces were the pools into which the sewers emptied. Here and there stood huge earthenware jars for the reception of human and household waste. In brief the general appearance of the place was mean and the smell nasty. But the granaries were full of rice. Three arsenals held bows and arrows, guns of every description (a few so ancient they were made by hooping iron rods together), thousands of tiny rockets with barbed tips ("they generally discharge them in showers of thousands at a time," one English officer remembered, "which were admired for their beauty but never dreaded by us"[10]), heaps of padded cotton jackets with thin metal plates sewn across the chest, and much else. In the temples the English found images of all shapes and sizes: a large white elephant, a woman with a child issuing from her breast (unwitting copy of a Jesuit Mother and Child, it was decided), three Buddhas fifteen feet high. As for the private houses, they were quite charming and comfortable behind the blank faces they presented to the street. Little gardens lay tucked between high walls. Elegantly furnished apartments with delicately carved doors and windows opened upon tiled courts. In one house Jocelyn came across a decorated box eight feet square and pierced by a small circular door, inside which he found to his astonishment an enormous couch covered in silk. Another house, by all appearances the property of a high mandarin, showed the marks of sudden departure, with half-smoked pipes and cups of untasted tea in the hall, and in the back rooms a confusion of female clothing, tiny shoes, cosmetic paints, fans, ornaments. Even Jocelyn was not above stuffing his pockets with some of these articles. They were, he observes in his memoirs, "lawful *loot*"—and hastens to explain the Indian word to readers who might not understand the meaning though they could not mistake the act.

So the English took Tinghai, looting it a little yet behaving on the whole much better than the Chinese can have expected. "No one has been killed in cold blood that I am aware of," Thom wrote to Matheson a week or so later, "and only one or two cases of rape have occurred—perpetrated it is said by the sepoys."[11] The *Blonde* with Thom aboard had arrived the day after Tinghai fell. The *Melville* had preceded her. Anchoring just outside the harbor on the evening of Sunday, 5 July—she had heard the rumble of Bremer's nine-minute cannonade as she came past Keeto Point—she started in first thing Monday morning behind the *Atalanta*, and as luck would have it struck bottom approximately where the *Wellesley* had touched two days before. This time there was no backing off. A pinnacle rock ten feet below low water held her so firmly that she swung broadside to the tide, heeled over, and might have foundered had her crew not rushed to close her lower deck ports. Captain Elliot and Admiral Elliot went ahead on the steamer. Forty-eight hours later the seventy-four was pulled off and brought the rest of the way in. But her pumps worked without ceasing, and it was obvious that she would have to be careened and her bottom mended.

This mishap complicated things for the Elliots. They had intended (though the chief superintendent's heart was not in it) to push on to the Peiho as soon as Chusan was occupied, but of their three line-of-battle ships, one could not sail and another had not yet arrived. Besides, careening a seventy-four required another vessel of equal size to haul her over (at Trincomalee they used a hulk for the purpose) and that meant tying up the *Wellesley* for weeks and weeks—or waiting for the *Blenheim*. They decided to wait, and moved their things to the *Wellesley*. They went ashore and looked about, smelled the *samshu* lying stagnant in the gutters (it almost made Thom sick), and saw the extent of the destruction in the village. It was much greater, decided Captain Elliot, than it need have been. "I know not why," he wrote privately to Auckland, "we should have landed very nearly two thousand men to march up a height without works and lying exposed to the fire of a formidable force of ships of war within three hundred yards of it." Nor did he know why Bremer should have thrown such a weight of metal against the village "when there was no sort of difficulty in taking possession of the half dozen pop guns on the beach."[12] But what was done, was done, and perhaps the very frightfulness of the landing had saved a worse carnage by persuading the Chinese not to defend Tinghai.

Burrell set up headquarters inside the town, commandeering for the purpose the high mandarin's house that Jocelyn had discovered. Gutzlaff and Thom did the same; their principal work would be to interpret for the newly appointed civil magistrate, Captain Caine of the 26th. Not many Chinese remained in Tinghai. Most of these stayed carefully invisible.

Some took their cue from the invaders and began to break into vacant houses, rifling the rooms and escaping with their plunder into the country. At first Burrell let them go. After a few days, however, when it became apparent they would carry half the town away if given the chance, he posted sentries with orders to shoot, and several Chinese were killed. It was impossible, however, to seal all the exits or quite strip the inhabitants of their ingenuity. Thom gave one earnest and imploring young man permission to carry his mother outside the walls for burial, only to have the guard at the gate lift the lid of the supposed coffin with the tip of his bayonet and reveal yards and yards of the richest silk. "A more subtle, lying, and thievish race it never was my luck to live amongst" was the interpreter's morose conclusion.[13] It bothered him that he could not understand the local patois, whereas Gutzlaff, with his knack for language and his generally greater self-confidence, seemed quite at ease.

Foraging parties went looking for fresh food. There were no wheeled vehicles on the island and only a few ponies (with difficulty six were rounded up for Burrell's staff), but there were footpaths everywhere, many of them paved, and three-quarters of an hour's walk took you out of sight of Tinghai. The countryside was very pleasant. Little valleys wound down to shallow coastal plains diked with stone against the sea. The flat land was covered with ripening rice; the terraced hillsides bore yams, sweet potatoes, eggplant, and beans; on the heights dwarf oak, red-flowering arbutus, and the wild tea bush grew. Here and there were clumps of trees, a solitary temple, farms composed of so many cottages they became in effect small hamlets. In some of these the foraging parties stopped, to paste up proclamations claiming the island in the queen's name, to buy eggs or a bullock (for $20), a milk goat and her kid (for $5). The peasants, "regular clodhoppers" Thom thought, gaped and stared and laughed rather unpleasantly "as Chinamen laugh." The older or more important people maintained a dignified reserve, a coolness even, that caused Thom to abandon the popular notion that the Chinese disliked their own government and would join the English if they got the chance. He felt quite safe, however, even though the parties he accompanied were lightly armed and never large—until on the seventeenth the comprador went missing.

The comprador's name was Pu Ting-pang. He had worked for Jardine Matheson, had come up to Chusan with the expedition (which needed compradors and shroffs just as any group of foreigners did), and happened to be out buying livestock for the commissariat when some Chinese soldiers caught him, slung him pig-fashion from a pole, and carried him away. At the news a chill fell upon the town. Perhaps this was the long arm of the mainland mandarins at work. If it was, the fellow must be rescued before his captors could remove him from the island, so search parties were sent out; Jocelyn was given the largest and instructed to head directly for the island's northwest coast. For two days he, Thom, and forty Cameronians threaded their way through the hills that make up the interior of the island. It was hot; some of the Cameronians had bowel trouble; everywhere the inhabitants, forewarned by unseen watchers, melted quietly away. Then on the third day things changed. A village stood its ground and threatened to overwhelm the little party, and Jocelyn got clear only by some quick thinking and a single well-timed volley. So he gave up the search and allowed himself to be brought back to Tinghai by steamer. It was clear that the comprador was out of reach, clear too that on Chusan the English could no longer count on protecting their own. This was to have unpleasant consequences.

But for the moment Admiral Elliot and his cousin were preoccupied with other matters. They still had Palmerston's letter to deliver and sent the *Blonde* to Chinhai at the mouth of the Yung River to put a copy ashore. Back it came unopened. An unsealed Chinese translation had accompanied it, however, so its contents (the two plenipotentiaries felt sure) must have been read. On the twenty-seventh the *Blenheim* arrived at last, five months out of Portsmouth. Three days later the *Wellesley* had herself towed through the islands by two steamers and on 1 August, in thick weather with a strong wind on her starboard quarter, set sail for the Gulf of Chihli and Peking.

16

At the Peiho

Twice before the English had approached Peking: with Macartney in 1793 and with Amherst twenty-three years later. But though the published accounts of these two embassies were well known, and perhaps even to be found in the great cabin of the *Wellesley*, no one on board that seventy-four or the ships that went with her—*Blonde*, *Volage* (commanded now by Admiral Elliot's son), two corvettes, *Madagascar* steamer, and two transports loaded with coal—knew firsthand what a venture of this sort was likely to produce. As for the Tao-kuang emperor and his court, they looked at the approaching English as usual through the wrong end of the telescope.

They were perfectly well aware, of course, that the English expedition had reached the coast, sailed up it, and taken Chusan. An elaborate imperial postal service carried reports and memorials in abundance towards Peking, routine ones on foot, extraordinary ones by horse or horse express, so that what the Ningpo *taotai* (intendant of circuit) wished to report of the goings on at Chusan could be known at the capital within a week of his reporting them, what Commissioner Lin chose to say of Canton within little more than two. Information of this sort passed, moreover, directly to the emperor. He had no foreign office and took care of the barbarian affairs himself, brushing his autograph instructions directly upon the margins of memorials, reviewing with his grand councillors (in audience just before dawn) exactly what ought to be done, exhibiting in every way the greatest conscientiousness and system. Yet all this—the foot stations every five to ten miles, the horse stations every thirty, the army of couriers managed through an ingenious arrangement of warrants and tallies, the methodical processing of papers at the Peking end, and last but not least the personal attentiveness of the emperor—all this marvelous machinery for communication and decision making was powerless to insure that the imperial government would appreciate what the foreigners were really up to, would appreciate it and meet it head on. For at this downward stage of the dynastic cycle, the imperial court was afflicted with a peculiar kind of paralysis.

The emperor received, he did not initiate. Memorials flowed to him in streams, in floods, and he responded manfully with what the foreigners called edicts but might better have called exhortations, inasmuch as they rarely did more than attempt to reestablish what had existed before. In the provinces, meanwhile, the governors-general, the governors, and the *taotais* whose memorials the emperor so faithfully examined were as passive as he. They and the prefects, sub-prefects, and district magistrates beneath them were very thinly spread. None came from the area he governed; each expected to be rotated out of the area he was in; so each depended in day-to-day administration upon his yamen clerks and upon the local gentry. These acknowledged his special virtue, certified by possession of the *chin-shih* degree, and expected him to govern as the emperor governed, by the example of his own right conduct. But suppose something went wrong? It was not easy for a *taotai* or what have you to put that something right, unless clerks and gentry were with him, in which case the thing usually did not go wrong in the first place. Yet he was responsible before the emperor, just as the emperor was responsible before Heaven; he alone was to praise—and to blame. When, therefore, something occurred to break the even surface of public life, the high civil servant tried not to see it. He pushed it out of sight, or he reported just enough of it so that the news, when it reached Peking from another source, would not infuriate the emperor. Barbarian affairs fitted naturally into this last category. They were always disagreeable. They were usually difficult to hide. As a consequence the dreadful things the *fan kuei* did—the riot at Chien-sha-tsui, the affray off Kowloon, the battle at Chuenpi, the blockade of the Canton River, the assault on Tinghai—became known at Peking promptly enough, but became known in a form that largely concealed their seriousness, big matters being reduced to small matters and small matters to nothing at all. The truth was that the English intruders were resolute and dangerous. That ought to have been apparent. To Peking, looking darkly through a glass held backwards, it was not.

Add to this China's general and seemingly invincible ignorance of the West. Lin Tse-hsü had once thought that the red-haired devils were utterly dependent upon his country's rhubarb. He thought so no longer. But Lin was an unusually perceptive man, studying his subject from an unusually advantageous spot; the run of Chinese opinion was less well informed. England, it held, was distant and primitive, without laws, education, or culture. It was true she showed a certain cunning at naval architecture. (One reason the English men-of-war were so hard to sink, the Chinese understood, was that their sides were built up in two layers "with sand in between. The outside is covered with copper and iron, also in two thicknesses. When a cannon ball strikes the ship, it moves a little and that is all."[1]) Yet even in military matters England betrayed notable weaknesses. At the very moment the two Elliots left Chusan, Yukien (Yu-ch'ien), the governor of Kiangsu Province, was providing the emperor with a considerable list. One weakness was particularly comforting to Yukien (he was responsible for the Yangtze's mouth). "Take our fort at Woosung," he wrote. "From the bottom upward there is the stone base, then the clay base, and finally the fort itself. It is an elevation far above the level of the barbarian ships. If they shoot upward, their bullets will go down and consequently lose force." But the most serious weakness of the English was simply their excessive reliance upon guns. They did not know how to fight with bows and arrows, swords, or fists. "Moreover their waists are stiff and their legs straight. The latter, further bound with cloth, can scarcely stretch at will. Once fallen down, they cannot again stand up. It is fatal to fighting on land."[2]

One could multiply this sort of thing indefinitely. When a year later the English attacked Chinhai, Yukien had an opportunity to revise his appraisal. At that moment, however, the English were approaching the Peiho and meant to negotiate not fight.

They covered the five hundred miles between Chusan and the Shantung Peninsula out of sight of land, rounded the peninsula on 5 August, moved cautiously westward across the Gulf of Chihli until they reckoned to be opposite the Peiho's mouth, and anchored in eight fathoms of water while a strong east wind blew itself out; then they resumed their approach, sounding regularly, until the water had shoaled to six. That was as far in as they dared go. A seventy-four drew three fathoms, almost twenty feet, and they were still miles from shore (Barrow had been right). At dawn on the tenth all anyone could see from the *Wellesley*'s maintop was water. The coast remained invisible and with it the Peiho, though where it debouched could be pretty well guessed from the junks that came and went.

Captain Elliot pursued one of these junks in the *Madagascar*, seized several of her seamen, and had Morrison instruct them to act as pilots. Hesitantly they intimated to Dicey, the steamer's skipper, that there were extensive mud flats in the gray distance ahead and that the channel through them was impassable at low tide because of a bar. As it was afternoon and the tide on the ebb, Elliot waited until dawn Tuesday, then set off again in the pinnace of the *Wellesley* accompanied by several ships' boats under Lieutenant Bingham of the corvette *Modeste*. He had dressed his unwilling pilots in seamen's jackets and had made them coil their tails under straw hats so that they would not be recognized. It was in vain, the poor fellows were too frightened to be of any use, and the tide, which was in, by covering the mud flats made the channel invisible. But Elliot noticed a number of bamboo stakes poking out of the water, guessed that they marked the entrance, and headed for them. Sure enough there was a bar, with a depth of ten or twelve feet. Then the little flotilla was over and into the channel, the bottom dropped away again, and land became visible four or five miles ahead, very low, absolutely flat, with a break of a quarter of a mile where the Peiho must be.

All junk traffic had ceased. Elliot's pinnace overtook one small boat, but the man in it was so terrified that Elliot was glad to let him jump overboard and splash ashore. Two forts squatted in the mud at the entrance to the river proper. No one challenged from them, no one fired a warning shot; they seemed abandoned and in need of repair. The river too was empty. A mile or so upstream, however, Elliot observed a mandarin boat driving several junks before it. Leaving Bingham behind, he gave chase, and to his relief—he had begun to wonder whether in this waste of land and water he would ever make contact with anybody—the boat let him approach. Morrison had previously prepared, in Chinese, a request that the authorities receive Palmerston's letter and agree to negotiate at the Peiho. This request was handed to a mandarin in the boat; he indicated it would have to be forwarded to his superior a little distance inland. For two hours Elliot sat patiently while a silent, unfriendly crowd collected on the bank, and Bingham brought his own boats close up just in case. Then a mounted messenger appeared. He carried a chop from Kishen (Ch'i-shan), the governor-general of Chihli Province, acknowledging the receipt of Morrison's paper, intimating that the arrival of the English in these waters was not unexpected, and promising that the whole matter would be referred to Peking at once.

While the fleet waited in blustery rainy weather for Peking to reply, Dicey brought the *Madagascar* over the bar just to prove he could do it. He took her out again next day, however, for she drew almost twelve feet and even at flood tide went aground several times. A number of deep-sea merchant junks appeared, gorgeously painted things as high out of the water as a two-decked ship. Men standing along their sides sounded the bottom with long bamboo poles and called out the depths as they approached the bar. Coasting junks moved again too. Boats from the warships stopped several of these in search of provisions, and not all of the searchers stuck to the letter of their instructions. A seaman from the *Volage*, surprised in the act of looting by the captain of one junk, shot the captain dead upon his own deck and was promptly put in irons. On the thirteenth an officer from Kishen's yamen boarded the *Wellesley* with gifts of meat, poultry, and fresh vegetables. Over the next two days he came and went repeatedly, often by the *Madagascar*, so that the English got to know him well, and at last "Captain White" (as they called this man) announced that he was authorized to receive Palmerston's letter for transmission to Peking. But there would be a further delay of at least ten days while the letter was digested there.

A third of the men in the fleet were down with a mild form of dysentery, the result of bad water taken aboard at Chusan. Already the two plenipotentiaries had dispatched the *Blonde*, the *Modeste*, and one transport two hundred miles to the east to look for fresh water and provisions among the islands off the Liaotung Peninsula. (Right into the twentieth century, charts of these waters show a "Blonde Island" and an "Elliot Group.") Now the rest of the warships and the other transport scattered upon the same errand; even the *Wellesley* managed to obtain three dozen head of cattle in this way. By the twenty-seventh, however, they were all back at the Peiho, and when Admiral Elliot could discover no sign that the Chinese were preparing for serious negotiations—the dreary landscape was again empty of junks, mandarin boats, or activity of any sort—he got ready to nudge matters with a show of force. Guns and stores were taken out of the *Modeste* to lighten her, and she and the *Madagascar* were told to cross the bar and bombard the forts. At that moment, to the intense disappointment of Bingham and many other junior officers, "Captain White" appeared. He bore a message from Kishen. The barbarian headmen were invited to a parley on the thirtieth. For the first time in a quarter of a century, a diplomatic encounter with the West was to take place in the vicinity of Peking.

The parley was held on a piece of open ground near the south fort. The Chinese had made an enclosure out of canvas screens, with a causeway and a floating pier so that the English could approach from the river. To this enclosure came Captain Elliot (his cousin, the admiral, felt neither well enough nor sufficiently experienced to attend) accompanied by a few officers, Jocelyn among them, and some sailors and marines. Kishen was already there, a vigorous fellow Elliot thought, not much over fifty (he was in fact a good deal older), impressive in blue silk robe and white satin boots, with a ruby button on his straw summer hat and a peacock's feather drooping between his shoulders. The two retired into a marquee lined with yellow silk. Meanwhile Jocelyn and the others were put into little tents seating five persons and made to eat an interminable succession of Chinese dishes, some interesting and some not. Later they tried to reconnoiter the fort and were turned back. Later still an honor guard performed curious evolutions for them with matchlocks, swords, and bows and arrows. It was a long day; for the boats' crews, idle at their oars among the reeking mud flats, it was a very long day. Elliot and the governor-general remained closeted six hours.

What kept them so long was not the requirements of decorum, the meal of many courses that Elliot too was obliged to consume, or the having to pass everything through Morrison's mouth, with a good deal of fumbling. (Kishen apparently had an interpreter of his own, but the fellow cannot have been much use.) What took time was the attempt to reconcile two positions that were essentially irreconcilable.

Oddly, things went very easily in one respect. Elliot had expected to be treated in a high and mighty manner, even higher and more mighty than usual because of the proximity of Peking. Kishen surprised him by being, on the contrary, "perfectly unaffected and quiet."[3] Once only he made as if to assert a difference in status between himself and the chief superintendent—between the Celestial Empire and little England—and that was when he referred to England's having twice sent tribute embassies to Peking. Elliot caught the remark the moment it passed Morrison's lips and emphatically denied its truth, insisting that Macartney and Amherst had come as ambassadors and that Queen Victoria was the equal of any sovereign in the world, and Kishen "had at once the good sense to resume his far more imposing tone of sensible moderation." He surprised the chief superintendent, too, by shaking hands on parting. In matters of substance, however, the two were hardly closer at the end of six hours than they had been at the beginning.

Chusan did not detain them long. When Kishen protested that the emperor could not possibly renounce this or any other portion of the empire, Elliot replied that he probably would not have to; his government viewed the island as no more than a convenient station for the expedition presently on the coast. Once the real matters at issue had been resolved, it would find it as easy to give that island up as it had found the giving up of other places it had once possessed. The opium question was not so simply got over. Kishen came directly to the point. Was England's queen prepared to forbid the export of the drug from her dominions? Elliot declined to say, having no authority to speak upon the subject. He could not help remarking, however, that more than half the opium reaching China grew elsewhere than in Her Majesty's dominions (he meant, of course, Malwa). Her Majesty, therefore, was powerless to cut off the flow of the drug to China. Moreover European experience with ardent spirits taught that sobriety could not be compelled or virtue legislated. If the Chinese people were determined to smoke opium, no act of violence would stop them. Only the gradual influence of instruction and example would wean them from their "vicious tastes."

It was an almost Confucian argument, and Kishen, it seemed to Elliot, was "powerfully impressed." When the conversation turned to money, however, Kishen's reaction was quite otherwise. He was impressed all right, but in a different way.

For Palmerston's letter was absolutely emphatic on the point that where costs and expenses were in question, Peking must pay—pay for the confiscated opium; pay for the expedition; pay, by implication, for those injuries whose infliction upon the English in the previous year had made the expedition necessary; pay, too, for the hong debts. Even from Elliot's account, which alone we have, it is impossible to miss Kishen's mounting sense of astonishment as the calendar of required payments unrolled. That the English had been mishandled was conceivable or could be conceded for the sake of controlling barbarian feelings. That the emperor should confer a treasure in silver upon a people whose illicit trafficking in opium drained the empire of that metal was absurd! The Chinese version of Palmerston's letter lay open before the two men. At last Elliot, with Morrison's help, put his finger on the place where payment was demanded. Here, he announced, was the test. From this hung the question of peace or war. Kishen gave no sign of yielding, and Elliot turned to mark that fact in pencil on the margin of the letter.

Before he could do so, recounts Elliot, Kishen "stayed my hand," pointing out that he was only one of half a dozen men of importance whose opinion the emperor was bound to solicit, begging time for further consultation. And as the parley continued, sometimes at the level of amicable discussion, sometimes with a good deal of heat, it dawned on Elliot that for all Kishen's apparent obduracy he was edging towards an understanding. Peking, he seemed to be saying, would give ground if it had to. In that case the problem was how to arrange things so that it could give ground with dignity, in a face-saving way.

Lin Tse-hsü might provide the answer. Something clearly was happening to Lin. The determination and probity with which he had gone about extirpating the drug traffic had impressed much of the foreign community and ought to have earned him the highest honors and rewards at Peking. Yet Kishen, who was in daily contact with the capital, invoked his name only to darken it, saying of him what Elliot had said in the excitement of the opium surrender crisis a year and a half ago, confirming Elliot's bitterest predictions. "Great moral changes," Elliot had warned then, "can never be effected by the violation of all the principles of justice and moderation," and Lin, by recklessly violating them, "is hastening on in a career of violence which will react upon this empire in a terrible manner."[4] Now, listening to Morrison's running translation, Elliot almost imagined that he heard his own echo from that distant time. For Kishen was saying that Lin had indeed treated the English rudely and with excessive violence. Of course the English must not be so vain and foolish as to demand huge sums of silver by way of compensation. Still, they were entitled to know that the emperor meant to recall Lin to Peking, where he would be dealt with severely. A new high commissioner would go south—Kishen intimated that he himself was that man—and south the English must likewise go, to Canton, where trade had always been conducted and where alone matters might be put right. Meanwhile let the English do nothing rash or hasty. That was the main thing.

So Elliot returned to the *Wellesley*, persuaded (in spite of the apparent rejection of all the demands rehearsed in Palmerston's letter) that the Chinese were anxious to avoid war and would make Lin their scapegoat to avoid it. As Kishen wanted to consult his government again, the *Wellesley* sailed up to inspect the place where the Great Wall winds down to the sea. By 10 September she was off the Peiho once more. On the fourteenth out came "Captain White" with two letters. One, from the court, announced that negotiations would be arranged for Canton. The English should not, however, assume that they would obtain there the things they wanted. The other, from Kishen, implied that on the contrary they *would* be accommodated. Thus do we Chinese preserve appearances, the letters seemed to say, ruling out all shape and manner of concession even as we prepare to make a few.

Should the fleet then leave the Peiho? It did not have the capacity to strike inland at Peking. Five weeks had taught it that, lacking steamers of shallow draught, it could not blockade the river effectively. If full-scale war had to come, it must be fought in the south, and until the monsoon changed the whole length of the coast, a matter of another month at least, the fleet would have difficulty getting south to fight it. So a pause was unavoidable. Captain Elliot was confident that such a pause would operate to encourage "peaceful impulses" at the imperial court. These impulses existed, he felt sure. They were founded on the perception that a war to keep the foreigner out of China might actually bring him in—they were founded, that is to say, on an appreciation of England's power. "It may be taken for certain," he wrote the foreign secretary, "that the Court is perfectly conscious of our naval prowess. And it is notorious that it entertains the utmost dread of our enterprising spirit."[5] Peking was not in a belligerent mood. It would use a breathing spell to prepare concessions. It was obliged by the rules of the charade, however, to dress those concessions in the garments of condescending superiority and gentle reproof, and it would do this better if it had time and obscurity in which to work the details out.

Elliot might of course have drawn another and more pessimistic conclusion from these weeks of idling amid mud flats, salt water, and mist, where the land was hardly distinguishable from the sea and the imperial ministers talked out of both sides of their mouths. He chose, however, to be cheerful and to calculate advantages from moving the site of negotiation to another place. He had not wanted to come to the Peiho anyway, and his cousin, the admiral, who appears from the correspondence to have been tired, indifferent, or both, did not dispute him. So the order to sail was given. For a while the fleet lingered off the north coast of Shantung, loading flour and bullocks for the troops on Chusan. Then it rounded the tip of the peninsula and headed south with a favoring wind. The two plenipotentiaries knew that they had not accomplished what Palmerston had expected them to accomplish. They counted, however, on making up for that at Canton.

17

The Blockade and the Barrier

With the disappearance of the expedition at the end of June, a great quiet had descended upon the Gulf of Canton. It was the season when trade slackened and merchants retired to the relative comfort of Macao. Very few foreigners remained at the factories; at Whampoa there were only the *Kosciusko*, with two thousand bales of cotton to Matheson's consignment, and the *Panama*.

Parker went home. Save for one trip to Whampoa to care for a sick ship's captain, he had not left Canton in almost two years, and he was suffering from one of his periodic bouts of self-doubt. In June with the approach of the expedition, he had closed the hospital and come down to Macao. On 5 July he sailed for New York.

Bennet Forbes went with him, worn out by overwork and by the effects of a fall from a horse, and Jauncey, whose wounds were serious, went too. The entire Protestant Mission turned out to see the medical missionary off. A strange sight it must have been, this band of brothers in the gospel bonds crowding around their departing colleague, with emaciated "Black Ben" in one corner and the nearly helpless skipper of the *Hellas* in another, but if anyone felt uncomfortable at the juxtaposition of Christ, commerce, and the pernicious drug, no one left any record of it. During the voyage, which lasted five months, the three passengers got along together very well, so well, indeed, that when Parker went on to England the following spring to raise money for the Medical Missionary Society, Jauncey contributed $300 towards his passage and persuaded Jardine, Matheson and Company to give an equal sum.

The harmony was to a degree natural. Old China hands saw pretty much eye to eye on things; the differences of opinion grew sharp only with distance and unfamiliarity. Charles King was an exception, however. Time and experience had not diluted *his* purpose or softened *his* high moral tone, and things might not have been quite so pleasant on board the *Niantic* had he gone along.

In January he had published a long critique of the opium surrender crisis, a critique that, while far from taking the Chinese side of things, was decidedly hard on the English and the Americans. They had behaved badly, and the Americans had behaved particularly badly because, instead of staying their hand until the English stopped bringing opium to China (and the Chinese lowered their barriers to Christ), they had accepted the bond and gone deep into the transshipping business—had been, in a word, both cowardly and grasping. The righteous tone of the piece drove Forbes to a furious reply. Matheson too was annoyed. It happened that King had been doing agency work for him in Canton. "I begin seriously to think," he wrote Jardine, "of discarding our friend King, whose business, subsisting as it does exclusively by his extensive negotiations with us, would be extinguished were we to drop him. Let him then try how he could get on without the aid of the drug against which he is waging so unfair a crusade, making a tool of Bridgman."[1] A week or so later he *did* drop him, and King and his wife left for home by the overland route. Bridgman and Williams were sorry to see him go. Few others can have been. "He was very unpopular here," was one American's verdict.[2]

The opium traffic, chief target of King's incautious moralizing, of course survived his departure and in the summer of 1840 was carried on in much the old way. The *Mor* came in from Bombay with her first cargo of Malwa, the *Ariel* from Calcutta with Patna and Benares. New vessels made their appearance: for Dent the brigantine *Poppy*, for Jardine Matheson the clipper brig *Spy* (built at Calcutta and named for still another of Cooper's novels) and the full-rigged ship *Falcon*. Whether the fast crabs and scrambling dragons ran again as John Rees had intended is uncertain. Run or not, however, the receiving ships lay as always in the gulf, selling there for local delivery as well as to junks from some distance away.

Jardine Matheson remained the giant in the business. That autumn Matheson estimated that of 6,500 chests on the coast at the moment of writing, 3,700 lay in vessels connected with his house, 800 with Dent, 600 with the Portuguese, 300 with "Daddy" Rustomjee, 150 with Innes—and so on. Competition was keen just the same, and prices modest; you were lucky if you got $400 for Patna or Benares, $500 for Malwa. In his correspondence Matheson called them "whites," "greys," and "chintzes" still.

The very scale of Matheson's operations gave him an advantage. With so many clippers and country ships on the Calcutta and Bombay runs, he could afford to pair one or two with small vessels permanently on the coast. Thus the *Red Rover* teamed up that summer with the schooner *Jardine*. When a Hughesdon Brothers' brig invaded the *Ann*'s station, Matheson instructed Denham, her master, to make an offer for her entire cargo—something he had the resources for, and most of his rivals did not. His vessels were everywhere. They even accompanied the expedition to Chusan.

The first news from that place, brought down by the *Enterprize* steamer at the end of July, was not encouraging to opium men. "We look with some uneasiness to Admiral Elliot's prohibition of the drug trade at Chusan," wrote Matheson, "as indicating the same sort of disaffection which gave us so much alarm and trouble on the part of Captain Elliot. But as they have," he continued, "no mode of raising money for the expenses of the war unless from the drug sales in China, we think they cannot avoid giving it some toleration."[3] By this Matheson meant that, once the barrels of silver aboard the *Marion* were exhausted, the expedition would find that it could not raise what it needed for day-to-day operation except by selling bills. It would find, too, that no one had ready money with which to buy its bills (in more homely terms, cash its checks) except the opium men—always providing, of course, that the opium men still sold chests. Perhaps Admiral Elliot understood this already. Opium vessels approaching Chusan found that they could not do business in the immediate vicinity of the fleet, but they easily overcame that difficulty by moving a little distance away. "We should think it your best plan," Matheson wrote the *Spy*, "to be always cruizing about [between Chusan and the mainland] so as to fall in with the Chinese trading junks going backwards and forwards. And if you do not fall in with them at once, continue moving about till you discover their track."[4] Matheson did not expect men-of-war to interfere, and none did—indeed, Lieutenant Bingham of the *Modeste* remembers that Chinese smuggling craft sometimes themselves approached a man-of-war. "On one occasion the *Cruizer* had a bag of dollars thrown on board her at night, a boat coming with an opium order next day; and Fokie could hardly be convinced that he had mistaken the vessel."[5] In the Gulf of Canton, meanwhile, the European opium vessels and the warships of Captain Smith's squadron became so neighborly that when the *Colonel Young* went aground near the Typa in a fierce September storm, Smith undertook to protect her from the water people until Innes could get her chests out.

So the war and the traffic moved comfortably forward side by side.

About neither was Bridgman easy in his mind. The arrival of the expedition had invigorated him; the death and destruction inflicted upon the Chinese at the foot of Joss-House Hill did not. He read through the Parliamentary debates of April and found in them no trace of Christian spirit, "not a sentence . . . worthy of the occasion." It was untrue that Peking only pretended to be hostile to the drug. "The opposition of this government to the opium trade has been long, steady, and strong—the prohibitions have been as clear and as explicit, and the measures to carry them into effect as constant and as vigorous, as the combined wisdom and power of the emperor and his ministers could make them, during a period of forty years."[6] It occurred to him to publish (in translation) an edict of Lin's reminding the Cantonese that they had very little time left in which to give up the drug. "While the period is not yet closed, you are living victims. When it shall have expired, then you will be dead victims."[7] Dead by strangling! Bridgman did not doubt that Lin meant what he said.

Others too took opium seriously and contributed to the *Repository* on the subject, Hobson a long piece on the evils of smoking, Abeel a short one. And the three London Missionary Sociey men—Hobson, Lockhart, and Milne—encountered the problem at short range. It happened that Medhurst, the man who had coasted Shantung with Stevens in 1835, went to England shortly after that trip taking with him a Chinese named Choo-tih-long, whom he baptized there. In the spring of 1840 Choo appeared at Macao, announced he wished to become an evangelist, and was engaged by the three Englishmen as an assistant. There was something odd, however, about the fellow. For one thing he was quite unnecessarily proud, the consequence (it was thought) of having been raised so much above his station during his two years in England. Then on a Sunday in June, Milne smelled opium in his room. Choo was all denial. A few weeks passed, and Milne smelled the smell again. This time he searched and unearthed the "black horn boxes a little larger than a thimble"[8] in which the experienced smoker keeps his *chandu*. They belong to a friend, explained Choo. With growing uneasiness Milne, Hobson, and Lockhart questioned the fellow, questioned him again, until in the end he admitted that the horn boxes were his and that he smoked. They tried to make him see the error of his ways. It was in vain. Christians in England, he reminded them, indulged in far worse habits, "smoky tobacco, drinky rum, brandy, wine." They laid down a simple probationary routine. He would not follow it, would not remain in the house, came late to prayers or did not come at all, and early in August was discovered in bed with the implements for smoking all about him. So at last they sent him packing. It had been, just the same, an unnerving experience.

How did men like Choo obtain their opium? The thing could not be blamed entirely upon conniving mandarins. "The opium smugglers," Williams wrote home a little later, "have been furnishing arms and ammunition to the opium purchasers, that they may resist their own officers and introduce the drug. Government boats have been shot at and sunk by these ruthless Christians—oh that that reverend name should be thus desecrated!" Indeed, Williams was forced to admit that "all the knowledge, strength of mind, wit, invention, and moral power that education in Christian lands gives a man only makes him tenfold more the child of hell and servant of the devil than is a thoro'bred heathen."[9] It was a profoundly discouraging thought.

Nevertheless, Williams and the other Protestant missionaries did not turn their backs on the English and Parsee merchants. That summer Bridgman went out of his way to deny that the opium traffic was simply and directly the merchants' doing and desire. "We doubt not that nine-tenths if not every one of them would abandon it at once and for ever, provided it were disowned and disapproved of by their government, and a well-regulated and honorable commerce in all other articles opened and ratified with the Chinese."[10] Now this was perhaps going it a bit far. Innes was hardly a promising candidate for the no-opium pledge, and there were numbers like him. But China opened was what Bridgman most desired. It is not surprising that he imputed the same ambition to the merchants.

Besides, as long as China was *not* opened, all the old exasperations and annoyances were bound to crowd forward again and take a missionary's mind off those children of hell and servants of the devil whom he met riding at the Barrier or strolling along the Praia Grande. It happened that about this time Williams found particular pleasure in Abeel's company. "We often walk together and discourse sweet communion," he wrote his brother. Occasionally, however, the two would stop to talk to some Chinese, hoping to instruct and enlighten the unfortunates a little, only to discover that they were simply not being listened to. Worldly things alone interested the Chinese; it was altogether usual for them, after hearing about Jesus and being exhorted to forsake opium and other sins, "to ask the price of your jacket and discuss the size of your nose."[11] They exhibited, in short, a most dreadful shallowness of character.

"I think that in all things the Chinese are decidedly inferior to the Europeans," wrote Jean-Henri Baldus, the French Lazarist, at approximately the same time. It was not their relative standing in the martial or mechanical arts that prompted the comment, it was exactly the sort of thing that bothered Williams: the absence of true feeling, the laziness, the venality, the public display of sin. (In Honan, where Baldus labored, there was a perfect craze for cockfighting, and prostitutes accosted him at every turn.) How colossally smug, too, they were. They assumed as a matter of course that the crowned heads of Europe, the kings of France and England even, were tributary to their emperor. "Just the same they have acquired a considerable respect for English guns since encountering a few."

It was impossible, of course, that this new-found respect should extend to English missionaries and their American brethren. With scorn Baldus noticed that there were none of *these* gentlemen about him in Honan. "They have made their appearance on the coast only, like commercial travellers armed with a prospectus; they have done no more than toss Bibles from shipside upon the beach."[12] But there was this to be said for Englishmen in general: they were even now trying to pierce the wall of China's exclusiveness. If their efforts succeeded, the true faith would at last be able to speak freely and openly to China's millions. And though that work, Baldus noted with sadness, was done at the sword's point, one might remember what the blessed St. Thomas once had said. It is wrong to compel by force the conversion of the heathen, but it is not wrong to make him listen.

Perhaps the war was a blessing in disguise. Peter Parker certainly thought so. In a letter written ten days before he sailed, he announced himself "constrained to look upon the present not so much as an opium affair, or an English concern, as a great design of Providence to make the wickedness of man subserve his purpose of mercy towards China."[13] For the Dents and the Mathesons, the warships and the regiments, the Chinese ought almost, then, to feel grateful.

The thirty-nine-article statute of the previous year was still operative, the campaign to suppress opium still on. Neighbor spied upon neighbor, houses were entered and searched, quantities of the drug were seized and destroyed, and addicts crowded the Canton jails and the sanitarium outside the wall. What Lin had done was to shift from an attack on the smugglers and brokers to one that reached the smokers too. His failure to drive away the receiving ships and to compel the clippers to return to India with cargoes intact had taught him not that his work was useless but that it must be ever harder pressed. Just the same it troubled him that the English lingered in the outer waters. His disquiet grew intense when he discovered what they were doing with their blockade.

A blockade, Whitehall had long ago decided, was to be applied not to the full length of the China coast (as Jardine had suggested) but only at selected points: the Gulf of Canton, Amoy, the Chusan-Ningpo area, and the mouths of the Yangtze and Yellow rivers—this was what Palmerston's February instructions had laid down. Then in April there had issued an order in council for the general seizure of Chinese ships and cargoes, an order, by the way, that was as close to a formal declaration of war as Whitehall was to come, it being difficult to withdraw an ambassador from a court you have never been allowed to accredit one to. The idea, of course, was to hurt the Chinese in the pocketbook and make them more willing to come to terms. Besides, seized ships and cargoes could be sold to cover a part of England's expenses. Only warships, however, were to do the work. Letters of marque were not to be issued, and the Jaunceys and Inneses not encouraged to go privateering.

So a selective blockade coupled with the taking of ships and cargoes everywhere was what the expedition was expected to undertake. The closer you got to China, however, the less the thing made sense. It did not matter so much that the Yellow River, being quite unnavigable in its lower reaches, was useless for commerce and not worth closing.* It mattered a good deal that a blockade at Canton, if prolonged into the winter, would choke off an entire season's export of tea as well as put an end to the movement of silks, cotton, and other legitimate articles. As for seizing merchant junks, they sailed in hundreds to the Straits of Malacca; were Her Majesty's ships to fall upon and seize them there? Was the coastal junk trade to be indiscriminately plundered? Perhaps Palmerston thought in terms of a war with the French or the Dutch. If he did, he had picked the wrong model. Unlike Paris or The Hague, Peking would not much mind an interruption of exports and a spoliation of shipping. The Chinese of the maritime provinces would mind both terribly, however. If one object of the English expedition was to obtain freer commercial access to these people, antagonizing them with blockades and ship seizures was an odd way to go about it.

Admiral Elliot did not at first grasp this. Entering Singapore on 17 June aboard the *Melville* with Whitehall's instructions fresh in hand, he noticed a junk sailing blithely out, sent the *Blonde* to catch her, and put marines aboard three others in the harbor. Then the governor protested that activity of this sort would ruin Singapore's commercial reputation, and Elliot let them go. Arriving two weeks later off Macao, he discovered that to find prize crews for all the junks that came and went in the gulf was quite out of the question; there were too many of them. Elsewhere on the coast, he was told, it would be the same. And as he sailed north, talking to his cousin, Captain Elliot, and to other officers with local experience, all thought of systematically sweeping up the Chinese coast and deep-sea traffic went out of his head. Later some of the opium men complained that this was unfair. Since London would not compensate them promptly for their confiscated chests, let the expedition pay them out of prize money. The plenipotentiaries paid no attention, much to Auckland's relief when he heard about it—and Matheson's too. Matheson knew that the taking of a single junk "with funds for the drug for instance, would go far irretriev-

*The Yellow River was loaded with silt and carried a widely varying volume of water. Where it emptied—in those days to the south of the Shantung peninsula—the coast was absolutely flat and featureless. There were no ports of any consequence, great shoals extended some distance out, and foreigners had never charted the waters and rarely ventured close.

ably to destroy the confidence of the Chinese" and make doing business in opium or anything else very difficult.[14] He was glad, therefore, that the April order in council became so quickly a dead letter.

The blockade was another matter, however, and as seizing vessels is a common way of stopping up a place, some merchant junks became prizes without benefit of the order. Before ever the main fleet had left Chusan for the Peiho, Bremer (who remained behind) had sent the *Cruizer* and two steamers to shut Chinhai. There they intercepted junks and brought them over to Tinghai, until the Chinese themselves closed the river and no more junks came out. A little later the *Alligator* appeared off Amoy, battered sixteen foolhardy war junks into the rocks and shallow water, and lay for a week picking up anything that sailed. Bremer would have put ships at the mouth of the Yangtze too had not the two seventy-fours been tied up, one with a hole in her bottom, the other serving as careening hulk. It was at Canton, however, that the blockade and the seizures that went with it were most keenly felt.

The blockade began at the very end of June. It was applied by the ships of Captain Smith's squadron: the 44-gun *Druid* (which Smith himself now commanded) and four lesser vessels, among them the *Hyacinth* and *Larne*. Turn and turn about they lay off the Bogue in pairs, making sure that no western vessel (English or otherwise) did a *Thomas Coutts* on them, stopping any junk that tried to pass. If the junk was small they let it go, knowing perfectly well that it would immediately enter or leave the river (as the case might be) by one of those channels to the west that made up the inner passage. If it was large, a salt junk perhaps—their draught, it was said, compelled them to use the Bogue—it received a prize crew and went off to Capsingmun. As early as 10 July the warship that guarded that anchorage had seven or eight of these handsome vessels lying under its guns. The masters of two more had run them ashore to avoid a similar fate.

Now, bumptious and thieving as the *fan kuei* notoriously were, they had never systematically preyed upon shipping. It was the Chinese who habitually stopped the trade when the barbarians needed disciplining, not the other way around! The blockade and the detaining of salt junks made the authorities very angry. In June there had been rumors that Englishmen were to have prices put upon their heads. Now suddenly it was a fact. An edict appeared offering amounts that descended as the rank descended: $5,000 for a man-of-war's captain; $100 for a plain soldier, sailor, or merchant taken alive; $20 for his head. A seventy-four burned to the waterline commanded $10,000. Even the little *Louisa*, which Johnston used in Elliot's absence, was worth $100. At the same time forts were alerted and reinforced, channels blocked and barricaded, and the Tanka people encouraged to build fireboats and use them. No sooner had these bounties been announced, however, than most of the English men and ships disappeared to the east. They could no longer be reached. In their absence the foreigners at Macao became the target.

On 11 July, Williams, Hobson, and a merchant captain named Strachan, out walking for pleasure on the Lappa, were approached by several men who (as Diver recounts it) "from sheer malevolence, and doubtless encouraged by Commissioner Lin's late edict, struck Williams a violent blow on the leg, and severely injured Dr. Hobson's arm with a huge stick."[15] A few days later an American riding near the Barrier was dragged from his horse and beaten. Two English naval officers were attacked at knife point, and there were several other incidents, but the Chinese did not actually capture anyone—until early in August they took Stanton.

Stanton, Abeel, and some others had arranged to go swimming early one Thursday morning at Casilha's Bay, where the Dutch had been stopped and driven off two centuries before. It was a lonely place quite close to the village of Wanghia; between that village and the Barrier small bodies of Chinese soldiers were camped. Abeel and the others were late. When they reached the beach, they saw nobody; Stanton, they decided, was not coming; they had their swim and returned to town. Towards noon, however, Mary Gutzlaff grew anxious and went to Abeel. (Mary was back from Manila with her young cousins, the Parkes girls; Stanton occupied a room in her house.) Abeel raised the alarm, the beach was searched, and fishermen were induced to drag the bay. No sign of Stanton. Friday passed. On Saturday the rumor spread that he had been seen at the Bogue, his clothes torn and his head bloody. By Sunday afternoon it was known for certain that he was a prisoner. He had indeed gone swimming and been jumped, bound, and carried off to Canton.

The news put his countrymen into an uproar. If such a thing as this went unpunished, Macao would quickly become unsafe for them all. Captain Smith hurried over from Capsingmun, where merchantmen and warships alike lay that season, and went straight to Pinto. The governor was sympathetic; perhaps he did something too, for on Tuesday the local *taotai* left Macao for the north, presumably to consult his superiors. When the *taotai* returned, however, it was noticed that there were more soldiers at the Barrier than there had been before. Additional men were rumored to be at Chinshan (Ch'ien-shan-chai) three miles to the northwest, where the Macao subprefect had his yamen. Eight war junks lay in the inner harbor. It looked as if the Chinese, having dealt successfully with a single Englishman, meant now to move against them all.

This was in fact Lin's intention. He could not reach the English at the outer anchorages; he would make one last attempt to deny them Macao. Stanton, of course, was a nobody. That was clear from his interrogation, a part of which Lin had conducted himself. But the English were attempting to obtain his release through Governor Pinto—as if Macao were Portuguese soil, not a piece of China on which the Portuguese were graciously permitted to perch. To let one foreigner go at the bidding of another was, in any case, to show weakness and would simply make the *fan kuei* bolder. So Lin must act at once. Fortunately his land forces were in excellent shape, their numbers swelled by hundreds of recently engaged mercenaries. (From Canton someone sent Bridgman a description of these fellows lifting sixty-pound stones on the ends of seven-foot shafts to demonstrate their fitness.) On the Monday of the *taotai's* return to Macao, Lin was part way down the river inspecting these forces. In a few more days he would be ready for a decisive blow.

The *fan kuei* struck first. Already the *Hyacinth*, *Larne*, and *Enterprize* steamer lay in Macao Roads. On Tuesday, 18 August, the *Druid* and one transport came over from Capsingmun. The transport carried Bengal volunteers (two companies of these, much delayed by the gales in the Bay of Bengal, had reached the gulf so late they had remained there). That afternoon old Thomas Beale led Smith to a house in the northwest corner of the town, introduced him to Gideon Nye its occupant, took him up on the roof, and let him study the Barrier and its southern approaches. Wednesday morning Smith put 180 sepoys and an equal number of marines and armed seamen aboard the *Enterprize* and two longboats, appointed the corvettes and the *Louisa* as escorts, and towards noon set the little flotilla in motion up the east side of the peninsula. Several hundred people kept level with it on foot, going out through the St. Lazarus gate, crossing the Campo, and coming finally to a low hill west of Casilha's Bay. There they stopped. Below, on the narrow sandy waste where horse races were sometimes run, rose the New Temple. Beyond it lay the brick and granite Barrier wall with its scattering of guardhouses and its single great gate. During the night the eight war junks in the inner harbor had been hauled up close to the west end of the Barrier. They lay there now, motionless, indeed for the time being immovable as the tide was out. Soldiers were visible about the sand battery on the far side of the Barrier; more mustered from the New Temple, from troop boats, and from the village of Wanghia around to the left.

From their vantage point above this scene, the mixed crowd of spectators watched the English ships round the tip of land above Casilha's Bay, the steamer towing the two longboats; watched them approach and take up line against the Barrier's eastern end; watched as the thirty-two pounders of the corvettes began to fire. The Chinese fired back. But their battery had been built to command the wall and gate, not the water; its guns had to be dragged on clumsy wheelless carriages out from the shelter of the banks of sand before they could be brought to bear, and then were scarcely capable of hurting anything at the range of one-third of a mile that Smith chose to maintain. So when the six-inch iron balls of the English came bounding in, the Chinese gun crews lost heart and went looking for shelter. An hour or more of leisurely pounding, and Smith sent in several boatloads of armed seamen. The battery was occupied, the guns spiked; a light artillery piece the *Druid* carried was hoisted ashore and turned upon the Barrier itself. Then the marines and the sepoys landed and rushed the wall and gate. The war junks were afloat now and firing, and a single gun planted near the New Temple fired bravely too, until the English silenced both with musket fire. The soldiers melted away in the direction of Wanghia. The junks, relatively undamaged because a low ridge down the spine of the isthmus had caught most of the English shot, upped anchor and withdrew towards Chinshan. Many of the native spectators made off too, probably convinced that the English were about to press south and take the town. The English came no further, however, they did not even prepare to hold the Barrier; they fired tents, stores, magazines, everything that would burn, picked up such of their cannonballs as were readily recoverable (Bridgman estimated they had fired no less than six hundred), and by seven in the evening had reembarked and were on their way back to Macao Roads.

Their casualties were exactly four wounded. The Chinese alleged losses as small, at the same time claiming that the English had been driven off with many dead and much damage to ships, but their actions belied their words. Abeel had watched the battle with Bridgman and Williams. "When I went out," he remarked later of his walk to the observation hill, "my ears were offended by the usual appellation 'foreign demon.' When I returned I did not hear, and since that I have not heard, the epithet once." The day after the battle the three missionaries sallied forth again, past the hill, the temple, and up the narrow isthmus. "Never had the Chinese appeared so civil, indeed so deferential." Right through the Barrier gate they went and out upon the ground beyond, "ground seldom trodden by European or American feet," climbed over the deserted sand battery, counted the spiked guns (they numbered twenty-seven), and noticed that the Chinese who were out sightseeing too seemed almost glad to find their soldiers gone. "To understand this feeling," explained Williams later to his brother, "it should be mentioned that a body of soldiers is one of the greatest annoyances to a Chinese village that can infest it. Many of the soldiers fled into town, only to leave it again this morning for the country, and today there is not a soldier in the place." Eventually a few came back, removed the guns, unspiked them, and set them in a small redoubt three-quarters of a mile to the north where the isthmus joined the main island. But from that day forward, wrote Bridgman at the end of September, "not a Chinese soldier, except in disguise, has been in Macao, nor have any of the war junks or troop-boats returned to their former anchorages in the inner harbor."[16]

On the last day of August the *Druid*, *Larne*, and *Columbine* engaged a large force of armed junks that made as if to molest the shipping at Capsingmun. The wind being light, the junks got away over the Fansiak flats—plainly the gulf was not yet secure for westerners. As for Stanton, he remained in his Canton prison. The town, however, was safe (Matheson and his friends took to riding beyond the Barrier even), and so it remained throughout the war. Though Captain Smith cannot have foreseen it, his sudden successful attack had the consequence that more than a century would pass before the Chinese again threatened Macao.

18

Chusan

On 12 September, Torrette died suddenly at Macao at the age of thirty-eight. He lacked a month of completing eleven years' service with the *procure*, eleven years during which the strength of the French Lazarist mission in China had risen from two to more than a dozen.[1] The increase was a tribute to Torrette's energy and skill as procurator. It was a tribute, also, to Catholic Europe's rediscovered enthusiasm for Christ in China. And by an odd coincidence, at almost the very moment Torrette died, something happened deep inside China that was practically certain to give that enthusiasm fresh impetus and a cutting edge—though the thing itself was grim enough. On 11 September they killed Perboyre.

It was Rameaux who informed the *procure*, in a letter whose opening contrived to strip the fact of the darkness and despond that generally surround an undeserved and brutal death. "I bring you glad tidings," it began. "After enduring pains and tortures of a sort quite unheard of in China before, pains and tortures born unflinchingly for the pure faith, our dear Jean-Gabriel has at last received the martyr's palm."[2] The execution took place, it seems, outside Wuchang. Maresca, Rizzolati's assistant (and a newcomer to the Italian branch of the China Mission), gave Rameaux the details, though neither he nor any other European was actually present.

Several common criminals accompanied Perboyre to the place of execution. These the executioners beheaded; next they advanced upon Perboyre, who had only a moment to kneel and pray before he was seized, tied to a sort of cross, and strangled just as the opium broker had been strangled at the St. Antonio Gate three and a half years before—"a death different from the others," explained Maresca, "and more honorable, but more painful too as it takes longer (I do not know how long)."[3] Then a strange thing was observed. It happened that Maresca was in Hankow, opposite Wuchang, when two Chinese Christians brought him the news. He at once sent his own people to discover what they could. When they had crossed the river and reached the place of execution, they found the common criminals gone. Perboyre's body, however, was still upon its cross. Now a man strangled (wrote Maresca) is usually horrible to look upon. The face is discolored, the eyes and tongue stick out, agony is written all over the contorted features—but this was not the case with Perboyre. He seemed alive, though sleeping. "His eyes were cast down, his mouth closed in a natural manner; in his expression there was not a trace of suffering," and Maresca was told that, seeing this, "the Heathen wondered a great deal." Except for a cloth about his loins, the dead man's clothes were gone. Maresca's people managed to obtain the cloth, some strands of hair, and the cord by which he had been strangled. For a price they were able to substitute a hand barrow filled with earth for the one in which Perboyre was to be transported to the criminals' burial ground. In this way his body received decent interment "in a consecrated place with other faithful."

The cloth, the hair, the cord, and some clothes with the dried blood of previous tortures upon them passed through Maresca to Rameaux, who in his letter promised to forward them to the *procure*. Eventually they must be sent to the Lazarist mother house in Paris. There they would rival the relics of the martyred Clet and by their presence give silent proof that Our Lord's purpose had been well served by the triumphant submission of this His servant. But the joyful news of Perboyre's death did not allow Rameaux to forget the possible imminence of his own. "They are after me again, not just in Hupeh but in Kiangsi and other provinces." It surprised Rameaux that some officious Christian had not already betrayed his hiding place. The vicariat, he was sure, was in for a general persecution, though fortunately his flock was "too dispersed and above all too poor to much excite the cupidity of the mandarins. You will understand, nevertheless," he added (in the letter Torrette did not live to read), "that this war with the English makes us all fearful."

The letter did not reach Macao until long after Christmas. Hundreds of miles to the east, meanwhile, Englishmen were dying as miserably as Perboyre had died and for a good deal less reason.

Burrell's failure to recover the kidnapped comprador together with other incidents suggestive of the long arm of the Ningpo mandarins had led at the end of July to a further chilling of the atmosphere on Chusan. Foraging parties discovered they could no longer buy fresh food. The peasants hid their eggs and drove away their cattle, while in Tinghai vegetables and poultry quite disappeared from the markets. Then many of the soldiers took to seizing what they could—old men fishing the canal had their catch snatched from them, if a cock crowed it seldom crowed again. But of course this only made things worse.

A second exodus emptied the town. Shops shut, entire streets of houses stood deserted; coming ashore from his ship, the *Scotland*, Robert Strachan (the same who had been attacked on the Lappa while walking with Hobson and Williams) at first saw no one at all. Later "I found on the door of a house 'Jardine Matheson and Co.' written in chalk letters, and discovered these premises had been taken possession of by Mr. A. Jardine."[4] Strachan was told that if he wanted a house too—Gemmell and Company wished him to stay a while to see whether cloth could be sold and teas bought on the island—he must apply to Captain Caine.

"Called at the *Mor* and saw Andrew Jardine," his journal continues. "Her captain and Jardine had to give the Commodore their written promise they would not dispose of the drug in the anchorage, ere the vessel was permitted to come in. She has now some one hundred chests on board. I understand she will sail in ten or twelve days, proceeding along the coast collecting silver, and will then go to Macao. I have been asked for opium in the streets of Tinghai," but none was in fact being sold there because Bremer forbad it. Down at the harbor Strachan talked to officers from the *Melville*. Using the great capstans of the *Blenheim* she had been careened on the third try and the hurt inflicted by the pinnacle rock laid bare. It was severe. For a distance of twenty-eight feet forward of her sternpost, itself badly damaged along with her rudder, the great timbers of her three false keels had been torn away and hung only from the main. To repair this sufficiently so that she could be sailed would require weeks; to repair it fully could not be done this side of Bombay.

On the summit of Joss-House Hill the Irish of the 18th assisted by Madras sappers and miners labored to build a fort. To make the approaches steep it was necessary at several places to dig away the sides of the hill. Presently it was discovered that the earth being moved was not part of the hill at all but a great accumulation of coffins. For a while the men tipped the coffins over the side of the hill. Later the smell became a nuisance, and efforts were made to burn the bodies on pyres improvised from coffin scraps. The work dragged, it was muggy and very hot—Chusan lies on a level with New Orleans—and there were frequent interruptions for duty parades and guard, which meant putting on a tightly fitted coatee and stiff leather stock, two broad belts worn X-fashion across the chest and held in place by a third around the waist (bayonet and cartridge box were suspended from these), and an enormous shako weighing two or three pounds that fell off if you ran. Had native labor been available, things might have been easier. Hardly a prospective coolie was to be seen, however, let alone hired or pressed. The regiments still had more than five hundred camp followers among them, but five hundred was not very many—in India a single European regiment was entitled to fully half that number: to eighteen *bhistis* (for example), twenty-seven washermen, and more than a hundred hospital attendants. The fact was that the regiments on China service had not been able to re-cruit to full authorized strength. All accounts agree that as a consequence the men were overburdened with housekeeping duties.

The 18th was quartered in the village at the foot of Joss-House Hill. It was battered and burned, and filthy with decaying fish and spilled *samshu*, but it gave better shelter than canvas could provide; the commissariat was here, and the transports close by. The 49th stayed aboard ship. Later it was put into tents on a piece of high ground to the west of the harbor. The artillery, the sappers and miners, and the Bengal volunteers camped on the flat rice fields between Joss-House Hill and Tinghai. The 26th (Cameronians) went right into the town, to a bare hill in the north-west corner that seemed in several ways the most favorable location of all. But the men were put to a great deal of work scarping steps, cutting pathways, and leveling ground for tents, and had moreover to fetch their daily rations under the hot sun over a distance of a mile and a half, so that they felt the want of coolies even more than the rest.

The rations they fetched were a disaster. Quantities of rice were to be had from Tinghai's captured granaries, but only the Madras sappers and miners and the Madras gun lascars would touch it. The European troops ate bread—after months aboard ship the flour was sour, the bis-cuits moldy and full of worms. None of the cattle shipped live in the spring had survived as far as Chusan. Salt beef and pork ought to have taken their place. It was discovered, however, that most of the butts were spoiled; many, it was now remembered, had smelled offensively while being loaded at Calcutta. In the harbor lay several merchantmen, one of them Jardine Matheson's *Syden* (the former *General Wood*), quite filled with provisions of a better sort: Irish porter, Hamburg beef, biscuit, beer, wine, tongues, and other delicacies. But though the officers (who messed comfortably on board the *Marion* and other transports) were glad to purchase in this quarter, Burrell's commissariat would not. It went right on issuing salt meat that was green in color and stank, and the men, finding they could not barter the putrid stuff for poultry or eggs, went right on throwing it away. In the end several hundred butts had to be car-ried back unopened to Singapore, to be disposed of there as manure.

The men were no better handled in other respects. Oglander, the one-armed veteran of the Peninsula Campaign who had thrown up his sick leave and his local rank of major-general to accompany his beloved Cameronians to China, had of course died at sea. On the hill where the 26th was camped they buried him, "with great decorum and propriety" observed Mountain,[5] these being the chief qualities to be expected of the run of regimental officer. Many were quite elderly, a captain in his fifties seeming nothing unusual. Few had seen active service. At best they knew how to take care of themselves. They ate well, drank too much (though not of the cheap and debilitating liquors the men got hold of), and followed Oglander to the grave rather more slowly than did the rank and file. Their commander now was Burrell. "He is old," wrote Thom, "and seems to me to be what we call in vulgar Scotch a haverel"—meaning a garrulous half-wit.

Burrell's incompetence had swift consequences. Many of the men were camped on ground little better than a swamp. In the rice fields they drank water so muddy a bucket of it deposited two inches of sediment in as many minutes. As for the *bhistis* of the 26th (there were only seven of them), they filled their skin bags from the canal just outside the town wall—and the canal was connected to the sewers. "Even the natives hold their noses. . . . Unless we can manage to get the canal and town cleared out, I fear that we shall be getting some contagious distemper among us. The climate moreover is moist and mosquitos swarm in amazing numbers. Let no man come here without mosquito curtains, else he will bitterly repent of it."[6]

No one yet recognized the connection between mosquitos and the intermittent fever from which so many now began to suffer, a fever that was thought to be the work of vegetable matter decaying in water under circumstances of prolonged heat. Decomposition produced a noxious vapor, a miasma or "mal'aria" such as settled each summer upon Rome and killed unwary visitors there. To avoid it you shunned low wet ground, especially at night (when the effluvium was particularly dangerous), and prayed for cooler weather. Sometimes, however, the stuff rose and settled even on the higher ground. The 26th, it was observed, did not escape it.

Dysentery was better known and more seriously regarded. It had killed Oglander, and as the summer of 1840 advanced, the Cameronians went sick with it by scores. There were no deaths in July. In August, however, a dozen rank and file died. September was not far along before it became clear the toll that month must double. The 18th, the 49th, and the Bengal volunteers contributed their share. For every death ten men went to hospital or were confined to quarters. By the middle of the month Burrell was told that a third of his force was quite unfit for duty, and at this point an alarm sounded of a far more dramatic sort. Captain Anstruther was missing and presumed taken.

The disappearance in July of Pu Ting-pang, the comprador, had not put an end to expeditions into the countryside. Foraging parties moved as before, though larger and more generously armed, and restlessness brought out a number of the more energetic officers. One of these was Anstruther of the Madras artillery, a big man in his early thirties with an unusually ugly face and a beard of "rufus red." Anstruther made it his habit to explore in the hills beyond Tinghai, alone except for an elderly gun lascar, sketching for pleasure and making preliminary observations for a map survey. On the morning of 16 September he and the lascar left the gun park as usual, passed through Tinghai's north gate, followed a paved footway for about three-quarters of a mile, and turned left up a hill. At the top of the hill they took a number of sightings. Then they started down the other side, meaning to return home by a pretty valley that led around to the harbor. Part way along this valley, however, Anstruther began to feel uneasy. He was used to the Chusan peasants, in fact sometimes amused himself by sketching them and by carrying on a kind of conversation with them in sign language of his own devising, but the ones who were collecting now did not seem at all friendly. By a grove of trees through which the pathway ran they thickened to a crowd, so Anstruther turned left up the hill, hoping to regain Tinghai. One of the crowd, however, made a rush at the lascar, and Anstruther had to go back to help. It was obviously too late now to escape over the hill, the only hope was to follow the valley to its end; Anstruther and the lascar pushed on, their only weapon the iron spade the lascar carried for driving sighting stakes.

"I am," he wrote,[7] "but a bad runner, and my poor old servant was worse, so I went slowly along the valley, turning round now and then to keep the Chinese at bay. Meantime the whole population of the valley gathered with loud shouts in our front, and it was evidently a hopeless job. I could not get my old man to leave me and try to escape unnoticed, so we went on together, and at a turn in the path, which had now crossed to the southern side of the valley (which lies east and west), I was opposed by a few scoundrels with sticks and stones. I charged them, and they got all round me, and then my poor old man ran back about eighty yards, where he was met by the crowd following us, and struck down. I have an inexpressible reluctance to write what follows—but must. I attempted to force my way towards him, but could not, and I saw the inhuman villains pounding his head with large stones as he lay with his face downwards. I cannot doubt that he died."

A moment later they overpowered Anstruther too, but instead of dashing his brains out tied him hand and foot, stuffed a gag into his mouth, and gave his knees a couple of smart blows with a bamboo. Then they put him into a sort of sedan chair "which was evidently kept ready for some such purpose" and hurried him by a roundabout route to the southwest corner of the island. "Here we waited till nightfall, my conductors comforting me by repeating the word Ningpo and drawing their hands across their throats." At Ningpo late the following afternoon Anstruther was brought before a magistrate and questioned. (The interpreter at this interrogation was Pu, the kidnapped comprador, though Anstruther did not realize it at the time.) Later he was taken to a prison and put into a wooden cage. Irons were placed upon his ankles, an iron ring about his neck, and his handcuffed wrists were locked to the ring by a short length of stick. In this condition he remained throughout the night and for the better part of each day, his knees drawn up to his chin. Five or six days later they brought into the prison a number of like cages containing survivors of the armed brig *Kite*.

The *Kite* had brought stores from Madras to Tinghai and had then been hired to help the frigate *Conway* and two lesser vessels survey the lower reaches of the Yangtze, for the Elliots wished to complete what Jauncey and the *Hellas* had set out to do in May. For this purpose she received six carronades, a number of marines and seamen from the *Melville*, and a Royal Navy lieutenant named Douglas. Returning from the Yangtze in mid-September—her ten-foot draught unsuited her for river work, and she was rife with dysentery—she struck a submerged sandbank beyond sight of the coast, swung broadside to the rush of tide, went over with a crash that killed her master Noble and his baby son, and slowly righting settled into the sand. A dozen seamen and marines, some desperately ill, escaped drowning by climbing into the tops. Lieutenant Douglas, the chief mate Witt, two lascar cabin boys, and Noble's young wife Ann got away in a jolly boat, and after drifting helplessly for two days (the tidal currents made oars useless) reached the Chekiang shore. There they were immediately apprehended, put in neck chains, and hurried on foot towards Ningpo.

Their progress was distinctly unpleasant. It rained incessantly, their captors led them through towns and villages clamorous with hostile curiosity, and at one place someone ripped the wedding ring from Ann Noble's finger. Later they were put in cages. "Mine," explained Mrs. Noble, "was scarcely a yard high, a little more than three quarters of a yard long, and a little more than half a yard broad. The door opened from the top. Into these we were lifted, the chain around our necks being locked to the cover. They put a long piece of bamboo through the middle, a man took either end, and in this manner we were jolted from city to city to suffer the insults of the rabble, the cries from whom were awful."[8] Later still the cages were loaded onto canal boats, and in this way they reached Ningpo. There Mrs. Noble was lodged next to Anstruther. Her cell was small and dirty, grating made up two sides of it so that she had very little privacy, and she continued, she claims, to sleep in her cage. Douglas and Witt were close by. In the next court were the brig's other survivors.

Boatmen had lifted them from the wreck; soldiers had brought them to Ningpo, in cages, exposed like Mrs. Noble to the jeers, spittle, and hair-pulling of the crowd. Those who tried to resist had been beaten so badly that two marines were dead of it. Their corporal, already far gone with dysentery, seemed certain to follow—when Anstruther first saw the poor fellow he was lying unconscious on his back, his feet on the edge of the opened lid of his cage, smelling dreadfully. That night he died. In the course of the next few weeks two more marines and a seaman died too.

There were, however, no more acts of positive ill-treatment. All that the little group had to endure was prison life. It bore hardest on the lascars—they included several caught on Chusan—for though taken out of their cages like the others, the manacles remained on their legs and their quarters were extremely cramped. (One of the captured Englishmen, a certain John Scott, ascribes the poor treatment these Indians received to their tendency to show fear when threatened and to their habit of eating rice with the fingers and invariably spilling some. But perhaps to be Indian was to be on the wrong side of a Chinese color bar.) The rank and file English did better. After a time they were moved to an unused joss-house on the other side of Ningpo, given one large room, fed twice a day on rice, vegetables, and weak tea, and left to their own devices. The best treatment was reserved for Ann Noble and the officers. Several times they were invited to audiences with the local mandarins. Mrs. Noble, who was pregnant, went dressed in gaily colored Chinese clothes that made her feel vaguely improper. The mandarins inquired about the movement of soldiers and ships, displayed two of the *Kite*'s carronades recovered somehow from the wreck, and wanted to know whether she had carried opium; but their questions (put through Pu, the comprador, who was evidently a prisoner too) were never pointed or pressing and seemed in the end the expression more of idle curiosity than of anything else. Somehow they got it into their heads (or so Mrs. Noble believed) that the young Englishwoman of twenty-six was Queen Victoria's sister, with the consequence that they provided her with a female attendant and put an old bedstead in place of her cage. Anstruther, Douglas, and Witt were made more comfortable also and allowed small freedoms.

Nevertheless they remained prisoners of the Chinese, and the fact of their being so—first rumored, later formally conveyed—made the English very angry. The *Melville* was at last repaired. This left the *Blenheim* free to go to sea again, and Captain Sir H. Le Fleming Senhouse, her commander, offered to sail over Chinhai and "batter down the place."[9] Bremer declined the offer. He did not think Admiral Elliot would approve. He did, however, give the word to start picking up merchant junks wherever they could be found. Then the *Madagascar* came in from the north bearing confidential dispatches on the outcome of the Peiho venture, and on 28 September the *Wellesley* herself dropped anchor.

The two plenipotentiaries had intended to continue south without interruption, so as to be able to open negotiations at Canton (or know that Kishen played them false) by the middle of October. Once at Chusan, however, they were persuaded to pause. It was partly a matter of ships. The *Wellesley* needed a refit; the *Melville*, though on an even keel once more, had her masts to step and the stores taken out for the careening to recover; a number of other vessels had touched bottom over the past few months, some like the *Atalanta* quite heavily, and as "the worm" seemed very destructive in these seas, Admiral Elliot wanted to heave down the suspects to inspect their copper. There was also this bad business of sickness in the Chusan garrison. (The Elliots very quickly adopted the prevailing low opinion of Burrell, who in any case was half incapacitated by illness.) Something, moreover, had to be done about the prisoners at Ningpo.

Steps had already been taken to quarter the troops more sensibly. The artillery had left the rice flats for the village by Joss-House Hill, the Bengal volunteers had moved to a hillside northeast of the town; the Cameronians would have gone back aboard their transports had not so many been occupied by stores from the *Melville*. Now a whole street of houses in the north part of the town was set aside for them. They moved on 2 October, and ten days later the 49th left its tents on Harbor Point and went into houses too. Efforts were made to obtain better food. No supplies could be expected from the south, the winter monsoon was blowing in full earnest and for the next two months nothing would come up from Canton except an opium clipper or two, but the Elliots had brought tons of wheat and wheat flour and more than a hundred bullocks down from the north. Now they sent the *Nimrod* and a transport back to Quelpart, off the coast of Korea—the *Modeste*, cruising idly about those waters, had found off Quelpart's southeast tip a little island on which cattle grazed unattended. While the *Nimrod* patrolled the channel, preventing with occasional warning shots the indignant owners from crossing over, a party of Royal Irish went ashore, herded the animals out to a point, provoked them into a stampede, and managed to trip a number over a rope. In two days of this hilarious sport almost sixty head were captured. They were hobbled, brought down to the transport, and carried back to Chusan.

In the matter of Anstruther and the survivors of the *Kite* there was less the plenipotentiaries could do. Very early in October, Captain Elliot went over to Chinhai and on the beach there met a high mandarin to whom he insisted that the prisoners must be instantly released if the promise of peaceful negotiations made at the Peiho was to remain binding. But this meeting produced nothing, though the English remembered it for the mandarin (who was "aged and infirm" and of an "easy temper"[10]) and their first sight of Chinese cavalry (two hundred men mounted on small but sturdy horses and carrying bows and arrows); subsequent talks arranged from the little island of Just-in-the-Way made it plain that the Chinese did not think the detention unreasonable. Anstruther had been drawing maps. Douglas and his men had gone ashore and injured innocent villagers. (In fact the surveying squadron of which the *Kite* had been a part repeatedly landed parties to commandeer fresh meat and vegetables and in one pitched battle killed several Chinese.) "Were now officers of the Celestial Empire to proceed at the head of military parties to the anchorage of the Honourable Nation's vessels, would the Honourable Admiral quietly leave them to their own ways, or would he not of a certainty seize them in like manner?"[11] It was a fair question—and after a while the Elliots stopped thinking in terms of an immediate release. On the Chinese side there developed an equal willingness to compromise. The elderly but good-natured mandarin whom Elliot had met on the beach was Ilipu, governor-general of Kiangsu, Kiangsi, and Anhwei. Ilipu had recently been made special high commissioner to the coast of Chekiang; he had reached Ningpo in August, when fight fiercely was still the order of the day; later word had come down to him that the English were not to be molested as they made their way south. They held Chusan, he had the Ningpo prisoners; it seemed an excellent basis for a truce.

So a truce was arranged. No more hostilities on the Chekiang coast—the English to be left alone there. No more seizing of junks (the thirty collected in Tinghai harbor had already been released), no more blockading of ports, and, implicitly, Anstruther and the others to be permitted every reasonable comfort but not set free. Admiral Elliot announced these terms on 6 November. Eight days later he set sail for the

south, taking with him his cousin and the three seventy-fours. Long before he sailed, however, things were beginning to look up for those who
remained on Chusan.

A determined effort was made to establish control over the entire island. Garrisons were posted at several points along the coast, parties of
soldiers moved with fresh pugnacity through the valleys; in Tinghai itself
Captain Caine and his men flogged or cut off the queues of Chinese who
stole or otherwise misbehaved—for every Englishman knew that what
the "fokies" could least abide was the loss of their tails. (In high spirits as
they prepared to leave South Africa for China the previous April, Bingham and the other officers of the *Modeste* had jokingly promised the girls
of Cape Town some. Perhaps they obtained them now.) The result was
that confidence of a sort returned. The town filled up again. Poultry and
vegetables reappeared in the markets, bullocks were once more to be had;
it even became possible to buy Nanking pears, Kiangsi walnuts, and
oranges from Fukien. Lockhart, who had arrived early in September to
see what the Protestant Mission could do, soon thought nothing of walking miles into the interior to distribute tracts and medicines. With
Burrell's encouragement he opened a native hospital. Gutzlaff and Thom
helped, Morrison was there as long as the plenipotentiaries lingered,
Mary Gutzlaff and the Parkes girls arrived in the *Falcon*; for a time the
two Jardine nephews and Donald Matheson were resident too, so that the
place had something of the air of a little Canton. Gangs of coolies cleaned
out the sewers. The hot weather broke, frost nipped the air and drove the
Chinese into padded cottons of light blue; piece by piece the smashed war
junks by the seawall and the doors and windows of vacant houses went
to feed the fires of the troops. By Christmas the more sporting of the
officers were shooting duck and woodcock.

But though fresh cases of malaria ceased with the coming of cold
weather, and improved rations and water meant that fewer men came
down with dysentery, those who were already sick got worse not better.
"I was present at the burial of seven in one afternoon," observed an
officer of the 26th early in November. "When this sickness will stop God
only knows. There seems to be a fatal indifference to our sufferings.
Eleven officers have applied for leave to go to Calcutta."[12] They did not
receive it, though Jocelyn (who was probably in no worse shape) managed to trade on his excellent connections and start home with dispatches. The officers were at least well housed and had plenty of Indian
servants. The rank and file, in billets without window glass (rain and a
cutting north wind soon drove in the oiled paper used instead) or packed
into improvised hospitals like the pawnship that served the Cameronians,

sank steadily lower and as the autumn advanced died in appalling numbers. Samuel Ellis, the Trafalgar veteran who commanded the marines and whose men kept relatively healthy because they were scattered about the men-of-war, remembers going one day to visit the Cameronians and finding "four hundred and sixty persons of the finest regiment of the expedition when we arrived in China, lying on mattresses on the floors of several rooms of an extensive building," many obviously dying, others sick with "dysentery, diarrhoea, and ague fever," and all so crowded he could barely thread his way among them.[13] Burrell put four hundred of the more hopeless of the island's garrison onto transports for Calcutta. Those who survived the voyage could scarcely crawl ashore when they arrived. Four hundred more in rather better condition were sent to the Philippines, but the Spanish would not allow even the officers to land, fearing (they said) a repetition of the awful scenes of 1824, when cholera introduced from English vessels had provoked a general massacre of foreign residents. After several weeks of riding at anchor off the Manila waterfront, the two ships with their miserable cargo weighed again and set sail for the Gulf of Canton. By the end of the year only nineteen hundred men remained on Chusan of the thirty-three hundred who had landed there. Many of these were quite unfit for duty. The Bengal volunteers had lost half their strength, the Cameronians two-thirds; if negotiations failed and further hostilities became necessary, it was a question what the Elliots would have to do their fighting with.

Fortunately reinforcements were already on the way. From India came six hundred men of the 37th Madras Native Infantry (over nine hundred sailed, but headquarters and several companies were lost in a typhoon in the China Sea). And from England there approached a truly remarkable engine of war, an engine that would in the end prove successful beyond all expectations. She was named, appropriately, the *Nemesis*.

19

Up the River to Canton

The Nemesis *was* a paddle steamer of 660 tons burden launched on the Mersey late in 1839 by John Laird for the Secret Committee of the East India Company. Except for deck, spars, and sundries, she was built entirely of iron. If that were not novelty enough, her dimensions and some of her fittings were unusual too. She was long in proportion to her beam, 184 feet against 29 if you forgot the paddle boxes, and her bottom was almost perfectly flat. This, though it held her draught to a maximum of six feet (much less if she was lightly loaded), guaranteed that she would slip dreadfully beating to windward, so she was equipped forward and aft with centerboards in open cases, each capable of being lowered by a hand winch to a depth of five feet. Her rudder was equipped with an equivalent movable extension. She was two-masted and rigged fore-and-aft. Just behind the paddle boxes, which were connected by a raised platform that served as a bridge, rose a single tall funnel. Two pivot-mounted thirty-two-pounders, several six-pounders and swivels, and a rocket launcher made up her armament. And though she carried only half the crew of an 18-gun corvette like the *Larne* or the *Modeste,* she was almost their equal in tonnage—and in appearance, being half again as long, seemed actually larger.

Her commander was William Hall, a Royal Navy man past forty years of age who had received his master's warrant more than fifteen years before and had risen no higher. Hall had studied steam at Glasgow; he had made steamer passages across the Irish Sea and on the Hudson and Delaware rivers; as a very young man had accompanied the Amherst embassy to China. With him now went two other Royal Navy men as first and second officers. The rest of the officers and crew were civilian. The *Nemesis* was not commissioned under the articles of war. She was not listed with the ships of the East India Company's navy. She was to all appearances a private armed steamer. Hall was to take her around to the

Indian Ocean and there receive his instructions, but even this much (oddly) was supposed to be a secret. When the *Nemesis* sailed from Liverpool early in 1840, it was publicly intimated that she was bound for Odessa.

In fact she barely reached Lands End. Navigating at night on a compass inadequately corrected for the iron in her frame, she ran on the rocks off St. Ives, would have foundered but for the eight watertight compartments into which she was divided, and was obliged to put into Portsmouth. Laird and a dozen workmen hurried down from Birkenhead to replace her damaged plates, and on 28 March she sailed again. "It is said," reported the *Hampshire Telegraph,* "that this vessel is provided with an Admiralty letter of license or letter of marque. If so, it can only be against the Chinese; and for the purpose of smuggling opium she is admirably adapted."[1] That was not far from the mark.

The long voyage around the Cape is worth following because the *Nemesis* was the first iron steamer to attempt it (the *Enterprize* had come out to India in 1825, but she was wooden) and because, too, her near disaster off Africa's southeast coast, and Hall's recovery from it, say a good deal about the capability of both and make the extraordinary China performance of the next two years more nearly understandable. Fuel was a problem: at seven or eight knots in a reasonable sea the *Nemesis* exhausted the 130 tons in her bunkers in less than two weeks. Consequently, Hall adjusted his course to catch following winds, put in to shore for coal or wood wherever it was available, and did not reach Cape Town until 1 July, ninety-five days out of Portsmouth. It was beyond Cape Town, however, that the real trouble began. The wind was favorable so Hall, choosing to rely entirely on canvas, stripped the paddle wheels of half their float boards to lessen the drag. This was a mistake. Four days out it began to blow a gale. Six days out, at three in the morning, a tremendous following sea struck full on the port quarter, and the *Nemesis* broached to. She recovered, but at first light it was discovered that a large piece of her starboard wheel, weakened by the removal of the boards, had broken off and was hanging from the rim. Worse, a perpendicular crack had appeared in the three-eighths-inch plates of the hull just before the after sponson beam. It extended down each side of the ship for a distance of two and a half feet. As the vessel worked you could slip your hands between the ragged edges. The *Nemesis* was breaking in two.

For a while the weather improved. Still under sail but with the port wheel working, the steamer limped unseen past Port Natal (as Durban was then called) and headed for Delagoa Bay three hundred miles further up the coast, where if necessary she could be beached. Meanwhile the dangling piece of starboard wheel was hauled up on deck, mended, lowered over the side, and bolted in place once more. As the piece weighed three-quarters of a ton, this took several days. Then it came on to blow again, this time from a different quarter, which made for a distressing cross swell. Because of this swell and because she was built to ride low in the water, the *Nemesis* began to take the sea over her stern. False gunwales of timber were rigged, the after pivot gun dismounted and lowered into a bunker, but still the water came in. More alarming was the lengthening of the cracks down the ship's sides. Every conceivable remedy was attempted. Planks were nailed to the deck fore and aft over the threatened section and bolted at either end to the sponson beams. Small iron plates were maneuvered over the rents and fixed in place by bolts passing through the rivet holes (the rivets had to be extracted first) into stout pieces of oak laid against the inside surface. Not, however, until the vertical iron ribs on either side of the rent were themselves bolted together and the bolts tightened was the deadly tendency checked, and by that time the break in the ship's side ran from the deck to a point far below the waterline. So much water was coming in that it threatened to put out the fires and stop the engines—upon which, of course, the pumps depended. Again and again the paddle wheels buried themselves in enormous waves and almost refused to turn; men had to stand constantly by to help the engines over dead center.* For five days the steamer struggled up the coast. Then the gale abated, and on 27 July she passed the cape that guards the southern approach to Delagoa Bay, steamed twenty miles across smooth water, and anchored off Lourenço Marques.

Lourenço Marques was a miserable place, low, malarial, barely subsisting on driblets of ivory and gold dust and on the export of slaves to Brazil. Practically no ships called there except an occasional American whaler. Hall exchanged ceremonial visits with the Portuguese governor, whose official residence, one-storied but dignified by a porch with two white pillars, rested among sandhills near the dilapidated fort, then bought some timbers he noticed piled on the shore, and set about bracing the steamer's sides. Guns and coal were taken out, she was hauled well up on a sandy beach, guards were posted to keep the natives off (and the crew from getting liquor), and the work began. Where the tear extended, seven feet down each side of the hull, the broken iron plates were removed and new ones riveted in their place. Six of the newly acquired timbers were introduced into the bunkers, raised until they lay horizontally against the ship's ribs three to a side, one above the other, and bolted

---

*To move the paddle wheels, 18 feet in diameter with floats 7 feet long, the *Nemesis* was equipped with 2 engines (one for each wheel) with 44-inch cylinders and a 4-foot stroke. Their estimated combined horsepower was a mere 120, by Hall's own confession not nearly enough.

home. Two more were placed lengthwise along the deck, inside the paddle boxes, and similarly fastened to the sponson beams. Barnacles were scraped, other minor repairs made, and in twelve days—the men worked under the promise of double pay—the *Nemesis* was afloat again.

She stopped briefly at the Portuguese port of Mozambique, at Johanna in the Comoro Islands (whose sultan tried to overawe a rival with the steamer's presence), for a month sailed eastward across the Indian Ocean, under canvas except for the difficult passage through the Maldives, and early in October reached Point de Galle on the southwest coast of Ceylon. At Galle, then the island's chief port (Colombo did not have a breakwater), decks were caulked and bunkers filled with coal brought down from Calcutta. Hall went calling upon Governor Mackenzie, and so fired the governor's son, Stewart, that the young man begged and received permission to accompany the ship to China.* Hall's destination was known at last. On reaching Galle, he had been handed a dispatch from Fort William instructing him to proceed directly to the Gulf of Canton (Auckland had in fact expected him two months earlier), and this dispatch he was permitted to publish. The whole ship's company was therefore in the highest spirits when the *Nemesis* weighed at dusk on 14 October.

To Penang on the west coast of Malaya took a full ten days because the Indian coal burned badly and clogged the furnaces and because quantities of barnacles fouled the steamer's bottom. (She had been scraped twice, at the island of Principe and again at Lourenço Marques, but barnacles seemed to collect more rapidly on iron plates than on the copper sheathing of a wooden hull.) Three days of coasting brought her to Singapore. There she took aboard all the coal she could carry, so much coal that bags of the stuff covered her deck, and on 4 November set sail on the last leg of her voyage with the winter monsoon in her face. Twenty-one days later, at dawn, Moller of the *Press* heard guns in Macao's harbor, hurried down, and was astonished to see the long hull of a steamer lying among the small craft in front of the Praia Grande. None of the other steamers had ever come in so close—Pinto was sure she would go aground and warned Hall so—and the Chinese seized the opportunity to have a close look. But Hall did not linger. The Elliots, he learned, were

*James Matheson knew the Mackenzies well, entertained young Stewart when he reached Macao, and recommended him to Captain Elliot who arranged that he serve as military secretary to the plenipotentiaries in Jocelyn's place. Mackenzie's coming may have pleased Matheson on another score too. "We are but few Highlanders in this part of the world," he had written two years before to a London friend who was arranging to send him the *Inverness Herald*. The Mackenzies were large landholders in Ross and Cromarty. Matheson came from Loch Shin in Sutherland, just to the north.

not there. Off he went that very morning across the gulf to the *Melville,* which returned his salute exactly as if the *Nemesis* were a regular man-of-war.

The *Melville* lay at Tongku, Captain Smith having advised a general shift there from Capsingmun early in October. Between Castle Peak and the island that gave the anchorage its name there could be found, at any given moment, perhaps a dozen warships, among them the 26-gun frigates *Calliope* and *Samarang* just in from South America, with merchant ships besides. Passage boats ran regularly to other places in the gulf; at Tongku itself a sort of floating Wapping had grown up, whole streets of boats moored in regular lines, carpenters here, blacksmiths and tailors there, with gambling shops and drink shops ("nor are temptations of a softer kind wanting," added the *Press*).[2] When the mandarins, who did not like this at all, sent runners to take down the names of the boatmen, the boatmen turned upon them, drove two into the water where they drowned, tied the rest to their own boat, covered it with oil, set fire to it, and burned the poor wretches alive.

If Legrégeois got wind of this shocking incident, he did not think it worth mentioning. His infrequent letters to the Rue du Bac that autumn were largely taken up with the work of the *procure*. In mid-September three fresh recruits had arrived from France, giving the Missions Etrangères over a score of European priests in or on the borders of China.[3] News dribbled in from the north: Ann Noble's capture, the decision to move the negotiations back to Canton, the dreadful sickness and mortality on Chusan. "There are more than two thousand Catholic Irish among the troops, and Mr. Jermingham does not cease to bother me about sending them a chaplain or going up myself." (Jermingham was Legrégeois's Catholic friend aboard the *Wellesley*.) Putting Missions Etrangères priests on Chusan would, to be sure, present a difficulty; Chusan was part of Chekiang Province, and Chekiang belonged to the Lazarists. "But as those fellows can't speak English, I may get up there myself before I leave for Europe."[4] Legrégeois still had hopes of being called home, perhaps to a procureship at Rome.

Instead he was forced into hiding again. The mandarins, it seemed, were after Pinto about the man responsible for Paul and the letters, so on 18 October, Legrégeois left his house and took refuge in the Italian *procure*. (He went to Joset because Torrette was dead, and he barely knew Guillet his successor.) Then on the twentieth two couriers appeared and said that Taillandier was taken.

Louis-Alphonse Taillandier was an arrival of the previous January who had recently set off for Szechwan accompanied by couriers and a Chinese seminarian named Augustin Ko. A few miles the other side of Canton their boat had been stopped by magistrates' runners who demanded eight thousand taels in silver (or more than $11,000). The couriers had been sent to fetch the money, that was why they appeared now before Legrégeois, but Legrégeois was as unable as he was unwilling to raise so huge a ransom. Ten days later he learned that Taillandier and Augustin were in prison at Canton.

The information came in a letter from Coolidge and Shillaber, two Americans who remained at the factories for Jardine Matheson. They knew about Taillandier and Augustin because, through the hong merchants, they were able to visit Stanton from time to time—and Stanton was lodged in the very place to which the new captives had been taken. What the two Americans reported was not encouraging. Taillandier had dysentery, Augustin had been severely beaten, and one of the couriers was said to be giving the authorities a great deal of information about stations in the interior.

Legrégeois wondered whether to appeal for help to his own government. For the first time in months a French presence on the China coast was actually discernible. The ship that brought the three recruits in September had brought a French consul too. A French frigate lay at Singapore, a corvette at Manila; Barrot, the consul-general at the latter place, was under instructions to follow events in China and protect French ships and merchants there. No one in Paris, however, had mentioned missionaries. Besides, to risk warships in the Gulf of Canton was folly while things remained uncertain in the Levant.

For the "eastern question" was hotting up again. Mehemet Ali's son, Ibrahim, and his army remained obstinately in Syria. Palmerston was more than ever determined to have them out. But it was clear they would never budge as long as France stood silently behind them, and as Palmerston frankly disliked the French (quite in the spirit of '93, his cabinet colleagues were dismayed to see), he had no compunction whatever about arranging things with Austria, Prussia, and Russia behind France's back. Together the four powers would force Ibrahim to evacuate Syria. An agreement to that effect was signed in July. In August an English fleet began patrolling the Syrian coast, along which ran Ibrahim's lines of communication. Public opinion in Paris was thoroughly aroused; war with England seemed a distinct possibility; if it came (the September overland might tell), common prudence required that news of it find France's frigate and corvette well away from the English seventy-fours at Tongku.

So Legrégeois did not expect much from his appeals to Barrot and Consul Challaye. He went instead to Captain Elliot. Elliot listened sympathetically, agreed to make inquiries, but promised nothing. He was preoccupied with matters of a far graver sort.

The situation towards the end of November was this. Leaving a decimated garrison on Chusan and the Anstruther-Noble party still in prison at Ningpo—they fared better now, food and clothing reached them, and someone even sent them two cases of gin (though Anstruther discovered to his dismay that half the bottles were full of water)—the two plenipotentiaries had come down to the gulf. They took at face value Kishen's implied assurance that a settlement could be reached at Canton and meant to negotiate one there. It would not contain all Palmerston asked for; they had, in fact, already written asking permission to settle for less. The first effort to make contact had gone awry when the Bogue forts fired on the *Queen*. On 29 November, however, Kishen himself reached Canton from the north. At once the ingratiating "Captain White" of Peiho memory presented himself at the *Melville*'s gangway, and a few days later negotiations began.

Not many of the private English were pleased. Kishen, it was widely believed, had deliberately sweet-talked the plenipotentiaries away from the dangerous vicinity of Peking and treating with him now would not get anybody anywhere. What a shame that the regiments and ships brought to China over such a distance and at such cost were not being put to serious use! "Gunpowder," began a piece inserted among the *Press*'s usual advertisements for hams, cheeses, jams, and seidlitz powders. "Large arrivals, but it does not go off at all." Insults "continue to be offered by the Chinese and taken by the British." As for war, "the low, wretched imitation of this article which the house of Palmerston and Company have lately manufactured for this market is wholly unsuited to it. A good description, of a bold pattern, well got up and properly finished, would we are confident be found to answer."[5] But Elliot was not to be nudged or prodded in this way.

Innes pursued him on an old personal score. The Parliamentary papers of the previous spring, for some time now available on the coast, had revived in the public eye the affair of the eight purloined chests and with it Elliot's threat to throw the Scotsman bodily out of China. Recollection made the hot-tempered fellow furious. Had you attempted any such thing, he announced in a public letter, I should have seized a gun and shot you through the head! Matheson's opinion of Elliot was more mixed and circumspect. He did not trust Elliot on the matter of opium, knowing his hostility to it to be of long standing—and in those same Parliamentary papers entirely transparent. It was quite possible that the chief superintendent wished to sacrifice the traffic for the sake of better relations with

China. "But I cannot help feeling," he wrote Jardine two days before the *Nemesis* came in, "that the Admiral and he are now acting under the orders of the supreme Government of India, who will naturally make a strong effort to support so lucrative a source of revenue until the Saints at home compel them to abandon it."[6] It gratified Matheson, moreover, that Elliot put Jardine Matheson first on the public notices he sent the merchant community from time to time and that he confided his plans to the house, asked its advice, and showed it little favors. As November passed into December, Matheson began to admit to himself that perhaps Elliot really was on the right course—that perhaps a settlement really could be arrived at with little or no fighting and in a very few months.

Elliot himself had no doubts at all. He might have, had he known with what pain and disappointment Auckland received the news that negotiations were to be resumed at Canton. It was a bad time of year to learn anything from Calcutta, however. The clippers that reached there were waiting for the first opium sale of the year, and all Elliot had was a September letter that appeared to assure him he was free to act as he thought best. The prospect of his doing so with honor and profit seemed suddenly the brighter, too, because of what happened at this moment to two of the chief actors on the scene.

One of the two was Lin. What Elliot had heard during that six-hour disputation with Kishen was confirmed when he came south. The high commissioner was in disgrace, the immediate cause being a memorial he had sent the court—a memorial in which, while admitting that opium continued to be bought and sold, he had repeated his usual assurances that the evil would be extirpated in the course of time. Reaching Peking in August simultaneously with the news that an English fleet lay off the Peiho prepared to give the court no time at all, this memorial had thoroughly annoyed the emperor, and his comments on it (the *Repository* quickly had a version) were acid. "Externally you wanted to stop the trade," he wrote, "but it has not been stopped. Internally you wanted to wipe out the outlaws, but they are not cleared away." By incompetent meddling, moreover, Lin had "caused the waves of confusion to arise" and "a thousand interminable disorders" to sprout. "In fact you have been as if your arms were tied, without knowing what to do. It appears that you are no better than a wooden image."[7]

Lin had responded with a far longer memorial in which he argued that sickness and the sheer expense of the expedition were bringing the English, despite appearances, to the end of their rope. What else could the emperor do anyhow save persevere? It was no use temporizing with these foreigners, "the more they get the more they demand, and if we do not overcome them by force of arms there will be no end to our troubles.

Moreover there is every probability that if the English are not dealt with, other foreigners will soon begin to copy and even outdo them." The Emperor was not impressed. "If anyone is copying," Waley has him note, "it is you, who are trying to frighten me, just as the English try to frighten you!"[8] He had already decided to get rid of Lin, and Lin probably knew it; the express letter with news of his recall, dated the end of September and received two weeks later, cannot have come as much of a surprise. So Lin surrendered his seals of office, collected his belongings, said his goodbyes. Hundreds of people blocked his palanquin as he moved about the city, crying his praises and showering him with presents (most of which Lin insisted on returning). There was a farewell dinner at the yamen of his subordinate Iliang, governor of Kwangtung, in the course of which he learned that his great friend Teng, the former governor-general, had also been ordered back to Peking in disgrace. Lin went down to Whampoa and (among other things) visited the *Kosciusko* and the *Panama*. Then word came that he was to remain at Canton after all to help Kishen, and he waited, practicing his calligraphy a little and writing verses—but Kishen, when he arrived, did not ask his advice.

The dismissal of Lin encouraged Captain Elliot in the belief that a settlement was possible; the resignation of Admiral Elliot left him the better able to reach one. The admiral had been unwell for months, "an old complaint, palpitations of the heart," Matheson called it, and on the twenty-ninth (the day of Kishen's arrival) told his cousin he could carry on no longer. Next day he landed at Macao, looking very ill, but declined a chair and walked the short distance to his cousin's house. A few days later he was aboard his son's *Volage,* bound for England—and Captain Elliot was free to fashion just that combination of threats and offers as seemed to him best.

The three seventy-fours and most of the other men-of-war were sent to anchor off Boat Island, just below the Bogue. The 37th Madras native infantry and the two companies of Bengal volunteers left their camp on Sawchow Island, went aboard transports, and moved up too. Watering parties landed boldly on Chuenpi; boats from the warships sailed right under the guns of the fort. On 4 December, Kishen apologized for the firing on the *Queen.* On the twelfth Stanton received his freedom, hurried down to Macao in a schooner, and went at once to Legrégeois with word of Taillandier—and a letter. "The mandarins wish to know my nationality, my excuse for travelling," wrote the Frenchman. "I answer them always in Latin, I write only in Latin, so that they can discover nothing. I am in a tiny prison with fifty common criminals, with only the clothes I stand up in. My companion has been so cruelly beaten he is like to die."[9] In fact this dismal recitation, Stanton explained, was a little out of date. Taillandier now occupied Stanton's old cell and Shillaber had managed to get money, food, and clothing to him.

So Elliot's show of force was beginning to have its effect. Offer and counteroffer made up the other side of the coin. There were no grand encounters between the two chiefs like the one held three months before in the north. Kishen would have preferred to deal with Elliot at Macao, through the Chinshan subprefect, but Elliot insisted on doing the thing from the *Wellesley* where she lay at anchor a mile or two below Chuenpi. So Kishen's messages came to the great cabin of the seventy-four, brought by "Captain White" or by an old comprador of Dent's, and Morrison translated them on the spot, and they were studied and answered (without the *pin* of course)—in this way the negotiations proceeded.

For Elliot their starting point was perforce the draft treaty that Palmerston had sent out the previous spring: freedom to live and trade at the five ports of Canton, Amoy, Foochow, Ningpo, and Shanghai; the cession of an island or islands, or, if the Chinese absolutely refused (this was the only area in which Palmerston allowed a little leeway), the establishment of a secure English enclave somewhere on the mainland; above all money—money for the unpaid hong debts, money for the confiscated opium, money for the expenses of the expedition. These were the things that Palmerston expected the Elliots to obtain. Of course Captain Elliot could not obtain them and had never expected to be able to! On 1 December he wrote Palmerston that he was sure of a settlement within ten days. On the thirteenth he wrote Auckland that, while no settlement had actually been reached, one was definitely in prospect. It did not include all that the draft treaty laid down. He would in fact be stopping "far short of the demands of the government. But we shall have . . . sown the seeds of rapid improvement without the inconvenience of indefinitely interrupted trade; and we shall have avoided the protraction of hostilities, with its certain consequence of deep hatred" and its likely consequence that the French or the Russians tried to get into the act.[10] For this a settlement on modest terms was well worth having.

Just the same he had to obtain at least a *part* of what Palmerston wanted. Kishen offered $5 million paid over the space of a dozen years. Elliot countered with seven million in half that time—and Amoy and Chusan. The money issue resolved itself without much difficulty at six million. But to open, let alone cede, two places in addition to Canton was more than Kishen dared do. Elliot offered to drop Chusan in favor of a second port unnamed. He made the offer on 17 December; Kishen kept silent; "there are large forces collected here," Elliot warned with perfect truthfulness, "and delays must breed amongst them a very great impatience."[11] The sepoys of the 37th went ashore to practice-fire their muskets. Passage boats advertised themselves to carry sightseers to the battle, which surely was imminent—even Elliot could not dillydally forever. But Christmas came and went.

Several other Americans joined Coolidge and Shillaber at Canton. Together these two sold the *Kosciusko*'s cotton and loaded congou for Jardine's, while Warren Delano put teas into the *Panama* for Russell and Company (whose chief he was now that Forbes was gone). Bremer was approached and agreed to allow both vessels past the blockade. This made Dent extremely angry; the only teas he had, Matheson was sure, were inferior lots purchased in small quantities from smugglers. Bremer stood firm, however, and on 4 January the *Panama* came out and set course at once for New York. The *Kosciusko* was not so lucky. Near Second Bar she took the ground. Chop boats would have to be brought down from Canton to lighten her, and Matheson was afraid serious fighting would break out before she could get clear.

He was right; Elliot was losing patience. By now the four hundred Chusan invalids turned away from Manila had arrived in the gulf, half of them well enough to fight. An opium clipper just down from Chusan brought the rumor that in Peking the war party was again in the ascendancy. Elliot decided to wait no longer. On Tuesday, 5 January, he gave Bremer (who commanded now) word to prepare an assault. On Wednesday, Bremer sent Belcher of the survey bark *Sulphur* to reconnoiter the south side of Chuenpi. On Thursday the assault was delivered.

A ship that approaches the entrance to the Canton River leaves Lankit and tiny Boat Island to port and very shortly comes abreast of twin promontories something less than three miles apart. On the left is the hill of Taikoktow; on the right is the headland of Chuenpi. Beyond Chuenpi the eastern shore of the river falls back to describe Anson's Bay, then juts out again in a second headland that is actually part of the island of Anunghoi. On the western side the shore recedes too, then advances slightly to form the Little Taikok. At this point the river is only two miles wide. Right in the middle lie the little islands of North and South Wangtong. Further up is Tiger Island, the hilly island with the cleft summit from which the Bocca Tigris or Bogue takes its name.

A double gauntlet then, first Chuenpi and the Big Taikok, then Anunghoi and the Little Taikok with the Wangtongs in between, provided there are forts at all these places—and there were. Chuenpi had one at the foot of the hill and a second, a sort of fortified watchtower, at the top. At Anunghoi there were two forts side by side. The Big Taikok had a fort, the Little Taikok had a fort, North Wangtong was heavily fortified too. A great iron chain buoyed by rafts ran across the water from Anunghoi to a rock between the Wangtongs. To the west there was no chain and the forts there were smaller than those on the eastern side, but the western channel was relatively shallow and little known—merchantmen did not like to go that way and seventy-fours, it was thought, would not dare. What with the forts and guns, what with the chain, the big barbarian ships constrained to move slowly, and the fire rafts and war junks collected in Anson's Bay, it must have seemed to many Chinese on the morning of 7 January that they had an excellent chance of beating off the English.

In fact they had no chance at all. Each fort was the shape of the letter D, the straight side parallel to the water, the curve running up the slope behind. From a distance they were quite pretty, like rows of swallows' nests; close up you saw, between the frowning blocks of granite, port lids painted to resemble tigers' heads. But their guns, both those of Chinese construction and the ones bought from the foreigners, were lashed to solid blocks of wood, which made them almost incapable of elevation or deflection, and were served by powder so inferior that, though North Wangtong and Anunghoi were only a mile apart, the shot from one were in no danger at all of striking the other. The walls that ran up the slopes behind them were completely without fosse, bastion, or embrasure, so that a party attacking from the landward side had only to plant its scaling ladders and be in. Worst of all, they were too scattered to be mutually supporting. If the English wanted to they could take them one by one.

Bremer did not see the need; he planned a combined land and sea assault on the outer group. His fleet lay off Boat Island. At first light Thursday the *Nemesis* received as many of the six hundred sepoys of the 37th as her single deck would hold. The *Enterprize* and *Madagascar* steamers took the remainder, one company of Bengal volunteers, and some Manila invalids. In longboats went eight companies of marines under Ellis, over a hundred armed seamen, and a party of Royal Artillery with one twenty-four-pounder and two sixes. By nine in the morning these not quite fifteen hundred men had landed without opposition at a sandy cove on the south side of Chuenpi and were moving through the hills towards the forts, dragging the guns with them. Meanwhile the *Nemesis*, her deck clear, was working into position to bombard the Chuenpi watchtower. The *Queen* preceded her, towing Herbert's 26-gun *Calliope* to a place from which the frigate's broadside and that of the *Larne* and *Hyacinth* could rake the lower fort. The *Druid, Samarang, Modeste,* and *Columbine* set a course for the Big Taikok. The three seventy-fours remained motionless off Boat Island.

It was nearly ten o'clock when Major Pratt of the 26th, commanding, with young Stewart Mackenzie of Ceylon as his aide-de-camp, brought the head of the column to the top of a ridge just east of the Chuenpi forts. On the far side of a little valley rose the hill with the fortified watchtower. The lower fort could not be seen; presumably it was somewhere near the bottom of the slope beyond. In the valley itself were a number of wood and earth stockades (apparently the Chinese had taken alarm and tried to mend their landward defenses) whose occupants began to shout and bang away with muskets and gingals the moment the English appeared. Clearly they were not to be taken by surprise. So Pratt paused for fifteen or twenty minutes to let the rest of his men come up, then gave the order to advance.

Down went the marines and seamen, the three pieces firing over their heads, while the sepoys and Manila invalids worked their way around by the flanks. At almost the same moment the *Nemesis* and the *Queen* began firing at the watchtower. It fired back, but as its nine guns were mounted to hit vessels a good deal further out, its shot passed harmlessly over the steamers, or else (from the poor quality of the powder) started high and fell short, while almost every round from the *Queen*'s sixty-eight-pounder and the *Nemesis*'s two thirty-twos found their mark. In a few minutes the tower fell silent. Then the steamers stopped firing too. From their decks marines could be seen moving just beneath the walls. One put his musket through an embrasure, took aim, fired, stepped back to reload, then coolly repeated the process. Others scrambled over the wall. For a moment the yellow banner on the flagstaff wavered uncertainly as if a struggle were going on beneath. Next moment it fell, the English flag rose in its place, and Pratt himself appeared upon the parapet waving his cap at the steamers' crews cheering wildly below.

Meanwhile *Calliope* and the two corvettes had been pounding the lower fort a few hundred yards upstream. Hall hurried the *Nemesis* to their support, deliberately coming in close and moving with such impetuosity that he struck a submerged rock, "which gave the old barky a terrible list to port, but fortunately did not stop us; ranged up almost within biscuit throw of the walls, and poured in a round of grape and canister from both guns, which must have killed a considerable number of them for we observed them falling dead and wounded out of their ports."[12] This murderous final blow was probably unnecessary. The sixteen Chinese guns were silent, the men-of-war had stopped firing, and a boat from the *Hyacinth* was already pulling towards the shore. But the survivors would not give up. They made for the rear of the fort and would have escaped up the hill had they not run straight into Pratt's men, who forced them back. Many stumbled into the water and died there under a crossfire from pursuers and ships' boats. Others met their end in the fort itself. Visiting the place a few days later with Delano and others from Russell and Company, William Low, one of Harriet's younger brothers, found the inside of the fort a charnel house, bodies everywhere, many horribly burned or disfigured "in consequence of carrying their powder in a belt around the body, and a rope lit, which they use for firing their matchlocks."[13] A considerable number got away along the shore. Of the rest only a few were allowed to surrender, for the English were already acting upon a principle that in time became second nature to them. "The slaughter of fugitives is unpleasant," explained Armine Mountain later, "but we are such a handful in the face of so wide a country and so large a force that we should be swept away if we did not read our enemy a sharp lesson whenever we came in contact."[14] None of Pratt's men had been killed, and only a few dozen wounded.

At the Big Taikok the twenty-five guns of the fort were pounded into silence by broadsides at two hundred yards' range, after which the boats went in. Bingham, landing at the head of a party from the *Modeste,* met thirty Chinese on a gun platform, chased them up the slope, then discovered that his pistol would not fire because the cap had fallen off the nipple. The Chinese, however, were more frightened than he. They wanted simply to get away. So a few prisoners were taken, guns disabled by driving shot wrapped in wet canvas down their bores, and the English withdrew.

The final act of the day was played out by the *Nemesis.* A little fleet of war junks lay at the bottom of Anson's Bay, and though they made no move to interfere, Bremer sent Hall against them the moment the lower Chuenpi fort had fallen. The junks, about fifteen in number, were moored in shallow water partially shielded by a sand bar. It was a position no ordinary man-of-war dared approach, except perhaps slowly, sounding as it went, but the *Nemesis,* with her less-than-six-foot draught, steamed straight in, and when she had closed to within a few hundred yards began to fire shot and shell. The junks replied. Then Hall launched a Congreve rocket, the steamer's first, from the tube mounted on the bridge. By an extraordinary chance its flaming carcass struck square upon one junk's deck and penetrated the magazine, or else ignited loose powder leading to it, for the junk blew up with a roar, scattering wreckage in all directions, and presenting to the astonished English a spectacle so dramatic that it naturally invited comparison with the destruction of the 120-gun *Orient* in Aboukir Bay forty-three years before. The junks were astonished too. They cut their cables and tried to run. A few got away. Most were abandoned by their crews and were burned later by the English coming up in longboats. The *Nemesis,* meanwhile, continued along the principal waterway, reached a small town whose startled inhabitants fled in panic, found two more junks, destroyed one, and took the other in tow. By dusk she was back at the fleet, having accomplished in a day much more that Bremer or anyone else can have expected.

Friday morning she loaded fresh shot and shell. Bremer intended to force the second group of forts at once. The three seventy-fours came up, preparations were made to cut the great iron chain, a bombardment began and suddenly the *Wellesley* flew the signal to break off. A small boat had reached her with the Chinese announcement of a cease-fire, which Bremer proposed to observe.

His captains were astonished, his junior officers furious, yet it was Captain Elliot himself who had suggested the thing, that very morning, to Admiral Kuan through some prisoners released by Pratt. Compassion moved Elliot, no doubt. From Anson's Bay, Matheson reported him "full of compunctious feelings, not perhaps unnatural, at having to attack and slaughter beings so helpless" as the Chinese.[15] There was another reason, however, for wishing to spare the second group of forts as well as the defenses further up the river, a reason Matheson in particular understood. Matheson had gone up to Anson's Bay not to commiserate over the toll of Chinese dead and dying but to get the *Kosciusko* out. She came out all right that Saturday, dropped down to Tongku, and began to shift her cargo—a million and a half pounds of congou, with a little gunpowder and imperial thrown in—into three ships bound for London. But it was obvious that she would have stayed at Second Bar, and perhaps been sunk there, had Bremer continued his assault; and it was obvious that the remaining teas of the season were not going to get out, or the cotton already accumulating at Tongku get in, as long as fighting continued. The inner passage could not possibly handle the volume. It had to be the river.

Twice running Elliot had salvaged the trade of the season. It was something he valued above his reputation with the officers of the expedition, above his standing with Palmerston even. He meant to salvage it again. That was why he wanted a cease-fire and, if possible, an immediate settlement.

At first things went very much his way. Negotiations with Kishen resumed, while on Chuenpi and Taikoktow the English buried the Chinese dead and attacked the forts with pick, crowbar, and captured Chinese powder. (A premature explosion dropped a large rock on Bingham's right leg, injuring it so badly he had to retire to Matheson's house at Macao to convalesce.) On the twentieth Elliot was able to publish the terms of a tentative Chuenpi Convention: Hongkong to be ceded outright; an indemnity of $6 million to be paid over a period of six years; official intercourse between England and the empire to be direct and on a basis of equality; and trade to reopen in the river immediately after the Chinese New Year. On the twenty-first what were left of the forts were handed, with appropriate ceremony, back to Admiral Kuan. The fleet dropped down to Tongku, the *Columbine* went off to Chusan to tell Burrell to evacuate—for abandoning the island to the Chinese, though not actually part of the Chuenpi Convention, had been agreed upon—and the *Enterprize* sailed for Calcutta with dispatches. By the same steamer Elliot wrote for Mrs. Elliot and little Frederick. Auckland had invited them over from Singapore the previous autumn; they were both well, and Calcutta gay, his letters said.

Gaiety, however, was not the mood of certain private English. They continued to be furious with Elliot for having let two vessels past the blockade. They noticed that the *Enterprize* had left without picking up the mail and suspected darkly that this was done on purpose so that Auckland should not have *their* opinion of what Elliot was agreeing to. Their opinion was that the terms were inadequate and very probably a snare. Nothing Elliot touched could be anything but foolishness. "I really believe, had it been ever so favorable, it would have been impossible to please the cankered minds of several of our neighbours under the influence of Dent," wrote Matheson to Jardine.[16] But though Matheson himself regretted the omission of access to a northern port, he was content on the whole with what Elliot was obtaining and grateful for Elliot's "firm and friendly" conduct with regard to the *Kosciusko*. When it appeared that Dent meant to carry his complaints about the chief superintendent all the way to London, Matheson wrote Jardine to "pay liberally any lawyer or other qualified person who will defend him in the newspapers."[17]

Legrégeois too was grateful. On the seventeenth Taillandier turned up at the Bogue and, after spending a night on board the *Wellesley*, came down to the *procure* (to which Legrégeois himself had returned the moment Chuenpi fell). His release must be the English chief's doing. "Would any other man in his position, with so much business on his hands, have troubled himself to think of a poor foreigner?"[18]

Hongkong was occupied. On the twenty-sixth Bremer landed with a large party and formally took possession. "Elliot says that he sees no objection to our storing opium there," Matheson wrote Jardine, "and as soon as the New Year holidays are over I shall set about building." Did Kishen realize what he had done in handing over the island? "He expects it perhaps to be as dependent as Macao, and will be very much surprised when in a few days he sees a proclamation to the inhabitants taking them over as subjects of the British crown."[19]

The proclamation duly appeared on 1 February. Next day Johnston took the *Madagascar* and went from place to place along the shore, stopping to let Samuel Fearon, his interpreter, read the proclamation aloud. Not many Chinese could be collected to listen, and few of these can have understood a word. A week later Abeel, Williams, and half a dozen other Protestant missionaries came over from Macao in a rented lorcha and walked about for two days. "A continued chain of uncouth, naked, rocky, poor, uncultivated, and uncultivable mountains," it seemed to one of the party as they climbed wearily over the central spine. But good water was plentiful, on the south side there were substantial villages, and in the end it was agreed that Hongkong might after all form "a substantial foundation in the providence of God, on which to establish . . . the true principles of commerce, justice, and the Christian religion."[20]

It was time for trade to reopen in the river. Several Americans went up to the factories by the inner passage to join the handful of their countrymen already there. Many English prepared to follow—and still nothing happened. Elliot took the *Nemesis* to Second Bar to confer with Kishen. With him went Captain Rosamel of the French corvette *Danaide*, just arrived from Manila but forbidden by Bremer to enter the river. (A few days later the October overland arrived with the news that the English fleet had bombarded Beirut and that war between France and England was imminent, whereupon the *Danaide* slipped out of the gulf "sans tambour ni trompette.") While the conference proceeded, Hall's officers climbed a nearby pagoda and discovered English names carved in the bricks at the top. Some bore dates as far back as 1785. Cheerfully the officers added their own. Later the entire Cohong came aboard the steamer. "Old Howqua is a very fine old man, now nearly seventy-five years old, with hair and moustache as white as snow. The others are fat, jolly-looking fellows who appear to know what good eating is, particularly old Mowqua."[21] It was all very amusing, but Elliot withdrew to the gulf with nothing settled.

Kishen was stalling again; he would not put his seal to the convention; he pleaded illness, want of instructions, anything. Many westerners thought that Hongkong was the reason for his holding back. "People at large, soldiers, mandarins high and low, are all furious at the Imperial Commissioner," wrote Callery, the Missions Etrangères man, "and maintain that he has gone far beyond his powers in thus ceding ground." An imperial edict for his recall had been issued, the emperor was sending reinforcements, what the Chinese said (reported one American from Canton) "is that neither money nor land can be given to the English, and if they wish trade they must knock head and chin-chin." And though

Elliot retained for a while his confidence in the January settlement, indeed seemed to Callery "quite idiotic over it," by the middle of February even he was wavering.[22]

It was not that he doubted Kishen. It was simply that Kishen appeared to be no longer master in his own house. Three officers were reported on their way to replace him, there were unmistakable signs of military activity about the Bogue—reluctantly Elliot decided on a second blow. First he must make sure of Chusan; it would never do to have the Chinese fall suddenly upon the feeble and unsuspecting garrison there. On the fifteenth the *Alligator* brought word that evacuation was imminent. (In fact Anstruther, Mrs. Noble, and the other Ningpo prisoners were brought over from Chinhai some ten days later, after which the ships and men headed south.) In the gulf Elliot made one last vain appeal to Kishen. On 26 February the attack was delivered.

A small battery had been established on South Wangtong Island, which the Chinese for some reason did not occupy. While its guns shelled the Chinese works on North Wangtong half a mile away, setting fire to a number of wooden sheds and generally disheartening the garrison, the *Blenheim* approached the nearer Anunghoi fort, anchored without haste, clewed all up, and when her seamen were safely out of the tops delivered a first starboard broadside. The *Melville,* passing majestically to port, engaged the farther fort; the *Queen* steamer fired shells and rockets; while up the western channel (which Belcher had reconnoitered) went the *Wellesley,* the *Druid,* the four 26-gun frigates, and the *Modeste,* to take North Wangtong from the flank and rear and to silence the Little Taikok. For three-quarters of an hour the bombardment continued, ceasing from time to time so that the smoke could clear away (for there was very little wind), then resuming with a roar that echoed and reechoed like thunder from the neighboring hills. Belcher describes the *Calliope* anchoring within musket range of the fort on the west end of North Wangtong, the *Samarang* taking up station "very prettily under her stern. . . .The crossfire of the two vessels was beautiful, it acted like masons—chipping off the alternate angles of the nearest embrasure" before turning upon the next. In the face of such deliberation and method the Chinese were helpless, and at last their guns, which as usual had done little more than cut up English spars and rigging, fell wholly silent.

Then up from South Wangtong came marines, armed seamen, and five hundred sepoys of the 37th and stormed ashore. "Opposition there was none," continued Belcher.[23] "The unfortunate Chinese literally crammed the trenches, begging for mercy. I wish I could add that it was granted," but the sepoys in particular were bent on killing. When Belcher, in an effort to intervene, went down into a trench and tried to lead some terrified Chinese out, "two were shot down whilst holding my shirt; and one of my gig's crew, perceiving my danger, dragged me away exclaiming 'they will shoot you next, sir!' " It was discovered that the senior officers on the island had taken what boats there were and fled up the river—before even the landing began, some said.

It was otherwise with Admiral Kuan. When the forts at Anunghoi were occupied (it was done with very little fighting an hour or two after North Wangtong fell), his body was found among the dead, a bayonet thrust in the chest. Later that afternoon a detachment went ashore on the Taikok side, climbed the hill, and came upon a large Chinese camp quite deserted. It was put to the torch and burned all night; the glare, observable for miles around, advertised to all who saw it that the Bogue had indeed fallen.

The great iron chain was at once dismantled, and a light squadron of frigates and lesser craft moved resolutely up the river. Past Second Bar it went, the *Nemesis* leading with Hall and Elliot on the bridge. Just above First Bar and the reaches where merchantmen normally anchored, the squadron encountered Douglas's *Cambridge,* now Lin's first western warship, lying close against the east bank and protected by war junks, a mud fort, and a powerful line of rafts. The junks were dispersed, the fort was stormed, small boats were dragged across the rafts and launched on the farther side, and a boarding party went up one side of the old Indiaman while her Chinese crew decamped over the other. She had hardly fought at all, being moored head and stern in such a way that only her bow guns would bear, but she burned handsomely when the torch was put to her, until the flames reached her magazine and she blew up with all masts standing. So much for Lin's foresight and ingenuity! The English casualties were eight wounded, and one Marine from the *Modeste* accidentally killed by his own percussion musket.

All this by the evening of 27 February. For the next three weeks the ships of Herbert's light squadron—including eventually the 42-gun *Blonde* down from Chusan, four 26-gun frigates, four corvettes, steamers, lesser craft, and transports with elements of several regiments—roamed the channels and waterways of the river and delta country, and in a series of actions that were never costly and never long in doubt, made themselves masters of virtually everything touched by tide between Canton and the sea.

They moved first up the Whampoa Passage, storming sand batteries, ripping away chains and barriers, seizing Howqua's fort, and after several days came within sight of the city. Their near approach produced general consternation. Tens of thousands of people fled the city. Even Lin sent his family upcountry. "Canton never looked so desolate," wrote James Ryan, an American still at the factories, adding that the few Chinese he encountered "scowl upon every one of us in a way indicative of a greater dislike than I have ever before observed."[24] The last few miles of the Whampoa Passage were too shallow, however, for anything much larger than a schooner, so the ships withdrew to Whampoa and from that point tried the waterways that reached due west. Elliot himself pushed along one waterway north of French Island, the waterway later named after him, and discovered that it led to the Macao Passage just west of Honam Island, where the inner passage from Macao terminated. Some of the smaller men-of-war were immediately sent this way, and it was now that there took place the curious incident of the Chinese officer who suggested that his fort and the English, to avoid injury while preserving the necessary appearances, fire only unshotted guns at each other. But it was the *Nemesis* again that undertook the most startling and dramatic excursion of them all.

There had been a short truce of the sort Elliot always welcomed and his critics became apoplectic over. The Chinese had used it to strengthen their defenses and make overtures to the Americans. Elliot was annoyed. A reminder, he feared, was in order. He happened to be at Macao, and it suddenly occurred to him to navigate the full length of the inner passage, from the ocean to Canton—westerners often went that way, of course, but western vessels never. So with a couple of longboats in tow and Morrison and Thom along to interpret, he took the *Nemesis* out of the inner harbor, picked a Chinese off a junk to be his pilot, and very early one morning disappeared up the Broadway.

He was gone two and a half days; for this length of time the expedition did not know where the plenipotentiary was. Then the *Nemesis* reappeared at Whampoa. She had left the Broadway a dozen miles above its mouth and turned due north up a waterway that wound past villages, through rice fields, near an occasional low and barren hill. She had encountered—surprisingly, for why should the Chinese expect intruders here?—small forts, masked batteries, parties of matchlock men, and had overwhelmed them all with shot, shell, rockets, and boatloads of armed men sent in with a rush. The first afternoon she had steamed through Hsiang-shan, where the dying Lord Napier had been so cruelly delayed eight and a half years before. It was a town of thirty thousand inhabitants, Williams had estimated as he passed that way five years before, a town with two conspicuous pagodas. "The day will come when instead of pagodas, spires of churches will rise above Hseangshan, and its people worship the God of the Bible."[25] But all that the years had brought thus far was this devil-ship—in shape like an enormous weaver's shuttle, huge carriage wheels on either flank, smoke spewing from a tall thin tower amidships—that chased two war junks up the town's main street and caught and burned one at its northern limit.

The *Nemesis* had spent the first night anchored in a passage so narrow that, had the Chinese attacked, she could hardly have maneuvered, let alone have turned around. On the second day she had encountered more forts and batteries and had been very nearly stopped by a double line of piles packed with stones—apparently the Chinese had been expecting something—an obstacle she had overcome by rigging tackle, laying alongside, and pulling the piles one by one like teeth. At anchor that night her officers had made out, way to the east, what surely must be the high rock of Lankit. On the third day the waterway she was following had grown so narrow and so shallow that a short distance past Tsznai, when she was only ten miles from the factories (though no one knew it), she had been forced to turn back and take a more easterly course. At last, shortly before noon, she had come out into the main channel of the river a little bit above Second Bar. In two and a half days, moving quite alone through strange and dangerously constricted waters, she had sunk nine war junks, destroyed works mounting more than a hundred guns, and fixed her bizarre and alarming image upon the minds of thousands of ordinary Chinese, demonstrating, as Bremer put it to Auckland, "that the British flag can be displayed throughout these inner waters wherever and whenever it is thought proper by us, against any defence or mode they may adopt."[26] Why should Canton resist any longer?

As usual, however, the Chinese were slow to take instruction. Williams had earlier predicted that more fighting would be necessary—"the body social of the Chinese is too inert, too lifeless, for the whole body to be affected by a rap on the heel; it must be on the head"[27]—and though it was Peking he had in mind, his prescription fitted Canton too. On 13 March, the day the *Nemesis* disappeared up the Broadway, elements of the light squadron took a fort in the Macao Passage only three miles south of the factories. Ryan heard the firing, brief but heavy, and next morning was told that Kishen had left for Peking in chains—which was true; Lin himself had seen the fellow off from a quay east of the factories. On the sixteenth the squadron attacked another fort higher up the passage. "Our regular troops sank two of their dinghies," wrote Lin in his diary, "and shattered the mainmast of one of their warships; after which they retired."[28] In fact the English had carried all before them. On the eighteenth they mounted a general assault upon the city's river front.

A chain of rafts was brushed aside; hundreds of river craft were sent flying, among them smug boats recently purchased for the water forces; the small forts on Honam and the mainland were silenced, the twenty-five guns on Dutch Folly overwhelmed and the tiny island occupied. Early in the afternoon marines and armed seamen landed on the factory square, chased the ragged guard of Chinese soldiers into Hog Lane, and shot many down as they crouched there behind their rattan shields. Then the English withdrew to their ships. On the twentieth, however, they came back, the flag was raised, and from the great hall of the New English factory, Captain Elliot announced that hostilities were again suspended. Trade was to resume, this time positively and for certain.

20

The City Spared

The Samarang *and the* Melville sailed for England, the
first to be paid off, the second to be repaired. The *Madagascar* and *Queen*
steamers sailed too, for India, and for the latter purpose. Bremer went
with them. He was anxious to see personally to the Calcutta end of the
expedition, though Auckland had not asked him to and was astonished
he should absent himself from the coast at such a time. His health,
moreover, was bad. At Calcutta it got worse. He and the *Queen* did not
start back to China until the end of May.

In his absence the naval command fell upon Senhouse of the
Blenheim, sixty years of age to Bremer's fifty-four but Bremer's junior in
rank by virtue of having obtained his captaincy in the autumn of a distant
year while Bremer had obtained his in the spring. The expedition got a
new military commander too; for Auckland, the moment he learned of
the terrible mismanagement on Chusan, had induced the commander-
in-chief in India, Sir Jasper Nicolls, to give him Sir Hugh Gough, the
number two man in the Madras army, and Gough, leaving wife at Ban-
galore but taking son, son-in-law, and nephew with him, had sailed for
China three days before Christmas. Gough was not a young man. At
sixty-one he had only three years' advantage of Burrell. Energy, however, and a wiry frame quite belied a head gone silver. People soon discovered that he climbed Hongkong's peaks like a goat. Thoughtfully
they named one after him.

Down from the north came the transport *Pestomjee Bomanjee* with a
dreadful tale of arriving at Chusan direct from England and finding the
English gone, of sending a watering party ashore on Keeto Point and
having Stead her master attacked, perhaps killed, certainly carried off
by villagers. Senhouse ordered the *Columbine* up to investigate. She discovered nothing; when Gutzlaff landed with an armed escort and tried to
put questions, everyone melted into the hills. Thereafter the schooner

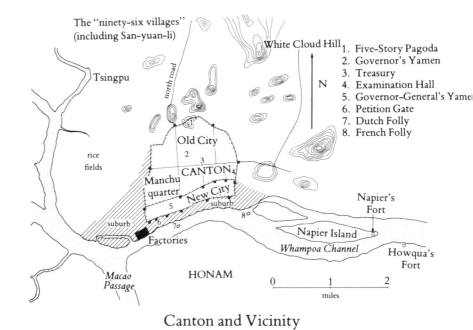

1. Five-Story Pagoda
2. Governor's Yamen
3. Treasury
4. Examination Hall
5. Governor-General's Yame
6. Petition Gate
7. Dutch Folly
8. French Folly

Canton and Vicinity

Omega and the brig *Ann* undertook to warn any transports that might approach.

The two vessels were in a position to do so because week after week they lay among the islands selling—not for a long time had the opium traffic been so brisk. Five or six other ships flying the Saint Andrew's cross of Jardine, Matheson and Company could be found at stations along the coast, and in the Gulf of Canton were still more vessels belonging to that house, perhaps careened for coppering (as the *Harriet* was in May), perhaps transferring treasure, loading provisions, or receiving the drug. (The *Governor Findlay* disappears from the firm's letter books about this time. The *Syden*, lately become the *General Wood* again, is flagship and chief floating warehouse now.) Dent, the Rustomjees, and others directed lesser flotillas and single vessels. From India came the usual relentless flow of chests.

Heavy weather delayed the first Bengal drug of the year (six thousand chests knocked down for prices close to Rs. 800, almost what opium had fetched before the whole uproar began), so that the *Red Rover* did not enter the gulf until 7 March, with the *Rob Roy*, *Poppy*, *Falcon*, and *Sylph* close behind. The *Mor* arrived on 10 March with sixteen hundred chests of Malwa and sailed for Bombay again with half a million in silver. The *Ardaseer* would have arrived from Bombay too, but lost her masts in the Karimata Passage and had to put into Surabaya to refit. Next month the *Ariel*, *Cowasjee Family*, and others brought consignments from the February sale; more vessels were expected; and so it went, in such volume that prices on the coast did not top $400 and after a while fell slightly below. But the traffic was its old self again, reliable and safe. "The opium bond in force before Lin's time is to be revived," wrote Matheson to Jardine, adding that in his opinion this was "quite unobjectionable."[1] When Elliot suggested that the senior naval officer at the Bogue stop schooners and other small craft carrying opium into the river, Senhouse refused. Was opium not a perfectly legitimate article of Indian produce? Neither Elliot nor he had the power to restrict it, and Elliot's suggestion was tantamount to asking him to assume "the vicarious office of head of the Chinese river revenue police"[2]—a thing he would not do! Obviously no other officer was going to do it either. In their letters of instruction to coastal skippers, Jardine Matheson no longer bothered to conceal references to the drug with "whites," "greys," or "chintzes."

The legitimate trade was almost as easily revived. For a time the authorities tried to arrange things so that only the Americans should benefit. They alone were to handle cargo at Whampoa, and to them were offered now the rewards posted for Englishmen alive or dead (Elliot it seemed was worth $50,000). Discord between red-haired and flowery-flagged devils would surely result, blows follow; eventually the Americans might be maneuvered into doing Peking's work for it—was not using a barbarian to catch a barbarian a tried and true imperial device? But Elliot had not stormed the Bogue for the purpose of resurrecting the transshipping business for neutrals. He made it clear that American vessels would leave the river with teas only if English vessels loaded freely too, and as for blood money, though Delano and his compatriots were anxious to turn every dollar they could, it was not going to be in any such manner as this! There remained the problem of confidence. At the approach of the English light squadron many Canton merchants had fled into the countryside, and days passed before they could be persuaded to return. Return they did, however; the factories filled again (Matheson and Andrew Jardine went back into the Creek), and by the second week in April twenty-six English merchantmen, eleven Americans, and one Frenchman lay at First Bar properly secured and served by licensed compradors. Raw cotton and piece goods moved westward in chop boats; silks and teas moved the other way. Ships of more than one thousand tons burden were unloaded and loaded in as little as seven days. Nothing was allowed to interfere with the work: when some riotous seamen killed a peasant on one of the Whampoa islands, "the affair was hushed up by a compromise of money," reported Senhouse (who happened to be passing by), "that being now hardly noticed which formerly would have stopped the trade."³ And as April drew toward a close, it became clear that Elliot was going to do what he had set out to do. The business of the year was going to be saved.

This did not make a resumption of hostilities less likely. If it were the ravaging of the light squadron that had induced the Chinese to open Canton to trade, "similar operations at other points along the coast," observed the *Repository*, "will very likely lead to similar results."⁴ A quick descent upon Amoy, an expedition up the Yangtze—Gough was ready for either, though he wanted first to secure things in the Canton area. Even Elliot leaned in the direction of a blow somewhere.

Elliot might not have had he still had Kishen to deal with—Kishen, that rarity among high mandarins, a man as sensible and candid as himself. Not many weeks before, in the interlude between the first and second Bogue battles, Kishen had sent Peking a quite surprising memorial, which Morrison had somehow obtained (Elliot forwarded a copy to London); a memorial frankly detailing the weaknesses of Canton's defenses and the spinelessness and venality of the men manning them; a truly remarkable paper, Elliot thought, direct, accurate, the work of an "honest advocate of timely yielding"⁵—which was perhaps how Elliot liked privately to characterize himself. Its immediate outcome, however, had been Kishen's recall in disgrace, and the three officers appointed in his place were not, it seemed to Elliot, cast in Kishen's mold.

The first to arrive, an elderly professional soldier named Yang Fang, had, it is true, advised Peking that the English must be allowed to continue trading. It took their minds off fighting and obliged them to curb their men-of-war a little. The emperor, however, was no longer to be beguiled by this kind of talk; the loss of Hongkong, conveyed by Iliang in February behind Kishen's back, had quite made up his mind. "If trade were the solution of the problem," he noted, "why would it be necessary to transfer and dispatch generals and troops?" (Several thousand men were even then marching towards Canton from neighboring provinces.) As for allowing special privileges to rice-bearing merchantmen from India, as had recently been suggested, "this is the source of opium, whom are you deceiving?" Of course it was desirable to keep the English inside the Bogue, only there could they be got at, but as soon as men and cannon had been collected, Yang Fang and his colleagues, Ishan and Lungwen, must "cut off their rear, close in on all sides, and recover Hongkong." When Ishan and Lungwen memorialized Peking to exactly this effect—they had not yet reached Canton and so spoke with a confidence

Yang Fang could not feel—the emperor allowed his brush a rare expression of commendation. "These views are quite proper," the vermilion endorsement ran. "We only await the news of victory with the greatest impatience."[6]

Thus both the English and the Chinese prepared to resume fighting. The only question was who would strike first, and where.

Late in March an English attack on Amoy had been agreed upon, but Elliot dilly-dallied—"whimsical as a shuttle-cock" Gough thought him. "Here we are at the island of Hongkong in the most delicious state of uncertainty. You are aware the trade is open. Captain Elliot only thinks and dreams of this, as if it was the sole object of the frightful outlay of money expended and expending." In the anchorage west of Kowloon lay a couple of dozen transports quite idle. Senhouse was making one over into a coal hulk; most transports brought coal in ballast, and it was a nuisance to have to shift cargo every time a steamer came up to fuel. All the same Gough was bothered. Though Whitehall, he knew, was committed to financing the China expedition, Fort William faced immediate running expenses of Rs. 400,000 a month. The hire of transports came to almost half that sum.

Since Elliot could not make up his mind to launch the Amoy venture, why not at least permit the occupation of the heights above Canton? It would exercise the troops. It would also secure the city. "Had my advice been followed," Gough wrote privately to Madras on 24 April, "Canton would be now virtually in our possession." Instead delay compounded delay, profiting only the Delanos, the Dents, the Mathesons, and other merchants. How divided and quarrelsome these fellows were! "They only agree in one thing, that is in their abuse of Elliot, who, to do him justice, takes the matter very stoically."[7]

Next day, to Gough's surprise, a council of war aboard the *Marion* fixed the second week of May for the sailing of the Amoy force. Senhouse went up to Canton to pull out the light squadron. To date nineteen million pounds of tea had been shipped, he noted, "and a very large amount of English goods landed. . . . I went through a great part of the suburbs, where everything was perfectly tranquil, the shops full of valuable articles and every civility shown."[8] But would this tranquility last if his corvettes and frigates left the river? Senhouse did not believe Elliot when he said that what happened up the coast need not affect Canton, that the English could be at peace there and at war everywhere else.

Then suddenly Elliot himself took alarm. He was at Macao, ill; news of warlike preparations came down to him from Canton; Herbert of the *Calliope*, who kept the factories with a guard of marines (his frigate lay in the Elliot Passage west of Whampoa), counted boatloads of Chinese soldiers passing the factories daily on their way into the city. The forts on Honam and the mainland were being rebuilt, war junks collected and fireboats prepared (or so the compradors of several agency houses reported); Elliot himself had received an odd communication from Yang Fang. Veteran soldiers in large numbers, it ran, reach me from the interior. Already they outnumber yours. Therefore only a peaceful arrangement is available to you—"cast not aside the words of an old man, but open your heart and let your bowels of kindness be seen."9 Yang insisted he stood entirely on the defensive. His words nevertheless conveyed menace. So Elliot warned Gough and Senhouse that troops could not be spared for Amoy after all, and prepared to go up to Canton to look around.

He went on 11 May, aboard the *Nemesis*, taking Mrs. Elliot with him. At the factories Herbert told him that more boatloads than ever were going by. All along the waterfront masked batteries were building, some mounting guns of unusual caliber specially cast at the nearby town of Fatshan. Elliot was disturbed and served She Pao-shun, the Canton prefect, with a written warning to dismantle the batteries and disperse the troops. Then the *Nemesis* carried him back to a council of war aboard the *Blenheim*, the upshot of which was that the Amoy venture was shelved: the force collected at Hongkong was to be held for use against Canton. Neither Gough nor Senhouse was pleased. Gough disliked any change of plan; Senhouse feared that as Canton had already twice been spared, a movement against it would only result in its being spared a third time. But Elliot had his way—he was after all plenipotentiary, what Senhouse in his correspondence sometimes coldly calls "the Minister"—and it was agreed that unless the Chinese gave immediate signs of reversing their warlike preparations, the English would occupy the heights north of the city.

Elliot returned to the factories, this time alone. Almost the whole of the force in the gulf set sail for the Bogue. The Chinese river pilots had fled, the small craft whose duty it was to buoy the dangerous places were nowhere to be seen, but Belcher had the *Sulphur*'s boats out, and except for two transports that got hard aground the fleet moved up the river without mishap. The *Wellesley* went only as far as the Wangtongs. Senhouse, however, wanted the *Blenheim* close to Canton. Under sail when the breeze and tide were right, towed by the *Atalanta* when they were not, the big seventy-four crept up to First Bar, turned west leaving Danes and French Islands to starboard, and after several hours of feeling her way along the deep but little-known passage that subsequently bore her name, anchored in five fathoms a little beyond Dent Point—where no ship-of-the-line, Senhouse proudly pointed out, had ever been seen before. From her maintop Canton was clearly visible. It was late in the afternoon of Friday, 21 May.

At the factories, meanwhile, the foreigners went on with their business. Teas moved at the furious rate of more than half a million pounds a day, and Elliot, to keep them moving, made no public announcement at all about the men-of-war and regiments coming up the river. Nevertheless anxiety was in the air. The *Nemesis*, her boilers constantly fired, rode at anchor not far from the factory stairs. Close by were the *Louisa* and Dent's armed schooner *Aurora*. To the east, near Howqua's Fort, lay the frigate *Alligator*; to the west, at the top of the Macao Passage, the brig *Algerine* and the corvettes *Modeste* and *Pylades*. Native boats hurried to and fro carrying nervous Cantonese to safety; and at last Elliot decided that the foreigners too must get away.

At first light, therefore, this same Friday, 21 May, while the *Blenheim* was still below First Bar, he published a circular advising the English and the Americans (there were no Parsees) to quit the factories, and at five in the afternoon boarded the *Nemesis*. Except for a few Americans too preoccupied with the tea business to heed the warning, not a soul remained. The houses were empty, the square deserted; midnight approached. Suddenly, remembers Coolidge (he was one of the Americans staying behind), the stillness was broken by the crash of cannon. Coolidge dashed to the roof. From the garden of the New English factory a gun was firing into the blackness of the river. Along both banks other guns winked and flashed; to the west flames illuminated great clouds of oily smoke. The Chinese had launched a surprise attack.

It very nearly succeeded. Fireboats chained two by two and filled with raw cotton soaked in oil had been sent with the tide against the three warships at the top of the Macao Passage. They moved unheralded and unlit; the first pair was a bare musket shot from the *Modeste* when a sentry saw the dark shapes and shouted the alarm; then they burst into flames, five pair of them, and came on, blazing furiously, so close that many of the water braves who had steered and set fire to them were shot from the deck of the corvette as they tried to get away in small boats. Behind them came war junks. From the shore the masked batteries (there was an especially large one on the Shameen, the piece of low ground opposite the top of the Passage) took aim at the vessels silhouetted against the glare. Cramped for sea room, without wind to make sail in or light to see by, the English could not move. The *Louisa* and *Aurora* were in especial danger; even Chinese shot would hole them if it struck. Desperately they hauled and slacked their cables in the hope that the Chinese gunners—who must be having trouble sighting as no fireboats had come this far—would continue to mistake their location.

The *Nemesis* alone raised anchor. Her fires were already lit, and in ten minutes from the time of the alarm she had steam up and was feeling her way westward. Even so she would have come up too late to prevent the blazing monsters from falling athwart-hawse of the corvettes and the brig and engulfing them in flames had not the Chinese chosen to launch their attack on the last of the ebb. This made for a rate of drift so slow that the English had time to put boats into the water, grapple the fearsome weapons, and tow them aside; and when, an hour later, fireboats from above Whampoa were sent against the *Alligator* with the first of the flood, the same was true. So the *Nemesis*, when she reached the top of the Macao Passage, was free to steam to and fro with both pivot guns playing, which so dismayed the Chinese that they fired the second wave of fireboats prematurely, and much of the third wave not at all. The ebb had ceased. In the uncertain current many of the blundering, blazing things went ashore, igniting everything they touched and giving the *Nemesis* and the three sailing men-of-war (which warped into position for the purpose) the illumination they needed to begin the work of silencing the masked batteries. Dawn broke before they were finished. The Shameen battery was particularly stubborn. The *Nemesis* had funnel and both paddle boxes riddled there, and at the height of the action Captain Hall burned himself seriously when, a hung rocket threatening to explode and kill everybody on the bridge (Elliot included), he coolly plunged his arm up the launching tube and pushed the sputtering thing clear. By early morning, however, the river was quiet. A few half-sunk and smouldering hulks, a few blackened waterfront buildings, considerable flotsam and jetsam on the surface of the water, and some bodies cast up here and there were all the Chinese had to show for their savage and unexpected attack.

They were disappointed, and not unnaturally the factories were made to feel it. At first light one of the *Morrison*'s boats tried to slip away to Whampoa. It was intercepted, forced to the bank, and its occupants assaulted and dragged into the city—all but a boy named Sherry, who was apparently killed on the spot. Two of the seamen had bullets in them, the others were losing blood from cuts and gashes, and one was unconscious when Coolidge later encountered them—for Coolidge was a prisoner too. Early that morning he had been caught as he left his factory, saved from instant death only because some coolies cried out that this was a flowery-flag devil not an English one, and led away into the city. He survived. So did the wounded. Forty-eight hours later they were brought to the Consoo House, and there, on Monday afternoon, Major Pratt and his Cameronians found them. "I cannot tell you with what feelings of goodwill we looked on every one of those redcoats," wrote Coolidge shortly afterwards from Dent's *Aurora*.[10] Although he was unhurt and the others recovered, their feelings of outrage and the anger of most of their countrymen persisted and if anything grew stronger. The surprise night attack upon the English had been treacherous enough. This day-time assault on an unarmed boat known to be American, the killing of young Sherry (son of the New York harbormaster; the *Morrison*'s skipper could not forget that the parents had asked him to keep a particular eye on the boy), the maltreatment of the wounded while they were being held in the city—these, decided Bridgman, were nothing less than barbaric acts. Never had the *Repository* sounded so fierce as now it sounded.

But the Chinese attack had failed, though it sputtered on downriver, where a few days later fireboats sent against the *Wellesley* and the merchant shipping scorched a dozen lascars from the *Scaleby Castle* so badly that several of them died. Ishan, to whom the emperor had entrusted the overall command, prepared now for the inevitable English blow. The morning of his capture Coolidge had been led close by that officer's headquarters near the east wall, and had seen in passing something of the bustle and activity there: messengers coming and going, soldiers and guns moving purposefully towards the river. The Chinese apparently expected the English to strike somewhere between French Folly and the factories. Gough, however, had a different plan. He meant to avoid the suburb and the flooded rice fields immediately adjacent and get at Canton from the northern heights. His only problem was how to move his regiments there.

Inadvertently the *Nemesis* discovered how. Pursuing a junk west of the Macao Passage, she came upon a waterway leading north, steamed up it marauding as she went, and returned hours later her rigging decked with Chinese flags and banners, her crew wearing scraps of Chinese clothing, and on her bridge as fine a collection of queues cut from the heads of captured "fokies" as you could wish to see. She also brought news of a landing place from which it should be possible to reach the northern heights—a place called Tsingpu. Belcher reconnoitered it, Senhouse gave his approval, transports had already brought the regiments to the Macao Passage by the route the *Blenheim* had taken; on Monday, 24 May, the grand flanking movement began.

A noon salute to honor the queen's birthday, which auspiciously it was, and the *Hyacinth*, the *Modeste*, and three brigs of the light squadron turned east at the top of the Passage and ranged in line opposite the factories while Pratt and three hundred Cameronians went ashore. (It was now that Coolidge was rescued.) Next these five warships and their attendant craft systematically cleared the full length of the Whampoa

Channel and wrecked the naval arsenal on its south side. The task required forty-eight hours and a good deal of hard fighting, for there were well-served batteries at several places, and shoal water bothered the big vessels badly—the *Atalanta*, for one, took the ground so hard she had to have her coals out and be lashed at low water to two junks before she could be refloated.

All this, however, was no more than a diversion. The main force struck off for Tsingpu with the *Sulphur* in the van, Belcher's other survey vessel the *Starling* in the rear, and in between the *Nemesis* towing strings of boats: chop boats; mandarin boats; upcountry tea boats eighty feet long with arched roofs that slid back for ease of loading; longboats from the men-of-war; boats of every shape and size. Bingham, with the fleet again (his right leg partly mended), says that there were even "flower boats," though they cannot have carried their usual fair cargo. By the time she had picked up the last, the *Nemesis* had sixty to seventy boats in tow. On her deck rode Gough, Senhouse, and three hundred men of the 49th. Behind came Burrell's five hundred Royal Irish, Ellis's four hundred marines, a brigade of armed seamen under Bourchier of the *Blonde*, three companies of the 37th, a company of Bengal volunteers, Royal and Madras artillery (Anstruther commanded the latter), sappers and miners, followers, and stores. In all more than two thousand men, a little army really, moving to battle aboard a prodigious tail of boats!

Naturally it slowed the steamer down, and it was dusk before the bizarre flotilla reached Tsingpu. The 49th went ashore at once, the guns and stores followed; the rest of the men stayed in the boats and snatched what sleep they could. At first light Tuesday they too disembarked, and the whole force moved east and south. Almost at once the headless body of an Indian camp follower was found, murdered (no one doubted) for the advertised money reward. The weather was sultry, the terrain all ups and downs with bits of flooded paddy and a surprising number of burial grounds. Soft earth and closely clustered gravestones gave the guns a good deal of trouble, so that after a while the single twenty-four-pounder was left behind, only the twelves, the lesser pieces, and the rocket "frames" with nine-pounder rockets continuing. Everywhere were Chinese pickets. They waved swords and spears and shouted fiercely but were careful to keep their distance.

From Tsingpu to the edge of the city was hardly two miles, so it was not nine o'clock when the English advance guard came within gingal range of the city wall, and Gough paused to make his final dispositions. His objective was a hill a few hundred feet high, lying midway along the city's north wall and surmounted by a large, red, five-storied tower. If he could place a few men and guns upon this hill, all Canton, he was satisfied, would be his. First, however, the wall itself, which skirted the northern slope of the hill, had to be got over. It was in a state of considerable disrepair. Bushes and small trees grew from it, and the ditch in front, which the tide had perhaps once filled, was now completely dry, but it was solidly built, upwards of twenty-five feet high, and before it could be approached at all several outlying forts had to be dealt with. Gough directed Bourchier's naval brigade to rush two at the northwest corner. The 49th and the 18th were to take a couple further east. As soon, therefore, as the gun lascars had manhandled a few light pieces into position, the little army moved off again, in smothering heat and with many of the men suffering from diarrhea. The armed seamen had a few moments of real fighting. The Chinese who faced them did not immediately run, and from the city wall, which was very close, came a galling fire that mortally wounded one officer from the *Nimrod* and cost another a leg. The 49th and the Royal Irish had nothing to do but race each other (their opponents fled incontinently), so that Gough, coming up in person to congratulate them—he was Irish too, and they knew it and cheered him wildly—very quickly stood upon the rampart of the higher of the two forts and gazed south over the provincial city.

What he saw was acre upon acre of dull reddish roof littered with woodpiles and household laundry. Not an avenue, not a square or public garden, nothing to break the monotony but temples, flagpoles, a few trees, and two pagodas over a hundred feet high. Beneath this enormous expanse of tile, within the six miles of wall, lived half a million people— and more in the suburbs besides. Canton was the seat of the provincial examinations; to the Canton treasury came millions in tax revenues each year; a governor had his yamen in the center of the Old City, a governor-general his yamen in the southwest corner of the New—command of Canton meant a great deal (or so Gough believed). And if, this very Tuesday, he had led his two thousand men straight up five-story-pagoda hill, as Senhouse later said he wished he had! But Gough did not attack, not Tuesday afternoon nor Wednesday either. After that it was too late.

He hesitated because he did not know how large Canton's garrison was. Everybody knew it to be much reinforced—by ten, twenty, some said thirty thousand men—and if these were the numbers the assault would have to be carefully prepared. That meant bringing up scaling ladders, carcass rockets (the *Blenheim* had a supply), shot and shell for the bombardment of the parapet. The guns themselves had to be got to the heights overlooking the north wall. (At the moment some were still back among the gravestones; two with broken axletrees would probably never come up at all.) Meanwhile Gough's flanks and rear needed looking to. Late that very Tuesday morning a column of Chinese had come suddenly at Tsingpu from the western suburb, and though Hall had driven them off with a scratch force of seamen, Gough felt obliged to detach Ellis and several companies of marines to that quarter. Just beyond the northeast corner of the wall, moreover, there was an entire encampment of Chinese troops, very active, with officers on ponies constantly coming and going, and as it threatened his left flank Gough sent the 18th and the 49th to break up the place—a thing that cost him several hours and casualties besides. The men were tired, the heat oppressive, the rain clouds threatening. He simply could not launch his main assault at once.

Wednesday at dawn a courier brought a letter from Captain Elliot. It reminded Gough that the object of the movement against Canton was to show the Chinese that the English could not be bullied. For this the occupation of the northern heights was enough; there was no need to enter the city, that would in fact be unwise, since forcible entry was certain to cause injury to an "immense unoffending" body of Cantonese, and such injury would more than cancel the gain. You and I agree—and I hope (added Elliot) that Senhouse, whom I know less well, will agree too—that "the protection of the people of Canton, and the encouragement of their goodwill towards us, are perhaps our chief political duties in this country." Therefore, once all armed resistance "without the walls" had been quelled, Gough's army must rest on its arms.[11]

"Without the walls"—Gough was not happy with the wording, and Senhouse, when he read the letter, was even less. About ten o'clock a red-button mandarin appeared on the parapet waving a white flag. (Extraordinary, thought MacPherson, the overbearing Chinese have at length come to know the use of the white flag.) Burrell and one of the younger Goughs went forward to discover what the fellow wanted. An end to the fighting, came the answer through Thom, to which Sir Hugh replied that he would observe an armistice for several hours so that red-button could produce his own commanding general—Gough would not deal with anyone less. Hours passed. No general came. Gough lowered his white flag and went on with his preparations. The Chinese, however, did not lower theirs, which turned out to be convenient, for the path by which the English guns and ammunition reached the heights was well within range of the walls, and a determined fire would have been annoying. All afternoon and evening, in heavy rain, the work went on. What was Elliot doing, away there on the other side of the city? His letter, with its implicit command to cease hostilities, had been thirty-six hours old when it arrived!

What Elliot was doing became clear first thing Thursday morning. The rain had ceased. Everything was ready. The guns were to begin firing at seven, the men to go forward in four columns at eight; Gough himself was making the final arrangements—when, as Belcher tells the story,[12] a white flag flapped again on the Chinese parapet and the English heard indistinct shouts of Elliot's name "as if he had been their protecting joss." Belcher guessed at once what was up. Gough and Senhouse would not believe him, but there was a naval lieutenant, resolutely climbing the hill. "That officer," said Belcher, "is the bearer of our destiny." He was right; the man in question, from the corvette *Pylades*, carried a dispatch prepared at ten the previous evening, a dispatch he had spent half the night stumbling up from Tsingpu to deliver. Gough received it in silence. The assault on five-story-pagoda hill was not to take place. While the chief superintendent discussed with the Chinese what they must do to save Canton, Gough's force was to stay exactly where it was.

When Senhouse in his turn had read, he said simply, "I protest."

21

San-yuan-li

Both Gough and Senhouse committed their feelings instantly to paper. "Heights of Canton at 6 a.m.," their notes to Elliot began. Sir Hugh did not conceal his indignation at being reined in "just at the moment of commencing the assault—sure of carrying the walls, according to all human certainty, within half an hour and with little loss."[1] Besides, Elliot's cease-fire had put his little force in a most precarious position: heavily garrisoned city in front, hostile and unknown countryside behind, communications with the fleet uncertain. Sir Le Fleming was positively apoplectic. He had long felt that the chief superintendent, so much his junior in the service, a boy of four when he was fighting at Trafalgar, did not lean upon his age and experience as he ought to do. And now this supremely supine, insufferably interfering act! Senhouse could not bear it, and in a while withdrew to the *Blenheim*—to see to his ships, he said; to avoid Elliot, Belcher avers; in any case to write Bremer an immense dispatch that mingled narrative of the campaign with Elliot's sins in respect to it. Senhouse was already ill with "marsh fever." For the moment, however, his pen marched indefatigably on.

Meanwhile Elliot went ahead with the settlement. He was perfectly aware that officers and men keenly resented being deprived of the storming of the wall and the occupation of five-story-pagoda hill. But he did not share Gough's confidence that these operations would prove decisive. More likely Gough would find that he must go down into the city after all; and should two thousand men then manage to penetrate such a rabbit warren of a place, Elliot was pretty sure what the consequences would be: "The disappearance of the municipal authorities and the police, the flight of the respectable inhabitants, the sacking of the town by the rabble, its certain desolation, its not improbable destruction by fire, and our own hurried departure from the ruins."[2] (Elliot wrote later, in London, with leisure and every inducement to marshal his arguments, but it had

296

been, I think, his opinion at the time.) Was it to smash the entire fabric of commerce and government that he had sent a force up the river? His object had been simply to demolish the forts, disperse the army, and drive Ishan and his colleagues away, and by so doing make it safe for the English expedition to move north to its real work in the Yangtze—this, and perhaps lay hands on the treasure that the Canton authorities were said to have collected. So when, by Wednesday evening, the offers made him aboard the *Pylades* had become substantial, he had granted a truce and sent the lieutenant off to stop Gough.

The truce was only till noon Thursday. In the very early hours of Thursday morning, however, final terms had been agreed upon: $6 million, or exactly the figure of the abortive Chuenpi Convention; the thousands of soldiers not part of the normal Canton garrison to be removed some distance from the city; compensation for the damage done to the factories (the morning of Coolidge's capture the rows east of Hog Lane had been pillaged and partially wrecked), for the injuries suffered by the Americans, and for the burning two years before of the Spanish brig *Bilbaino*. This was the Chinese undertaking. In return the English were to leave the river, abandoning all the forts and anchorages they had occupied, even North Wangtong. Not a mention of opium, the bond, or the twenty thousand chests, not a mention of Hongkong, Chusan, or any other place along the coast. Nothing about resuming trade at Canton on the old basis, a new basis, *any* basis; nothing about an intercourse of equals at Peking. It was a settlement entirely local, quite temporary, for particular purposes only—yet Senhouse was sure it would be represented to the emperor as very much more. For he could discover in its terms no admission that Canton had been beaten, and this being so, why should Peking take it for anything less than a comprehensive and mutually acceptable adjustment of all the differences between China and England?

Canton, however, knew very well it had been beaten. The Monday of his release Coolidge had seen soldiers deserting their posts and mandarins "in the greatest possible dismay, like frightened children."[3] Frederic Wakeman, Jr., who has made Canton in this period his particular study, relates how hour by hour the city threatened to fall apart. Soldiers plundered or fought among themselves, townspeople hid; Ishan, proceeding in retinue near the Great Buddha Temple, was stopped by coolies demanding to know how he would save the city, and by decapitating several only added to the terror and confusion. "Since the army crouched in one corner, conducting halfway measures and not marshaling to meet the enemy"—Wakeman is quoting from a Chinese account—"the people clamored like rushing water, saying that the soldiers were not to be depended on. The city would certainly be destroyed, and the barbarians would enter to burn and loot. And so, supporting the aged and leading their children by the hand," they besieged the yamens, begging the authorities to meet the *fan kuei* with "measures of expediency."[4] On Tuesday, accordingly, She Pao-shun, the prefect, had gone to Elliot aboard the *Pylades* in the Macao Passage. Matheson says that Howqua went with him, that they offered a certain sum down and a certain sum later, and that they were refused. Next day, however, She improved upon the offer. Ishan was instructing him, and Ishan knew that it was time to buy the barbarians off.

So Canton understood perfectly what had happened to it—understood, too, that this time the ransom (for ransom it was) would have to be paid promptly. In January, Kishen had agreed to $6 million spread over six years. It was to be six *days* now. By nightfall Thursday boxes of *sycee* lay on the *Hyacinth's* deck, and more came aboard the *Modeste* and the *Nimrod* over the weekend. The withdrawal of troops went briskly too. Saturday a great column left by the northeast gate, Yang Fang in a palanquin at its head, officers riding alongside, threaded its way through a village occupied by the 37th, and by its unsoldierly appearance and dejected manner made the sepoys laugh. Several days passed before the last million of the ransom was turned over. But Canton on the whole showed remarkable alacrity and good faith. It was the country that made trouble, particularly the "ninety-six villages" along the main road west of White Cloud Hill—so much trouble that one of these villages, San-yuan-li, has become legendary because of it.

The country people did not like the way Canton had been behaving. There was plenty of antiurban sentiment among them anyway, and when the English forced their way up the river and the *Nemesis* began roaming inland waterways spreading terror where the *fan kuei* had been only a rumor before, they naturally made the provincial city their scapegoat. The peasants did this out of instinct. The gentry arrived at the position more intellectually, reasoning as Confucians do that calamities have moral causes and that if barbarians carried fire and sword into their midst it must be because spiritual degeneracy rotted somewhere. It did not rot in themselves, of course. It was to be found in the mercantile community of Canton and among the higher officials stationed there, many of whom were Manchu—Kishen, Iliang, Ishan for example, though not Lin or Yang Fang or the new governor-general, Ch'i Kung.

Though the country people looked severely at the city people, their bitterest feelings were reserved for the foreign devils themselves. It was not a matter of patriotic sentiment. Patriotism comes last to peasants, I suppose, and China in any case was not a nation but a universality, inspiring in the Chinese a profound sense of cultural and ethnic self-sufficiency with which flags, national anthems, and other French and American inventions had nothing at all to do. What moved the peasants was plain distrust of strangers. They were xenophobes. The English raised that xenophobia to its most intense level. The peasants, moreover, had an instrument for expressing that xenophobia. They had their officially inspired and directed militia.

Throughout the empire it was normal for the gentry to hire mercenaries (or "braves") when times were bad and normal for the gentry to form village militias when times grew worse. Kwangtung Province was peculiarly suited to these arrangements, its people being accustomed to arms and more than a little feisty. No part of China, indeed, less fitted the classic European vision of a Cathay ruled by persuasion and sweet reason. Clan warfare was endemic; villages built walls, collected arms, and had at each other like the Hatfields and the McCoys; and among the poor, who of course did most of the actual fighting, a military tradition developed that would someday fill Chiang Kaishek's armies with Kwangtung men. Commissioner Lin had taken care to profit by this martial readiness. He had sent fishermen and Tanka people to join Kuan's marine; he had added hundreds of braves to the troops who were supposed to drive the English out of Macao. (These were the men of whom Bridgman had heard, lifting weights on the factory square to qualify for their $6 a month.) Though Kishen, to save money, had disbanded the militia and let most of the braves go, in the winter of 1841 the popular mobilization had begun again, at first frowned upon by Ishan (who came to Canton to quell troublesome barbarians and did not relish arming a people with a reputation for being troublesome too), later blessed when he saw that the gentry were determined to go ahead anyhow. Thus when She Pao-shun arranged the ransom, when the city stood shamed and the countryside lay open to Gough's men, a formidable popular force was already in being, ready and eager to fight.

It moved in bands hundreds strong, each under a banner inscribed with the characters "righteous people" and the name of a particular village. The bands were led by local gentry; the day Gough's men reached the north wall, a dozen notables from the San-yuan-li area met, laid plans, swore a blood oath, and went out to rouse the countryside. Along with their individual banners the bands carried a common flag, black (to ward off evil spirits), taken from the Buddhist temple at San-yuan-li, but it was the banners, not the flag, that counted. These peasants with their cudgels and hoes, their swords and spears and occasional matchlock, would never have risen had not the villages from which they came already seethed with anger against the foreigner. And when they marched, they marched for their villages.

Their anger was brought to fever pitch by the excesses of Gough's men. English patrols out looking for food too often improved the occasion by looting. At one place a temple was entered, the tombs opened, and the contents deliberately examined. "The bodies were all embalmed," writes MacPherson. "They were buried in their clothes, the cap and button denoting in death as in life the rank of the wearer." Each right hand held a fan, each left hand a piece of paper with characters on it. "The features presented a dried and shrivelled appearance, and there was a strong pungent aromatic smell perceptible on raising the lid."[5] For the ancestor-worshipping Chinese this was plain wanton desecration. Worse probably occurred, for Elliot found it necessary to warn the Indian camp followers to mind their behavior, and the *Repository*, adding boats' crews, spoke darkly of "doings of which it is a shame to speak."[6]

So the tinder was ready. On Saturday, 29 May, the very day old Yang Fang led his regulars out the northeast gate under the derisive gaze of Captain Duff's 37th, the match was put to it. An English patrol entered a hamlet several miles to the northwest of the city, broke into a house, and attacked the women there. "About 12 o'clock the following day," Gough writes, "I perceived numbers of men, apparently irregulars, and armed for the most part with long spears, shields, and swords, collecting upon the heights three or four miles to my rear."[7] These were the soldiers of righteousness, moving at last; it was obvious even at this distance that they increased and were approaching; and as Gough dared not wait until they hemmed him against the city wall, he went forward to disperse them, taking with him a wing of the 26th under Pratt (it had come around from the factories on Thursday), the three companies of the 37th under Duff, the three of the 49th, the one of Bengal volunteers, and some Royal Artillery with rockets.

At first everything went capitally. Pratt and Duff met a column and scattered it with so little trouble that Gough ordered the 49th and the Bengal volunteers back to camp. Once beyond musket range, however, the Chinese turned and formed again. More were collecting all the time. It was fearfully hot. Though storm clouds were gathering, the sun for the moment beat mercilessly down. It made the men sick and dizzy; it struck the deputy quartermaster-general, a certain Major Becher, dead at Gough's side. Peering north through sweat that half blinded him, Gough saw masses of Chinese on every hill. They waved banners and shouted, the rockets dropping among them had no apparent effect; where Gough had earlier put their number at four thousand he put it now at seven, and they moved with a determination he had never before seen.

So Gough ordered a second advance. The 26th was sent to the left; the 37th moved directly forward, with the Bengal volunteers (hastily re-

called) on their right. Again the Chinese gave ground, but by now the
storm had broken. It was raining torrents, you could not see twenty feet
in front of you, and Gough sent runners with the order to disengage.
Withdrawing through flooded rice fields in such a downpour was, however, easier said than done. "The rain had completely obliterated every
trace of a footpath," writes MacPherson.[8] "There was nothing but one
sea of water before us. The thunder and lightning were awful"—and the
Chinese, instead of using it as a cover for their escape, turned and pursued
the English. Flintlocks were useless in such heavy rain, bayonets had no
reach, if a man stumbled he went up to his knees in water, and on the
raised pathways (when they could be found) it was possible to proceed
only in single file. The result was a series of confused and desperate little
struggles, the Chinese setting ambushes, rushing the flanks, pressing the
rear, always trying to pick off a man here, a man there, for which purpose
they used (among other things) an instrument resembling a long shep-
herd's crook.

One company of the 37th found itself in particularly serious straits.
Duff had sent it just before the storm broke to open communications
with the Cameronians. He assumed, when he withdrew his other companies, that it was safely with Pratt. It was not, it remained out in the rain
and gloom, sixty sepoys and their three English officers fumbling
through the paddy, their muskets useless, darkness descending, all about
them Chinese shouting and lunging. For a time the rain let up, and the
sepoys, drying their muskets with scraps of lining torn from their tur-
bans, managed a few ragged volleys that gave their tormentors pause.
Then it began to pour again, and the Chinese closed in. What saved the
sepoys was their profound contempt for the enemy—they used on them
the word otherwise reserved for the scavenger pig of the Indian village—
and the good sense of their officers, who eventually gave up attempting
to move and formed a square. In a square two companies of marines
found them, fired a few volleys (they were armed with the new percussion musket), and brought them out. Only one man had been killed,
though a dozen were seriously wounded.

Indeed Gough's dead over the entire seven days came to exactly two
officers (Becher and the officer from the *Nimrod*) and twelve other ranks.
It was an astonishingly light bill, particularly when Sunday's fighting is
considered, for on that day the English had certainly been outnumbered:
seven hundred men had gone out to meet ten times that many, and had
returned. The peasants, however, did not see it this way. They thought
they had struck a mighty and successful blow—had not the *fan kuei* fled
in confusion through the rain and the thunder?—and as the news of victory spread from village to village, thousands of fresh volunteers flocked

to join the black flag of San-yuan-li. So when, next day, Monday, the thirty-first, Gough looked north over the hills and dales of the "ninety-six villages," he saw the irregulars collecting again, dark masses of them. By two o'clock they numbered, he estimated, ten to twelve thousand. Once again they moved slowly but purposefully towards the English lines. What was he to do?

To sit still was to risk, as before, being caught with no room to maneuver, so Gough prepared to send the 37th and the 49th to scatter the horde a second time. Meanwhile, however, he informed She Pao-shun that if it came to fighting, he would immediately denounce the truce and count himself at liberty to strike at Ishan's regulars where and when he pleased. If it was to be war again to the northward, it should be war also—if it suited him—to the south.

The upshot was that the prefect left the city and hurried over in person to assure Gough that the irregulars had assembled without the knowledge and against the wishes of the authorities. This was not true; though they marched for their villages it was the gentry who led them, and it was official Canton that had asked the gentry to do so; but Gough accepted the assurance, it being coupled with an offer to send the irregulars packing. Then She Pao-shun, accompanied by the Nanhai magistrate (no longer Lu but another), the Panyu magistrate, and one of Gough's own officers, crossed to where the advance elements of the army of righteousness stood upon a little hill, and told the notables at its head that peace had been signed and that the English must be allowed to leave unmolested. One by one the notables withdrew. Leaderless, the immense crowd of peasants gradually drifted away.

That was the end of the affair. Next day Gough took his men and guns back to Tsingpu, had the *Nemesis* tow them down to the waiting ships, and shut himself up in the cabin of the *Marion* to write Auckland an official account of all that had happened. In this account San-yuan-li figured only incidentally and not under that name. It had been an interesting episode, it had been for a time an alarming episode—but it had effected nothing. Gough saw no reason to make much of it.

It was otherwise with the Chinese. For them San-yuan-li was instantly a great popular victory. All about the countryside the heroic tale spread: how, when the bannermen and green standard troops proved unable to control the marauding foreign devils, the gongs of San-yuan-li had called the common people to arms; how they had risen by the thousands and tens of thousands, wives with husbands, hoe and mattock in hand, and had fallen upon the *fan kuei*, killing many (including a general with a head as big as a bucket), driving the rest towards the provincial city; and how they would have cornered and killed them all if the authorities had not stepped in. Canton believed this. "Mowqua told Mr. King yesterday," wrote Coolidge from the factories early in June—he meant not Charles King, who of course had left China, but Edward King of Russell and Company—"that if the mandarins had not interfered, the twenty thousand villagers who rose against the British troops would have made an end of them."[9] Peking heard the story. Before many weeks had passed the governor-general of Fukien and Chekiang was imploring the emperor to raise similar armies of righteousness throughout the empire. In time San-yuan-li entered the realm of patriotic legend, becoming part of the intellectual baggage of all Chinese—"a Bunker Hill and an Alamo," as Wakeman puts it, "rolled into one."[10]

It had more immediate consequences too. In September, when She Pao-shun went to the examination hall to administer a prefectural exam, the candidates shouted, threw inkstones, abused the Nanhai and Panyu magistrates when they tried to smooth the waters, and in the end forced She to resign. These candidates had not forgotten the act of betrayal on the hill outside Canton. They had not forgotten the prefect and those same two magistrates ordering, in the presence of a barbarian officer, the soldiers of righteousness to disperse. San-yuan-li had politicized the rural scholars as it had politicized the peasants. They hated the foreigners; they distrusted their own officials; they had experienced, briefly and intoxicatingly, their own power. This configuration would be repeated, would spread across China and be ever more intensely felt, until in the end it brought down the Manchus and with them the Confucian system of elitist government. For though the emperor and his ministers were content to manage the barbarians in the old, familiar way, the gentry and the peasants were not—were determined, instead, to throw the barbarians out—and as the years passed, threatened ever more furiously to chuck the emperor, dismiss his ministers, and do the job themselves.

The English had no inkling of this. They withdrew from the river, sorry they had not been allowed to storm Canton, but carrying with them the pleasurable feeling that they had earned $6 million in a mere eight days. On 5 June, Elliot published the terms of the Canton settlement. On the seventh he announced a public auction of lots on the north shore of Hongkong, at the same time urging the English mercantile community to move its business there. The auction was duly held and thirty-four lots sold, at prices ranging from $80 to $900. (Jardine Matheson bought the largest and choicest parcel, several lots side by side, which gave the house three hundred feet of sea frontage.) Meanwhile plans were made to send the expedition up the coast to Amoy and beyond, as originally planned.

There was a difficulty, however, in getting the expedition under way. Though the ships and regiments had left the unwholesome confinement of the river for presumably healthier Hongkong, the physical condition of the force was visibly deteriorating. Diarrhea turned to dysentery, malaria appeared where simple agues had been before; Mac-Pherson, tending the sepoys of the 37th in the great bamboo and mat shed that did duty as a hospital, noticed with astonishment that half-healed old wounds, small sores, and even scratches easily suppurated and grew gangrenous. The fact was that the men were exhausted. And for once the sailors were as exhausted as the troops.

The seventy-fours had spent weeks up the river; the frigates and the lesser craft had spent as much as three months there. Alarms and skirmishes in cramped waters, with the continual backbreaking work of warping by hand off mudbanks and up narrow waterways (there were, of course, not nearly enough steamers to go around), had tired both officers and men, and the eight days with Bourchier's naval brigade on the heights above Canton had worn them down still further. Now the lists of sick grew longer and longer. The *Conway* resembled a floating hospital (she had been east four years), the *Alligator* and the *Sulphur* were hardly better, the *Modeste*, in the Typa trying to wash away layers of accumulated river mud, rarely mustered twenty seamen fit for duty. On 13 June, Senhouse died of a violent fever compounded by fatigue and, it was said, extreme vexation. Twelve sailors from the *Blenheim* carried his coffin to the little Protestant cemetery at Macao. Frigate captains were his pallbearers, Gough walked in the procession; Pinto came and brought an honor guard to fire three volleys over the grave. But Elliot was spared the embarrassment of attending in death the man he had so bitterly disappointed in life. At the moment he was sick in bed himself.

Civilians suffered too. Samuel Fearon, the interpreter, was desperately ill. Libois, whom Legrégeois groomed to take over the management of the *procure*, lay for weeks at death's door—which greatly alarmed the procurator as it threatened to prevent his leaving China. One old China hand actually died. "It is with great grief I have to announce," wrote Matheson to Cosmo Innes of Edinburgh on 2 July, "the death of your brother, which took place at four o'clock yesterday morning, after a protracted illness of which the first symptons had developed nearly two years ago at Manila."[11] Innes, it seemed, had been diagnosed of an ulcer, had refused to take care of himself or pay attention to his doctor's orders, and had grown steadily worse and worse, until at the end he was confined to his couch, could eat nothing, and was quite unable to speak. Though he had done quite well in the opium traffic, his insistence on making his own way in his own vessels (he had recently sunk nearly

$30,000 into a new brig) had swallowed all his gains, and he died owing Jardine Matheson money. Matheson waived the debt. Perhaps he paid for Innes's monument too. There it stands in the Protestant cemetery, not far from Senhouse's and nearly as tall and fine.

Gradually the sickness abated. Bremer returned from Calcutta bringing the *Queen*, the April overland, and his own appointment as joint plenipotentiary in Admiral Elliot's place. The *Calliope* sailed for India with half of the $6 million in silver, the *Conway* (still sickly) for England with the other half. Ann Noble went too, with a new baby, ten thousand dollars raised by public subscription, and the satisfaction of knowing that her reminiscences (which the *Press* was printing) had gone into a second edition. To Palmerston, Elliot wrote that the expedition would start north soon after the middle of July. Then the weather took a hand.

For days the boat people had been prophesying trouble. On Tuesday, 20 July, Elliot and Bremer quit Macao for Hongkong in the cutter *Louisa*. There was a light wind, but towards noon it died away, and the tide being contrary the little craft anchored for the night off Lantao. The water was glassy smooth, the air sultry; at dusk the great black clouds that gathered every evening to the northeast grew blacker than ever, and thunder rumbled among the hills. Then darkness descended, a breeze sprang up, and squalls followed, each heavier than the last. By dawn it was clear that a typhoon was passing over the gulf.

It struck hardest about Hongkong. The wind, which came first from the northwest but wore around by degrees to the east, grew steadily stronger and stronger until the fiercer gusts laid even quite large vessels gunwale under. If a ship's ground tackle held and her master had had the foresight to house his topmasts, send down spars, and otherwise make everything secure, she rode out the storm with no great difficulty, for there was very little sea, the wind in that confined space tending to flatten the surface of the water. The danger came when a ship dragged anchor or snapped her cable. Warships, transports, and merchantmen crowded the Hongkong anchorage, and so heavy was the rain and so thick the spindrift that a ship loose could be right on top of a ship moored before either knew it. Even for the snugly secured there were perils and spectacles enough. Broken spars flew horizontally through the air, small boats leapt intact from their davits, mainmasts bent like bows. Most frightful of all was the sight of scores of native craft running before the blast, the men half paralyzed with fear, the women and children clutching each other in mute despair, visible one moment, lost to view the next, driving helplessly towards the Hongkong shore until they foundered or broke up or were smashed to pieces upon the rocks. On the island things were not much better. MacPherson, making his morning rounds, was pinned to the ground when the 37th's makeshift hospital collapsed on top of him, struggled free, helped injured sepoys to other shelters, and saw them blow down too. All along the sea's edge was an indescribable confusion of smashed timbers, bilged boats, and dead Chinese. Torrents of water rushed down the gullies; avalanches of mud and rock swept huts and their inhabitants away. The bazaar was wrecked. On the drenched ground torn matting and splintered bamboos mingled with what remained of the household belongings of the Chinese.

Wednesday afternoon the typhoon blew itself out. For four days the weather was quiet though unsettled. Then on Monday a second typhoon struck the gulf. From this double blow the expedition did not instantly recover.

It was not that many ships had actually been lost. A couple of merchantmen with broken backs; a few transports and lesser craft gone hard aground; several passage schooners (the unfortunate *Black Joke* among them) wrecked on this island or that; the *Snarley Yow* missing somewhere between Hongkong and Macao with Jardine Matheson treasure; the *Rose*, no longer Russell and Company's but Heerjeebhoy's, missing on her way down from Namoa—that was about the extent of it. A score of vessels had had masts snapped or cut away, and a price had been paid in broken rudders, smashed bowsprits, and battered hulls for ground tackle that did not hold. But none of the seventy-fours or frigates had suffered anything for which they remotely needed to be docked. The *Nemesis*, coolly riding to both bowers under Kowloon's lea, had suffered nothing at all.

Nevertheless, every ship was a mess and every regiment bedraggled. Stores were scattered, canvas torn, barracks reduced to matchwood. Worst of all, it was discovered that except for one small stock in the hands of a Macao merchant (who made a killing because of it), there were almost no fresh masts and spars to be had closer than Singapore—and scarcely a vessel but needed some. Men-of-war carried spares in relative abundance. They figured to replace top hamper after any serious action. Even they had trouble now, and though masters paid good money to ransack wrecks and thought nothing of using the stump of a foremast to tongue a mizzen, getting the expedition's transports promptly into sailing order was a thing quite out of the question.

So the expedition's departure had to be put off once more. At this juncture the *Good Success*, arriving from Bombay with her usual cargo of Malwa and raw cotton, brought news that caused it to be postponed still further. She had been close to the gulf when the first typhoon struck; she had lain close-reefed for eighteen hours, rescued forty-six Chinese from a sinking junk, and on the twenty-third dropped anchor in Macao Roads.

Aboard her was the May overland. When its contents had been examined, everyone's thoughts turned to Elliot.

Elliot was not immediately available. The *Louisa* had had a very hard time of it in the first typhoon. She had been blown all about the outer islands, lost her skipper, and at last been wrecked. How Elliot and Bremer got themselves and the crew to safety in spite of the hostility of the island people and their near capture by a mandarin boat is a story in itself. They stepped ashore at the Bar Fort on the twenty-fourth, Bremer in dirty white trousers and blue seaman's frock, Elliot looking no better, and learned that Elliot would soon cease to be master of the scene. Her Majesty's government was sending a new man to take charge of things in China.

22

A Winter of Waiting

One would give a good deal to know what Charles Elliot thought and felt when he learned that he was through. He left no diary, no private papers, and never set down his reminiscences, nor did his wife though she survived him. There are only his official dispatches to go by (to the end of 1839 they had, of course, already been published at Parli; .nent's request)—these, what people said of him, and a long but sober vindication of his conduct, which he prepared when he reached London, sending it over to Downing Street with the prayer that it might be laid before Parliament (it was not). What people said of him was mostly bad. The chorus of disapproval on both sides of the world was so intense and so prolonged that a family friend, the civil servant and minor poet Henry Taylor, felt obliged to enter the fray on Elliot's behalf, preparing a digest of his dispatches which is said to have greatly influenced the Duke of Wellington (and was subsequently translated into German), later putting him in the verse play *Edwin the Fair* as Earl Athulf. "I must be patient," reflects that noble lord towards the end of this interesting piece, "yet it frets my heart, amongst my many cares, to be reviled by shallow coxcombs whom I daily save, rescue, redeem, snatch from a rubbishy tomb. . . . God help them!" For a poet Taylor was surprisingly generous with verbs.* But still we do not feel that we know Elliot well.

Perhaps he resembled what his little son grew up to be, a man (remembers someone who knew Frederick at Haileybury in the 1850s) "with an indescribable air of noblesse, an imperturbable temper, a ready flow of talk, a keen and subtle wit, and an utterly calm and cheerful disposition."[1] Elliot's letters while confined at Canton were not nearly so

*Taylor became acquainted with the Elliots through the Colonial Office, where both he and Charles's younger brother, Frederick, worked. *Edwin the Fair* appeared in the summer of 1842. Later Taylor addressed Elliot directly with *Heroism in the Shade*. "His glory blossoms in the shade," this ode avers, "unseen save by the few"—which was true enough, Elliot being then in Texas.

frantic as Napier's had been; the jeers and insults thrown at him month after month by the two Canton newspapers and a segment of the English merchant community (not to mention Innes) seem never to have ruffled him; and at least one serving officer testifies that he continued to be personally popular with the expedition long after his wisdom and judgment had ceased to command its respect. The *Times* estimated him differently. When, in the autumn of 1841, it learned he was approaching England, it announced as a certainty that he would try to slip into the country unnoticed and thereafter hide his face. Elliot did nothing of the sort. His movements were perfectly open and his manner assured; Greville, the diarist, meeting him one November day at dinner, reports that he held a large company spellbound with his account of the China business, an account in which tales and amusing anecdotes mingled with the sharpest cuts at Senhouse and Gough. The dispatches of the latter had long since reached the press, of course, but if London society expected the recalled plenipotentiary to be put out of countenance by what they or anybody else said, it was very much mistaken.

Just the same, the recall had every appearance of being justified, for Elliot had not done what he had been told to do. He had received a considerable force of ships and men, had used that force haltingly and sparingly, and in the end had accepted terms far short of those he had been expected to obtain—all the while raising insubordination to the level, as it were, of a first principle. "Throughout the whole course of your proceedings," protested Palmerston, "you seem to have considered that my instructions were waste paper, which you might treat with entire disregard, and that you were at full liberty to deal with the interests of your country according to your own fancy."[2] How could Her Majesty's China business possibly be conducted as it should if her servants behaved like this?

Elliot replied that it had been a very peculiar war, a war so strange, and fought so far from home, that he who carried it on was bound to deviate from the letter of his instructions. In his case, moreover, the instructions he deviated from were based on what he himself had reported; if his opinion changed, his instructions (he assumed) must change too. Or, as he put it a little later apropos of his accepting Hongkong in place of Chusan: "It is clear that we have all been instructing ourselves, Lord Palmerston, the Governor-General of India, and myself, in this expedition of experiences, so heavily visited by sickness and accident and storm."[3]

Over the course of seven years' contact with the Chinese, Elliot, one feels, really *had* instructed himself. He had discovered, for example, that if anything was to be got from the emperor or his ministers, they must be approached circumspectly, with only a hint of menace. "The language in which the demands of Her Majesty's government is pressed," he had once written Palmerston, "can hardly be too profoundly respectful. To consult the situation and prejudices of the Government is as necessary as to awaken their fears."[4] He had perceived that from a practical point of view good relations with Canton meant more than a treaty with Peking, since it was on good relations that trade depended, and trade must be his first concern. Had not the pauses imposed upon the river campaign in the winter and spring of 1841 made possible the movement of thirty million pounds of tea worth in duties to the treasury £3 million? He had come to see that, though the Chinese must be knocked about a little, reason alone being incapable of shifting them, it was foolish to land armies, fight battles, and occupy their towns—the thing cost more in bitterness and hostility than it could possibly return. "We are all wrong to think of waging war with China in any way but by our ships," Greville has him saying at that November dinner.[5] Perhaps he had also learned to feel a certain compassion for these people, a certain fondness even. His detractors were only too sure that he had.

But Palmerston had never intended a learning experience, for himself, Elliot, or anybody else. For years he had left the chief superintendent with partial instructions—with no instructions at all, some said—because what happened or did not happen in that distant quarter of the globe could hardly disturb Whitehall. An expedition involving three seventy-fours, half a dozen regiments, and hundreds of thousands of pounds put the matter in quite a different light, however. Such an expedition must obtain what it was sent out to obtain. Very early in 1841 Palmerston had begun to fear that it would not.

The failure to bring the Chinese to terms at the Peiho had been disquieting. There might be good practical reasons for moving the negotiations back to Canton, but must Captain Elliot, in his exchanges with Kishen, put up with language so charged with condescension, language so very like what the Chinese directed at tribute-bearers from Korea or the Liu-chiu Islands? In unconcealed irritation Palmerston returned Elliot samples of the humiliating stuff, samples drawn from Elliot's own dispatches, each offending passage carefully underlined. That was in January. In February, Palmerston received Elliot's request that he soften his instructions—and declined to do so. By March, with news from China up almost to Christmas time, he was beginning to agree with Emily Eden, Auckland's sister, that "the Chinese have bamboozled us, that is the plain truth."[6] Then there arrived, on 8 April—carried to Calcutta by the *Enterprize* steamer, to Suez with the 12 March overland from Bombay, and across France by semaphore—word of a decisive January battle at the Bogue. For a moment the prospects seemed bright.

"SUCCESSFUL TERMINATION OF THE AFFAIR WITH CHINA," cried the *Times*. Forty-eight hours later, however, the full overland was in hand, with details of Elliot's Chuenpi Convention, and Palmerston knew that in return for Hongkong and $6 million, Chusan had been given up and the guns stopped.

His disappointment was extreme. Hongkong as far as he could judge was a barren island without a port, without a town, without houses even, and as the English would not be sovereign there (cession of sovereignty required the emperor's signature), it could hardly become more than a second Macao. The $6 million did not cover the cost of the confiscated twenty thousand chests, let alone pay the hong debts or the expenses of the expedition; besides, the Chinese had years in which to pay and would almost certainly raise the money by levying increased duties on English goods. As for the abandonment of Chusan, that meant no additional opening for trade up the China coast—"a capital point in our view." Yet the force at Elliot's disposal had carried all before it! It was past belief. "*All* we wanted might have been got," wrote the youthful Victoria to her uncle Leopold, king of the Belgians, when the foreign secretary had explained things to her a little, "if it had not been for the unaccountably strange conduct of Charles Elliot (*not Admiral* Elliot, for *he* was obliged to come away from ill health), who completely disobeyed his instructions and *tried* to get the *lowest* terms he could."[7] In his letter of recall Palmerston did not put the matter quite so harshly. This, however, was the unflattering estimate that went the rounds of London's clubs and salons; the *Times*, which made it a point to give its public what its public wanted, hastened to ring changes on the same theme; and though it was only Easter, long before England could know anything about Gough checked on the heights above Canton, the city spared, the river evacuated—long before these things, in fact, had even happened—from every quarter pressure grew to put the China business into abler and more trustworthy hands. Elliot must go.

On the last day of April, therefore, the cabinet decided to recall the chief superintendent. A certain Sir William Parker had already been selected to replace Charles Elliot's cousin, George, as commander-in-chief, the East Indian Station (which meant naval commander in China). Gough was to remain at the head of the land forces. To complete the triad the Melbourne administration turned to Sir Henry Pottinger, a veteran officer of the Bombay army who, in thirty years of travel and political work along the northern littoral of the Arabian Sea, had acquired a considerable reputation for skill and daring. It was Pottinger who had arranged in 1839 for the Bombay troops to pass through Sind on their way to Afghanistan. Early in 1840, just turned fifty and somewhat low in spirits, he had retired to England. There his spirits revived, he grew rest-less, and the suggestion that he become sole plenipotentiary and chief superintendent at £6,000 a year (twice what Elliot was getting) found him willing and ready. "A better man you could not have," observed one correspondent in a letter that reached Macao with Elliot's recall. "I really congratulate you, for he is up to all the tricks and chicanery of the native courts, and rely on it will not allow himself to be humbugged."[8]

Not to be humbugged. That was the chief consideration now.

Pottinger and Parker left London with the June mail. There had been talk of their turning aside to Calcutta for a talk with Auckland, but the season was already far along (no one knew anything about the sickness or the typhoons, of course) and at Bombay, where they rested a week and read Auckland's letters, it was decided to make straight for China in the new steam frigate *Sesostris*. She reached Macao on the evening of 9 August. Next morning Elliot came out to meet them, there was a formal landing to a salute from Portuguese guns, and the whole party repaired to James Matheson's house, where Gough happened to be staying. "Sir Henry delivered your letter of introduction," Matheson wrote Jardine, "and we gave him a dinner to meet the commercial community, on all of whom and ourselves he has made a favorable impression." Two weeks passed before Elliot sailed. The interval passed without unpleasantness, Elliot in good spirits laughingly telling Matheson that he had long ex-pected to be replaced, that he had in fact "sent home his resignation per *Enterprize* steamer in January." Matheson was sorry to see him go. He had not forgotten the affair of the *Kosciusko*; and though he had no inten-tion of trying to justify Elliot's general policy and would not argue that Palmerston was wrong to bring the fellow home, he did wish to give him credit where credit was due. The March business of hostilities suspended and trade resumed, for example—how much wiser that had been than carrying the war immediately to Canton. "I hope you will give Captain Elliot a friendly reception,"[9] he wrote Jamsetjee in Bombay and John Abel Smith in London. Then Elliot was off, Elliot's wife and child and Bremer and his lady accompanying him aboard the *Atalanta*. Much bat-tered, that steamer was retiring from the China service too.

Nevertheless there was no denying that Elliot's departure meant a stiffening of England's stance. Pottinger was barely known about Macao when he published the warning that bringing the Chinese to terms must henceforth take precedence over buying their teas. "The English," ob-served Bridgman approvingly, "now *make war*."[10]

It was in the north they meant the fighting to be. "We have received orders to prepare for sea immediately," wrote an officer of the Royal

Irish towards the middle of August. "Everything is in a state of confusion, and the decks of the ship present an extraordinary appearance—guns, howitzers, provisions, water casks, rocket tubes, brought on board and thrown down in a heap."[11] Early that summer Fort William had dispatched drafts for the three European regiments already under Gough's command and an entire fresh regiment, the 55th. Stores also had reached the gulf: thirty-two-pound shot by the thousands, musket cartridges by the tens of thousands, powder by the ton, four hundred of the new percussion muskets with fifty thousand caps to match, salt meat, flour, peas, lime juice, and from Singapore three thousand gallons of arrack. (Among the medicines was a quantity of opium.) By mid-August some of the new men were sick or dying and some of the stores scattered or destroyed, but enough remained to make a fair force for a campaign northward. On the twenty-first it sailed—the 18th, the 55th, parts of the 26th and 49th, with artillery, sappers and miners, and marines—in fifteen transports accompanied by the *Wellesley*, the *Blenheim*, and half a dozen ships carrying stores and coal. Seven lesser men-of-war went along and four steamers. (One was the iron *Phlegethon*, very like the *Nemesis*—indeed, it was John Laird who had built her, in his Birkenhead yard.) The *Nemesis* herself was one of the four. Though she had been worked desperately hard all winter and spring, been hit repeatedly, and run aground more times than anyone could remember, her engines were in excellent condition and the strengthening timbers put in at Delagoa Bay entirely secure and sound.

Fair winds brought the fleet the three hundred miles to Amoy by the twenty-fifth. Along the shore where Thom had tried to deliver Palmerston's letter there stretched now a stone battery faced with sod a mile long, but the two hundred guns it contained were as clumsily mounted and as poorly served as ever. It was no trick at all, after first pounding it for an hour or two (with astonishingly little effect, it was later discovered), to land men at its near end and roll it up from the flank. After this the city itself offered no resistance. A party of Royal Irish scaled a wall, opened a gate, and let the rest of the little army in. For a week bad weather held the fleet motionless. Then the wind settled into the south, and Gough, first arranging to leave a garrison on the island of Kulangsu, reembarked and continued up the coast.

The south wind did not hold, however. It was time for the monsoon to change. For days there was no wind at all; then it began to blow from the northeast with squalls and fog, and the fleet scattered. The transports and sailing men-of-war moved north some distance out. The steamers, their coal running low, kept close to shore and picked up wood where they could find it. Thus the *Nemesis* touched Shipu fifty miles below Chusan, burned or blew up the junks and forts that attempted to oppose her there, and collected twenty-five tons of the fuel. Approaching Keeto Point on the same errand, McCleverty of the *Phlegethon* met Dent's *Ariel* and *Lyra* and Jardine Matheson's *Ann*, and was told that a few days earlier the *Lyra*'s mate, on shore trying to buy provisions, had been attacked, beaten, and carried off. The assailants came from the vicinity of the same village where Stead of the *Pestomjee Bomanjee* had disappeared the previous March. McCleverty landed with a scratch force of armed seamen from his own steamer and the three opium ships, burned the village, marched on the nearby town of Kokgi, and burned it too. When the *Nemesis* arrived two days later there was a second landing and a second round of burnings—to relieve everyone's feelings, says the steamer's biographer—until the whole valley was ablaze with spreading fires. A just measure of retribution, remarked Admiral Parker when he heard of the affair. "I sincerely hope that it may have the effect of checking similar acts of atrocity on the part of the Chinese."[12]

By 25 September the last of the fleet had rounded Keeto Point and lay at anchor off Just-in-the-Way, a dozen miles east of Chinhai. Chinhai was next in line for attack. But the coast there was exposed to the northeast monsoon, which for the moment continued to blow fiercely, so it was decided to turn to Tinghai. Reconnaissance disclosed a half-completed battery in front of Joss-House Hill, a battery running the full width of the valley and actually longer than the one at Amoy (though it had very little stone in it). Once again, however, the Chinese had left their flanks up in the air. On 1 October, Gough put the 55th and the 18th ashore west of the battery and sent them up the hill immediately in front. It was a lovely day, the first for some time without rain, and everyone was in good spirits. Climbing the hill with his men, Gough was struck harmlessly on the shoulder by a spent musket ball. Minutes later an ensign of the 55th was hit and killed, for the Chinese resisted bravely, one man standing erect waving a large red banner until a thirty-two-pound shot from the *Phlegethon* literally cut him in two. Then the hill was Gough's, and while the 55th made straight for Tinghai, the 18th turned and pushed down into the battery. By two in the afternoon Joss-House Hill had fallen and the Chinese had fled. Signs of the previous English occupation were everywhere. The 18th, searching for billets, discovered its old company numbers in chalk on the doors of a number of houses. Someone found Oglander's gravestone set into a doorstep (in retaliation the house was razed). Patrols went briefly into the countryside, a permanent garrison was arranged, and on the seventh the rest of the force boarded transports and headed for Chinhai.

Here the going looked to be a good deal more difficult. Chinhai lay on a narrow peninsula between the mouth of the Yung river and the sea. At the tip of this peninsula, commanding both the town and the mouth (which was effectively staked), was a great rock over two hundred feet high, with very steep sides and a citadel on top. To scale the rock without first silencing the citadel was unthinkable, yet on its sea side the water was so shoal that seventy-fours and frigates could hardly hope to get within a mile of it in any sort of sea. South of the river, moreover, the Chinese had numerous field works and a considerable army. The ranking mandarin on the spot was Yukien, the man quoted earlier with regard to the curious English habit of binding the legs so tightly that once fallen they could not get up. Formerly governor of Kiangsu and now special high commissioner for Chekiang, Yukien was a determined and even ferocious fellow who, on reaching the province just after Anstruther and the other Ningpo prisoners were set free, had boasted that only death should have released them from *him*. He had driven home his point by having Pu Ting-pang, the kidnapped comprador, decapitated and his head hung in a cage. With Yukien present, the defense of Chinhai was certain to be tenacious.

Even so the place was carried in less than a day, by a military operation Mountain thought "the prettiest and smartest we have yet had."[13] At dawn Gough put fifteen hundred men ashore a few miles east of the mouth of the river and, while one column made as if to threaten the Chinese from the front, sent another swinging around behind. There was some brief, sharp fighting, and the Chinese broke and fled in confusion towards the river. Meanwhile Parker had the *Wellesley* and the *Blenheim* towed at the top of the tide to within thirteen hundred yards of the citadel rock's north face, where they anchored, settled gently into the mud, and deliberately pounded the citadel into silence. Then the marines and seamen climbed the rock, chased the garrison down its back side, scaled the town wall, and drove the garrison out the west gate. The Chinese losses were heavy. Bodies chequered the south bank where Gough's men had forced their way through to the water. There were hundreds of prisoners too. Gough let them go, though not before the tars guarding them had gleefully cut off their tails.

That afternoon Yukien tried to commit suicide by throwing himself into a pond. Attendants dragged him out and hurried him to Yuyao thirty-five miles in the interior, where he tried again (by swallowing opium) and succeeded. With his disappearance all resistance ceased. On 13 October the four steamers with the *Modeste* and two brigs in tow moved up the river and landed a force just short of Ningpo's east gate.

The gate was opened, the men marched in to the music of "Saint Patrick's Day in the Morning" played by the band of the Royal Irish, and the second city of Chekiang Province fell without a shot.

But Ningpo was as far as the barbarians got.

To have arrived there at all was something of an accident. The only place the expedition had categorically been told to seize was Chusan. Its premature evacuation the previous February had annoyed Palmerston so much that he had sent Bremer orders to reoccupy it at once, without waiting for the new plenipotentiary to appear. Amoy had been attacked because it was close to Canton, accessible in both monsoon seasons, and important for its sea trade with distant points like Singapore. Chinhai was the obvious place at which to deliver a second letter to the emperor, a letter Palmerston had drafted explaining frankly that Elliot was recalled for disobeying instructions and intimating that his successor was not likely to make the same mistake. If this letter could not be delivered at Chinhai, the natural thing to do was to continue on to Ningpo. Now Ningpo was taken; less than a hundred miles to the west lay Hangchow, the provincial capital and southern terminus of the Grand Canal, the place made famous in Europe by Marco Polo. If Hangchow could be occupied or even simply threatened, Peking might come to terms that very autumn.

By this time, however, Gough had very little to threaten Hangchow with. He had put five hundred men on Kulangsu and garrisons of equal size at Tinghai and Chinhai. He had had casualties and sick. The result was that, of the twenty-five hundred men he had started north with, not seven hundred in fit condition were still with him, and from these he had to find guards and patrols for a city said to contain a third of a million people. The *Nemesis* and the *Phlegethon* pushed further up the Yuyao branch of the river. Peasants crowded the banks and watched with stupefaction as the iron monsters steamed by. At Yuyao itself, where a stone bridge blocked the way, only the weather was hostile, the rain coming down in buckets and giving Parker rheumatism. To the rear rose an impressive ring of mountains. Ahead the plain settled gradually towards an invisible sea. It was attractive country, absolutely flat, highly cultivated, dotted with villages neatly tiled in blueish gray—and useless without men to garrison it. Native couriers sent overland to Hangchow did not come back. Someone thought of approaching the city by sea, but the Hangchow estuary was well known for its high tides and wicked tidal bore; the *Phlegethon*, reconnoitering that way in January, was very nearly flung upon a sandbank and lost. Gough would have evacuated Ningpo long before this, but Pottinger and Parker were afraid this might be taken as a sign of English weakness. So the garrison remained.

It took up quarters in public buildings near the river, on which a warship or two always lay. Mountain put pickets at every gate and sent patrols at irregular intervals through the city's principal alleys; Gough himself walked the nearly five miles of wall every day after dinner. On Wednesdays there was a public mounting of the guard in an open space before the so-called "Bell Pagoda," and when the weather was fine the men drilled there. Towards Christmas the rains ceased, frost set in with occasional snow, and life became remarkably healthy. The cold was little problem, for though Fort Williams had been advised about a winter campaign too late to send out blankets and greatcoats, it was no trick to devise bedding and even a kind of uniform out of the wadded cotton quilting the Chinese used. The men messed well off local eggs, poultry, pork, and Chinese bread. Their officers went shooting for wild fowl outside the walls, and in the evenings sat over charcoal braziers or before improvised fireplaces (four or five Chinese musket barrels made an excellent grate) in which burned furniture and window frames from abandoned houses.

There was a darker side to life at Ningpo, however, and in the end it colored everything else. The Chinese were civil enough when confronted, say, by a subaltern and a file of privates on patrol, but let that subaltern walk alone about the town and he risked being abused, pelted with refuse, or worse. On these occasions some officers used the flats of their swords. Unfortunately the flat made very little impression on padded cotton: "I might as well have beaten a pillow," remarked one after an encounter of this sort, adding that he would in future carry a good stout stick "to break the noddle of the next Chinaman who shall trespass on my dignity. They are a most insolent race. Still it is no doubt galling to have foreign barbarians strutting as lords, where a short time ago their only quarters were *cages*."[14]

The reference was to the Ningpo prisoners of a year before. The English had not been in the city an hour when they came across the building in which Anstruther, Mrs. Noble, and the others had been kept, saw on the walls the sketches and mess accounts they had left, and discovered their cages. Methodically they tore the building apart and used the timbers for firewood. For that whole episode had been thoroughly shameful, and though Anstruther took it lightly enough—happening to accompany the entering party, he saved his own cage and sent it home to Madras— many of his countrymen did not at all enjoy being reminded of their disgrace.*

*Even Anstruther did not wish the business to be totally forgotten. When William Milne, Jr., arrived a year later to open Ningpo's first Protestant Mission, he discovered the following graffiti on the city's principal pagoda:

P. Anstruther, *prisoner 16 Sept. 1840 to 23 Feb. 1841*
P. Anstruther, *free and master 13 Oct. 1841*

The English would have dealt severely with Ningpo anyhow. They were hundreds of miles from Canton and its inhibiting tea trade; besides, there was the question of money. China *must* pay—that had always been the intention and the plan—and with the fighting in its second year and likely to go into a third, it behooved everybody to seize as much silver (or as much property convertible into silver) as they could. Prize agents had been appointed and a prize court arranged for Singapore; officers and men of both the land and the sea forces could expect, when the campaigning was over and the accounts rendered, to share in the profits of the expedition—provided always that there were any.

There had been some thought of demanding a ransom at Amoy. One might actually have been demanded had there been a mandarin of rank to demand it of. For Ningpo, much worse was in mind. Elliot himself, throwing his usual forbearance to the winds, had recommended shortly before he went home that the place be destroyed if it did not pay up handsomely. Pottinger had entered the city on the thirteenth quite looking forward, he admitted, to a general plunder, and though the absence of resistance had obliged him to abandon the notion, he wanted every kind of public property—junks, yamens, granaries, whatever—seized and their contents sold or carried away.

The proposal made Gough nervous. Pottinger, he complained privately (he was beginning to find himself in Elliot's accustomed role of the sober old-timer trying to restrain the hotheads), seemed to think that Peking would submit if the Chinese in the provinces were treated harshly enough. "Now this might apply to France, where the people's voice must have a strong influence on the acts of the Government, but in China it is chimerical. The Government care not for the people, and I verily believe the most annoying thing you could do is to prove to the people by our moderation and our justice that our characters are foully belied."[15] He, Pottinger, and Parker often dined together, and they argued the point. In December, again over Gough's objections, a 10 percent levy on private property was decreed. Meanwhile the official looting of public stores went gaily forward. The great bell from the pagoda started off for Calcutta with a quantity of copper from the foundries at Chinhai. The government granary was opened and all comers were invited to buy rice at the ridiculous price of a dollar a sack, with the result that crowds came, and the prize fund grew fatter by a thousand dollars a day. Not much *sycee* was discovered, only a little sugar and saltpeter, but in the treasury there was an immense heap of the copper and lead cash that the Chinese used in daily commerce, and these the prize agents threaded on strings, packed into sacks, and sent off to India too—one account says $160,000 worth.

And as the winter wore on and this bold spoliation of public property was matched by the intermittent and even more bitterly resented theft of private goods, the atmosphere at Ningpo grew more and more tense. Gutzlaff was civil magistrate and undisputed king of the place, the only foreigner around who knew Chinese, for the expedition was as short of interpreters as ever: Thom at Chinhai and Medhurst at Tinghai (not the Medhurst of the *Huron*, but his son) were his nearest rivals. Day after day Gutzlaff dispensed a summary justice so bold and so effective that a local poet composed a song about it. As Arthur Waley translates the piece, "Daddy Kuo" (that was what the Chinese called him) sits on his dais briskly settling matters of fraud, theft, and petty disorder, when suddenly he pauses, takes brush and paper, and in a large hand writes out the English case for the war: twenty thousand chests wrongfully confiscated, twenty thousand chests that must be paid for; and the people in the courtroom read, and some dutifully copy, which makes Daddy chuckle and offer everybody biscuits. But Gutzlaff did more. He raised a native police force. He also recruited and directed spies. Early in the winter of 1842 his spies told him that bodies of troops were concentrating to retake the city.

Indeed they were. A certain Iching, cousin to the emperor, had been dispatched from Peking with orders to drive the English into the sea. From his headquarters first at Soochow, later in a village hardly fifty miles northwest of Ningpo, he collected troops from half a dozen provinces and raised militia too. In an effort to keep Iching off balance, Gough led little expeditions into the countryside, to Yuyao again and along the southwest branch of the Yung River as far as Fenghwa. His men met soldiers and braves, chased them smartly across frozen rice fields knee-deep in snow, destroyed arms and ammunition, and returned to Ningpo in great good spirits with trophies and a little *sycee* for the prize fund. Nevertheless the threatening concentration continued. At last, on the night of 9 March, the Ningpo garrison was surprised by a sudden and vigorous assault.

It was launched simultaneously upon the south and west gates and for a time, in the darkness and confusion, seemed likely to succeed. Perhaps it would have if Iching had managed to put in motion anything like the numbers he had intended, and if heavy rain and the breaking of the frost had not made the approaches to the city almost impassable for mud. The picket at the south gate was overwhelmed and forced to retreat along the top of the wall. The attackers broke into the city and got as far as the central market. There, however, they were checked and driven back; meanwhile at the west gate, where the assault was heaviest, the English held. At dawn 150 of Gough's men dragging a single field piece cleared the ground immediately before that gate, pushed on into the suburb, met a small army of Chinese jammed in a narrow street, and cut it to pieces with grape and repeated musket volleys, each file firing, retiring to load, then coming up to fire again. In ten minutes the street was choked waist high with dead and dying; even Peninsula veterans allowed that they had never seen so many bodies in so confined a space. The Chinese dead approached five hundred; the English did not lose a man. An assault on Chinhai the same night got nowhere. After that the Chinese attempted nothing beyond a few fireboat attacks, the largest of which (at Tinghai using several dozen flaming craft) accomplished nothing either.

Though the English could not be dislodged or made to suffer significant losses, they were certainly not left in peace. Chusan stayed quiet enough. The Chinese there were resigned to an indefinite occupation; the English stuck close to their fortified camp about Joss-House Hill and patrolled the neighboring waters relentlessly.* On the mainland, however, it was impossible to keep aloof and safe. Even before the night assault on Ningpo there had been attempts at kidnapping and murder, and now they multiplied. Several men of the 55th were fed poisoned food, with fatal consequences in one case. A private of the 49th was discovered in a bag, "his hands tied behind him to his legs, which were doubled back. Three or four more lashings were about him, and a large walnut, with hair wound round it, had been forced into his mouth, the sides of which were cut to admit it. He was quite dead."[16] On a single afternoon the Chinese managed to abduct one of the *Modeste*'s marines and two of Anstruther's gun lascars. Gutzlaff did his best, but his native police were nearly useless, particularly after their chief was kidnapped and killed. Gutzlaff himself narrowly escaped injury when an infernal machine exploded near him in the street; no sensible officer went anywhere without a two- or three-barreled pistol in his pocket. After a time the occupiers themselves began to lose all restraint. They scoured the countryside, they put houses to the torch, they brought suspects back tied together by their tails and set fire to the quarter where the private of the 49th had died. A good many Chinese had already quit the city. Many more left now. Those who remained burned and plundered without hindrance. Whole sections of the city were gutted; the rest assumed a more and more desolate and abandoned air.

Very little of this ugly aspect of things comes through in the official dispatches. These are as brisk and breezy as ever, as expressive of soldiers' duties nobly performed, of gallant deeds calculated to afford the highest

*On one of these patrols the *Nemesis* happened to strike a submerged rock, which tore a large hole in her bottom. The water poured in and threatened to put out her fires, but Hall, calmly running her aground on the nearest sandy beach, let the tide ebb, dug the sand away from about the tear, applied a patch, and was away with the flood. It was his boast that nothing could stop his iron ship, and nothing did.

satisfaction to the public and the crown. A week after the Ningpo assault, Gough took a mixed force of soldiers and armed seamen up the river to Tzeki. There he attacked and scattered a small army that had collected on the hills north of the town. It was a spirited action, the Chinese for a change were competently handled and fought with great determination, and the compliments Gough addressed to his men (and to Parker, who had personally led the seamen) were in consequence even warmer than usual. But one officer did not feel at all good about the affair. Towards the end of the day he happened to come across a curious and macabre scene. "Two British sailors and a soldier about fifty yards apart from each other formed the points of a triangle, in which some six or eight Chinese were running helplessly about over the paddy fields, some disarmed and others with swords in their hands. Our three men were loading and firing at them as coolly as if they were crows, and bayoneting to death those who fell wounded." The officer tried to stop them. They paid no attention; and another soldier, coming up, took a shot himself and said: "If we don't kill them now, Sir, they will fight us again, and we shall never finish the war."[17]

Never finish the war! It was certainly dragging on longer than anyone had supposed it would. And it was not going to be finished there in Chekiang Province—that was more than ever the opinion towards the end of this weary winter of hostility and waiting.

23

Hongkong

Pottinger did not pass the entire winter in the north. Shortly after the new year he set sail in the *Blenheim*, paused briefly at Kulangsu to inspect the little garrison and squadron that watched Amoy from that island, and early in February 1842 arrived at Hongkong.

He found the place a good deal changed. "Two thousand Chinese laborers are building a road right round the island," Legrégeois had reported excitedly early the previous summer.[1] This was not true, nothing so ambitious had in fact been undertaken; yet there was a road as Pottinger could see, the Queen's Road, along the northern shore. The tops of the spurs that come down to the water had been sliced away, the gullies filled or bridged; from East Point (where Jardine Matheson, despite its initial land purchases, was doing the bulk of its building) past Possession Point and on to the northwest tip of the island, you could drive now with perfect ease—as one foreigner regularly did, in a carriage and pair brought over from Manila for the purpose. Along this road, which was almost four miles in length, there had grown a straggling ribbon of a town, a town of eight thousand, one count suggests, containing among other things three-score ships' chandlers, two dozen brothels, and a single confectioner. The Tanka people, who formed perhaps a quarter of the Chinese population, lived in boats moored close against the shore, boats fifteen feet long and five to six wide, with a single mast and sail, and amidships a cabin with a low curved roof. The rest of the Chinese made do for the most part with mat sheds of the sort the July typhoons had torn to pieces. But there was a fair amount of construction in pisé, a mixture of clay, broken stone, and lime pounded between wooden forms—and a certain amount even in brick. The jail was brick, Captain Caine's magistrate's office was brick, so were the land office and the post office; on the waterfront you saw godowns of brick set upon stout stone foundations, and on the terraces overlooking Queen's Road stood private bungalows in brick, granite, or a combination of the two.

Pottinger was impressed and a little anxious too. On his first visit the previous August he had confirmed Alexander Johnston, his deputy superintendent, in the office of acting governor. Johnston had spent a good deal of time on the island and had worked hard to develop it. Pottinger was aware, however, that her Majesty's government intended that Hongkong should be kept only until the war was over and the claims against Peking settled. Then it would probably revert to the Chinese, and when it did the money sunk in it would be lost—Pottinger was certain the treasury had already thought of this. Any day now the overland would bring him instructions not to spend on the place a penny more than he absolutely had to. Looking around him at "Queen's Town" (it was not called Victoria yet), observing to what extent it had become a base for the expedition and a refuge for the foreign residents, Pottinger could not help agreeing with Auckland and the dismissed Elliot that to let the island go would be a pity.

It was unhealthy, to be sure. Wherever ground was cleared or terraces cut, the intense moisture and the burning sun brought on the "Hongkong fever," as malaria was locally called, and though things had become better with the cool dry winter weather, they would grow worse when summer came again. Sickness had already so reduced the 37th Madras Native Infantry that the survivors were sent home at the beginning of March.* The two remaining companies of Bengal volunteers withdrew, and there were many who wished Burrell away too, lest the removal of Gough by death or accident should put that "notable imbecile" (as Matheson called him) in Gough's place. It was already clear, however, that only a court martial would dislodge Burrell. He stayed on, supervising the garrison from a vessel in the harbor, doing very little to make it less sickly, but doing it comfortably and at great public expense.

Hongkong had another disadvantage: it did not take Canton's place in the tea trade. Teas were leaving the gulf in almost normal quantities, but they came as usual from Canton, that was where the Chinese tea men were still to be found, and so, perforce, interested foreigners had to be there too. Late that winter the American and French flags rose over the factory square for the first time since the strangulation affair of three years before. Although the union jack did not rise with them, very few English merchants supposing it safe for them to move back yet, English ships loaded quite normally at Whampoa. The transshipping business did not revive.

Opium was another matter. Coasters and clippers no longer bothered with Lintin or the other outer anchorages. They paused sometimes in Macao Roads, and a few lay from time to time at Whampoa, but Whampoa

*For the gallantry and steadiness of the single company cut off near San-yuan-li in May, the 37th was shortly appointed a grenadier regiment. It was the first of a deluge of honors that descended on persons and things in this war—a deluge that spared Charles Elliot, however.

was still an iffy place. Before putting the *Jardine* to station there, Matheson thought it prudent to change her name to *Lanrick* (after Jardine's recently purchased Perthshire estate) and to superscribe her delivery chits with a fictitious "Thomason and Company." Only Hongkong was both convenient and entirely safe. A great many opium vessels came directly there, and as a matter of course the harbor master, a Royal Navy lieutenant named Pedder, inserted them into the lists he kept and that Samuel Fearon's new *Hongkong Gazette* and the older journals published, lists showing (among other things) the cargoes each vessel carried. Ballast and government stores were there; coals, cotton, and rice; but opium too—and specie, everybody understanding perfectly how you acquired that commodity on China's coasts. It was specie the *Red Rover* brought when she reached Hongkong from Amoy early in November. At the end of February she was in again, this time from Calcutta, first clipper of the season (as in 1830, 1831, and so many other years), with no nonsense about her cargo, no concealing its nature under "whites," "greys," or "chintzes." That winter, according to Pedder's lists, every fourth vessel that touched Hongkong carried the drug.

It was not that the quantity leaving India was greater than before. If anything it was less: at the first Calcutta sale of 1842 five hundred fewer chests were sold than in the previous January, and in Bombay the export was down a little too. Demand along the coast was sluggish, Patna and Benares drifting as low as $400 a chest, Malwa as low as $350. There was, however, a special reason for vessels in considerable numbers to keep at the traffic. If the drug sold with difficulty, English manufactures sold hardly at all. Jardine's coasters carried cottons and woolens, tried hard to get rid of them, and got rid of very few. Though some cloth and a much larger volume of raw cotton found buyers in Canton, the buyers did not want to—and in many cases could not—pay silver for what they bought; they paid instead in kind. "It is vain," wrote Matheson, "to expect from the Hong Merchants a single dollar in cash for our large annual consignments of cotton and other goods, for which we are therefore compelled to take Chinese goods in exchange, chiefly Tea; and the more plentiful money is in the hands of other buyers, the more difficult we find it to obtain Teas on suitable terms."[2] Teas were something Matheson very much wished to have. Without hard coin he could obtain them neither in the best grades nor at reasonable prices.

Of course the expedition, by what it purchased, might have provided the necessary ready money. Not many distant consignors, however, were good judges of what the expedition needed. "Beer, porter, and pickles are poured into this market ten times as much as a whole army would consume, supposing it to eat or drink nothing else," complained Alexander Matheson.[3] The firm's new Hongkong godown was full of the stuff and gin too (rum would have sold more easily)—the fact was that the only article that could be depended upon to sell steadily and for cash was opium. That was why Jardine Matheson put so many vessels to the work. "It is the command of money which we derive from our large Opium dealings, and which can hardly be acquired from any other source, that gives us such important advantages."[4] When a Singapore correspondent inquired as to whether the house would accept consignments from a Chinese of that place, Alexander Matheson replied of course it would; it would be happy to have the drug "even one chest at a time, from anyone, be he Chinaman, Jew, or Gentile. It is the sort of business we are most desirous of cultivating."[5]

Never had the traffic been so open or so hotly pushed. Though opium could be landed without fuss at the godowns off Queen's Road, the general practice still was to store it in receiving ships—for Jardine's that meant the *General Wood* (sometime *Syden*) moored a few hundred yards from shore. From her, Captain Morgan managed the Jardine Matheson fleet as Grant, Parry, and Rees had managed it from her predecessors. To her came fresh supplies of the drug, to her came the treasure generated by its sale; indeed, Jardine's command of silver made that firm banker to a great many of the resident foreigners, merchant and missionary alike. Gough himself banked with Jardine's and by March of this year was overdrawn more than a thousand dollars. "You can repay in any manner most convenient," James Matheson wrote him at Ningpo, adding that he hoped Gough would occupy his old quarters in the firm's Macao house when next he came south.[6]

To the *General Wood* came also the brigs and schooners whose job it was to distribute the opium: the *Ann* and the *Harriet*, the *Hellas*, *Kelpie*, *Omega*, *Spy*, and four or five others. Demand for coasters was so brisk that anyone with a bottom to sell announced it, if at all plausible, as exactly suited for running opium. Builders in Calcutta and other places continued to lay down specifically for the purpose. From America came schooners of an unusually advanced design. Dent obtained the *Zephyr* from that quarter; Matheson was so impressed by the sailing qualities of the New York pilot schooner *Anglona* that he was on the point of making a bid for her when, the Boston-built *Ariel* (90 tons burden and not to be confused with Dent's clipper bark of the same name) happening to beat her in a race around Lintin, he turned and bought the *Ariel* instead.

He sent the *Ariel* at once to the east coast. The traffic there was so open, the English presence so marked, and the determination of the local authorities so enfeebled that life at the larger opium stations assumed an almost domestic air. At Namoa, Brig Island had been occupied outright. Visiting the place briefly in February, Abeel noticed a bridle path cut around the island and saw crews from the opium ships riding there on little Chinese ponies. He does not say so but perhaps they were joined in this exercise by Royal Navy men, for relations between the two services were friendly and close. When pirates in suspicious numbers collected off Chinchew, a corvette stationed herself there to overawe them. When a junk crammed (it was thought) with gunpowder entered the anchorage at Chimmo, up came a 16-gun brig, grappled the thing, towed it to shore, blew it up, and then bombarded Chimmo town for good measure. Opium afloat, it seemed, was entitled to the same protection that teas, silks, and cottons received, and if a coaster should be reported missing, like as not it was one of Her Majesty's ships that sailed to find her.

There were, in fact, a number of dramatic disappearances that autumn and winter. In September the *Madagascar* steamer, back at last from Calcutta and hurrying up the coast after the expedition, caught fire in heavy weather 150 miles east of Hongkong and after hours of desperate work (the fire had its seat in the coal of the aft starboard bunker and would not be quenched) had to be abandoned. Dicey and a few others managed to reach land and were taken prisoner, but by pretending that they were Americans, corresponding only through Ryan and Delano, and raising a substantial ransom, they persuaded their captors to conduct them to Macao and deliver them into Bridgman's friendly hands. Meanwhile a much worse disaster struck the transport *Nerbudda*. Beating up the coast with stores and 170 Indian camp followers, she was driven off course and wrecked on the coast of Formosa. Her master and the handful of other Europeans she carried got safely away and were picked up by an opium schooner. There had been only a few boats, however, and the camp followers and the lascar crew remained stranded on the wreck—a shameful fact that sent a corvette up from Hongkong the moment it was known. The corvette hunted everywhere. Not one of the poor Indians could be found. Months passed, and then it was the turn of Jardine Matheson's *Ann*. The *Ann* had been keeping the Chusan opium station. In March 1842 Denham was instructed to turn that station over to the *Omega* and come south, collecting Dent and Jardine treasure as he came. (The previous October, Dent had proposed that the ships of the two houses carry treasure for each other and make opium sales on joint account, and Matheson had agreed to the first suggestion though not to the second.) Denham started, disappeared, and a rumor reached Amoy that he had run aground on Formosa like the *Nerbudda* before him. Without waiting to be asked, Captain Smith of the *Druid* sent the *Pylades* to search. Again a blank—Jardine's had to reconcile itself to the loss of a useful vessel, an experienced skipper, and $50,000 in silver—but at least the Royal Navy had tried.

In the Gulf of Canton the only disappearance to rival these was that of old Thomas Beale, observed one December evening walking near Casilha's Bay, discovered a month later half buried on the beach with so little flesh on his bones that his clothes alone identified him. No one, however, suspected a repetition of what had happened to Stanton at the same place a year and a half before. Beale's extreme age and the burden of his debts (he owed the Missions Etrangères alone $5,000) had driven him, it was supposed, to suicide, or else his death had been an accident. Certainly it was not the long arm of the Canton authorities that had struck him down. They were too cowed for that.

From time to time, it was true, those authorities tried to refortify the river between the Bogue and Whampoa. In would go a steamer or a corvette, sink a few junks, tear out a few stakes, blow up a fort here and a masked battery there, and come quietly out again. That was the extent of the fighting in this part of China. That was all the war there was.

The *Water Witch* arrived with the September overland and news that Melbourne's government had finally fallen, that Peel and his Tories were in at last. Laird's most recent iron steamer, the *Medusa*, coming up from Singapore against unusually persistent head winds, exhausted her coal, burned bulwarks, wardroom furniture, and everything except her boats, and when literally within sight of Macao was obliged to turn and run all the way back to Camranh Bay. The 74-gun *Cornwallis* experienced, of course, no such difficulty. She arrived at Christmas and went immediately to Chusan to take the *Wellesley*'s place, and the *Wellesley*, fore and main masts buttressed with timbers because the years at sea had decayed them so, sailed for England carrying Mrs. Noble's cage, three enormous brass guns from the Bogue forts, and a number of officers (of whom Ellis was one). The *Melville* went home. The *Larne* went home. The *Hyacinth* went home (her crew would not sign on for another hitch). James Matheson departed. Though not seriously ill, he assured Jamsetjee, "I am summarily ordered off by the doctors to avoid the risk of getting worse should I remain over the hot weather."[7] Bingham went. Mackenzie and MacPherson went. Lancelot Dent was off—and Legrégeois too.

Still, the arrivals more than outweighed the departures. Macao was livelier than ever, houses scarce, rents high, the Praia Grande always crowded. Hongkong, at the other lip of the gulf, could not offer what the old town could. It could not, for example, put on such a ball and midnight supper as Pinto invited Pottinger to on the occasion of the queen of Portugal's birthday. The future lay with the island, however, not with the town—or so Pottinger must have decided—for at the very end of

February, four weeks after reaching the place, he collected his Superintendency from its old Macao quarters, clerks, letterbooks, Fearon the interpreter, and all and brought the whole show over.

Roberts and the Shucks followed in March. Roberts went immediately to Chek Chu (the later Stanley) on the island's south side, where there was a considerable village, and barracks were being constructed. It could be reached over the island's spine by a bridle path from Happy Valley. Lewis and Henrietta settled in Queen's Town and began to raise (by public subscription) money for not just one chapel but two. The first, a substantial brick structure right in the bazaar, was intended for the natives. The second, on Queen's Road, would serve the West.

Bridgman and Williams did not immediately join them. They remained instead at Macao in the house they kept together. Bridgman had at last finished the enormous *Chinese Chrestomathy in the Canton Dialect* and seen it through the press. He still had the *Repository* to edit, however, and he was accumulating materials for a Chinese grammar. Liang A-fa's son, Atih, was staying with him; Bridgman had it in mind to have the young man help him revise Liang's Chinese New Testament. When, at the end of March, Commodore Kearny of the American frigate *Constellation* asked him to join that vessel as interpreter, he was lost to the mission for the two months spent up the Canton River. Williams himself was extremely busy. He had his share of the *Repository* to write, the finished copy to print and bind, and a little manual to finish—*Easy Lessons in Chinese* it was cheerfully if inaccurately called. What with proofreading, printing, binding, and his usual translating work, he hardly found time to write home. A move just now would complicate his life unmercifully.

For the time being the Browns too remained at Macao. The school they kept for the Morrison Education Society had survived their absence of half a year at the Straits (they had gone for Mrs. Brown's health), and on their return in September they had managed to add sixteen boys to the half dozen survivors of the original enrollment. Some of these students had since been dismissed for stupidity or removed by their fathers, but most stayed on, boys ten to thirteen years of age, studying Chinese in the morning and English the balance of the day (it was English the parents particularly wanted, as likely to prove useful in a commercial way). When June approached and preparations were being made for the first public examination, it was gratifying to discover how keenly these young people appreciated the instruction they were receiving. "The English schools are much better than the Chinese," wrote one, "because the English learn of many useful things, such as astronomy, geometry, algebra, true religion, and many others," while the Chinese buried their heads in classical literature. How much more difficult Chinese was than English, wrote another. Though he and his fellows had studied Chinese for years, "none of us can write a Chinese letter *well*." But the greatest difference was that whereas the Chinese looked to the past, the English looked to the future. "Therefore the Chinese are always about the same, while the English become better and better. I do not mention the Americans because they are descended from them."[8] Sooner or later the school would move to Hongkong—Dent had given $3,000 for that purpose just before he sailed, and Pottinger had promised a plot. For the moment, however, things went very well as they were.

It was the same with the Medical Missionary Society. Parker was still on his travels, poor health had driven Diver home, Howqua refused to reopen Hog Lane, so nothing at all could be done at Canton. But Hobson's Macao hospital flourished. Two native assistants worked there, Lockhart helped with the more serious operations (he was part-time surgeon to the Superintendency and often busy at Parker's naval hospital); at any given moment you found several dozen resident patients, and outpatients besides. Pottinger had already offered a piece of land for a Hongkong hospital. When Parker returned, it should be possible to take patients at the factories again. The only question was the old familiar one: did all this tending of the sick, the injured, and the disfigured open the way for Christ?

Indeed, was it sufficient, was it effective even, to distribute books and tracts? Hobson had once thought so, but he was no longer certain; "our experience now teaches us," he and Lockhart advised their London society, "how immensely important and absolutely necessary it is that the living voice be used."[9] Fortunately the way seemed at last a little clearer for that voice. It was beginning to be lifted now at places outside the gulf.

On 7 February, David Abeel sailed for Kulangsu to open the Protestant Mission's first station on the Fukien coast. (His vessel, just in from Sydney with coals and general cargo, had been chartered to carry opium, which explains why she stopped at Namoa and allowed the missionary to look around.) Abeel carried a letter of introduction from Pottinger and on reaching his destination was pleasantly received by Major Cowper, the garrison commander. Cowper found him a house and got him carpenters and masons to repair the ravages of looters. The house was inside the English lines—Kulangsu is three miles in circumference, Cowper could not occupy it all—which meant that Abeel was not free to move entirely as he pleased. There were sentries, and after dusk there was a watchword. He was safe, however. His knowledge of Chinese recommended him highly to Cowper and the other officers. Before long he was able to cross the half-mile wide channel and visit Amoy. Best of all, he had the Chinese of Kulangsu to work among. It was true he encountered in them that mixture of indifference and contempt so painfully familiar to him from his Canton and Macao days. Asked after several months' instruction what God he worshipped, a boy who lived with him replied: "Oh, I am not at all particular, anyone whose birthday happens to come along."[10] Still, Abeel was able to collect a congregation of sorts; to hold Sunday services in Chinese and count on an average two dozen listeners; to feel, in short, that the long preparation was over and the true work of the Protestant Mission begun.

Bridgman too was encouraged. "Three stations, including many tens of thousands of Chinese, are now accessible under British rule," he wrote.[11] Hongkong was one, Kulangsu another, Tinghai a third—for Milne had gone there the same February, and Lockhart (who had worked in Chusan during the first occupation) was thinking of going there too. As the mission spread along the coast, its numbers increased in proportion. Ill health had driven William Boone of the American Episcopal Board up from Batavia; at Macao he had lent a hand with Brown's school; but when Abeel sailed for Kulangsu, Boone went with him, returned shortly to fetch his wife, and on the second trip up brought Thomas McBryde of the Presbyterian Board and an unattached medical missionary named William Cumming. Thus the Kulangsu station was suddenly served not by one missionary but by four. At Macao there were fresh faces also: Dyer Ball for the American Board, William Dean for the Baptists, young Walter Lowrie for the Presbyterians. Many of the missionaries, the newer ones especially, had wives, and there were children everywhere. The Browns, the Deans, the McBrydes each had one; Catherine Parkes bore Lockhart a daughter (they had married the previous spring); the Boones had two children; the Balls had two and expected another; Henrietta Shuck had three and was expecting too. A contrary current caught poor Mary Gutzlaff. Her first child died in January a few days after birth, and Mary, ill and dispirited, sailed for New York with three little blind Chinese girls. Other deaths would follow, small children too often accompanying their mothers to the grave, but for the moment all was prosperity in the Protestant nursery—and the mission, men, women, and children, approached two score.

As for the war and the opium traffic, which was its occasion and perhaps its cause, the Protestants were not happy about either. Opium, they knew, was addictive (they used the word). It was debilitating, about as harmless a luxury as idolatry is an innocent recreation. But dreadful as the opium traffic was, China's moral condition was worse; and it was upon China's moral condition that they fixed their gaze.

True evangelicals, they knew that the state of the soul determines everything else. Social institutions and practices simply reflect the depravity, or it may be the moral health, of man. In the proper ordering of priorities, therefore, bringing Christ to China came before taking opium away. What cried out to be saved was not China's body but her soul, and if opium was bad for her body, were not its purveyors yet breaking down the same barriers that kept Christ's message out?

Always it came back to China shut or China opened. Not many of the missionaries moved as far and as fast as Henrietta Shuck, who as early as the summer of 1839—the summer of Chien-sha-tsui and the forced evacuation of Macao—was confessing "how these difficulties do rejoice my heart; because I think the English government may be enraged, and God in his power break down the barriers which prevent the gospel of Christ from entering China."[12] The war once under way, however, and pursuing its desultory course, they laid the accumulated exasperation of years upon its outcome. It is apparent from their letters. Williams begins by thinking the opium traffic a serious impediment to missionary work, in the spring of 1839 is delighted (as we have seen) at the check it is receiving, in the spring of 1840 decides that the quarrel is really not about opium at all, and thereafter plays endless variations on the theme that the English regiments and ships are God's ax appointed to chastise the Chinese and force them to listen to the Word of Life. "Although war is bringing its train of horrors upon this heretofore peaceful land," he will write before the summer of 1842 is over, "and the still sorer scourge of opium is slaying its thousands, we will encourage ourselves in the name of the Lord. The cause of the war is exceedingly objectionable, and so has been many of those in ages past which at the end have brought blessings upon the scene of their devastation. The evils resulting from the traffic and use of opium are terrific, far exceeding, we fear, those of the war; nor do we see how they are to be removed until the moral principle of the Gospel is brought to assist the weak efforts of the people to resist the temptation."[13]

Only Christ can save China from opium. But only war can open China to Christ. And the war actually in progress has been occasioned by the traffic in the drug.

One is reminded of the principle by which Rasputin is alleged to have led his life. To be saved, you must repent. To repent, you must have something to repent of. Sin, therefore!—it is the only road to salvation. To the Protestant missionaries it appeared more and more obvious that four hundred million Chinese would never attain the Christian life save by the road that led through opium and war.

Parts of the Catholic Mission hardly noticed these things. Away in Szechwan, for example, Bertrand was gloomy enough, but it was not the fighting or the drug that depressed him: it was the two years of terrible harvests followed by a crop the locusts destroyed, it was the famine and plague, the brigandage, the instances of cannibalism even. Pérocheau, his vicar apostolic in succession to the deceased Fontana, noticed that native Christians were sometimes confused with the distant marauding English and that robbers grew bolder because so many soldiers had been withdrawn to fight them. From the lower Yangtze valley Faivre relates how a fellow Lazarist happened to be near a powder magazine when it blew up, flinging stones and burning timbers in all directions and killing several hundred people. The magazine was at Shanghai, for use against the barbarians, but Faivre's comment was very much a passing one. The explosion attracted his attention only because the priest in question escaped unhurt—clear evidence that God protects those who devote their lives to Him. Faivre cannot have forgotten his coastal trip in *Red Rover*. He cannot have forgotten that clipper's trade. But he had long since reached his pastoral station and, like Bertrand, was fully occupied with the work there. That work proceeded with very little attention to opium, war, or a possible change in the empire's external relations.

Yet even for Catholics it was different on the coast. Huc, a recent French Lazarist arrival, found it comparatively easy to move about China once he had put salt water behind him. He moved due north through Kiangsi and Hupeh, visited Peschaud, Laribe, Rameaux, and Baldus in that order, and stopped near Wuchang long enough to inspect the grave of Perboyre (a young Chinese Christian led him to the little hill where the martyr and Clet lay buried side by side); he passed through Peking, was briefly mistaken for a Russian, and at last arrived in Mongolia (or Tartary, as it was often called), which Rome had recently confided to his congregation and where another Lazarist already worked. His reaching Mongolia at this time and by this route is perhaps the best possible evidence that Indian opium and English belligerence endangered Catholic missionaries hardly at all, that what had happened to Perboyre was an accident and not likely to be repeated. At the beginning of Huc's six-months' journey, however, there had been a difficult moment: the getting out of Macao and up the waterways past Canton (this in the winter of 1841, when there was intermittent fighting in the river). Paul, the Cochinchinese courier who betrayed himself by dropping things upon the deck, had been caught within miles of Macao. So had Taillandier and Augustin Ko. Where English and Chinese actually confronted one another, the Catholic missionary found it by no means simple to turn his back and cultivate his garden. He *had* to take a position—and the position he took was not so very different from that taken by the Protestants.

He recognized opium for the terrible thing it was. "A mind brutalized, a body enfeebled, the premature death of the smoker followed by the sale of all his and his wife's and children's worldly possessions and their descent into a life of misery and crime—these are the normal consequences of this fatal passion," Baldus once observed, adding that he did not think most Europeans cared, "and particularly the English, in whom love of humanity never prevails over love of gain."[14] But Baldus also admitted that the Chinese took to the drug much too readily. Was not this a sign of their dreadful inner condition? As for the English, they were even now shouldering their way with sword and gun into regions of the empire where, until this moment, the foreigner had moved humbly, stealthily, sometimes not at all. It would be foolish not to recognize the opportunity their boldness offered, seize it, and let it serve the cause of the true Catholic church.

The church needed help. Unassisted, without secular intervention or support from any quarter, it had entered China many years before and had spread and flourished. Now it slowed, stood still, slipped backward even, so that to preserve his flock and keep it from actually diminishing was the limit of Baldus's ambition in his own Honan. The trouble was with the material. The Jesuits of a previous age had esteemed the Chinese too highly. "I think," Baldus felt compelled to point out, "that in all things they are decidedly inferior to the Europeans, whom indeed the Lord seems to have regarded as his second chosen people."[15] (This had to be the case, otherwise the true faith would not have flourished in Europe for the past eighteen centuries.) Persecution and martyrdom did not drive the Chinese to Christ. The example of Perboyre was evidently quite lost on them. What they required, if they were ever to embrace Christianity, was the assurance that their own mandarins wished them to—or would at least allow it. In the grand old days, when the Jesuits were visibly welcome at Peking, they had had that assurance. They had it no longer; they must recover it; if they did not, he, Baldus, would spend the rest of his life moving secretively from one little community to another, never raising his voice, never venturing into strange places, baptizing no one whom the accident of being child, servant, or apprentice to a present Christian did not bring within his reach.

"We stand here, awaiting the Lord, ready to preach when we shall be called to that work. . . . But who will unbind our lips, who will shift from the path the enormous rock that blocks our way? Will it be the English, who, they say, are disposed to try?"[16]

In the course of 1841 three Missions Etrangères priests, two French Lazarists, three Jesuits who happened to be Frenchmen too, and three Italian Franciscans reached Macao from Europe.[17] It was the largest addition to the Catholic Mission in years. With it came a decree detaching Hongkong from the see of Macao and confiding it to Joset, procurator of the Roman Propaganda, a decree that must have issued the moment Rome learned that England had assumed formal possession of the island.

When Joset, however, prepared early in 1842 to take up his commission, the Portuguese protested loudly, would not admit the validity of the papal decree, and gave him three days to pick up and get out of Macao. Poor Joset! He had never intended leaving the town. From the hut off Queen's Road that became his refuge now, he approached Johnston and warned him that Portuguese animosity might pursue him right across the gulf. Johnston laughed, told him not to worry, and promised to help him get established. Established the Propaganda very soon was, in a proper stone building, the first *procure* on the island—with plenty of Irish Catholic troops to minister to. When Joset himself died suddenly the following August, his work went confidently on.

The Portuguese turned next on Legrégeois's successor, Libois, for they were not at all pleased to see Jesuits in China again, and the three newcomers of that society, with Joset gone, had taken up quarters in the *procure* of the Missions Etrangères. Pinto summoned Libois, tried to get him to send the three away, and when Libois would not, saw to it that the *procure*'s mail was overcharged or deliberately delayed. Libois paid little attention, however, and as for the Jesuits, though they left, it was only for Chusan. There they set up, temporarily, their own *procure*.

Two Italian Franciscans and Danicourt went with them, and by another ship two more French Lazarists. Guillet, Torrette's successor as procurator, was anxious to claim the island; it was, after all, part of the vicariat apostolic assigned to Rameaux. Yet would any of these gentlemen have dared spend a week on Chusan—would the two Spanish Dominicans who went to Kulangsu and were received there by Major Cowper as cordially as Abeel had been have dared expose themselves there for a day—had the English not seized the places first? It looked very much as if, on the coast at least, the Catholic Mission rode the coattails of the English expedition.

In June, Milne counted nine Catholic priests in and about Tinghai. "Higher motives activate Protestant missionaries," he assured his London society, "than mere ambition to emulate those of a spurious faith." Nevertheless it was disquieting. Late that summer Williams had it on good authority that a ship bearing sixty-two had recently reached Singapore, and though some of these were obviously intended for the Philippines and other places in east Asia, a great many were sure to come his way. "They have twenty men to our one," he warned the American Board, adding that he trusted "God is with the unit." How fortunate it was that England and not some other power battered at China's gates.

"What a difference it would make in all our plans and prospects if Portugal or Spain or Russia, or even 'young France' or Protestant Holland, were in the ascendant."[18]

The priests of the French *procures* naturally looked at the matter differently. "At last we have reached Macao," wrote one of the new Missions Etrangères men. "Here we are at the gates of China, that strange land that ever thrusts aside the proffered torch and is content to remain in darkness. For almost three centuries true religion and enlightened polity have counselled her to turn and enter the family of nations. In vain; her isolation feeds and sustains an immense and grotesque self-satisfaction; always she has preferred to close her ears to the message of salvation. But now, suddenly, everything is altered. Soldiers appear unannounced and uninvited to execute upon her body the terrible and sublime decrees of Heaven. All about the empire the cannon growl and roar."[19]

This was how Blanchin put it, with an enthusiasm that time did not have the opportunity to temper—for he died suddenly three weeks later. Reading him, one cannot help feeling that he at least had wished that the soldiers and the cannon were French.

France did take an interest. The Mediterranean war scare that had driven the *Danaide* from the gulf came to nothing and did not recur, so the corvette was able to return and follow Admiral Parker and the English fleet as they moved north in August 1841. Meanwhile the government of Louis Philippe dispatched a proper mission aboard the 46-gun *Erigone*, with instructions to find out what was going on along the coast of China and to protect French interests there. It was, in fact, the *Erigone* that brought the three Jesuits and two Lazarists from France. She reached Macao Roads shortly before Christmas; early in February 1842, Cécille, her captain, managed to meet the Chinese provincial authorities privately outside Canton; in March, Dubois de Jancigny, the head of the mission, met them too. Handshakes were exchanged in place of the kowtow. If prompt, direct access to mandarins of rank was the measure of a foreigner's importance, the French had acquired importance very quickly and cheaply indeed.

When, however, the mission suggested to Ishan and Ch'i Kung that China face the reality of her situation and concede open ports, resident ambassadors, and payment for the confiscated opium, those gentlemen were astounded—however convey such a thing to Peking? And when the French intimated that their own sovereign was ready to mediate the war with the English, the Chinese were put at once on guard. Barbarians were by nature cunning. Were these *fo-lang-chi* trying to take advantage of England's undeserved successes and China's temporary weakness? Jancigny, in fact, had exactly this in mind.

Unfortunately he lacked both the means and the authority to intervene in any real way, and Cécille, the *Erigone*'s captain, would have protested had he tried. Cécille represented the navy. Jancigny, who had once
advised the Nabob of Oudh, spoke for foreign affairs. When another
corvette, the *Favorite*, reached the coast (the *Danaide* having departed),
Jancigny took her for himself. Thereafter Cécille and he moved and operated apart. Jancigny was supposed to look after France's commercial interests. These were small, however; France bought few teas, sold no
opium, and was represented in the factory community by no one the
measure of a Matheson, a Dent, or even an Innes. Religion might have
taken commerce's place. Guillet, who contrived to be the mission's interpreter and guide, did his best to promote the proposition that French
priests in foreign parts deserved the active support of French arms.
Cécille was privately sympathetic, Perboyre's example (or it may be his
relics) already exerted influence at home—but French public policy did
not permit the connection.* The missionaries who boarded the *Erigone*
atBrest had found they could celebrate mass only at three in the morning,
and then only behind closed doors. In the end all that the ships and the interviews did was show the flag for France, exactly as Cécille, for one, had
been instructed.

No other European power sent agents or an armed presence to the
coast during the war, not Holland, not Spain, not Portugal, though Russia followed the business closely—at Macao in early 1842 the rumor ran
that Russian officers were advising the Chinese on the Chekiang coast.
The United States was another matter. Americans did more business at
Canton than anyone except the English. They were next to the English in
numbers, mixed with them easily, spoke the same language. Like them
they were confined to the factories and to the curious style of life the old
Canton system imposed; paid *cumsha*, measurement duties, and tariffs
that varied with the rapacity of the mandarins; bought teas, smuggled
opium, and got proscribed for it (ineffectually, of course). If the English
had the gunner of the *Lady Hughes* on their conscience, the Americans
had poor Terranova on theirs. And they were Protestants if they were
anything—indeed, as the Protestant Mission was more than half American, the Americans understood more readily than anybody else why that
mission's future hung on China opened.

In March 1839 they, like the English, had been detained against their
will. In May, Bennet Forbes, Delano, Nye, and half a dozen others had

---

*The rope Perboyre had been strangled with, his pallet, clothes, hair, even his fingernails,
had reached the Paris house in the summer of 1841. Before the year was out, they and
Perboyre's intercession (obtained through novenas) had cured one young woman of
pleurisy, another of an ulcer on the arm, and a third of an unspecified leg injury that had
kept her bedridden for six months.

framed a vigorous memorial asking Washington to send a naval force; suggesting, too, that now was the time to compel Peking to accept a resident ambassador and open ports other than Canton. The memorial had gone to Congress. There papers had been requested just as they had been in England. The request, however, was not a partisan one, and the papers, though they reached clear back to the Terranova affair, were much too slim to break through floors and generated little argument. There was another difference. Forbes and the others did not repeat their memorial. From many quarters, instead, came the caution that the government should think twice before doing anything at all, and when it was learned that English newspapers represented America as anxious to join actively in bringing Peking to terms, there was a scene on the floor of the House of Representatives. Where England was concerned, Americans were suspicious to the point of touchiness.

This touchiness sometimes showed itself right in the gulf. Once, H.M.S. *Herald* and Russell's *Lintin* happening to anchor very near each other, and the frigate making known in a peremptory manner that it did not wish the sometime receiving ship to put out a kedge lest its bower be overlaid, the *Lintin*'s skipper stood on his taffrail and showered the frigate with such abuse that she felt obliged to send a boat's crew and forcibly fetch the fellow over. When he threatened to put a "Kentucky bullet" through his captors, they tied him up and left him to stew. For the most part, however, common interests and a common experience persuaded Americans actually on the spot to see the war and the Chinese as the English saw them. They tended, that is, to agree with John Quincy Adams, secretary of state at the time Terranova was strangled and now chairman of the House Committee on Foreign Affairs, who after much thought and a careful reading of the Parliamentary Papers came to the conclusion that it was not the confiscation of twenty thousand chests that had driven the English to arms. It was the arrogance of the Chinese, their persistent denial of normal, civilized intercourse. The war, Adams decided, was about the kowtow.

This was a line Americans resident in China were much inclined to take. Even in China, however, there were exceptions—Bridgman held opium to be the "proximate cause" of the war—and in Boston and other places along the eastern seaboard the exceptions became the rule. The public lecture in which Adams made his case was stormily received. One prominent journal refused to publish it. Sentiment formed at such a distance from China and so little familiar with Chinese exclusiveness turned easily and naturally against John Bull. The opium traffic was lucrative; England had gone to war to safeguard it; that was the whole, and shameful truth of the matter. It did not follow that America should actively intervene on China's behalf. To do so would be, practicably speaking, madness—besides, though England's motives were ignoble, the probable result of an English victory, namely, China opened, was much to be desired. But one could be thankful for what was going to be effected and still look askance at the agent.

So Washington did very little. The heavy frigate *Constellation* and one smaller vessel were sent to the China coast. Kearny, the frigate's commander, took her up to Whampoa in the spring of 1842, kept her there for nine weeks, and with Bridgman's help obtained mandarin interviews as promptly and impressively as Cécille and Jancigny had done. He did not meddle, however in the controversy between the English and the Chinese. He simply extracted compensation for the injuries done the previous May to Coolidge, poor Sherry, and the others. When the Frenchmen and their men-of-war followed the English expedition to the Yangtze, he and his frigate stayed quietly at the gulf.

That was the difference. The French did not take part in the war but, suddenly noticing it when it was part way through, danced around the edge half wanting to join in. The Americans waited to see what would happen when it was over. It was the English alone who fought. In the summer of 1842 they undertook to bring the thing to a final and decisive conclusion.

24

The Yangtze Campaign

The China war was not the only military business to occupy the English that year. Afghanistan was even more on their minds. Setting Shah Shuja on the throne at Kabul had been a gamble, and in the autumn of 1841 the gamble was found to have failed. The Bombay army had been withdrawn, the Bengal army was seriously depleted, Dost Muhammad was safe in Calcutta—but he had a son. And Shuja was not the man to overcome the stigma of being so obviously the creature of the English. In November there was a sudden rising at Kabul. Outnumbered, mismanaged, dispirited, the English garrison surrendered on terms and started for the Khyber with women and followers in bitter winter weather. It never reached the top of the pass; one survivor, a Scots doctor named Brydon, rode into Jalalabad on 13 January, covered with wounds and with his sword broken off at the hilt. The venture that had begun so brilliantly two and a half years before had ended in horror and disaster.

The news crushed Auckland, and as the weeks passed the news grew worse. What had happened at Kabul was repeated elsewhere. Though Jalalabad held and Kandahar too, Ghazni fell in the same circumstances of incompetence and treachery, and with the same dreadful results. If this was a general rising, a thing of genuine patriotic and religious feeling, it would be folly to attempt to reconquer the country—or so Auckland was inclined to think as, in a bitter and perplexed frame of mind, he received towards the end of February his successor Ellenborough.

Ellenborough did not agree. More confident than Auckland, with less delicacy of feeling (at Government House, which the two shared for several weeks, he exercised his cavalry escort in Auckland's sister's flower garden), and with less experience of India though he had once been president of the Board of Control, he reacted to the Kabul disaster as most Englishmen in England did. Though Afghanistan might have to be relinquished, England's reputation at arms must first be firmly rees-tablished there. And as he had always regretted that he was not himself a soldier, he was all the happier for the opportunity of directing, first from Calcutta and later from headquarters in the field, the force that should teach the Afghans the necessary lesson.

The consequence was that what held everyone's attention through-out almost the whole of 1842, in England and India alike, was the pre-paring, the setting in motion, and at last the triumphant advance of Ellenborough's Army of Retribution. The China war was nothing. As the *Times* observed: "It is impossible to view that contest with the same exciting interest that attaches to the terrible realities of our Afghan warfare."[1]

Nevertheless the China business had to be carried through—no one doubted that, least of all Ellenborough. On reaching Calcutta, Ellen-borough wrote Pottinger that China was costing a great deal of money, that every rupee was needed to repair the Afghan disaster, but that rather than recall regiments or postpone the departure of those already prepar-ing to embark, he preferred to press on and finish the business with all possible dispatch. It was exactly what Her Majesty's government wished too. The Whigs were out—not because of China (though they were blamed, especially for leaving Captain Elliot in charge so long), but be-cause of a succession of budget deficits and the natural erosion of office. There had been adverse votes in Parliament, a general election in which they were thought to have lost seats (in those days loose party affiliation made a delightful uncertainty of such matters), then more votes from which it became clear that indeed they had. Melbourne had resigned. Peel was prime minister now. That was why Ellenborough was replacing Auckland and why, at the Foreign Office, Aberdeen had taken Palmer-ston's place. But there was no question of putting new men at the head of the China expedition. Gough, Parker, and Pottinger were to stay. Their instructions would hardly vary from those Elliot had carried when he was recalled, which meant they would be essentially what Palmerston had issued when ships and men first went out in the spring of 1840. "The only objects which Her Majesty desires to obtain are satisfaction for the injuries to which Her subjects have been exposed and for the insults which have been offered to Her Crown, and the establishment of peace-ful and friendly commercial relations with China. . . . Her Majesty de-sires no acquisition of territory, nor any advantages for Her own subjects which should not equally be shared by other nations."[2] This was how it was put by Stanley at the War Office. Peel had confided to him the gen-eral superintendence of the final campaign.

For this campaign the China expedition was to be substantially rein-forced. Ellenborough's Army of Retribution required, of course, no naval support; the Mediterranean was quiet; so the Admiralty had no difficulty in sending Parker another seventy-four in addition to the *Cornwallis*, half a dozen frigates, several corvettes, and no less than eight steamers (many from the Indian navy, to be sure). Though some vessels of an earlier commission were coming home, the China squadron was therefore certain to be larger than it had ever been—it suffered, it must be remembered, hardly any losses since, except for the *Madagascar* burned at sea and another steamer that foundered after striking a rock off the mouth of the Yangtze (as will be seen), no men-of-war were lost to acci-dents and none to the Chinese. The land force gained too. The four European regiments were brought up to strength and kept there, and a fifth, the 98th, left England early in the new year. Additional horse and foot artillery were sent, sappers and miners from Madras, gun lascars by the hundreds, a fresh regiment of Bengal volunteers—and, to take the place of the 37th Madras Native Infantry, *five* other regiments of that corps. At the beginning of the winter Gough had commanded not many more than three thousand men. By early summer he commanded ten thousand.

And though this China war played second fiddle to the events un-folding beyond the Indus, the fact of its existence and the manner of its proceeding inevitably became known in England. Grey of the Reform Bill had a nephew on board the *Herald*; the Duke of Wellington had a nephew aboard the *Cornwallis*; Peel's son, William, served on the frigate *Cambrian*—one must suppose they occasionally sent letters home. Re-turning officers wrote at length and put what they wrote into print. Vis-count Jocelyn's *Six Months with the Chinese Expedition* appeared before the end of 1841, and as it was short and the author a man of some conse-quence (on reaching England, Jocelyn had married Melbourne's niece and gone to live at Richmond Park), it no doubt was noticed. Bingham, the *Modeste*'s first lieutenant, published his recollections in two volumes. MacPherson of the 37th did the same in one, first slipping excerpts into Bridgman's *Repository*—so did Stewart Mackenzie (he had been military secretary to the plenipotentiaries after Jocelyn). How Anstruther had been captured, the heroic story of Mrs. Noble, even her cage, were freely available to Londoners. On Tower Wharf squatted several huge Chinese brass cannon. And for 2s. 6d. the interested could explore the China col-lection brought over from Philadelphia by an old China hand named Nathan Dunn. It was housed near Hyde Park Corner in a pavilion espe-cially erected for the purpose. Models of palanquins, bridges, junks, joss-houses; carpenters' tools; a complete shoemaker's shop; the implements ambulatory barbers carry; porcelain, silks, hanging lanterns, objects and articles beyond number and sometimes beyond identification (they included an opium pipe and a watchman's rattle); most striking of all, eighty life-sized figures, carefully posed and costumed, of Chinese in every rank and occupation from mandarin to coolie—these occupied a single great hall 225 feet long. Queen Victoria spent almost two hours there with Albert. The Duke of Wellington visited the place three times.

And one day sixty-five tons of silver arrived at the London terminus of the Southampton Railway and was carried in wagons to the Mint. The *Conway* had reached Portsmouth with her part of the Canton ransom. In some quarters hope revived that the British treasury would now advance partial compensation for the confiscated chests. In Parliament the China lobby made strenuous efforts to see that it did.

That lobby's voice was stronger because at the June election Jardine had been returned for the little Devon borough of Ashburton, and Larpent and Hugh Hamilton Lindsay for other places. Palmerston too was friendly. But when Lindsay at last put the formal motion (Jardine hardly opened his mouth), it was enough for Peel to point out that the previous government, the government of which Palmerston had been a part, had regularly declined to honor Captain Elliot's guarantee until and unless the Chinese should be beaten and pay up. The Canton $6 million were a *droit* of the Crown. Lindsay's motion failed by a wide margin.

Elliot himself was about to take up a new position. The *Times* thought him "unfit to manage a respectable apple stall,"[3] but he was too determined, too engaging, and too well connected to be entirely cast aside. Texas had recently declared her independence. A chargé d'affaires was needed there. Palmerston appointed the former chief superintendent (at half his previous salary), Aberdeen confirmed the appointment, and in the spring of 1842 Elliot sailed with his wife and little son.

On the other side of the world, meanwhile, the reinforcements for the China expedition approached the Gulf of Canton. The greater part, including all seven new regiments, would not arrive until May or early June, but Gough and Parker did not wait—they began the final campaign without them. Steamers lifted Ningpo's garrison clear of that depressing place. Chinhai was stripped, drafts were collected from Kulangsu and Tinghai; the men-of-war and transports rendezvoused off Just-in-the-Way and moved into Hangchow Bay. On 16 May the *Nemesis* and the *Phlegethon* steamed ahead to reconnoiter. On the eighteenth the main force landed and attacked the walled town of Chapu.

Chapu lay on the north side of Hangchow Bay about half a mile from the open roadstead that served it for a harbor. A frontal assault was clearly unwise; the shore to the west was low and marshy, and to the east ran a short range of hills on which the Chinese seemed to be posted in considerable strength; so Gough decided to land to the right of these hills, send part of his force behind them, and with the rest roll the defenders up from the flank. As usual the Chinese were disconcerted by the deviousness of the approach, and for a time everything went well. But in a cup of land between two of the hills stood a joss-house with a single entrance, and here there occurred a bloody and unexpected check. Three hundred Chinese had taken refuge in the structure and, from the shelter of a stone screen just inside the door, fired boldly at anyone who tried to enter. The door was narrow; the defenders were almost invisible in the gloom; the first rush was thrown back with one killed and several wounded, and when Colonel Tomlinson of the Royal Irish tried to lead a second, two bullets took him instantly through the neck. Rockets and a six-pounder made no impression on the thick stone walls. It was not until powder charges had brought a part of them down and set fire to the wooden upper story that the place was carried and prisoners made of the few defenders who were not shot, bayoneted, or burned to death. After this the taking of Chapu itself was something of an anticlimax. The walls of the town were low and there were almost no men or guns on them; the Chinese had made their stand in the hills. Parker with marines and armed seamen joined Gough, the gates were forced, and the defenders fled towards Hangchow. The English did not follow. As always when local authority collapsed, many Chinese took to looting and plundering. Groups of them could be seen "hastening across the country laden with every kind of property; and perhaps occasionally a little quiet European foraging party, hunting ducks and fowls and pigs. For which, however," adds the observer with a perfectly straight face, "the peasants were generally very well paid."[4] It was lovely country, low hills near the town and a wonderfully fertile plain beyond, reminiscent (blue-tiled roofs notwithstanding) of the prettiest parts of Devonshire.

But Tomlinson was dead, as were a captain of the 55th and a dozen rank and file. Mountain ought to have been dead too. Three bullets had struck him in the body and all three had miraculously emerged without striking anything vital, but he would be flat on his back for weeks. Never had the Chinese resisted as furiously as they had at the joss-house. The English were impressed.

It was partly, of course, because many of the men they had been fighting were Manchus—"Tartars" almost everybody called them—the first they had actually met. (The English would have encountered Manchus at Canton if they had crossed the north wall.) Inside Chapu there was a whole Manchu quarter separate and distinct from the Chinese town, with houses laid out in lines like tents in an encampment. In this quarter lived a permanent Manchu garrison of men, women, and children. Most of the men were dead or gone. Apparently it was not easy to take a Manchu warrior prisoner; perhaps it was not easy to take his women and children either, for there were a number of these among the lifeless—poisoned, to judge by their swollen throats and blackened lips. G. Tradescant Lay came across one old woman hanging by the neck. (After importuning the Foreign Office for months, he was back in China with an interpreter's appointment.) Two young women tended an old fellow who looked as if he might have tried to cut his own throat. "Their heads were large and their hair bushy, their faces broad and flat," their feet unbound, and their expressions sullen and irreconcilable.[5]

Something must be said, before it is too late, about the Chinese army.

What particularly struck the English was the ridiculous show the Chinese made on the field of battle. It was not that a Chinese regiment was never a pretty sight. An Englishman who happened to be wrecked in 1819 on the island of Hainan observed one day, as he made his way on foot towards Macao, a body of soldiers exercising outside a city. Archers demonstrated their skill by shooting at a paper target fifty yards distant. Their bows were of horn and their arrows were specially constructed to make a singing noise in flight. Several hundred horsemen shot with the same weapon while riding successively at a trot, a canter, and a gallop. Then it was the turn of the matchlock men, in red jackets and blue nankeen pantaloons, carrying cartridge boxes containing thimble-sized bamboos filled with powder. Advancing to a point opposite wooden targets set eighty paces away, each man emptied a bamboo down his barrel, dropped in a ball, and sent it home by striking the butt of the piece against the ground. No wadding was used and no rammer. "The balls did not exceed that of the smallest sized pocket pistol; they seemed, however, to go with great force and precision." On the whole this Englishman, whom we know simply as "J.R.," was favorably impressed by what he saw.[6]

It was the kind of favorable impression, however, that one gets watching the yeomen at the Tower or a tableau in a well-constructed *son et lumière*. There was a theatrical quality about it; it was as if the Chinese meant to defeat their adversaries by dressing the part of the conqueror, executing the pantomime of ferocious combat, and leaving the rest to the imagination. Mackenzie describes how, when the Chinese came to meet the English, they were preceded by soldiers brandishing swords in both hands and uttering "strange cries varied by terms of opprobrium," and adds dryly that "one or two of these military mountebanks having been picked off by our men, they did not latterly exhibit their accomplishments so often."[7] Soldiers performed somersaults as they moved to the attack. Their rattan shields were painted with the heads of devils or ferocious animals, they wore tiger-head caps when they could get them—and their weapons were unbelievable.

The gingal (the Chinese had no field artillery) was reasonably effective. In size it resembled the wall piece known to Europe in the early eighteenth century or the elephant gun of the nineteenth. It was served by two or three men, was mounted on a tripod or else allowed to rest on a man's shoulder, and fired iron scraps or ball weighing half a pound to a pound. The Chinese musket, however, was a wretched thing, crudely made, of small caliber, with a touchhole large enough to admit a tenpenny nail. If the charge did not blow out the back, it escaped forward — for, as I have said, the ball went in without wad or ramming. Worst of all, the thing was a matchlock, which is to say it was fired by holding a slow-burning cord over a hole instead of by pulling a trigger. English line regiments had not been issued such a weapon since the reign of Queen Anne. To encounter it now was to put oneself perfectly in tune with the other military anachronisms of this strange land: bows and arrows; gunpowder so coarse and inferior that, when the English used it to blow up captured works, hundreds of pounds of the stuff sometimes did nothing but shake down bricks and dust; dart rockets with barbed tips, like the ones seen on Chusan in 1840; spears, halberds, and a curious thing like a hedge chopper fastened to the end of a pole; gongs for signaling, helmets of iron or brass, even chain mail. If the English had known that some Chinese generals prided themselves on their calligraphy (Lin was not alone in this) and anticipated victories by composing victory announcements in verse, they would have been more derisive still.

What should have attracted their attention, however, was less the matter of weapons and accouterments than the matter of organization and numbers. China's soldiers came in two sorts—one might almost say in two sizes. There were the Tartars or Manchu bannermen, so called because they organized themselves man, woman, and beast under flags or "banners." And there were the Chinese of the Army of the Green Standard. The bannermen had conquered China in the seventeenth century, and took care thereafter to maintain themselves in force about Peking and in the key provinces of the empire. Most cities of any consequence, especially in the north and along the lower Yangtze, had Manchu quarters like Chapu's. At their peak, however, the bannermen did not number a quarter of a million fighting men—England's army was fully half that size and when you added the Indian army became actually larger—so as a supplement the Ch'ing (or Manchu) emperors raised the Army of the Green Standard. This army was recruited from native Chinese. It was larger than the banner forces and much more evenly distributed. But it was distributed in smaller packets, some of them little more than a hundred men in size, and it early became intermingled with the administrative structure (the Ch'ing had no desire to see its military men autonomous) and assumed many of that structure's features. Officers were rotated from post to post just as mandarins were; they operated without the benefit of a clear chain of command just as mandarins did. High mandarins had military responsibilities as well as civil and checked and balanced their cousins in arms exactly as they did each other. The result was that the Army of the Green Standard was no more an army than the war junks of the provincial flotillas were a fleet. It resembled a constabulary. Asking it to concentrate and move decisively against the English, at Canton or Chapu or anywhere else, was a bit like asking Italy's *carabinieri* to throw the Austrians out of Venice.

Then, too, neither the green standard troops nor the bannermen were at their best in the second quarter of the nineteenth century. By that time China was already some distance down the path of dynastic decline. Mandarins helped themselves liberally at the public trough. A Malthusian pressure on the land drove rents up, forced peasants into debt, and in the end cost many their land, and this land, when bought by mandarins and other gentry, by paying less than normal taxes made intolerable the weight of taxation that fell upon the rest. In desperation the peasants drifted off to become thieves and beggars in the city, or else they took to robbing and stealing where they were; some, passing beyond the bandit stage, joined permanent brotherhoods of outlaws in the hills. The resulting increase in general insecurity exacerbated every other ill. Meanwhile the bannermen, obliged to support an increasing number of dependents on a fixed scale of pay (for their dependents multiplied like everybody else), vegetated unhappily in garrison, privileged paupers of little use either to themselves or to the state. The green standard troops were in an even worse condition. The decay of the civil service naturally hurt them too—besides, good iron is not beaten into nails nor are good men made into soldiers (runs the Chinese proverb). Officers who had become so by dint of little more than demonstrating that they could brandish a sword, pull a powerful bow, and lift a heavy stone, would not scruple to shortchange their men or, when desertions occurred, conceal the fact and pocket the difference. So the Army of the Green Standard, its pay in arrears, its arms old and neglected, its training largely *pro forma*, and its parts quite incapable of responding to Nathan Bedford Forrest's dictum about gitting thar fust with the mostest men, grew year by year less adequate to the task of coping with the English.

Which brings us back to what the English ought to have noticed. The fact of China's teeming millions inclined them to suppose that China's soldiers were numberless and her every army a horde. Yet of fighting forces in the western sense, forces a central government could assemble, move, and throw as one man against the enemy, China had very little. Few as the English were here on the other side of the world, for most land engagements they could put almost as many soldiers into the field as the Chinese could. In Canton, where the foreign presence had always been felt, where the long opium crisis had ripened and the first skirmishes of the war been fought, the banner garrison in the southwest part of the Old City had held steady at four thousand men, the green standard at three (both figures were paper figures, the true numbers must have been less), and nothing had been done to enlarge this force until reinforcements were ordered in from neighboring provinces early in 1841, as we have seen. These reinforcements were green standard men. They came from a dozen places, had never served together, and never expected to—if Ellis had troubles commanding marines from nine different ships, they were as nothing next to Ishan's. And in the end this army, though certainly larger than Gough's—large enough, indeed, to make Gough cautious—was not after all so very formidable in size. It had been that way at Tinghai on both occasions, and at Chinhai and Ningpo. Chapu was defended (it is Gough's estimate) by almost eight thousand men, but fewer than two thousand of these were bannermen, they were widely scattered, and at the joss-house after the first quarter of an hour they were actually outnumbered by their attackers. It was their stubbornness that had momentarily shaken the English. Along the Yangtze it would be the same.

Chapu was the port for Hangchow, seventy miles up the estuary—it had been the intention to move on that city next. A little reconnaissance, however, confirmed what the *Phlegethon* had previously discovered: the estuary was unsafe for ships. Venturing so far by road, against so large a place, without naval support or heavy artillery (the large pieces could not be manhandled over that great distance, and for draft animals the English had only a few captured ponies), was quite out of the question. So Gough put his little army back aboard the transports and went out to sea again.

To force the Chinese to the conference table by cutting the Grand Canal where it crossed the Yangtze, suppressing all traffic on the lower reaches of that river, and perhaps taking Nanking, had from the start been the principal alternative to a move against Peking itself. Gough and Parker knew that instructions to do one or the other would someday reach Pottinger and themselves. But the overland mail had been much delayed that winter, and when, from time to time, a particular mail did ar-

rive, it showed that Stanley delayed making up his mind about the 1842
campaign until he could discover what had been accomplished in 1841.
When at last he gave up waiting and framed instructions as well as he was
able, they amounted to no more than this: consult Ellenborough and each
other, then do what you think best.

Gough thought it best to take the expedition to the Yangtze. The old
objections to the Peiho—the poor anchorage, the impossibility of escort-
ing the army on its march to Peking with anything better than shallow-
draft steamers, the bitterness with which the Chinese were bound to fight
(and negotiate) when practically beneath the eyes of their emperor—were
as powerful as ever. Besides, the experience at Tzeki and more recently at
Chapu made Gough suspect that the Chinese might become really formidable if they put their minds to it. Some of his officers feared the same;
so did Augustine Heard, the veteran American merchant. "Nearly
everyone here seems confident that the Chinese will yield," he wrote
from Canton early in May. "I am not so. . . . They have learned a great
deal since the war began, and every six months shows that they are harder to beat than they were before. If they had a few Russian or French
officers or West Point cadets, they would soon show a different face."[8]
He did not mean on the water, of course, there they remained as ridiculous as ever; indeed, it probably annoyed Gough more than a little that his
colleagues of the fleet affected nothing but indifference and amused contempt where their opponents were concerned. But if Gough took his
army up the Yangtze, he would, he knew, have the fleet's constant and
close support. It was a thing he needed, and it would be given the more
willingly because a Yangtze campaign promised the men-of-war some
scope.

A Yangtze campaign also offered the Chinese the chance to practice
delaying tactics. Auckland had always been afraid that this was exactly
what they would stumble upon, that they would learn to abandon every
place the English threatened while always declining to treat, so that in the
end the English would be driven to declaring the war over unilaterally.
That hardly squared with Pottinger's instructions not to stop fighting
until a treaty had been obtained. Still, the Yangtze's advantages—for all
that the river lent itself to Fabian tactics—were in Gough's mind overwhelming. From Calcutta, Ellenborough wrote to urge them, Parker and
Pottinger were agreeable, and so it was decided that the Yangtze it should
be.

From Chapu the men-of-war and transports moved to an anchorage
on the edge of the Chusan archipelago, then early in June to one north of
Gutzlaff Island—within reach, but not in sight, of the Yangtze's mouth.
Few of the sea or land reinforcements had yet arrived, so Parker (in the

Cornwallis, the *Blenheim* being at Hongkong) commanded only twenty-five sail or so. The *Queen* steamer went south to fetch Pottinger. But it was not for the plenipotentiary that Parker waited, only for the weather to improve—that and the establishing of a safe passage through the shoals at the river's mouth. The *Nemesis* steamed ahead and scouted Woosung. Once, on a particularly dark and stormy night, Hall took his cutter right in to the beach, landed in front of the forts, and boldly peeped through an embrasure at the Chinese soldiers inside. Another time he stopped a fishing junk and discovered that her catch was packed in ice, which set him to intercepting others for the fleet at large, fresh fish being welcome in any wardroom and ice most satisfactory to cool wine and beer with now that the hot weather had begun.

On 13 June, with everything ready and the weather mending, Parker at last moved. Six of his smaller vessels had been posted as beacons along the edge of the Tungsha Banks, for there was nothing on the low and distant shore to take bearings upon, and everyone remembered how the little iron steamer *Ariadne*, moving in apparently safe waters a few days before, had struck a submerged rock, torn a hole in her engine compartment, and eventually foundered. (On naval charts you will still find an Ariadne Rock.) Even with the beacons it was difficult going; there were moments during the thirty-mile passage when her leadsman gave the *Cornwallis* only three or four feet to spare; but the surveyors had done their work well and no vessel took the ground. Two days were spent reconnoitering the approaches to Woosung, and at five-thirty on the morning of 16 June the attack began.

The *Cornwallis*, the *Blonde*, and three corvettes were towed to their firing positions by steamers lashed alongside. The several forts on the west bank of the Hwangpu River (Woosung lies at its mouth) fired furiously while this was going on, and as their guns had leisure to lay and were themselves not being shot at, they had some effect: the *Blonde* lost three killed, and Lay (who was aboard her) was slightly wounded. When the five warships had finally got into position, however, and had anchored and began to reply, the Chinese guns were gradually silenced, and the English pounded away unopposed. About eight o'clock they fell silent too; marines and armed seamen went ashore and, after a little sharp fighting, occupied the entire line. Wandering through a fort next day, a Royal Navy officer named Loch discovered that its outer wall, "cased round with piles, and with two and a half feet of mud and stones jammed between, was riddled like a sieve, and the guard-rooms and small magazine in the centre smothered in ruins. Broken gingals, dismounted and spiked guns, arrows, spears, matchlocks, shot and loose powder, besides hats and other articles of dress, were strewed about in every direction."⁹ Some of the guns had a rude sort of pivot mount that made it unnecessary to shift the entire block when correcting for deflection. Up the Hwangpu the *Nemesis* came across several gunboats hand-propelled by paddle wheels, two to a side. These unexpected bits of technical (or imitative) enterprise had done the Chinese no more good, however, than had their charming old-fashioned habit of inscribing their larger pieces with terrifying names: Robber's Judgment, Tamer and Subduer of Foreign Devils, and (in the case of one twelve-foot brass monster) Barbarian. There were all told 175 guns in the Woosung forts, or that at least is the English figure, but they were a heterogeneous lot, spread along hundreds of yards of river front, each piece immovable, and most of them indifferently served—no match at all for Parker's floating batteries.

Three days later Shanghai was taken by a double column of steamers towing men-of-war in the Hwangpu and elements of two regiments with artillery moving overland. There was no resistance to speak of. Loch, who accompanied the land force, remembers that as they drew near the north wall of the city, moving in single file along the earthen dikes that divided the fields (there were no roads in the western sense), they saw two guns pointing at them through a hole in the ramparts. The guns never fired. "We scaled the wall by an old house appropriately placed, found the ramparts deserted, and saw the townspeople flying. The gates were opened, the bugles struck up, and the troops marched through."¹⁰ Shanghai was known to be an important place commercially. Lindsay and Gutzlaff had visited it in the *Lord Amherst* ten years before, Medhurst in the *Huron* more recently. Just the same the number of trading junks and the volume of merchandise in the stone warehouses along the river front surprised everybody. The city was a natural terminus, not just for the Yangtze traffic—the Yangtze drained half of China—but for the coastal trade as well, junks from northern ports going no further south and junks from southern ports reciprocating, and though it was not an administrative center and therefore had no great circumference of wall and no Manchu quarter, it was obviously a very desirable place to have regular access to.

But that would have to wait. Though Parker pushed up a branch of the Hwangpu almost as far as Soochow, Gough had no desire to waste time and men on diversions . The campaigning season was well along, the reinforcements from England and India were entering the Yangtze at last; Pottinger had returned. It was time to start for the Grand Canal and Nanking. On the twenty-third Shanghai was evacuated. For two weeks the now much enlarged expedition remained at Woosung, in unsettled and squally weather, sorting itself out and waiting for the Yangtze to be reconnoitered beyond the point reached by the *Conway* two years before. On 4 July the *Phlegethon* came in with the news that a navigable channel had been established and marked. On Wednesday the sixth with a light southeast wind and clearing skies the ascent began.

Eleven sailing men-of-war ranging in size from the *Cornwallis* to a little 10-gun brig, four troopships (all men-of-war at one time—the *Belleisle* had been a seventy-four), ten steamers, two survey schooners, and forty-eight transports carrying men, guns, Indian followers, coal, and stores were drawn up in five divisions, each division led by a man-of-war, the whole anchored in line with room to swing. "It was a beautiful sight," remembers Keppel of the *Dido* at the head of the fifth division. "On a signal from Flag to fleet to weigh, in a few minutes you saw a white cloud three miles in extent moving up the river." When darkness fell (for there was no attempt to sail by night) or the wind backed around to the west, "the reverse took place and a forest of masts succeeded the white cloud."[11] What can Cécille have thought as he watched from the deck of the *Erigone*? He had brought her to Woosung at the end of June and lay there now unwilling to risk his frigate further without pilot or steamer, neither of which the English had any intention of furnishing to a Frenchman. Surely he was impressed. Nothing like this armada had ever been seen on the Yangtze before, and as it was the twilight of the sailing man-of-war, nothing quite like it would ever be seen there again.

Of course seventy-five vessels so disparate in size and sailing qualities could not ascend the Yangtze for almost two hundred miles and remain as Keppel describes them. For a considerable distance the river was ten miles or more from bank to bank. But the channel itself was nothing like so wide. Though it was far deeper above Woosung than below it, though it was buoyed by the advance party and continuously scouted by the shallow-draft steamers, sooner or later a vessel—a transport perhaps, under full sail with the wind aft and the tide helping—would miss the edge, shoal her water from eight fathoms to fifteen feet in little more than her own length (as happened to the *Modeste* on one occasion, Loch says), and take the bottom, which fortunately was almost everywhere soft mud. Before Nanking was reached nearly every ship in the fleet had gone aground at least once, and every grounding was an interruption; a ship that stuck fast at the turn of the flood sometimes waited an entire tide before she got free again. The worst offenders were the flagship and that "terrible old tub" the *Belleisle*. "Everybody is much dissatisfied with these large ships coming up, especially at the Admiral leading the way in that monster the *Cornwallis*," observed young Harry Parkes when the two grounded for the first time on the very first day of the ascent.* "If he

---

*Before she left China, Mary Gutzlaff had brought Parkes out to join his two older sisters, putting him with Morrison and her husband to learn Chinese. Though he was only fourteen, he traveled now in the *Queen* with Pottinger's staff. Years later, as Sir Harry Parkes, he became Her Majesty's minister to Japan and afterwards to China.

gets on shore, all the fleet will have to stay for him if it takes a week."[12] It was true; when the flagship broke her capstan one morning trying to weigh, the leading division did not stir for twenty-four hours. Meanwhile the other divisions were experiencing their own accidents and delays, so that Keppel's "white cloud" soon stretched from three miles to something nearer thirty.

Loch and Parkes kept extensive journals, Keppel a brief but pithy one, and we have three or four other firsthand accounts; all make a great deal of these delays and difficulties. Calms or contrary winds kept vessels motion-less in the heat and mosquitos for days. After the first sixty or seventy miles the banks drew together, there were occasional sharp bends, the tide was less felt and therefore less useful, and the current grew perceptibly stronger. At one place a large island split the channel. Keppel's *Dido* passed under sail after several tries. The *Blonde*, the *Modeste*, and a 16-gun brig ran afoul of violent eddies that "whirled them round and sent them down as helpless as boys' toy boats in a running brook,"[13] until in the end they had to be towed. Over the final two score miles to Nanking the tide helped not at all, and the wind was mostly westerly, so that a sailing vessel moved only when there was a steamer available to move her. The *Marion* with Gough aboard negotiated this stretch lashed side-by-side to Pottinger's *Queen* steamer. The *Cornwallis*, which Parker kept stubbornly in the lead, came up sandwiched between two such vessels. When she finally dropped anchor, it was thirty days since she had given the signal to weigh off Woosung; when the last transport arrived, it was thirty-six. Regiments on foot would have reached the city faster.

An overland march, however, would have accomplished not half what Parker's ships accomplished, and the army that made it would have been fit for very little when the march was finished. This was not because there was a great deal of fighting to be done before the Grand Canal could be cut or the former Ming capital taken. Above Woosung practically no resistance was offered anywhere along the Yangtze. A few fire rafts, launched amateurishly even by Chinese standards, came down on Parker's ships. Once or twice a handful of guns fired and were immediately smothered. That was all. The *Nemesis*, pushing up the inner passage to-wards Canton, had met a sturdier and more systematic defense than she encountered now on China's principal inland waterway.

There was a single exception. Forty-five miles short of Nanking, on the right bank of the river where the southern branch of the Grand Canal came in from Soochow, lay the important walled city of Chinkiang, and here, on 21 July, Gough's army fought an unquestionably major engage-ment. Two brigades went ashore and with lighthearted confidence at-tacked the place. A third advanced against a small entrenched camp on some hills to the southwest. The Chinese in the camp were dispersed without difficulty and with almost no casualties except from sunstroke. Chinkiang itself, however, suddenly became alive with bannermen who fought bitterly and skillfully even after the walls had been scaled and one gate blown in, and would neither surrender nor run but died where they stood, or else managed to avoid the English long enough to regain their own quarter and there make an end to themselves and their families. Afterwards, with bodies still lying about the streets, the city was looted, wrecked, and partially burned by Chinese, Englishmen, sepoys, and lascars, so that when Gough finally went away, leaving a garrison outside but blowing an enormous breach in the walls so that it could reenter instantly if need be, the desolation and the stench of death far exceeded anything experienced at Ningpo or at any other place. It had been a bitter experience—and in one respect the joss-house at Chapu over again on a greatly enlarged scale. For Gough estimated the Tartar garrison at a bit over two thousand men, while the two brigades that attacked, being the better part of six regiments with marines and armed seamen besides, were at least two and a half times that number.

But that was all the action Gough's men saw. As for Parker's ships, they fought not at all; they did not even bombard Chinkiang. They were indispensable, however, for two reasons.

The first was the sickness spreading through the expedition, the usual business of diarrhea, malaria, dysentery. Life on the Yangtze in midsummer was not exactly healthy. Keppel's *Dido* swarmed with rats. "The *Urgent* storeship has had dreadful sickness on board, having lost her master, officers, and all her crew but three men and a boy. It was not regular cholera but something like it," observed one officer, adding that the cause "was that the different stores, such as salt fish, oil, and ghee, broke loose in the hold, and the smell caused by their getting mixed produced the fever."[14] Such things did not happen on land. Indeed, a regiment under canvas with fresh food and good water was almost certain to do better than the same regiment in the confinement of the *Belleisle*'s orlop deck, where the 98th sweltered. Put that regiment to a serious overland campaign, however, across all sorts of ground and in all sorts of weather, and its sick list lengthened as sick lists had lengthened for the regiments on the heights above Canton. Add to this a hostile countryside, in which invalids left by the way (and stragglers too) got knocked on the head; stretch that campaign to several hundred miles and several months; and its losses, even if it fought no battles and suffered no casualties, became very great indeed. If Gough's army had been obliged to scour the Yangtze basin on foot, it would have been lucky to emerge at all. Moving as it did by ship, its sick went with it and no one straggled, and—best of all—it could not be reached or stopped.

This was one of the services the fleet provided. The other counted, possibly, for even more. The fall of Chinkiang would, it was supposed, alarm Peking considerably. It did; a full report of the disaster reached the capital on 26 July—though the ordinary post took two weeks to cover the seven hundred miles to the imperial city, special couriers could do the distance in four days—and prompted the court to give Kiying (Ch'i-ying), a high mandarin whom it had sent south some months before, full powers to negotiate seriously. Yet if all the English had done had been to take a town here and a city there, the temptation to spin the negotiations out, seeming to concede a great deal yet actually performing little, would have been very strong. What made Fabian tactics useless was the English stranglehold on the river traffic.

From the first a frigate had been assigned to lie off Woosung and intercept junks trying to reach or leave Shanghai. As the other warships moved upstream, they too plundered, burned, sank, or commandeered everything that moved. Gough had misgivings, the misgivings of the previous winter, and urged successfully that the trade in common articles of food down the Chekiang coast be left alone, but in the river his colleagues had their way. "Our period of operations is limited," Pottinger observed to him and Parker, "and we therefore cannot afford to follow half measures. The Government and people of England look to decisive results from the operations of the ample forces placed under the orders and guidance of your Excellencies," and as past experience suggests that the Chinese will be perfectly happy to go on trading space for time, we must "let the Emperor see that we have the means, and are prepared to exert them, of increasing the pressure on the country to an unbearable degree."[15]

The Grand Canal was the obvious point at which to apply that pressure. When the steamers came to the place where it left the river for the north, when they reconnoitered some distance up the magnificent waterway stretching in one unbroken line as far as the eye could see, they found that the rice fleets of the year had already passed and were beyond reach. There was plenty of local traffic, however, on the great artery, on lesser waterways crisscrossing the countryside, and on the Yangtze itself; and there were towns and villages besides. Yangchow, a city almost opposite Chinkiang, paid half a million dollars in silver to be left alone. It is a fair guess that many smaller places bought immunity too. There was no systematic ravaging; it was not intended to lay waste the Yangtze basin. But the fleet had to provision, it was under instructions to paralyze the movement of goods, and it was bored. Keppel remembers foraging in the most lighthearted manner. "The best plan was to catch a fat Chinaman, generally the chief of the village. The people always pleaded poverty as an excuse. Having dropped on to a chief such as I have described, I gave him until 4:00 pm to supply twenty-five bullocks or have his tail cut off, which had the desired effect."[16] Young Parkes went junk hunting in a cutter. "The junk sailed very fast and we could hardly keep up with her, but as we rowed as well as sailed we gained upon her, and when quite near fired into her several times; but she would not stop, and we actually had to board her by force. We immediately proceeded to cut away the masts, toss the sails overboard, and cut her up so that she could not move."[17] Loch, who was with the *Modeste* now—recently promoted to captain but too junior for a command, he had come out to China as a spectator and roamed pretty much as he pleased—saw abandoned junks being plundered by river thieves and helped turn the thieves out. Some of the junks were loaded with coal, which the steamers found extremely useful. Others carried rice, oil, dried fish, dried seaweed, sugar, *samshu*, and bales of common nankeen cloth, "besides ware and furniture of various descriptions. Salt we found in great abundance on board the largest and better finished. These appear to average about one hundred tons burden" and were beautifully built, with sterns forty feet high and a single great mast.[18] The English appropriated many for use as storeships, infirmaries, above all houseboats—almost every skipper had a houseboat, with living cabin amidships, sleeping cabin forward, cookhouse aft, a Chinese crew to man her, and a couple of honest tars in charge. But whether put to some such use, collected at anchor (as the *North Star* did with the Shanghai junks at the Hwangpu's mouth), or plundered and burned by the Chinese themselves—for local authority disappeared and more damage was done by lawless natives than ever the English managed to inflict—hundreds upon hundreds of junks were driven from their normal commercial pursuits.

It would have been bad enough on a lesser river like the Min. It was a catastrophe here. As Ilipu's principal assistant reminded Kiying on 5 August, the day the *Queen* brought the headquarters ship *Marion* to join the *Cornwallis* under the walls of Nanking, "the Yangtze River is a region like a throat, at which the whole situation of the country is determined. Now they have already cut off our salt and grain transportation and stopped the communication of merchants and travelers. That is not a disease like the ringworm, but a trouble in our heart and stomach."[19] It was time to come to terms.

25

China Opened

Ilipu was the elderly, mild-mannered mandarin who had met Elliot on the Chekiang coast in the autumn of 1840 and arranged the November truce. When early the following year it dawned on the emperor that Kishen, that "honest advocate of timely yielding," was in fact yielding much more than he ought to at the Gulf of Canton, and Ishan was sent in his place to drive the English out, Ilipu was simultaneously instructed to recapture Chusan. Of course the old gentleman was utterly without the means of doing so and pleaded excuses, with the result that he was recalled at the same time as Kishen, stripped like him of honors and titles, and sentenced to exile. Ilipu had not actually given anything away, however. (Kishen had surrendered Hongkong.) When, in the autumn of 1841, the English took Chinhai and occupied Ningpo, the governor of Chekiang remembered the old man's skill at managing the barbarians and asked for him back. Months passed; the request was renewed. Early in April 1842 Ilipu was given high military rank and ordered south. With him went Kiying, the officer just mentioned.

Kiying was considerably younger than Ilipu. He lacked Ilipu's experience with provincial administration—his career had been almost entirely in and about the capital—and he had never dealt with the English. This, however, actually gave him the advantage over Ilipu who, though in demand because he had once managed the barbarians successfully, was also suspect because of it. Too many Chinese had collaborated with the red-haired devils, in the opium traffic (else how did it continue?) and now in this war. Pu Ting-pang, the traitorous comprador, had been caught and decapitated, but there must be hundreds of other Pu's—as indeed there were: the *Nemesis,* for example, carried native firemen, and when out hunting junks employed two Chinese to hail her prey—and if so many ordinary Chinese kept on close and treasonable terms with the English, a high officer of state who got along with them certainly bore watching. Thus while Ilipu's reputation for barbarian management obtained him the April appointment, it denied him the chief direction of things. That would lie with Kiying.

It was Ilipu, however, who was to make the first overture. Indeed the English supposed, in what followed, that they were dealing with a brace of high commissioners and that of the two it was Ilipu who mattered. The misunderstanding quite suited the Chinese. The English, they knew, remembered Ilipu and liked him. If anyone could coax and cajole them into leaving the Yangtze, it would be he.

To coax and cajole was not at first Ilipu's commission, nor Kiying's either. They were to manage the barbarians all right, but that did not mean giving way to them. At times—as when the English unexpectedly abandoned Chapu or approached Soochow by steamer and then suddenly withdrew—Peking recovered its hopes for military victory and instructed the pair to do whatever was necessary to achieve one. Bit by bit, however, the difficulties and dangers both real and imagined drove Peking, with many backward glances, down a different path. The Yangtze lay wide open. Barbarians had never come that way before, and defensive improvisations however ingenious (one involved enlisting divers to approach the English under water and bore holes in their hulls) were not likely to be of much use there. Far more serious, however, was what might follow once the English had ravaged the river. It was hardly plausible that they battered at the empire's gates simply to trade. They had taken Hongkong; like all barbarians before them, they must have designs on this province or that; eventually they would try to seize the capital itself. The prospect made the court frantic, so frantic that it hurried reinforcements to Tientsin, and also (it was the key to a route traditionally used by invaders from inner Asia, and the English had reconnoitered that way) to the point where the Great Wall came down to the sea.

If the English reached Peking and took it, the shock and shame of the thing would destroy the dynasty. Preserving the dynasty was every Manchu's first duty. Chinese might place detestation of invading barbarians above mere considerations of dynastic survival. Manchus would not. And since the emperor's official entourage was dominated by the Manchu interest, since his chief councillor and virtual prime minister was a Manchu, it was probably inevitable that, as news from the south grew worse and worse, the task set Kiying and Ilipu should perceptibly alter. When they set out from Peking on 15 April, that task was to control the English by a combination of threats, conciliation, and calculated delay. In the end—though they had always to watch over their shoulders in case Peking changed its mind again—it was to make a settlement no matter what the cost should be.

On 9 May they reached Hangchow. On the eighteenth Chapu fell.

Two days later the pair made their first approach, Ilipu at Kiying's direction sending a minor military officer (whom the English jocularly christened "Corporal White") to see Gutzlaff. Weeks passed. The English evacuated Chapu and disappeared. Kiying was instructed to proceed to Canton and look into the possibility of recovering Hongkong—"why should the rebellious barbarians be allowed to keep it permanently?"—and then the English appeared again, entered the Yangtze, and took Woosung and Shanghai. Meanwhile the full extent of the Chapu disaster (at Chapu a regular Tartar garrison had for the first time been overwhelmed) became known at Peking, and Kiying's reassignment was canceled. On 20 June, Ilipu again sent "Corporal White" to sound the English out. Kiying's purpose was partly to discover what the English intended to do next, it being very difficult to predict where these wily barbarians, moving swiftly in their ships, would turn. But the burden of the overture, and of the ones that followed with increasing frequency, was that Pottinger should rein in his forces, cease ravaging the river, and prepare for a round of talks.

It was exactly what Pottinger was determined *not* to do. Elliot had been humbugged that way; he would avoid the same fate by imposing the most severe conditions upon any cessation of hostilities. Kiying and Ilipu must negotiate in person. Subordinates like "Corporal White," and a certain Chang Hsi who began to appear in August, would not be allowed to speak for them. The negotiators, moreover, must carry plenipotentiary powers, so that there could be no alleging the incapacity to concede this or do that, no pleas for time while Peking was consulted. The two conditions put Kiying in an awkward spot. It was unusual for principals in such a matter to meet face to face until the hard bargaining had been completed and the path cleared of possible indignities. The subordinates in question, particularly Chang (a retainer of Ilipu who had helped with the Chekiang truce of late 1840), were among the most experienced and trusted men at his disposal. And Kiying did not have plenipotentiary powers in the western sense. He did not even have detailed instructions. He carried a general mandate; he would be judged, as a *ch'in-ch'ai* always was judged, by what he in general obtained. Given Peking's vacillating temper, he would be well advised to put off negotiating a surrender until sentiment in the capital was unequivocally favorable to one.

So the English continued up the river, and Kiying and Ilipu followed uncertainly, keeping always to the south and east. Chinkiang fell. Peking at last authorized Kiying to act as circumstances required. By now, however, there was almost no time left. On Friday, 5 August, the *Queen* steamer brought Pottinger to join the *Cornwallis* before Nanking's walls.

This news, with its clear warning of an imminent assault, reached Kiying and Ilipu late that night at Wusih, seventy miles away, and alarmed them very much. Chang Hsi started for the city at once. Ilipu, who was suffering from heat prostration, hurried after him. Monday morning they conferred with Niu Chien, the Nanking governor-general, and that afternoon Chang went aboard the *Queen* carrying a request from Ilipu that the attack not take place. In the interview that followed, with Pottinger present and Morrison and Thom doing the interpreting, Chang took a surprisingly belligerent line. It was impossible, he asserted, for the emperor to admit that things had been handled badly at Canton. "How can he acknowledge any mistakes before you foreign barbarians?" The warning that the Peiho and Peking itself would be the next English objective drew from him the retort that the foreigners had thus far been unopposed only because of the kindness of the emperor, "who cannot bear to kill or injure human creatures," yet who would, if pushed too far, call upon his people to rise, men, women, and children—"every bush will be a soldier." When reproached by Thom for the maddening Chinese habit of designating the English in derogatory terms, Chang demanded angrily what did they expect. "You kill people everywhere, plunder goods, and act like rascals; that is very disgraceful; how can you say it is not like bandits? You alien barbarians invade our China, your small country attacks our celestial court; how can you say you are not rebellious?"[1] At this point, indeed, Chang by his own account pounded the table and spat upon the floor.* The English thought he was actually going to strike Thom. But the request to stay hostilities came from the gentlemanly and well-disposed Ilipu, the English had preparations to make, and so they held their hand.

On Tuesday, the ninth, Ilipu sent over what purported to be his commission as plenipotentiary. Morrison declared it inadequate; the *Cornwallis* moved to a position from which it could batter the walls at the point where they approached the river; a brigade went ashore and worked its way along the eastern perimeter. (Nanking, though much reduced in population, still covered a large area.) Once more it looked as if the dreaded assault was about to begin, so very early Thursday morning Ilipu promised an immediate ransom of $3 million and negotiations the moment Kiying should arrive. Approaching the *Queen* with this offer, Chang passed through swarms of small boats putting troops ashore, and feared the worst. Gough, however, needed more time for reconnaissance

*The diary of Chang Hsi, which Teng has translated, adds considerably to what we know about the Chinese side of the Nanking negotiations and informs Fairbank's treatment of them (upon which I have largely relied). Chang is the man who made the remark about the Yangtze being "a region like a throat."

and for landing his artillery—it included a Madras troop with proper horses, which left their transport now for the first time. On Friday a little progress was made. Major Malcolm, Pottinger's secretary of legation, produced the draft of a settlement and got the Chinese to receive it. But these signs of a lessened military resolve encouraged Kiying (who had now arrived) and Ilipu to resume the normal tactics of evasion and delay, a thing perhaps made easier for them by the fact that the talks took place not in the middle of the menacing fleet but in a temple some distance from the river. Their representatives at these talks—for Kiying and Ilipu were not ready to appear in person—could not show evidence of plenipotentiary powers, and they did not bring to a later meeting the draft settlement Malcolm had given them, with the result that it could not even be discussed. By Saturday afternoon, therefore, Malcolm was sure he saw humbug developing, humbug of the kind that had done Elliot in, and he announced that the guns would speak and the men move at dawn the next day.

He meant it. It was obvious he meant it. Anyone watching from the walls of the city could see that the English were numerous and ready. If something was not done immediately it was going to be Chapu and Chinkiang all over again. Very early, therefore, on the morning of Sunday, 14 August, Chang Hsi came a last time to the *Queen* and said that, if the English would call their attack off, Kiying's full commission would be produced and serious negotiations on the basis of Pottinger's terms immediately follow.

That was enough. At the temple later that same day Kiying's commission was examined by Morrison and Thom and pronounced sufficient. Next the skeleton text of a treaty was drawn up in both languages, and with a certain amount of coming and going between officers of the middle rank—Pottinger no longer insisted on face-to-face meetings—the terms were worked out. On the seventeenth Pottinger formally requested Gough and Parker to suspend hostilities. On the nineteenth the Chinese accepted Morrison's rough text and sent a copy˙ off for the emperor's approval. Next morning Kiying, Ilipu, and Governor-General Niu paid a ceremonial visit to the fleet, the little *Medusa* steamer bringing them down the east wall canal as far as the river, Parker's barge conveying them to the *Cornwallis*. There they were shown about the ship and offered tea and cherry brandy. It was the Englishmen's first opportunity to study Kiying, and they liked what they saw. "A fine manly honest countenance, with pleasantness in his looks" was young Parkes's verdict.[2] Niu by contrast seemed a dull fellow; Ilipu looked old and ill. There happened to be a picture of Queen Victoria in the great cabin. When her identity was explained to the three Chinese, they rose and bowed.

Time had to pass before Peking could signify its assent, and it passed in a state of rising Chinese impatience. The English were determined that the written text of the treaty should be correct in all particulars and in both languages. Not so the Chinese. "All their anxiety, which was too powerful to be concealed," remembers Loch, "was centered upon one main object—our immediate departure."[3] The days went by with more exchanges of visits and the negotiation of unresolved details. Pottinger, Parker, and Gough called on their counterparts, received a salute from a couple of crude Chinese pieces placed perpendicularly upon their breeches, and took tea and sweetmeats. (It was now that Anstruther shook hands with Ilipu, the man who had set him free.) Two days later Pottinger went right into the heart of the city. There, at a long working session, he broached the topic that was, after all, central to the war. That topic was the opium traffic, and if anything was needed to demonstrate how single-mindedly the Chinese concentrated on getting the English out of the river and on their way home, it was their reaction now.

"They unanimously declined entering upon the subject," writes Loch, "until Sir Henry assured them he did not wish to speak of it but as a topic of private conversation." They then showed considerable interest. They wanted to know why the English did not stop the cultivation of the poppy in their Indian dominions. Pottinger gave the stock answer: if opium was prohibited in British India, it would migrate to other places. The true remedy lay with the Chinese themselves. "If your people are virtuous, they will desist from the evil practice; and if your officers are incorruptible, and obey their orders, no opium can enter your country."[4] As neither was the case, would it not be better to legalize the drug, put a duty on it, and at least benefit the treasury? It was a point Pottinger felt strongly about, it was a point his government had much on its mind—and he pressed it warmly. But it was clear that the Chinese were not going to follow his advice.

So the settlement said nothing about the opium traffic. It did not treat the mission question either. Elliot's instructions had not breathed a word about that subject, nor had Pottinger's; though the men who translated and interpreted for the plenipotentiary were almost to a man committed to the rapid extension of Christianity, though the expedition as a whole was sympathetic, in all of the memoirs and correspondence there is nowhere a hint that Pottinger was under any pressure to include a clause that would explicitly open China to the cross. No missionaries as such were with the river force. No men of business, in opium or anything else, were with it either. Christ and opium! The bearers of the first were more insistent than anyone else that China be opened. The traffic in the second was unquestionably the occasion, and quite possibly the cause, of the war that began the opening. The Treaty of Nanking dealt directly with neither.

Instead it provided that the Chinese pay an indemnity of $21 million, six of these earmarked as compensation for the famous confiscated chests. The five ports of Canton, Amoy, Foochow, Ningpo, and Shanghai were to be open to English residence and trade. Consuls were to be permitted at these five places, the Cohong was to be abolished, and a rational schedule of customs duties arranged. Future relations between England and China were to be on a basis of perfect equality. The island of Hongkong was to pass to Her Majesty in perpetuity. Chusan and Kulangsu were to remain in English hands until the $21 million had been paid; indeed, the fleet would not leave Nanking until it had loaded the first six. These and a bit besides, in thirteen articles, were the terms agreed upon—though not, it must be pointed out, with Peking's unqualified assent. Right to the end Kiying had been obliged to manage his emperor as well as the barbarians and to practice as much deception on the one as he would have wished to practice upon the other. An edict of mid-August, for example, had commanded him not to meet Pottinger until a settlement was reached and the barbarian fleet had left the river. An edict five days later had declared that Foochow was on no account to be opened and that, at places that were, the foreigners were not to reside permanently. By taking Hongkong, Pottinger, too, had exceeded his instructions. All the same, there was no comparing the two plenipotentiaries. In confidence of action, in the openness with which each faced his master and was treated by him, the advantage lay all with the Englishman.

On the twenty-seventh Peking's permission—for as much, that is, as Peking had been told about—reached Kiying and was passed immediately to Pottinger. There was a day's further delay because Ilipu was ill. On the twenty-ninth, however, he felt well enough to be carried to the great cabin of the *Cornwallis*. There everybody who could squeezed in: Pottinger, Parker, and Gough, of course; Kiying and Niu Chien; Cécille, the *Erigone's* captain, just arrived from Woosung in a commandeered junk and given a suspicious welcome; more mandarins; and on the English side every officer of field rank or its equivalent, as well as Hall of the *Nemesis* and young Parkes (because Pottinger had taken to him so). The treaty was laid out in four silk-bound copies, each containing an English and a Chinese version. Morrison affixed Pottinger's seal. A mandarin did the same for Kiying. Pottinger signed. The Chinese triumvirate signed. Then there was a handsome lunch, the union jack went up at the mizzen and the yellow flag of China at the main, and the guns fired a twenty-one gun salute. "Some of the mandarins went to see this done," says Parkes, "but came running up again much frightened. Soon after this they took their leave. Each party seemed satisfied, and pleased with each other."[5]

The fighting was over at last. It was a moment for reflection, and Mountain for one seized it. "To see a crowd of mandarins in their cumbrous boots, long petticoats, and conical caps," he wrote a friend that evening, "like beings of another planet, mingled in amity on the quarter-deck of a British ship with our military and naval officers, is a sight novel and striking, which leads the mind to future visions of God's purposes, and to the hope that this day has begun an era of blessing to China."[6] It is doubtful, however, that any Chinese saw the matter quite this way. For them the blessing was not that the English had arrived but that most of the English were leaving. "There is quiet along the seacoasts," wrote Chang Hsi sometime later in the course of a visit to his parents. "Soldiers and civilians rejoice at their work, country people and villagers enjoy the good fortune of great peace, and flesh-and-blood relatives have secured the family happiness. How extremely enjoyable and fortunate this is."[7] There were even Chinese who assumed that their side had won. Laribe, the French Lazarist, reported from the interior not many months later that the green standard men he saw returning from the lower Yangtze carried themselves as men do who have met the enemy and cut them to pieces.

For many years, indeed, the Chinese did not perceive that anything fundamental had been altered by the war and by the treaty. If anyone had told them that an irreversible act of penetration had occurred, they would have looked incredulous. They recognized the power of the English ships and men. They did not feel obliged on that account to remake their view of the world. These particular barbarians had come by sea, to the coast and up the Yangtze, which was embarrassing because it had proved impossible to resist them there, but they were barbarians just the same. When China had caught her breath she would manage them in the old familiar way. Nothing of substance had been conceded. The living and trading area outside Canton, to which the English and other foreigners had been confined from time immemorial, was to be reproduced now at four other ports. (Canton city itself would be no more accessible to foreigners than it had been before, as the English to their annoyance quickly discovered.) Allowing consuls at these ports was entirely in keeping with the ancient principle that a community of foreigners ought to be superintended by a *taipan* drawn from among themselves. The placing of a resident English ambassador at Peking—certainly the sign of signs that China was at last entering the family of nations—figured nowhere in the treaty; it was, in fact, delayed for twenty years; and since the emperor, when it did occur, happened to be a minor, the question of his receiving a western envoy without the kowtow was avoided for another ten. What did it mean anyway, this family of nations? As Fairbank remarks somewhere, to the Chinese the phrase suggested a patriarch surrounded by obedient children. If that was the picture the mind's eye gave them, why should they treat the barbarians as anything better than rough country cousins?

The tenacity of the Chinese world view was amazing. So was the resilience and recuperative power of the state. Both survived Nanking for many years; indeed, if in the 1860s the westerners had quietly packed up and gone home, it might have been discovered that, though the Ch'ing dynasty was too far down the path of decline to survive, the system as a whole was not. The westerners, however, did not go home; they had never intended to. It does not require feats of hindsight to perceive that after this war and this treaty—which at best left the opening of China half effected—it was going to be China open all the way. Neither subterfuge nor open resistance nor pretending that it was otherwise could check the process.

How, then, further acts of penetration followed this war, some bloodless, others violent, and how the progression to a China fully opened was interrupted from time to time by furious efforts at reversal— one of which, the Boxer Rebellion, is probably better known to ordinary westerners than any other piece of modern Chinese history—is another and a longer story, and has no place in this book. By the turn of the century there was hardly a self-respecting western nation that did not move freely along China's coasts and up her rivers, that did not fly its own flag, direct its own gunboats, practice its own law, and effectively protect its own citizens on Chinese soil. The foreigners did not carve China up as they carved up Africa. They did not take her over as the English took over India and the Russians central Asia. They riddled her through and through, and in the end could live, work, travel, and proselytize in her with an absolutely colonial confidence, existing not so much in enclaves (though the more than forty treaty ports were the underpinnings of the system, the places where at any given moment most of the foreigners were to be found) as in a sort of special layer that ran through, but was separated from, the Chinese society around—and too often communicated with it in the old, serviceable, stultifying pidgin. They were very active people, these foreigners. They built factories, ran steamships, managed banks. They published newspapers, raised hospitals, founded universities. They preached, converted (here the Catholics kept their lead), and spread the fabric of Christian life, not simply in its devotional aspect, but in social service and education and technical training. They advised admirals, reorganized government departments, administered the post, and supervised the collection of the customs. When the things they tried to teach the Chinese did not take, they tried again. To change China involved an enormous amount of repetition.

To change China was a large part of what opening China meant. For the technical experts, the teachers, and the missionaries it was the whole of it. Whether the West went about the job properly, or ought even to have attempted it, is for us a moot question. It is otherwise to a great many Chinese, who return an answer as simple and even simplistic as the film they once made about the Opium War, with Lin (I understand) the spotless hero, Kishen the traitor, and Dent the dark-dyed villain. As for what the westerners *did* to China, the effect they had on her, that is debatable too and is nowadays usually approached by shifting the terms a little and asking—it is the explicit title of one well-known book and the implied title of a dozen—what was China's response to the West? Some day, perhaps, we shall reverse the coin and begin to look closely at how the West responded to China. Not to China before 1842, there has always been a great deal of attention to that, but to China after—particularly the West's response to the fact of China closing, the bitterness and the dashed hopes.

For China remained open for hardly more than a century. On 20 April 1949 the English frigate *Amethyst* was fired upon by Communist guns as she navigated a stretch of the lower Yangtze that the men-of-war of western powers had moved freely over for years and years, that Parker and Hall and the others must have been quite familiar with—was held motionless for weeks and then one dark night stealthily slipped her cables and got away down the river to the sea. She never reentered. Neither did any other western warship. From that moment, if a moment must be picked, China was closed again. If the door has since opened a crack, it is for a different purpose and with a very different hand upon the knob.

The Treaty of Nanking was signed on 29 August. For some weeks longer the expedition lingered outside the city. Parties of officers and men visited the famous Porcelain Tower, climbed to the top, and chipped pieces for souvenirs until Gough made them stop. It rained a good deal, in the intervals becoming sultrier than ever; sickness spread so alarmingly through the fleet and army that, though the instrument of imperial ratification had yet to return from Peking and the $6 million in instant indemnity were not completely in hand, Parker started a number of ships down the river. Some were in very bad shape indeed; the *Belleisle,* carrying the unfortunate 98th, was a floating disaster; but even skeleton crews were able to manage them. When the *Dido* went bow first into a rice field, Keppel laid out anchors, offloaded his guns into a couple of commandeered junks, and warped clear, all in less than twenty-four hours with half his men helpless. Although many soldiers and seamen died in the river and many more after they had reached the open sea, the bulk of the force survived. It could not have done so had it been obliged to move by land.

The rest of the coast felt the sickness too. At Kulangsu half the garrison was in hospital by the middle of August. Further south the "Hongkong fever" took its annual toll. (Among the dead on Hongkong was young Horatio De Quincey of the Cameronians, recently come out with an ensign's commission purchased for him by his grandmother. It was as close as his father, England's most celebrated opium eater, would get to the war that bore in a sense his name.) As the autumn advanced, however, cooler weather brought the usual improvement, and attention turned to other things. Early in October the last of the fleet cleared the Yangtze. There was a rendezvous off Chusan; then most of the ships and men set off on the first leg of the long journey home. Ahead of them on the *Auckland* steamer hurried Major Malcolm, Pottinger's secretary of legation, with the imperial instrument of ratification in his bag. Word reached the coast that survivors of the shipwrecked *Ann* and *Nerbudda* were alive on Formosa. Parker sent a 10-gun brig to fetch them; she returned with Denham of the *Ann* and nine other men; almost three hundred more, it seemed, had died on the island in the course of the past twelve months, starved, beaten, or deliberately beheaded by the mandarins there. The appalling story, when it reached London, quite eclipsed the Anstruther and Noble affairs and confirmed Englishmen in their general opinion as to who, between themselves and the Celestials, the real barbarians were.

This was some time after these same Englishmen had learned that the war was over. The news had arrived late in November, simultaneously with word of important successes in Afghanistan, and there was no mistaking which commanded the greater notice. The Nanking settlement was perfectly satisfactory. "It secures us a few round millions of dollars and no end of very refreshing tea. It gives an impetus to trade, cedes us one island in perpetuity, and in short puts that sort of climax to the war which satisfies our interests more than our vanity and rather gives over glory a preponderance to gain." The *Illustrated London News,* which advanced this judgment, nevertheless devoted twice as much space to the recapture of Kabul as it did to the Yangtze campaign. The *Times* was even less enraptured. No doubt Chinese arrogance needed piercing;

no doubt "that silly and presumptuous despot," the emperor, had to be brought down a peg. The war had arisen, however, over a quarrel that the *Times* had never been able to believe just, a⁻ 1 it had been fought in a manner that brought very little credit to British arms. What pleased the paper most, indeed, about the China news was the thought that its readers would no longer be obliged to hear by each Indian mail that the successors in arms to the heroes of the Peninsula were busy "sweeping away with cannon or bayonet whole crowds of poor pigtailed animals."[8]

About the Gulf of Canton there was considerably more enthusiasm. "China is not now fast shut up as beforetime but is in very truth a land of promise," wrote Lockhart to his London Missionary Society. "What changes there will be," observed Libois of the Missions Etrangères, adding a few months later that it seemed to him "easier than ever to get into China."[9] At Jardine's, however, Alexander Matheson wondered privately whether peace would be good for the firm. "For years to come we shall not be in a better position, or trade to so much advantage, as during the continuance of the war, especially if the opium trade is to be hampered, as I suspect it will be."[10] Fortunately it was not. Though excluded from the five treaty ports, the traffic prospered openly at anchorages nearby (Woosung serving Shanghai, for example) as well as at Hongkong and the old coastal stations like Namoa, until in 1858 Peking at last recognized fiction for fact and made the whole thing legal. Legal it remained for more than half a century. World War I had passed before the last chests of Indian opium were burned, with considerable publicity, on a Shanghai dock, and by that time the poppy was so extensively cultivated within China itself that prohibiting imports meant almost nothing. All that came later, however. For the moment what mattered was that the trade recovered from the uncertainties and interruptions placed upon it by the war, and resumed its normal course.

The year ran out. Early in December there was a short, sharp riot at the factories, with several deaths and a good deal of looting and burning. Peter Parker, who had returned from America to reopen the Hog Lane hospital and had brought a young wife with him, thought it prudent to slip her into the relative safety of a hong merchant's residence. Since the houses affected were those in the Creek, Dutch and New English that had been half wrecked in May 1841, and since the riot itself seemed to have been provoked by unruly lascars up from Whampoa, many agreed with Pottinger that the affair was no augury of the future (they were wrong). By now the bulk of the expedition had reached Hongkong. On 20 December fifty ships, Gough aboard one, sailed for Singapore, India, and beyond. Christmas came and went. On the thirty-first Pottinger sat in Government House on what was now incontestably English soil and gazed across the water at China two miles away. The *Good Success* unloaded raw cotton and Malwa practically at his feet; the *Red Rover* waited at Calcutta for the first opium sale of the season; the *Ariel* and the *Hellas* beat up the Fukien coast with chests for Jardine Matheson's floating drug depots. Gutzlaff played civil magistrate on Chusan with his usual insensitivity and gusto. Milne explored Ningpo (it pained him that women and children bolted at the sight of him). Bridgman prepared to conclude the month's number of the *Repository*. As the Lord has chosen England to chastise and humble China, he wrote, so will He likely employ her "to introduce the blessings of Christian civilization and free intercourse among her millions."[11] And Lin, the valiant and incorruptible, Lin who had tried and failed to make all this impossible, pursued the exile's life in cold and lonely Ili.

Far away in London on this last day of 1842, Peking's instrument of ratification having been safely delivered by Major Malcolm, the great seal of England was affixed to a copy of the Treaty of Nanking at the lord chancellor's house in Great George Street—and the war in every formal sense was over. That night Queen Victoria danced the new year in at Windsor Castle. Did anyone tell her that she was now Sister to the Emperor and Aunt to the Moon?

Having resisted so long in the matter of compensation for the twenty thousand chests, Her Majesty's government did not hesitate to resist a little longer. It was not until August 1843 that the holders of opium scrip (receipts for opium surrendered, which were often bought and sold like bills of exchange) were summoned to the treasury chamber in Whitehall and paid. What they received averaged about $300 a chest, far less than Dent, Matheson, and the others had originally clamored for—but much more, as many people pointed out, than they could possibly have realized by selling in the depressed China market of early 1839. In the end most felt that the figure was reasonable.

Jardine was not alive to agree. He had died in February at his Upper Baker Street house, aged fifty-nine, unmarried and not much noticed. It was otherwise with James Matheson. Good health and fortune preserved him for another thirty-five years. He sat regularly in Parliament, kept busy with this and that, and for a time served as chairman of the P and O—which by then was active on the China coast. Quite early he bought the island of Lewis in the outer Hebrides. Some say this made him the second largest landed proprietor in the United Kingdom. For his efforts to relieve the sufferings of his island tenants during the great potato famine he received, only naturally, a baronetcy.

What happened to all the other "Early Victorian Vikings" (as Arthur Waley likes to call them) it would be impossible as well as tedious to relate. Pottinger became governor of Madras but did not distinguish himself in the post. Charles Elliot served his country well if obscurely as governor successively of Bermuda, Trinidad, and St. Helena. Hall left the *Nemesis* for the Royal Navy proper, commanded steam yachts and frigates, and in the Crimean War took a seventy-four rebuilt as a 60-gun screw ship into the Baltic—she was in fact our old friend the *Blenheim*. It was Gough who rose the highest. Made commander-in-chief in India after Nicolls, he fought the two Sikh Wars, became viscount and field marshal, and was honored in death with a large bronze statue in Phoenix Park, Dublin, cast partly from cannon he had brought back from China. Little Winston Churchill was taken to see this statue dedicated, and never forgot it, but it is probably fancy to suppose that at the moment of the unveiling an Early Victorian Viking spoke somehow to a Late.

John Morrison died suddenly at Hongkong on the first anniversary of the signing of the Treaty of Nanking. A few days later Old Howqua succumbed to acute diarrhea at his home on Honam, leaving a large fortune and a name so well known outside China that years later his likeness was still to be seen at Madame Tussaud's. Lin also received that accolade. "The Author of the China War," his label read, adding (since it was what the English chiefly remembered him for) that he had destroyed British property worth £2.5 million! He had been called out of exile in 1845, given other posts, and was on his way to a fresh assignment when he died near Canton in the autumn of 1850. The *Repository* noted his demise with respect. Two years later it too was dead, of natural causes. Bridgman survived another decade and lies buried in Shanghai. Williams accompanied Perry to Japan (which he had visited before, you will remember), became secretary and interpreter to the American Legation at Peking, and after more than forty years in China retired to Yale, preceded in reputation by the enormous book that he called *The Middle Kingdom*—the book that made him the foremost American Sinologist of his day.

Perboyre obtained immortality in another way. He was beatified in 1889, the first of the China martyrs to be thus recognized. It was another eleven years before the same honor was bestowed on his older colleague and model, Clet.

The *Nemesis* was last heard of in Burma in the early fifties. The *Volage* became a powder hulk, the *Cornwallis* a jetty at Sheerness, the *Wellesley* a Thames training ship—until, under another name, she was sunk by German bombs in the fall of 1940. Russell and Company's first receiving ship was sold to the Chinese, who made a western-style man-of-war of her and stationed her near Canton. One night a flood tide threw her on a rock and she foundered. Then the Chinese cut away her masts except for part of the fore, hung out a lantern, and called her a lighthouse, the river's first. "When I last saw the stump of the mast twenty-eight years after," remembers Hunter, "a great bank of mud had formed round the hull, and a faint glimmer from a penny dip in a small paper lantern marked the last resting place of the *Lintin*."[12] As for the opium clippers, they went on with their lucrative, hazardous voyages until more often than not they just disappeared somewhere. That is what happened to the *Red Rover* one season in the Bay of Bengal.

Curiously, however, the china dinner service that Clifton had commissioned and put into this ship of his—this first of all opium clippers—survived. When Clifton's grandson, a Somerset solicitor, died at Crewkerne a few years ago, the service passed by bequest to Matheson and Company, Ltd., of London. For Matheson and Company is decidedly in existence today. In the late 1840s it succeeded Magniac and Smith, and it still handles the London business of Jardine, Matheson and Company—which is alive too and very active on the China coast. Of course the firm does not now traffic in opium. It got out of that a hundred years ago when the trade was at its height, when Indian exports to China sometimes reached eighty thousand chests a year. Nor does it do business inside China. That has not been possible for some time. But it does business *with* China—indeed, from its headquarters in Hongkong and its lesser offices about the Pacific's rim it keeps an eye out for whatever may turn up anywhere in that immense basin, and if the thing seems promising, moves into it as shrewdly, as forcefully, as aggressively even, as ever the first Jardine or Matheson did. There are none of that name in the firm any more, but there are others as enterprising, some third and fourth generation, and the proportion who are Scots is still high.

If you go around, then, to 3 Lombard Street, you will find *Red Rover*'s dinner service, and portraits and other things from the old days of the China trade, as well as a keen recollection of Jardine Matheson's beginnings and a still keener interest. The same is not true of the Ghazipur opium factory. Elsewhere in India there are reminders of the Opium War. In the old Bombay town hall now become a public library, just off the reading room where newspapers in English and eleven Indian languages doze upon the racks, stands a marble statue of Jamsetjee Jeejeebhoy, the first Parsee baronet, knighted in the spring of 1842 for his public services and his philanthropy, with never a hint upon his benign countenance that a part of his immense fortune was amassed out of the Malwa he consigned to Jardine's. In the museum at Fort St. George, Madras, they keep the cage Anstruther recovered from Ningpo and three Chinese war helmets picked up nearby. At Ghazipur, however, they have no time for antiquities. It is not much over sixty years since the last cake-maker sat to his work in the caking room there, petal sheets on one side, *lewah* and poppy trash on the other, brass cup before. Over the century or more that Ghazipur supplied opium for the pipes of China, there must have been thousands of those brass cups required. Surely a few are still lying around. But if you ask them to show you one, if you even ask them to describe one, they will look blank, it will be plain they do not know what you are talking about, and for a moment you will wonder whether the old Indian opium trade ever really existed at all.

Appendix
Notes
Sources
Index

Appendix

CALCUTTA OPIUM SALES

Tables showing as well as can be determined how many chests left India for China year by year are available in a number of places: for example, in the appendix to Hsin-pao Chang, *Commissioner Lin and the Opium War* (Cambridge: Harvard University Press, 1964). But I know of none showing prices and quantities at the Calcutta sales and accordingly give one for the crisis and war years:

Monthly sale	*Quantity sold*		*Average price per chest*	
	(P—Patna, B—Benares)		(in rupees)	
January 1839	P - 4,500	B - 2,500	P - 839	B - 732
February	P - 1,500	B - 1,000	P - 688	B - 620
April	P - 3,000	B - 400	P - 365	B - 390
May	P - 1,500	B - 1,000	P - 235	B - 197
July	P - 2,345	B - 818	P - 283	B - 304
January 1840	P - 4,000	B - 2,000	P - 438	B - 413
February	P - 1,600	B - 800	P - 610	B - 551
April	P - 2,500	B - 853	P - 540	B - 501
May	P - 1,400	B - 700	P - 644	B - 628
June	P - 1,769	B - 1,089	P - 736	B - 686
January 1841	P - 4,000	B - 2,000	P - 796	B - 699
February	P - 1,400	B - 700	P - 753	B - 667
April	P - 3,000	B - 1,500	P - 664	B - 630
May	P - 1,400	B - 700	P - 733	B - 669
June	P - 2,840	B - 1,287	P - 683	B - 660
January 1842	P - 4,000	B - 1,500	P - 787	B - 764
February	P - 1,400	B - 600	P - 828	B - 810
April	P - 3,000	B - 1,200	P - 785	B - 768
May	P - 1,600	B - 900	P - 841	B - 803
June	P - 3,014	B - 1,148	P - 683	B - 660

Approximate rates of exchange: Rs. 1 = 2 shillings
$1 = 5 shillings
$1 = Rs. 2½

Notes

The following abbreviations appear in the notes:

ABCFM	American Board of Commissioners for Foreign Missions papers
Annales	*Annales de la propagation de la foi*
Annales C.M.	*Annales de la congrégation de la mission*
Broughton	Broughton papers, Add. MSS 36,474
Carrington	Carrington papers
FO	Foreign Office series, Public Record Office
Forbes	Forbes papers
Heard	Heard papers
IOL	India Office Library (including India Office Records)
JM	Jardine Matheson papers
Lay	Lay papers
LMS	London Missionary Society papers
ME	Missions Etrangères papers
PP	Parliamentary Papers (Commons)
Press	*Canton Press*
Register	*Canton Register*
Repository	*Chinese Repository*
Squire	Squire papers
Times	London *Times*
USJ	*United Service Journal*
Williams	Williams papers

CHAPTER 1
1. T. A. M. Gennoe, *Notes on the Cultivation of Poppy*.
2. W. Eatwell, *On the Poppy Cultivation and the Benares Opium Agency*.
3. Sir George Birdwood, *First Report of the Royal Commission on Opium*, 1894, 60 (C7313), 667, PP.

4. Sir John Strachey, ibid., p. 652.

5. J. Elliot Bingham, *Narrative of the Expedition to China*, 1:88.

6. D. MacPherson, *Two Years in China*, pp. 245-46.

7. Bayard Taylor, *India, China and Japan* (New York, 1887), p. 494.

8. Quotations are from *Opium; the Diary of a Cure*, trans. Margaret Crosland and Sinclair Road (New York: Grove Press, 1958).

9. 1839 ed., 2:66.

10. D. Butter, "On the Preparation of Opium for the China Market," *Journal of the Asiatic Society of Bengal* 5 (March 1836): 171-79.

CHAPTER 2
1. Frederick W. Williams, *The Life and Letters of Samuel Wells Williams*, p. 170.

2. Elma Loines, *The China Trade Post-Bag*, p. 32.

3. Ibid., p. 34.

4. Ibid., p. 115.

5. Ibid., pp. 118-19.

CHAPTER 3
1. Letter to his uncle, 10 Aug. 1836, *Annales C.M.*, 3:229.

2. Hosea Ballou Morse, *The Chronicles of the East India Company Trading to China, 1635-1834*, 2:247-52.

3. William C. Hunter, *Bits of Old China*, p. 226.

4. 11 Mar. 1839, Canton Agency Consultations, China 262, IOL.

5. *Repository*, 2:372.

6. G. W. Keeton, *Development of Extraterritoriality in China* (London, 1928), 1:59.

7. Earl Swisher, "Extraterritoriality and the Wabash Case," *American Journal of International Law* 45 (July 1951): 566-67.

8. *Repository*, 2:211.

9. Ibid., pp. 356-72.

CHAPTER 4
1. Elma Loines, *The China Trade Post-Bag*, p. 164.

2. Ibid., p. 163.

3. *Repository*, 5:548-50.

4. David Owen, *British Opium Policy in China and India*, p. 87.

5. *Select Committee on the Trade with China*, 1840, 7 (359), 93, PP.

6. Ibid., p. 73.

7. 17 Apr. 1838, Lay.

8. W. W. Wood, *Sketches of China*, pp. 35-36.

9. *Select Committee on the Trade with China*, 1840, 7 (359), 95, PP.

10. William C. Hunter, *Bits of Old China*, p. 42.

CHAPTER 5
1. Michael Greenberg, *British Trade and the Opening of China, 1800-42*, p. 5.

2. Charles King in the *Repository*, 6:512.

3. 24 Jan. 1842, Bengal Proceedings, P/107/51, IOL.

4. Elma Loines, *The China Trade Post-Bag*, p. 160.

5. *Repository*, 2:27.

6. Peter Auber, *China*, p. 361.

7. *Hostilities between the Chinese and British Subjects Engaged in the Opium Trade, 1830-33*, 1840, 36 (156), 13, PP.

CHAPTER 6
1. Eliza Morrison, *Memoirs of the Life and Labours of Robert Morrison, D.D.*, 2:510.

2. *Correspondence Relating to China*, 1840, 36 (223), 5, PP.

3. Ibid., p. 12.

4. 11 June 1834, William Jardine Private Letter Books, vol. 3, JM.

5. *Correspondence Relating to China,* 1840, 36 (223), 18, PP.

6. 20 Aug. 1834, William Jardine Private Letter Books, vol. 3, JM.

7. *Correspondence Relating to China,* 1840, 36 (223), 10, PP.

8. Ibid., p. 13.

9. *Repository,* 2 Sept. 1834.

10. 18 Aug. 1834, William Jardine Private Letter Books, vol. 3, JM.

11. *Correspondence Relating to China,* 1840, 36 (223), 24, PP.

12. Ibid., p. 16.

13. *Register,* 26 Aug. 1834.

14. *Correspondence Relating to China,* 1840, 36 (223), 36, PP.

15. *Register,* 7 Oct. 1834.

16. *Correspondence Relating to China,* 1840, 36 (223), 44, 80, PP.

CHAPTER 7

1. *Correspondence Relating to China,* 1840, 36 (223), 115, PP.

2. Ibid., p. 197.

3. *Repository,* 3:363; 5:180.

4. Ibid., 2:4.

5. Ibid., 1:144.

6. G. R. Williamson, *Memoir of the Reverend David Abeel,* p. 64.

7. Eliza Morrison, *Memoirs of the Life and Labours of Robert Morrison, D.D.,* 1:136.

8. L. Kitzan, "The London Missionary Society in India and China, 1798-1834" (Ph.D. dissertation, University of Toronto, 1965), p. 131.

9. *Missionary Register* 12 (1835): 91.

10. Michael Greenberg, *British Trade and the Opening of China, 1800-42,* p. 139, note 4.

11. *Repository,* 4:310.

12. 22 Dec. 1837, Lay.

13. Frederick W. Williams, *The Life and Letters of Samuel Wells Williams,* p. 65.

14. Ibid., p. 83.

15. Ibid., p. 109.

16. 4 Nov. 1836, Lay.

17. *Repository,* 2:429.

18. Eliza J. G. Bridgman, ed., *The Life and Labors of Elijah Coleman Bridgman,* p. 21.

19. *Repository,* 5:372.

20. Ibid., 4:463.

21. Letter to LMS, 26 Mar. 1830, South China 1830-39, LMS.

22. 10 Oct. 1836, Lay.

23. Williams to Anderson, 5 Oct. 1838, South China 1838-44, ABCFM.

24. William Milne, *A Retrospect of the First Ten Years of the Protestant Mission to China,* p. 82.

25. Bridgman to Anderson, 7 Mar. 1838, ABCFM.

26. *Repository,* 1:145.

27. Maxwell of the *Alceste,* ibid., 8:590

28. Morrison, *Memoirs,* 2:503.

CHAPTER 8

1. 2 Apr. 1836, Williams.

2. Elma Loines, *The China Trade Post-Bag,* p. 187.

3. Williams to Anderson, n.d. (late 1837?), South China 1831-38, ABCFM.

4. Perboyre to Torrette, 7 Mar. 1836, *Annales,* 11:14.

5. Ibid., 14:73-80. Though dated 10 Aug. 1840, Bertrand's letter describes the routine of some years before.

6. Ibid., p 77.

7. Faivre to Etienne, 28 Feb. 1838, ibid., 12:185-86.

8. Ibid., p. 187.

9. Pupier to Dubois, 17 June 1825, ibid., 3:47.

10. Ibid., p. 46; Albrand to Directors, 22 Nov. 1834, ibid., 8:133.

11. Squire to the Church Missionary Society, 10 Nov. 1838, Squire.

12. Robert Morrison, *A View of China*, p. 122.

13. Faivre to Etienne, 28 Feb. 1838, *Annales*, 12:186.

CHAPTER 9

1. Faivre to Constant Nozo, 23 May 1839, *Annales C.M.*, 6:167-212.

2. John Slade, *Narrative of the Late Proceedings and Events in China*, pp. 177-78.

3. *Repository*, 5:572-73.

4. Danicourt to Sister Boulet, 10 Dec. 1837, *Annales C.M.*, 5:245.

5. Hsin-pao Chang, *Commissioner Lin and the Opium War*, p. 89.

6. *Repository*, 5:336.

7. James Matheson, *The Present Position and Prospects of the British Trade with China* (London, 1838), pp. 1, 59.

8. *Repository*, 5:412.

9. Ibid., p. 173.

10. *Correspondence Relating to China*, 1840, 36 (223), 190, PP.

CHAPTER 10

1. Squire to the Church Missionary Society, 10 Nov. 1838, Squire.

2. Russell and Company to J. M. Forbes, 17 Sept. 1838, Forbes.

3. Jardine to Jamsetjee, 11 Oct. 1838, William Jardine Private Letter Books, vol. 7, JM.

4. Jardine to Baylis, 16 Dec. 1838, ibid.

5. Danicourt to his parents, 22 Dec. 1838, *Annales C.M.*, 5:280-81.

6. Perboyre to Carrole, 12 Sept. 1838, *Annales*, 13:147.

7. 5 Dec. 1838, William Jardine Private Letter Books, vol. 7, JM.

8. Thom to Jardine, 8 Dec. 1838, unbound correspondence (local, Canton), JM.

9. *Register*, 13 Dec. 1838.

10. 1 Jan. 1839, William Jardine Private Letter Books, vol. 7, JM.

11. *Correspondence Relating to China*, 1840, 36 (223), PP.

12. *Repository*, 7:586-87.

13. Legrégeois to Directors, 10 Jan. 1839, vol. 323, ME.

14. 12 Dec. 1838, ibid.

15. 17 Dec. 1838, ibid.

16. Russell and Company to J. M. Forbes, 1 Jan. 1839, Forbes.

17. 4 Mar. 1839, ibid.

18. *Register*, 29 Jan. 1839.

19. Matheson to J. A. Smith, 25 Jan. 1839, James Matheson Private Letter Books, vol. 3, JM.

20. *Repository*, 7:605.

21. *Select Committee on the Trade with China*, 1840, 7 (359), 69, PP.

22. Matheson to T. W. Henderson, 9 Mar 1838, James Matheson Private Letter Books, vol. 3, JM.

CHAPTER 11

1. Matheson to Parry, 12 Mar. 1839, James Matheson Private Letter Books, vol. 3, JM.

2. Arthur Waley, *The Opium War through Chinese Eyes*, pp. 28-31. Compare with the undoubtedly exact but stilted translation in Hsin-pao Chang, *Commissioner Lin and the Opium War*, p. 135.

3. Russell and Company to J. M. Forbes, 16 Mar. 1839, Forbes.

4. John Slade, *Narrative of the Late Proceedings and Events in China*, p. 36.

5. Matheson to Jardine, 1 May 1839, James Matheson Private Letter Books, vol. 4, JM.

6. *Correspondence Relating to China*, 1840, 36 (223), 349, PP.

7. Ibid., p. 357.

8. Slade, *Narrative of Proceedings*, pp. 53-54.

9. William C. Hunter, "Journal of Occurrences at Canton during the Cessation of Trade, 1839," MS in the Boston Athenaeum.

10. *Correspondence Relating to China*, 1840, 36 (223), 367, PP.

11. Hunter, "Journal," 26 Mar. 1839.

12. G. R. Williamson, *Memoir of the Reverend David Abeel*, p. 187.

13. *Repository*, 7:628-33.

14. *Correspondence Relating to China*, 1840, 36 (223), 370, PP.

15. Hunter, "Journal," 26 Mar. 1839.

16. *Correspondence Relating to China*, 1840, 36 (223), 374, PP.

17. *Select Committee on the Trade with Chine'*1840,(359), 147, PP.

18. Slade, *Narrative of Proceedings*, p. 59.

19. *Repository*, 11:372.

20. 17 Apr. 1839, James Matheson Private Letter Books, vol. 4, JM.

21. Hunter, "Journal," 2 May 1839.

22. Bridgman's account of the visit is in *Repository*, 8:70-77; King's is in the *Times*, 1 Nov. 1839.

23. P. C. Kuo, *A Critical Study of the First Anglo-Chinese War*, p. 247.

CHAPTER 12

1. *Correspondence Relating to China*, 1840, 36 (223), 392, PP.

2. Ibid., p. 390.

3. Legrégeois to Directors, 13 Apr. 1839, vol. 323, ME.

4. Matheson to Jamsetjee, 3 Apr. 1839, James Matheson Private Letter Books, vol. 4, JM.

5. Matheson to Henderson, 29 May 1839, ibid.

6. Elma Loines, *The China Trade Post-Bag*, p. 71.

7. Thacker's testimony, in *Select Committee on the Trade with China*, 1840, 7 (359), 64, PP.

8. Williams to Anderson, 17 May 1839, South China 1838-44, ABCFM.

9. Parker to Anderson, 4 July 1839, ibid.

10. Legrégeois to Directors, 11 Apr. 1839, vol. 323, ME; Legrégeois to Dubois, 3 Apr. 1839, ibid.

11. W. H. Hughes, 15 July 1839, FO 17/36.

12. Matheson to John Rees, 2 July 1839, Coast Private Letter Books, vol. 1, JM.

13. Matheson to J. A. Smith, 24 Aug. 1839, James Matheson Private Letter Books, vol. 4, JM.

14. Adam Elmslie to William Elmslie, 3 Sept. 1839, FO 17/35.

15. G. R. Williamson, *Memoir of the Reverend David Abeel*, p. 192.

16. Arthur Waley, *The Opium War through Chinese Eyes*, pp. 64-65.

17. Adam Elmslie to William Elmslie, 5 Sept. 1839, FO 17/35.

18. Bell to Larpent, 6 July 1839, FO 17/36.

19. *Repository*, 8:637.

CHAPTER 13

1. Auckland to Hobhouse, 25 May 1839, Broughton.

2. Auckland to Hobhouse, 6 June 1839, Broughton.

3. Matheson to Captain Grant, 18 June 1838, James Matheson Private Letter Books, vol. 3, JM.

4. John Trotter, 2 May 1839, Bengal Proceedings, P/107/39, IOL.

5. Bethune to Maitland, 28 May 1839, FO 17/35.

6. "Memorandum on W. Strangway's letter of 20 Sept. 1839," by "T. W. W.," 21 Sept. 1839, China Foreign Office Instructions and Correspondence, 1839-40, IOL.

7. Auckland to Hobhouse, 23 Jan. 1840 and 16 Feb. 1840, Broughton.

8. Bombay Chamber of Commerce Resolution, 3 June 1839, FO 17/35.

9. Matheson to J. A. Smith, 6 May 1839 (enclosing Matheson to Jardine, 1 May), James Matheson Private Letter Books, vol. 4, JM.

10. *Select Committee on the Trade with China,* 1840, 7 (359), 124, PP.

11. Matheson to J. A. Smith, 24 Sept. 1839, James Matheson Private Letter Books, vol. 4, JM.

12. Jardine to Matheson, quoted without a date in Maurice Collis, *Foreign Mud,* p. 253.

13. Elliot to Palmerston, 3 Apr. 1839, FO 17/31.

14. John Cam Hobhouse, Baron Broughton, *Recollections of a Long Life,* 5:227-28.

15. 4 Nov. 1839, as amended 23 Nov. 1839. The text is reproduced in Elliot to Palmerston, 18 July 1840, FO 17/40.

CHAPTER 14

1. Legrégeois to Directors, vol. 323, ME.

2. Ibid., 10 Jan. 1840.

3. William C. Hunter, *Bits of Old China,* p. 53.

4. Legrégeois to Directors, 10 Jan. 1840, vol. 323, ME.

5. 2 Mar. 1840, in F. Combaluzier, "Martyre du bienheureux Jean-Gabriel Perboyre," *Neue Zeitschrift für Missionswissenschaft,* 9 (1953): 253.

6. Georges Goyau, *La Congrégation de la Mission des Lazaristes* (Paris, 1938), p. 216.

7. 15 Mar. 1840, vol. 323, ME.

8. Forbes to A. Heard, 21 Jan. 1940, BM-8, Heard.

9. Matheson to J. A. Smith, 17 Feb. 1840, James Matheson Private Letter Books, vol. 5, JM.

10. Robert Bennet Forbes, *Personal Reminiscences,* p. 155.

11. 29 Jan. 1840, quoted in the *Times,* 13 Mar. 1840.

12. Hansard's *Parliamentary Debates,* 3rd ser., 53:818.

13. Ibid., p. 940.

14. Ibid., 54:34.

15. 25 Apr. 1840.

16. Arthur Waley, *The Opium War through Chinese Eyes,* p. 96.

17. *Hampshire Telegraph,* 8 Feb. 1840, quoted in the *Times,* 10 Feb. 1840.

18. 18 Apr. 1840, James Matheson Private Letter Books, vol. 5, JM.

19. In Matheson to Baylis, 16 June 1840, Coast Private Letter Books, vol. 1, JM.

20. *Repository,* 9:2.

21. Milne to Mission House, 9 Mar. and 18 June 1840, South China 1840-47, LMS; Bull to Carrington, 5 May 1840, Carrington.

CHAPTER 15

1. Memorandum, Admiralty, 17 Nov. 1839, FO 17/36.

2. Memorandum, 20 May, in Elliot to Palmerston, 10 June 1840, FO 17/40.

3. Elliot to Palmerston, 10 Jan. 1840, ibid.

4. *Repository,* 9:106.

5. Palmerston to "the Minister of the Emperor," 20 Feb. 1840, China Foreign Office Instructions and Correspondence, 1839-40, IOL.

6. *Repository,* 9:223.

7. Ibid., p. 230.

8. Armine S. H. Mountain, *Memoirs and Letters,* p. 170.

9. Lord Robert Jocelyn, *Six Months with the Chinese Expedition,* p. 54.

10. J. Elliot Bingham, *Narrative of the Expedition to China,* 1:338.

11. Thom to Matheson, 15 July 1840, unbound miscellaneous correspondence, JM.

12. 20 July 1840, FO 17/40.

13. *Repository,* 9:231.

CHAPTER 16

1. Earl Swisher, *China's Management of the American Barbarians,* p. 78.

2. P. C. Kuo, *A Critical Study of the First Anglo-Chinese War,* p. 261.

3. Elliot's account of the parley is contained in a memorandum dated 31 Aug. 1840, FO 17/39.

4. *Correspondence Relating to China,* 1840, 36 (223), 387 and 385, PP.

5. Elliot to Palmerston, 21 Sept. 1840, FO 17/39.

CHAPTER 17

1. 17 Feb. 1840, James Matheson Private Letter Books, vol. 5, JM.

2. Bull to Carrington, 6 Mar. 1840, Carrington.

3. Matheson to Jamsetjee, 4 Aug. 1840, James Matheson Private Letter Books, vol. 5, JM.

4. Matheson to Paterson, 24 Sept. 1840, Coast Private Letter Books, vol. 1, JM.

5. J. Elliot Bingham, *Narrative of the Expedition to China,* 1:119.

6. *Repository,* 9:324, 416.

7. Ibid., p. 406.

8. Hobson, Lockhart, and Milne to the Society, 18 Aug. 1840, South China 1840-47, LMS.

9. S. Wells to Frederick Williams, 26 Oct. 1840, Williams.

10. *Repository,* 9:321.

11. S. Wells to Frederick Williams, 29 July 1840, Williams.

12. Baldus to the Congregation, 9 Sept. 1840, *Annales C.M.,* 8:137, 167.

13. Parker to Anderson, 24 June 1840, South China 1838-44, ABCFM.

14. Matheson to Jamsetjee, 19 Apr. 1840, James Matheson Private Letter Books, vol. 5, JM.

15. Diver to Anderson, 18 July 1840, South China 1838-44, ABCFM.

16. Abeel to Anderson, P.S. to 19 Aug. 1840, South China 1838-44, ABCFM; G. R. Williamson, *Memoir of the Reverend David Abeel,* p. 201; Frederick W. Williams, *The Life and Letters of Samuel Wells Williams,* p. 120; *Repository,* 9:327.

CHAPTER 18

1. When Torrette reached China in October 1829, he found one other French Lazarist at Macao (the aged and veteran Lamiot) and none in the interior. By the autumn of 1840 his colleagues at the *procure* and elsewhere, as far distant as Mongolia, were Baldus, Danicourt, Faivre, Gabet, Guillet, Huc, Laribe, Lavaissière, Mouly, Perboyre, Perry, Peschaud, Privas, Rameaux, Simiand, and Vautrin. Working with them were about twenty priests. The seminarians at Macao, carefully observed before they were brought in from the provinces and then kept in training for a surprising number of years, numbered ten.

2. Rameaux to Torrette, 15 Oct. 1840, in F. Combaluzier,"Martyre du bienheureux Jean-Gabriel Perboyre," *Neue Zeitschrift für Missionswissenschaft* 9 (1953): 263-64.

3. Maresca to Rameaux, 22 Sept. 1840, in ibid., pp. 260-62.

4. Strachan's journal is in FO 17/49.

5. Armine S. H. Mountain, *Memoirs and Letters,* p. 175.

6. Thom to Matheson, 15 July 1840, unbound miscellaneous correspondence, JM.

7. Anstruther's account of his capture is in *Repository,* 10:506-10.

8. Ann Noble's account of the loss of the *Kite* and her capture is in ibid., pp. 191-204.

9. Strachan's journal, 19 Sept. 1840, FO 17/49.

10. The Elliots to Palmerston, 6 Nov. 1840, FO 17/39.

11. From a Chinese communication (translation) in the Elliots to Palmerston, 18 Nov. 1840, ibid.

12. *Press,* 10 Mar. 1841.

13. Lady Ellis, ed., *Memoirs and Services of Sir Samuel Burdon Ellis,* p. 136.

CHAPTER 19

1. *Times,* 30 Mar. 1840.

2. 9 Jan. 1841.

3. The three were Berneux, Chamaison, and Maistre. Already with Legrégeois at Macao were Callery, Galy, Libois, Retord, and Taillandier. In Szechwan were Bertrand, Delamarre, Desflèches, Favand, Freycenon, Mariette, Papin, Pérocheau (styled Bishop of Maxula, also Vicar Apostolic of Szechwan in succession to the late Fontana), Ponsot, and Renou. Barentin

was at Hinghwa in southern Fukien. Verrolles was on his way from Szechwan to Manchuria to take charge of a new vicariat apostolic there. And a certain Ferréol, who had reached Macao at the beginning of the year, was moving towards Korea by a roundabout route deep in the interior.

Long before he reached his destination, Ferréol would learn that the three Missions Etrangères men who had opened the mission in that kingdom had been martyred near Seoul in September 1839—six days after Perboyre's arrest, though that was pure coincidence.

4. Legrégeois to Directors, 31 Aug. 1840, vol. 323, ME.

5. 2 Dec. 1840.

6. 23 Nov. 1840, James Matheson Private Letter Books, vol. 6, JM.

7. Hsin-pao Chang, *Commissioner Lin and the Opium War*, p. 212; *Repository*, 9:413.

8. Arthur Waley, *The Opium War through Chinese Eyes*, p. 120.

9. In Stanton to Legrégeois, n.d. (probably 12 Dec. 1840), vol. 304, ME.

10. Elliot to Auckland, 13 Dec. 1840, FO 17/39.

11. Morrison's translation of the Kishen-Elliot exchange is in Elliot to Palmerston, 5 Jan. 1841, China miscellany, vol. 4, IOL.

12. John Galbraith, 3d officer, in *USJ*, 1841, pt. 2, p. 240.

13. Elma Loines, *The China Trade Post-Bag*, p. 86.

14. Robert S. Rait, *The Life and Campaigns of Hugh, First Viscount Gough*, 1:230-31.

15. Matheson to Jardine, 13 Jan. 1841, James Matheson Private Letter Books, vol. 6, JM.

16. 22 Jan. 1841, ibid.

17. 23 Jan. 1841, ibid.

18. Legrégeois to Directors, 20 Jan. 1841, vol. 323, ME.

19. 22 Jan. 1841, James Matheson Private Letter Books, vol. 6, JM.

20. *Press*, 27 Feb. 1841.

21. *USJ*, 1841, pt. 2, p. 245. Actually there were two Howquas, Wu Ping-Chien, the old man described here, and his much younger son, Wu Ch'ung-yueh. The latter had become official head of the hong eight years before, but the elder Howqua continued to manage the business.

22. Callery to Tesson, 10 Feb. 1841, vol. 304, ME; Bull to Carrington, 17 Feb. 1841, Carrington.

23. *Repository*, 12:493.

24. Ryan to Thomasen, 27 Feb. 1841, unbound miscellaneous correspondence, JM.

25. S. Wells to Frederick Williams, 17 Dec. 1835, Williams.

26. 27 Mar. 1841, *USJ*, 1841, pt. 2, p. 425.

27. 1 Mar. P.S. to printed letter of 20 Jan. 1841, Williams.

28. Waley, *Opium War through Chinese Eyes*, p. 143.

CHAPTER 20

1. 31 Mar. 1841, James Matheson Private Letter Books, vol. 6, JM.

2. Senhouse to Bremer, 28 May 1841, FO 17/52.

3. Ibid.

4. *Repository*, 10:240.

5. Elliot to Palmerston, 22 Apr. 1841, FO 17/48. The memorial is here and also in *Repository*, 10:236-40.

6. Earl Swisher, *China's Management of the American Barbarians*, pp. 69, 67, 64.

7. Robert S. Rait, *The Life and Campaigns of Hugh, First Viscount Gough*, 1:168-71.

8. Senhouse to Bremer, 28 May 1841, FO 17/52.

9. Enclosure no.2 in Elliot to Palmerston, 16 June 1841, FO 17/48.

10. *Repository*, 10:418.

11. Elliot to Gough and Senhouse, 24 May, in Senhouse to Bremer, 29 May 1841, FO 17/52.

12. Captain Sir Edward Belcher, *Narrative of a Voyage Round the World*, p. 214.

CHAPTER 21

1. Armine S. H. Mountain, *Memoirs and Letters*, pp. 186-87.

2. Elliot to Aberdeen, 25 Jan. 1842, FO 17/61.

3. Quoted in Matheson to Jardine, 27 May 1841, James Matheson Private Letter Books, vol. 7, JM.

4. Frederic Wakeman, Jr., *Strangers at the Gate: Social Disorder in South China, 1839-1861*, p. 53.

5. *Repository*, 10:396.

6. Ibid., p. 530.

7. Gough's account of this day is in ibid., pp. 540–42.

8. MacPherson's account is in ibid., pp. 397–401.

9. Coolidge to Matheson, 4 June 1841, unbound miscellaneous correspondence, JM.

10. Wakeman, *Strangers at the Gate*, p. 21.

11. James Matheson Private Letter Books, vol. 7, JM.

CHAPTER 22

1. John Beames, *Memoirs of a Bengal Civilian* (London, 1961), p. 68.

2. Palmerston to Elliot, 21 Apr. 1841, FO 17/45.

3. Elliot to Aberdeen, 25 Jan. 1842, FO 17/61.

4. Elliot to Palmerston, 10 Jan. 1840, FO 17/38.

5. Lytton Strachey and Roger Fulford, eds., *The Greville Memoirs, 1814-1860* (London, 1938), 4:422.

6. Ibid., p. 364.

7. A. C. Benson and Viscount Esher, eds., *Letters of Queen Victoria* (London, 1907), 1:329.

8. *Press*, 31 July 1841.

9. Matheson to Jardine, 23 Aug. 1841; to J. A. Smith, 29 July 1841; to Jamsetjee, 24 Aug. 1841—all in James Matheson Private Letter Books, vol. 7, JM.

10. Bridgman to Anderson, 31 Aug. 1841, South China 1838-44, ABCFM.

11. *Times*, 9 Nov. 1841.

12. Parker to Auckland, 25 Sept. 1841, *USJ*, 1842, pt. 1, pp. 428–29.

13. Armine S. H. Mountain, *Memoirs and Letters*, p. 194.

14. "A Field Officer," *The Last Year in China*, p. 103.

15. Robert S. Rait, *The Life and Campaigns of Hugh, First Viscount Gough*, 1:236.

16. Alexander Murray, *Doings in China*, p. 130.

17. "A Field Officer," *Last Year*, p. 137.

CHAPTER 23

1. Legrégeois to Directors, 22 June 1841, vol. 323, ME.

2. Matheson to J. A. Smith, 8 Sept. 1841, James Matheson Private Letter Books, vol. 7, JM.

3. Alexander Matheson to F. Macqueen, 16 Apr. 1842, Alexander Matheson Private Letter Books, vol. 2, JM.

4. Matheson to J. A. Smith, 8 Sept. 1841, James Matheson Private Letter Books, vol. 7, JM.

5. Alexander Matheson to J. Purvis, 9 May 1842, Alexander Matheson Private Letter Books, vol. 2, JM.

6. Matheson to Gough, 5 Mar. 1842, ibid.

7. Ibid.

8. *Repository*, 11:340.

9. 30 May 1842, South China 1840-47, LMS.

10. G. R. Williamson, *Memoir of the Reverend David Abeel*, p. 233.

11. Bridgman to Anderson, 26 Mar. 1842, South China 1838-44, ABCFM.

12. J. B. Jeter, *A Memoir of Mrs. Henrietta Shuck*, p. 145.

13. Williams to the ABCFM, printed letter, 10 July 1842, Williams.

14. Baldus to Etienne, 3 Aug. 1835, *Annales*, 10:70-71.

15. Baldus to the Rue de Sèvres, 9 Sept. 1840, *Annales C.M.*, 8:122.

16. Ibid., pp. 165-66.

17. The Missions Etrangères men were Blanchin, de la Brunière, and Guerin, the Lazarists Carayon and Combelles. The Jesuits were Bruyère, Estère, and Gotteland. I do not know the names of the Franciscans.

18. Milne to his Society, 20 June 1842, South China 1840-47, LMS; Williams to Anderson, 3 Sept. 1842, South China 1838-44, ABCFM; Abeel to Anderson, 9 Jan. 1842, ibid.

19. Blanchin to Jurine, 14 Feb. 1842, *Annales,* 14:482-83 (rather freely translated).

CHAPTER 24

1. 23 Nov. 1842.

2. Stanley to the Board of Control, 31 Dec. 1841, FO 17/62.

3. 22 Nov. 1842.

4. W. D. Bernard, *Narrative of the Voyages and Services of the Nemesis,* 2:327.

5. *Repository,* 11:433.

6. Ibid., 18:230-31.

7. K. S. Mackenzie, *Narrative of the Second Campaign in China,* p. 145.

8. Heard to Bowditch, 8 May 1842, BL-7, Heard.

9. Granville G. Loch, *The Closing Events of the Campaign in China,* p. 39.

10. Ibid., p 46.

11. Sir Henry Keppel, *A Sailor's Life under Four Sovereigns,* 1:269.

12. Stanley Lane-Poole, *The Life of Sir Harry Parkes,* 1:29.

13. Loch, *Closing Events,* p. 91.

14. Alexander Murray, *Doings in China,* p. 193.

15. Pottinger to Gough, 1 July 1842, in Augustus Phillimore, *The Life of Admiral Sir William Parker,* 2:473.

16. Keppel, *A Sailor's Life,* 1:271.

17. Lane-Poole, *Sir Harry Parkes,* 1:32-33.

18. Loch, *Closing Events,* p. 99.

19. S. Y. Teng, *Chang Hsi and the Treaty of Nanking, 1842,* p. 32.

CHAPTER 25

1. S. Y. Teng, *Chang Hsi and the Treaty of Nanking, 1842,* pp. 38-41.

2. Stanley Lane-Poole, *The Life of Sir Harry Parkes,* 1:42.

3. Granville G. Loch, *The Closing Events of the Campaign in China,* p. 172.

4. Ibid., pp. 172-73.

5. Lane-Poole, *Sir Harry Parkes,* 1:48.

6. Armine S. H. Mountain, *Memoirs and Letters,* p. 211.

7. Teng, *Chang Hsi and the Treaty of Nanking,* p. 115.

8. *Illustrated London News,* 26 Nov. 1842; *Times,* 22 Nov. 1842.

9. 27 Oct. 1842, South China 1840-47, LMS; 18 and 17 Sept. 1842, vol. 304, ME.

10. To J. A. Smith, 24 Sept. 1842, Alexander Matheson Private Letter Books, vol. 3, JM.

11. *Repository,* 11:688.

12. William C. Hunter, *The Fan Kwae at Canton before Treaty Days, 1825-1844,* p. 153.

A Note on Sources

What passed officially between England, India, and China before and during the Opium War is recoverable with tolerable completeness from Parliamentary Papers (principally 1840, vol. 36; and 1843, vol. 35), from the FO 17 series in the Public Record office, from letter books in the India Office Library, from the collection of "China Papers" in the National Archives of India at New Delhi, and from the Broughton and Auckland papers in the British Museum. Dispatches covering land and sea engagements were regularly published in the *United Service Journal* and elsewhere. The weekly *Canton Press* and *Canton Register,* and Bridgman's *Chinese Repository* (which carried, besides articles, a monthly "Journal of Occurrences"), are full of information and opinion. And the London *Times,* though it often allowed the exciting news from Afghanistan more space, reported the latest China "intelligence" faithfully whenever the overland brought any.

Then there are the military memoirs. Charles Elliot left none, and apparently no papers either, so that the single biography (Clagette Blake *Charles Elliot, R.N., 1801-1875* [London: Cleaver-Hume, 1960]) is very thin indeed. Nineteenth-century lives of George Elliot, Gough, Parker, and Parkes (at the time only a boy) are thin too for the war years, and there is nothing at all from Pottinger. But a number of less important serving officers published personal reminiscences. Belcher, Cunynghame, Ellis, Jocelyn, Keppel, Loch, Mackenzie, MacPherson, Murray, and an anonymous "field officer" are of this number; Mountain's memoirs include a great many letters written during the war; Bingham's recollections (J. Elliot Bingham, *Narrative of the Expedition to China,* 2 vols. [London, 1842]) amount to a complete account; the same is true of the book Bernard wrote from notes and oral communications supplied by Captain Hall and other officers of the *Nemesis* (W. D. Bernard, *Narrative of the Voyages and Services of the Nemesis,* 2 vols. [London, 1844; reprint ed., New York: Praeger, 1969]). Finally, Lieutenant John Ouchterlony of the Madras sappers and miners combined his personal experiences during the second expedition with several of the memoirs just mentioned to produce a full dress military history (*The Chinese War: an Account of all the Operations of the British Forces from the Commencement to the Treaty of Nanking* [London, 1844; reprint ed., New York: Praeger, 1970]) that has yet to be superseded.

The relevant early chapters of Hosea Ballou Morse, *The International Relations of the Chinese Empire: The Period of Conflict, 1834-1860* (London, 1910; reprint ed., New York: Paragon, 1964), and recent books by Maurice Collis, Christopher Hibbert, Edgar Holt, and John Selby, make considerable use of these military memoirs, and in Morse's case considerable use of the official papers too. They do little, however, with what might be called the merchant component in the story, and nothing at all with the missionary. Among American merchants only Forbes, Hunter, and Nye left memoirs; of the English merchants, none did. (Slade's *Narrative* was written at Macao during the war and is properly of a class with the polemics by Matheson and Lindsay.) There survive, however, collections of merchant letters on both sides of the Atlantic: on this side the Carrington papers at the Rhode Island Historical Society in Providence, and the Forbes and Heard papers at the Harvard Business School; on the other side the much larger and more important Jardine Matheson papers in the Cambridge University Library. Working from the latter, Michael Greenberg (in *British Trade and the Opening of China, 1800-42* [Cambridge: Cambridge University Press, 1951; reprinted 1970]) has laid out with great skill and economy the growth of Jardine, Matheson and Company to the end of the war, and by extrapolation the growth of the country trade as a whole (of which the opium traffic was a part). With respect to opium itself there is Jonathan Spence's as yet unpublished "Opium Smoking in Ch'ing China," the testimony given by William Jardine and others before a Select Committee of Parliament (1840, vol. 7), David Owen's *British Opium Policy in China and India* (New Haven: Yale University Press, 1934; reprint ed., Hamden, Conn.: Archon Books, 1968), Louis Dermigny's enormous *La Chine et l'occident: Le commerce à Canton au XVIIIe siècle, 1719-1833*, 4 vols. (Paris: S.E.V.P.E.N., 1964), contemporary manuals of opium husbandry and manufacture, and a number of modern studies of opium and opium addiction (the Addens is particularly useful).

In proportion to their numbers the Protestant missionaries were better served by the memorialist than even the English officers managed to be, perhaps because a missionary widow will take up a pen where a service widow will not. So memoirs or biographies that are little more than memoirs exist for Abeel, Bridgman (by his widow), Lockhart, the elder Milne, Robert Morrison (by his widow), Parker, Henrietta Shuck, and Williams (by his son). There are more recent lives of Gutzlaff and Liang A-fa, a short biographical sketch of Parker in Jonathan Spence's *To Change China*, and a full-dress life of the same (so recent I have not seen it) by Edward V. Gulick. The *Chinese Repository* is a mine of missionary information; Protestant missionary journals in Europe and America paid some attention to China; but the principal source for the Protestant mission there before and during the war remains the several collections of papers: the very considerable American Board of Commissioners for Foreign Missions papers at Harvard and the London Missionary Society papers at London University; the much slighter G. Tradescant Lay papers (British and Foreign Bible Society) in London, Edward Squire papers (Church Missionary Society) in London, and S. Wells Williams papers at Yale.

Catholic missionaries did not leave memoirs. Aristide Chatelet's *Jean-Gabriel Perboyre* (Meudon: Librairie vincentienne, 1943) is detailed but suffused with hagiolatry. Louis Wei Tsing-sing's *La Politique missionaire de la France en Chine, 1842-1856* (Paris: Nouvelles Editions Latines, 1953) reaches back into the war and prewar years, drawing upon the archives of the French Lazarists and the Roman Propaganda. De Moidrey and Van den Brandt provide indispensable information on names and appointments. The letters by missionaries published selectively in the *Annales de la propagation de la foi* are often so informative that one wishes the editors of that money-raising journal had published them all. To these add the letters of French Lazarists in the *Annales de la congrégation de la mission* (also published but apparently not to be found outside the Paris house) and the letter books of the Société des Missions Etrangères.

For the Chinese side of the story I have had to rely on the Sinologists. To a surprising extent they too draw upon western sources, perhaps because Chinese habits of reportage were not nearly as well developed as those in the West: a memorial to Peking on the subject of a naval battle with the English conveyed, I would surmise, nothing like the detail, and conveyed it with nothing like the truthfulness, of the dispatch the English commander was simultaneously directing to the Admiralty. Just the same what the Sinologists have to contribute is indispensable. I wish they had published more. And if what I have fetched from their present stock is unsuitable or misused, if I went poaching for partridge and came home with a laying hen, it may in part be because I have had to read back into the early part of the century what they say about the middle. I remain, however, not one of them; the reader must recognize that this has been in the main a western account, written without benefit (for example) of the *Ch'ou-pan i-wu shih-mo* and the *Ya-p'ien chan-cheng*, without consulting FO 233 or 682. I might have called it "The Opium War through Western Eyes," were it not that I did not wish to appear to be imitating that marvelous man of letters (and Sinologist), the late Arthur Waley.

In *The Opium War through Chinese Eyes* (London: Allen and Unwin, 1958) Waley makes Lin Tse-hsü's diary the basis for a short, elegant, discursive account of the war. Hsin-pao Chang's *Commissioner Lin and the Opium War* (Cambridge: Harvard University Press, 1964) is a much longer, painstaking reconstruction of the coming and early course of the conflict; drawing upon Lin's diary and upon a wide range of other Chinese sources; not at all elegant, paying some attention to opium and none to Christian missions, and ending abruptly in 1840. Frederic Wakeman, Jr.'s *Strangers at the Gate: Social Disorder in South China, 1839-1861* (Berkeley: University of California Press, 1966) is a marvelous pioneer exercise in local Chinese history. Wakeman writes with an eye to the Taiping Rebellion. Because he begins with the San-yuan-li incident, however, he adds greatly to our knowledge of how the peasants and gentry about Canton reacted to the first English expedition. There is an old but still useful study of the war (with documents) by P. C. Kuo; Earl Swisher has translated that part of the *I-wu shih-mo* which touches the Americans in the years 1841 to 1861; Arthur Hummel supplies indispensable biographical information on Chinese of importance; Paul Cohen's book on Christian missions and Chinese antiforeign feeling in the 1860s is illuminating for more than the decade in question. I do not ignore a slightly earlier generation of Sinologists, nor a group much earlier still that includes Bridgman, Robert Morrison, and Williams. Lastly there are the articles and several books of John K. Fairbank, particularly his *Trade and Diplomacy on the China Coast, 1842-1854,* 2 vols. (Cambridge: Harvard University Press, 1953). It begins in fact well before the indicated date. There can be hardly a student of nineteenth-century China who is not intellectually in Fairbank's debt.

There remain to be mentioned a miscellaneous collection of things. The letters and journal of Harriet Low have been edited by Elma Loines (*The China Trade Post-Bag* [Manchester, Maine: Falmouth Publishing House, 1953]). W. C. Costin's *Great Britain and China, 1833-1860* (Oxford: Clarendon Press, 1937) is a useful but compressed—and not always accurate—review of the official English papers (FO 17 mostly) for that period. Hosea Ballou Morse's monumental *The Chronicles of the East India Company Trading to China, 1635-1834,* 5 vols. (Oxford: Clarendon Press, 1926, 1929; reprint ed., Taipei: Ch'eng-wen, 1966), is so full of things that one can only wish the company had not quit China so soon. There are half a dozen histories of Hongkong; there are regimental histories, commercial guides, books of travel and description. It would be foolish to list them all. What follow are the more important only, including those mentioned but not fully described in this note.

Addens, Tjako Johan. *The Distribution of Opium Cultivation and the Trade in Opium.* Haarlem: Enschedé, 1939.

Auber, Peter. *China.* London, 1834.

Baker, Wyndham. "An Artillery Officer in China, 1840-1842." *Blackwood's,* July-December 1964, pp. 73-86.

Ball, J. Dyer. *Macao*. Canton: China Baptist Publication Society, 1905.

Belcher, Captain Sir Edward. *Narrative of a Voyage Round the World*. 2 vols. London, 1843.

Berry-Hill, Henry, and Sidney Berry-Hill. *George Chinnery, 1774-1852*. Leighon-Sea: F. Lewis, 1963.

Bridgman, Eliza J. G., ed. *The Life and Labors of Elijah Coleman Bridgman*. New York, 1864.

Callery, Joseph. *Voyage sur les côtes de la Chine fait en 1838*. Tracts 289, IOL.

Carter, T. *Historical Record of the 26th or Cameronian Regiment*. London, 1867.

Chen, Gideon. *Lin Tse-hsü*. Peiping: Yenching University Press, 1934; reprint ed., New York: Paragon, 1961.

Coates, Austin. *Prelude to Hongkong*. London: Routledge and Kegan Paul, 1966.

Cohen, Paul. *China and Christianity: The Missionary Movement and the Growth of Chinese Antiforeignism, 1860-1870*. Cambridge: Harvard University Press, 1963.

Collis, Maurice. *Foreign Mud*. London: Faber and Faber, 1946; reprint ed., New York: Norton, 1968.

Congressional Documents.

    Canton Consular Letters. House Doc. 119, 26-1.

    Canton Consular Letters. House Doc. 71, 26-2.

    Kearny Correspondence. Senate Doc. 139, 29-1.

Cordier, Henri. "La Mission Dubois de Jancigny dans l'Extrême Orient, 1841-1846." *Revue de l'Histoire des Colonies Françaises* 4 (1916): 129-232.

Cunynghame, Captain Arthur. *An Aide-de-Camp's Recollections of Service in China*. 2 vols. London, 1844.

Danton, George H. *The Culture Contacts of the United States and China*. New York: Columbia University Press, 1931.

David, Sir John Francis. *China During the War and Since the Peace*. 2 vols. London, 1852.

————. *The Chinese: A General Description*. 2 vols. London, 1836.

————. *Chinese Miscellanies*. London, 1865.

Dennett, Tyler. *Americans in Eastern Asia*. New York: Macmillan, 1922.

Downs, Jacques M. "American Merchants and the China Opium Trade, 1800-1840." *Business History Review* 42 (Winter 1968): 418-42.

Eatwell, W. *On the Poppy Cultivation and the Benares Opium Agency*. Calcutta, 1851.

Eitel, E. J. *Europe in China: The History of Hongkong*. London, 1895.

Elliot, Sir George. *Memoir of Admiral the Honourable Sir George Elliot*. London, 1863.

Ellis, Lady, ed. *Memoirs and Services of Sir Samuel Burdon Ellis*. London, 1866.

Endacott, G. B. *A History of Hong Kong*. London: Oxford University Press, 1958.

Fairbank, John K. "Chinese Diplomacy and the Treaty of Nanking." *Journal of Modern History* 12 (March 1940): 1-30.

————. "Tributary Trade and China's Relations with the West." *Far Eastern Quarterly* 1 (February 1942): 129-49.

———, and S. Y. Teng. *Ch'ing Administration: Three Studies*. Cambridge: Harvard University Press, 1961.

Faivre, Jean-Paul. *L'expansion française dans le pacifique de 1800 à 1842*. Paris: Nouvelles Editions Latines, 1953.

Fay, Peter Ward. "The French Catholic Mission in China during the Opium War." *Modern Asian Studies* 4 (April 1970): 115-28.

———. "The Irrepressible Drug: Opium and the Opium War." *Bengal Past and Present* 90 (July-December 1971): 149-64.

———. "The Protestant Mission and the Opium War." *Pacific Historical Review* 40 (May 1971): 145-61.

"A Field Officer." *The Last Year in China*. London, 1843.

Forbes, Robert Bennet. *Personal Reminiscences*. Boston, 1876.

———. *Remarks on China and the China Trade*. Boston, 1844.

Gennoe, T. A. M. *Notes on the Cultivation of Poppy*. Benares, 1861.

Gretton, G. le M. *The Campaigns and History of the Royal Irish Regiment*. Edinburgh: W. Blackwood, 1911.

Gulick, Edward V. *Peter Parker and the Opening of China*. Cambridge: Harvard University Press, 1973.

Gully, Robert. *Journals Kept by Mr. Gully and Capt. Denham during a Captivity in China*. London, 1844.

Gutzlaff, Charles. *China Opened*. 2 vols. London, 1838.

———. *Journal of Three Voyages along the Coast of China in 1831, 1832, and 1833*. London, 1834.

Hansard's *Parliamentary Debates*, 3rd series.

Hibbert, Christopher. *The Dragon Wakes: China and the West, 1793-1911*. London: Longman, 1970.

Hobhouse, John Cam, Baron Broughton. *Recollections of a Long Life*. 5 vols. London, 1865.

Holmes, Edward M. "Opium." *Encyclopaedia Britannica*, 11th ed.

Holt, Edgar. *The Opium Wars in China*. London: G. P. Putnam's Sons, 1964.

Hoskins, H. L. *British Routes to India*. New York: Longmans, Green & Co., 1928.

Hsu, Immanuel C. Y. "The Secret Mission of the *Lord Amherst* on the China Coast, 1832." *Harvard Journal of Asiatic Studies* 17 (1954): 231-52.

Hummel, Arthur W., ed. *Eminent Chinese of the Ch'ing Period*. 2 vols. Washington, D.C.: U.S. Government Printing Office, 1943-44.

Hunter, William C. *Bits of Old China*. London, 1885.

———. *The Fan Kwae at Canton before Treaty Days, 1825-1844*. London, 1882.

———. "Journal of Occurrences at Canton during the Cessation of Trade, 1839." MS in the Boston Athenaeum.

Imlah, A. H. *Lord Ellenborough*. Cambridge: Harvard University Press, 1939.

Impey, Elijah. *A Report on the Cultivation of Malwa Opium*. Bombay, 1848.

Jeter, J. B. *A Memoir of Mrs. Henrietta Shuck*. Boston, 1846.

Jocelyn, Lord Robert. *Six Months with the Chinese Expedition*. London, 1841.

Keppel, Sir Henry. *A Sailor's Life under Four Sovereigns*. 3 vols. London, 1899.

King, Charles W. *Opium Crisis: A Letter Addressed to Charles Elliot, Esq*. London, 1839.

Kuo, P. C. *A Critical Study of the First Anglo-Chinese War*. Shanghai: Commercial Press, 1935.

Lane-Poole, Stanley. *The Life of Sir Harry Parkes*. 2 vols. London, 1894.

Latourette, Kenneth Scott. *A History of Christian Missions in China*. New York: Macmillan, 1929; reprint ed., Taipei: Ch'eng-wen, 1966.

———. *The History of Early Relations between the United States and China, 1784-1844*. New Haven: Yale University Press, 1917; reprint ed., New York: Kraus, 1964.

Lay, G. Tradescant. *The Chinese As They Are*. London, 1841.

LeFevour, Edward. *Western Enterprise in Late Ch'ing China: A Selective Survey of Jardine, Matheson and Company, 1842-1895*. Cambridge: Harvard University Press, 1968.

Lindsay, Hugh Hamilton. *Is the War with China a Just One?* London, 1840.

———. *Remarks on Occurrences in China Since the Opium Seizure*. London, 1840.

———. *Report of Proceedings on a Voyage to the Northern Parts of China in the Lord Amherst*. London, 1833.

Ljungstedt, Sir Andrew. *An Historical Sketch of the Portuguese Settlements in China*. Boston, 1836.

Loch, Granville G. *The Closing Events of the Campaign in China*. London, 1843.

Lockhart, William. *The Medical Missionary in China*. London, 1861.

Lubbock, Basil. *The Opium Clippers*. Boston: Charles E. Lauriat, 1933; reprint ed., Glasgow: Brown, Son, and Ferguson, 1967.

MacArthur, J. W. S. *Notes on an Opium Factory*. Calcutta, 1865.

McCulloch, J. R. *A Dictionary of Commerce*. 2 vols. London, 1839.

Mackenzie, Alexander. *A History of the Mathesons*. 2nd ed., London, 1900.

Mackenzie, K. S. *Narrative of the Second Campaign in China*. London, 1842.

McNeur, George Hunter. *China's First Preacher, Liang A-fa*. Shanghai: Kwang Hsueh Publ. House, 1934.

MacPherson, D. *Two Years in China*. London, 1842.

Malcom, Howard. *Travels in Southeastern Asia*. 2 vols. Boston, 1839.

Mason, Mary G. *Western Concepts of China and the Chinese, 1840-1876*. New York: The Seaman Printery, 1939.

Medhurst, W. H. *China: Its State and Prospects*. London, 1838.

Milne, William. *A Retrospect of the First Ten Years of the Protestant Mission to China*. Malacca, 1820.

De Moidrey, Joseph. *La Hiérarchie Catholique en Chine, Corée, et au Japon, 1307-1914*. Shanghai, 1914.

Morrison, Eliza. *Memoirs of the Life and Labours of Robert Morrison, D. D.* 2 vols. London, 1839.

Morrison, Robert. *A View of China*. Macao, 1817.

Mountain, Armine S. H. *Memoirs and Letters*. London, 1857.

Murray, Alexander. *Doings in China*. London, 1843.

Nye, Gideon, Jr. *The Morning of My Life in China*. Macao, 1873.

———. *Peking the Goal*. Canton, 1873.

Parkinson, C. Northcote. *Trade in the Eastern Seas, 1793-1813*. Cambridge: Cambridge University Press, 1937.

Philip, Robert. *The Life and Opinions of the Reverend William Milne*. London, 1840.

Phillimore, Augustus. *The Life of Admiral Sir William Parker*. 3 vols. London, 1880.

Rait, Robert S. *The Life and Campaigns of Hugh, First Viscount Gough*. London: Constable, 1903.

Schlyter, Herman. *Karl Gutzlaff als Missionar in China*. Lund: Gleerup, 1946.

Scott, John. *Manual of Opium Husbandry*. Calcutta, 1877.

Scott, John Lee. *Narrative of a Recent Imprisonment in China*. London, 1841.

Selby, John. *The Paper Dragon: An Account of the China Wars, 1840-1900*. London: Barker, 1968.

Slade, John. *Narrative of the Late Proceedings and Events in China*. Macao, 1840.

Spence, Jonathan. *To Change China: Western Advisors in China, 1620-1920*. Boston: Little, Brown & Co., 1969.

Stelle, Charles C. "Americans and the China Opium Trade in the 19th Century." Ph.D. dissertation, University of Chicago, 1938.

Steuart, James. *Jardine, Matheson and Co*. Hongkong: p.p., 1934.

Stevens, G. B., and W. F. Markwick. *Life of Reverend Peter Parker*. Boston, 1896.

Swisher, Earl. *China's Management of the American Barbarians*. New Haven: Yale University Press, 1951.

Taylor, Fitch W. *The Flag Ship: Or a Voyage Around the World*. 2 vols. New York, 1840.

Teng, S. Y. *Chang Hsi and the Treaty of Nanking, 1842*. Chicago: University of Chicago Press, 1944.

————, and John K. Fairbank. *China's Response to the West*. 2 vols. Cambridge: Harvard University Press, 1954.

Thayer, Thatcher. *A Sketch of the Life of D. W. C. Olyphant*. New York, 1852.

Tiffany, Osmond, Jr. *The Canton Chinese*. Boston, 1849.

Van den Brandt, Joseph. *Les Lazaristes en Chine, 1697-1935*. Peking: Imprimerie de lazaristes, 1936.

White, Ann Bolbach. "The Hong Merchants of Canton." Ph.D. dissertation, University of Pennsylvania, 1967.

Williams, Frederick W. *The Life and Letters of Samuel Wells Williams*. New York, 1889.

Williams, S. Wells. *The Chinese Commercial Guide*. 5th ed. Hongkong, 1863; reprint ed., Taipei: Ch'eng-wen, 1966. Based on an earlier work by John Morrison.

————. *The Middle Kingdom*. Rev. ed., 2 vols. New York, 1883; reprint ed., New York: Paragon, 1966.

Williamson, G. R. *Memoir of the Reverend David Abeel*. New York, 1848.

Wood, W. W. *Sketches of China*. Philadelphia, 1830.

Wu, Wen-Tsao. *The Chinese Opium Question in British Opinion and Action*. New York: Academy, 1928.

Wylie, Alexander. *Memorials of Protestant Missionaries to the Chinese*. Shanghai, 1867; reprint ed., Taipei: Ch'eng-wen, 1967.

Index